State Governance of Mining, Development and Sustainability

This book is dedicated to all the people and non-human beings that have sacrificed their lives and their well-being under the 'rolling and running of iron', for the sake of the useful mineral commodities we enjoy in a globalized world.

State Governance of Mining, Development and Sustainability

Tracy-Lynn Field

Professor, School of Law, University of the Witwatersrand, South Africa

Edward Elgar
PUBLISHING

Cheltenham, UK • Northampton, MA, USA

Published by
Edward Elgar Publishing Limited
The Lypiatts
15 Lansdown Road
Cheltenham
Glos GL50 2JA
UK

Edward Elgar Publishing, Inc.
William Pratt House
9 Dewey Court
Northampton
Massachusetts 01060
USA

A catalogue record for this book
is available from the British Library

Library of Congress Control Number: 2019950538

This book is available electronically in the **Elgar**online
Law subject collection
DOI 10.4337/9781784712648

MIX
Paper from
responsible sources
FSC® C013604
FSC
www.fsc.org

ISBN 978 1 78471 263 1 (cased)
ISBN 978 1 78471 264 8 (eBook)

Printed and bound by CPI Group (UK) Ltd, Croydon, CR0 4YY

Contents

Acknowledgements

The seed for this book was planted in a confrontation between the 'suits' and the activists on a street outside the Cape Town Convention Centre, South Africa in February 2014. The international Mining Indaba was taking place at this venue, while the attendees of the 'Alternative Mining Indaba' had convened a short distance away. Taking part in the street march to the Convention Centre, I observed the reactions of both sets of protagonists: Fury, outrage, anger and frustration on the side of the activists, shouting and dancing in the street; indifference, irritation and bemused concern on the part of the mining executives and their supporters, as they watched impassively. The rift between the two sides seemed intractable. 'How unproductive,' I thought, 'and how sad that we can't find a common language.' And so began a five-year journey into the languages we speak around mining, development and sustainability, and their translation into legal and economic concepts.

I am indebted to a wide range of people and institutions who have contributed to my intellectual growth and exposure to the contradictions of the mining industry over more than a decade. In particular, I must thank: Melissa Fourie and Catherine Horsfield of the Centre for Environmental Rights; Mariette Liefferink and (formerly) Koos Pretorius of the Federation for a Sustainable Environment; Lisa Chamberlain, Louis Snyman and Robert Krause of the Centre for Applied Legal Studies; Dr Caroline Digby and Ingrid Watson of the Centre for Sustainability of Mining and Industry; Dr Karl von Holdt, Professor Jacklyn Cock, Dr Gavin Capps, Dr Victor Munnik and Dr Sonwabile Mnwana of the SWOP institute, where I am also a research associate; Samantha Hargreaves of WoMin; John Capel, Jeremy Daphne and Hassan Lorgat of the Benchmarks Foundation; and Mohamed Ameermia of the South African Human Rights Commission, amongst others. I am also grateful to the South African Human Rights Commission for the opportunity to serve as an independent panelist into the hearings on the socio-economic rights of mining-affected communities, which allowed me to hear testimonies from a wide range of stakeholders on the problems besetting the mining industry. My colleagues Professor Elmarie van der Schyff and Dr Fola Adeleke joined me as co-researchers on a project entitled 'Re-imagining mining governance and regulation in a post-extractivist age', funded by the South African National Research Foundation, and I am thankful for their insights. The same goes for Professor Hanri Mostert and the team of researchers she has built around the

'Mineral Law in Africa' project. The intellectual inspiration and support of Professor Carmen Gonzalez and Professor Sara Seck are also acknowledged.

The PhD students who have accompanied me on this particular research journey, and whose own research extends some of the work in this book deserve a special mention: Louis Snyman, Maxwell Chuma, Ntombifuthi Monedi-Noko, Naledzani Mukwevho, and Melissa Strydom – thank you! I must also acknowledge the 2018 Masters Class in the course 'Comparative Law of Mining and Environment' offered at the University of the Witwatersrand, for serving as the guinea pigs for the first masters' teaching based on this book.

To Ben Booth and his team at Edward Elgar a huge thanks for your patience, support and encouragement over the book's long genesis. The University of the Witwatersrand granted me a sabbatical in 2017, which enabled me to make substantial progress on this book. I am thankful to my Head of School, Wesahl Domingo for her continuing support during the latter stages of this book. The completion of this book was facilitated by incentive grants from the South African National Research Foundation and the Wits University Council and a grant from the National Research Foundation's Competitive Rated Researchers Fund (Grant No. 98936).

The grounding and support of Dr Jacki Watts is a lifelong debt, and I am grateful for the interest and support of many other friends and work colleagues.

Finally, my wife Linda Meyer – your love, support and recognition is the foundation of my life. I cherish you every day. And to my precious children Evan, Charlotte and Tristan, thank you for bearing the sacrifice of my attention that enabled me to finally finish this work. This book is also dedicated to you.

Abbreviations

4IR	Fourth Industrial Revolution
AITC	Alaska Inter-Tribal Council
AMD	Acid Mine Drainage
AMV	Africa Mining Vision
ANS	Adjusted Net Saving
ANZMEC	Australian and New Zealand Minerals and Energy Council
ARO	Asset Retirement Obligation
ASM	Artisanal and Small-scale Mining
AUD	Australian Dollar
BEPS	Base Erosion and Profit-Shifting
CEA	Cumulative Effects Assessment
CEAA	Canadian Environmental Assessment Act
CIA	Cumulative Impact Assessment
CSR	Corporate Social Responsibility
EA	Environmental Assessment
EANRA	Environmental and Natural Resource Accounting
EIA	Environmental Impact Assessment
EIR	Extractive Industries Review
EIS	Environmental Impact Statement
EITE	Emissions Intensive and Trade Exposed
EITI	Extractive Industries Transparency Initiative
EJ	Environmental Justice
EJOLT	Environmental Justice, Liabilities and Trade project
EP	Equator Principles
ETS	Emissions Trading System
FPIC	Free, Prior and Informed Consent

GDP	Gross Domestic Product
GHGs	Greenhouse Gas Emissions
GMI	Global Mining Initiative
GNI	Gross National Income
GNP	Gross National Product
HIA	Health Impact Assessment
IAIA	International Association for Impact Assessment
IBA	Impact Benefit Agreements
IBRD	International Bank for Reconstruction and Development
ICCPR	International Covenant on Civil and Political Rights
ICESCR	International Covenant on Economic, Social and Cultural Rights
ICMM	International Council of Mining and Metals
IDA	International Development Association
IFFs	Illicit Financial Flows
IFI	International Financial Institution
IFRS	International Financial Reporting Standards
IGF	Intergovernmental Forum on Mining, Minerals, Metals and Sustainable Development
IIED	International Institute for Environment and Development
ILO	International Labour Organization
IMF	International Monetary Fund
IPCC	Intergovernmental Panel on Climate Change
ISO	International Organization for Standardization
IUCN	International Union for the Conservation of Nature
KP	Kimberley Process
LDCs	Least Development Countries
MAC	Mines and Communities
MCA	Minerals Council of Australia
MCI	Mining Contribution Index
MEM	Ministry of Energy and Mines (British Columbia)
MMSD	Mining, Minerals and Sustainable Development Project
MoE	Ministry of Environment (British Columbia)

MRF	Mining Rehabilitation Fund
MRRT	Mineral Resources Rent Tax
NEPA	National Environmental Policy Act (USA)
NGO	Non-Governmental Organisation
NMED	New Mexico Environment Department
NNP	Net National Product
NOAMI	National Orphaned and Abandoned Mines Initiative (Canada)
NPL	National Priority List
NPV	Net Present Value
OECD	Organization for Economic Co-operation and Development
OFC	Offshore Financial Centre
PWC	Price Waterhouse Coopers
PWYP	Publish What You Pay
RRT	Resource Rent Tax
RSPT	Resource Super Profits Tax
SDGs	Sustainable Development Goals
SEA	Strategic Environmental Assessment
SEEA	System of Environmental Economic Accounting
SIA	Social Impact Assessment
TSF	Tailings Storage Facility
TSM	Towards Sustainable Mining
UNCTAD	United Nations Conference on Trade and Development
UNDRIP	United Nations Declaration on the Rights of Indigenous Peoples
UNECE	United Nations Economic Commission for Europe
UNEP	United Nations Environment Programme
UPB	Unconditional Performance Bonds
USD	US Dollar
USGS	United States Geological Survey
VECs	Valued Ecosystem Components
VPSHR	Voluntary Principles on Security and Human Rights
WBG	World Bank Group

WMI	Whitehorse Mining Initiative
WSSD	World Summit on Sustainable Development
WWF	World Wildlife Fund

1. Introduction

1. INTRODUCTION

'All vulnerable things must perish under the rolling and running of iron.' So muses Oliver Mellors, the working class titular character in DH Lawrence's 1928 novel *Lady Chatterley's Lover*. This story is set in England's East Midlands, a region vastly transformed by coal mining at the turn of the twentieth century. As Mellors descends into the darkness and seclusion of the woods, he resents the 'evil electric lights' and 'diabolical rattlings' of the mining machinery. In the 'world of the mechanical greedy, greedy mechanism and mechanized greed, sparkling with lights and gushing hot metal and roaring with traffic' lay a 'vast evil thing', a thing '[r]eady to destroy whatever did not conform'. Through the character of Mellors, DH Lawrence voiced his own antipathies. Born in a coal mining village to a coalminer father and school-teacher mother, the author's hostility towards mining-led industrialization that pulsates throughout *Lady Chatterley's Lover* has been ascribed to his belief that mining dehumanized his father and destroyed the English countryside of his birth.[1]

More than one hundred years later, there are many who contend that mining is like a greedy, mechanized machine, now with global reach, that destroys all vulnerable things in its path. They might point out that mining has become one of the negative driving forces of the Anthropocene[2] – the term Crutzen coined in 2002 to supplement the Holocene and to signal human dominance of planet Earth.[3] They might add that mining has always been associated with

[1] For extracts from DH Lawrence *Lady Chatterley's Lover* Chapter 10, see www.gutenberg.net.au/ebooks01/0100181h.html, accessed 9 May 2019; see also Sparknotes, 'Lady Chatterley's Lover: Context', www.sparknotes.com/lit/ladychatterley/context, accessed 24 November 2018.

[2] SD Van de Veer, 'Still digging: Extractive industries, resource curses, and transnational governance in the Anthropocene' (2013) *Transatlantic Academy Paper Series* 1.

[3] PJ Crutzen, 'Geology of mankind' (2002) 415 *Nature* 23.

spectacularly unequal distribution of wealth, debunking claims that mining fosters equal development.[4]

Others contend, equally vociferously, that life as we currently know it could not subsist without the flow of mineral commodities, and that mining advances human civilization, sustainable development and poverty alleviation. In mineral-rich jurisdictions, for example, it is not uncommon to encounter metaphors characterizing mining as the engine of growth, the lifeblood or backbone of the economy or an instrument of national stabilization.[5] Importantly, many also argue that a sustainability transition to counter the global threat of climate change cannot take place without strategic mineral commodities.[6]

'Contention and ambiguity' – these are the words Bebbington *et al* use to characterize the relationship between formal (largescale) mining and development. They continue:

> 'Contentious' because mining has so often delivered adverse social, environmental and economic effects for the many, but significant gains only for the few; 'ambiguous' because of the abiding sense, among local populations as much as development professionals, that *just maybe* mining could contribute much more. In the coexistence of such divergent feelings about mining and its human and environmental impacts lie the seeds of much conflict.[7]

This conflict is both ideological and material, and, at times, deadly. Following policy and legal reforms spearheaded by international financial institutions (IFIs) and the mining industry since the mid-1980s, mining has expanded dramatically in the developing world.[8] On the minefields of mining's new frontiers, the stakes could not be higher: 'The life of the people involved; the physical survival of its members; the extractive companies' survival in the market; the biodiversity at stake; the plans for life and death executed by the illegal, armed groups that swarm the minefields.'[9] There is no shortage of

---

4 Anthony Bebbington *et al*, 'Contention and ambiguity: Mining and the possibilities of development' (2008) 39(6) *Development and Change* 965, 966.

5 For example, see World Bank, *Albania Mining Sector Reform, Restructuring and Future Prospects* (June 2009) 32; Government of British Columbia, *Province of British Columbia: Strategic Plan 2014/2015–2017/2018* http://bcbudget.gov.bc.ca/2014/stplan/2014_Strategic_Plan.pdf accessed 20 February 2019, 6.

6 Saleem H Ali *et al*, 'Mineral supply for sustainable development requires resource governance' (2017) 543 *Nature* 367.

7 Bebbington (n 4) 965.

8 Ibid.

9 César Rodríguez-Garavito, 'Ethnicity.gov: Global governance, indigenous peoples, and the right to prior consultation in social minefields' (2011) 18(1) *Indiana Journal of Global Legal Studies* 1, 35.

research detailing the social conflict stoked by mining,[10] and it is still the sector in which the greatest number of deaths of human rights defenders is seen.[11]

Conflict persists notwithstanding a concerted and apparently well intentioned effort on the part of the mining industry to come clean on sustainable development. By the end of the twentieth century, a number of converging negative trends were exposing mining companies to growing reputational risk, threatening market acceptance of their products and placing their social licence to operate at risk.[12] Following a number of smaller initiatives, the industry commissioned the Mining, Minerals and Sustainable Development Project (MMSD) to identify how it should respond to the societal expectation of sustainable development. The MMSD project became widely regarded as a 'symbolic point' in the mining sector's engagement with broader debates on development and sustainability.[13] Since that time, as this book shows, the mining industry and its supporters have engaged vigorously with issues of development and sustainability, albeit always from a vantage point that prioritizes the survival of the industry.

The MMSD project inspired a neoliberal, mainstream discourse on the sustainable development potential of the mining industry: a 'sustainable mineral development consensus' that has become widely adopted in developed and developing mineral-rich jurisdictions alike. Building on the earlier set of reforms aimed at promoting private investment in the mining industry, advocates of the consensus claim that sustainable development can transform mining industry practices and that mining can catalyze development that leads to poverty alleviation. The model of economic growth is private-led and extractives-based. The State plays a minimal role in production. It nevertheless plays a critical balancing and mediating function by facilitating and promoting mining while also regulating the industry to protect society from environmental and social (and, to a lesser extent, economic) impacts. The State is burdened with the expectation of preventing and resolving social conflict around mining and transforming the benefits associated with mining into more widely shared social goods.

---

[10] Bebbington (n 4) 969ff; RA Hodge, 'Mining company performance and community conflict: moving beyond a seeming paradox' (2014) 84 *Journal of Cleaner Production* 27; GA Okoh, 'Grievance and conflict in Ghana's gold mining industry: The case of Obuasi' (2014) 62 Part A *Futures* 51; D Kemp *et al*, 'Just relations and company-community conflict in mining' (2011) 101(1) *Journal of Business Ethics* 93.

[11] See further the discussion in section 5.2 of Chapter 3.

[12] Luke Danielson, *Architecture for Change: An Account of the Mining, Minerals and Sustainable Development Project History* (Global Public Policy Institute 2006) 18.

[13] John R Owen and Deanna Kemp, 'Social licence and mining: A critical perspective' (2012) 38(1) *Resources Policy* 1.

The sustainable mineral development consensus still holds sway, but it has come under increasing, left-leaning, critique. Critics claim that instead of leading to 'development' and 'sustainability', mining is simply 'extractivism'. This is a pejorative term highlighting 'activities which remove great quantities of natural resources that are not then processed (or are done so in a limited fashion) and that leave a country as exports'[14] – a phenomenon that has deep roots in colonialism, extractive capital and the imperialist State.[15] Critics maintain that the largescale material extraction of natural resources has failed dismally as a developmental strategy. Rather than leading to the development and poverty alleviation promised by the World Bank, other IFIs and the mining industry, extractivism has continued to position developing countries on the periphery of global systems of production, to dehumanize people and to destroy the environment. Instead of balancing and mediation, under extractivism the State colludes with multinational mining companies to maintain conditions that lead to 'adverse social, environmental and economic effects for the many, but significant gains only for the few'.[16] The sustainable development turn has done little to change these trends. Critics hold that extractivist policies, laws and regulatory systems (or their absence) generally facilitate highly unequal terms of trade, externalize social and environmental costs, allow for profits to be repatriated to the global North and guarantee a cheap labour force and compliant citizenry.[17]

The same critics have also observed a new strand of extractivism in 'progressive' left-leaning States in South America, a phenomenon Gudynas named 'neoextractivism' in 2010. States in which neoextractivism holds sway have not eschewed classic extractivist practices: they continue to position extractive industries as a pillar of development and externalize social and environmental costs. But unlike the minimalist State of private-led extractivism, the State plays a more active role. This may include State participation in production, such as State-owned mining companies, joint ventures and free carried interest in mining companies. In other instances, States have revised contracts and increased taxes in order to win a greater share of the benefits of mining for

---

[14] Eduardo Gudynas, 'The new extractivism of the 21st century: Ten urgent theses about extractivism in relation to current South American progressivism' (2010) *Americas Program Report* 1; Womin (IANRA), *Background Note and Explanation of Key Concepts*, Women, Gender and Extractivism in Africa: A collection of papers (undated) 6.

[15] Henry Veltmeyer and James Petras, *The New Extractivism: A Post-Neoliberal Development Model or Imperialism of the Twenty-First Century?* (Zed 2014).

[16] Bebbington (n 4) 966.

[17] Womin (n 14) 8.

purposes of national development.[18] These trends have also been observed in Africa, although here more commonly under the banner of 'resource nationalism'.[19]

Critics hold that neoextractivism binds resource-rich countries even closer to their nonrenewable, extractive industries, a situation that perpetuates international subordination.[20] Moreover, under neoextractivism social and environmental impacts have allegedly increased. Actions to confront and deal with them are 'still ineffective and even, on occasion, have been weakened'.[21] Under neoextractivism the State stirs itself to some attempt at balancing, mediation and transformation, but only insofar as economic benefits are concerned. Neoextractivism improves upon the neoliberal strategies of previous decades, but critical engagement with its tenets and approaches remains imperative. Critics refuse to see neoextractivism as a promising alternative, especially insofar as far as social and environmental outcomes are concerned.

Extractivism and neoextractivism both rest on the concept of development.[22] Spanning the divide between neoliberal and socialist approaches to economics, development is rooted in an ideology of progress driven by the project of Modernity. As Gudynas has argued, as a school of thought Modernity adheres to a Cartesian knowledge system (affirming the possibility of truth and falsity and excluding other knowledge systems), restricts ethical values to the human sphere, understands history as a temporally linear process (from conditions of backwardness to a brighter future) and stresses the duality of society and nature.[23] All these ideas are present in a contemporary ideology of progress that makes economic growth synonymous with development, to be achieved through increased investments and exports.[24] Extractive industries, inclusive of mining, oil and gas, enjoy pride of place in this paradigm because it is believed

---

18 Gudynas (n 14) 3ff.

19 See Michael Solomon (compiler), *The Rise of Resource Nationalism: A Resurgence of State Control in an Era of Free Markets, or the Legitimate Search for a New Equilibrium* (South African Institute of Mining and Metallurgy 2012). Unless otherwise indicated, references to 'neoextractivism' in this work include the trend of resource nationalism in Africa.

20 Gudynas (n 14) 5.

21 Ibid 7.

22 The connection between ideas of development, the sustainable mineral development consensus and neoextractivism is canvassed in Chapter 2.

23 Eduardo Gudynas, 'Debates on development and its alternatives in Latin America: A brief heterodox guide' in M Lang and D Mokrani, *Beyond Development: Alternative Visions from Latin America* Permanent Working Group on Alternatives to Development (Rosa Luxemburg Foundation, transl. 2013) 15, 31.

24 Ibid 18.

they will achieve this export-led growth.[25] The mandate to foster progress through extractives justifies the largescale appropriation and destruction of nature. Schools of thought as diverse as the dependency and Marxist theorists of the 1960s, the neoliberals of the 1980s and the progressives that emerged in the early 2000s have rejected ecological limits to perpetual economic growth, minimized the impacts of the extractive industries or argued that losses can be compensated for economically.[26]

As a viable alternative, intellectuals and activists have put forward the notion of postextractivism, understood as indispensable extraction of resources.[27] Postextractivism is one of many transition discourses that attempt to plumb alternatives to development rather than development alternatives, that is, ways of thinking that sidestep the Modernist obsession with progress, economic growth and the special role assigned to extractive industries. Under postextractivism, the intent would be to vastly reduce extraction, promote sustainability through recycling, close 'unfair' material and resource flows, reduce emissions and radically reduce pressure on ecosystems.[28] Acosta links postextractivism to the mission of 'serious and responsible degrowth' in the global North,[29] and envisages a 'well thought-out transition' from the current state of obsession with economic growth and extractivism/neoextractivism:

> Overcoming extractivism and its colonial shackles is a fundamental condition to overcome underdevelopment. However, on the way out of an extractive economy, it will be necessary to continue such activities for some time. A well thought-out transition, firmly adopted by society, will be needed. It should become very clear that a solution to this complex dilemma of societies that are rich in natural resources yet remain cursed to an almost inevitable impoverishment will not be reached by maintaining, or worse, deepening extractivism.[30]

The theory of postextractivism is noble and resonates with current broadranging debates on planetary and social boundaries to growth and development.[31] However, calls for a well thought out transition and the firm adoption of a fundamentally new paradigm must reckon with the dynamics that hold an extractivist/neoextractivist paradigm in place with such strength. Why is the position

---

25 Ibid 25.

26 Ibid 28.

27 Arturo Escobar, 'Degrowth, postdevelopment and transitions: A preliminary conversation' (2015) 10 *Sustainability Science* 451, 455.

28 Womin (n 14) 8.

29 Alberto Acosta, 'Post-growth and post-extractivism: Two sides of the same cultural transformation' (2016) 3(1) *Alternautas* 50, 59.

30 Ibid 61.

31 These debates are outlined in section 5 below.

of States towards mining so entrenched, notwithstanding strong resistance? Is it the case that the State simply promotes the extractive industry and colludes with mining companies in a manner that is blind to the suffering of people and environment? And what exactly would need to be undone in the move towards a 'well thought out transition'?

2. ARGUMENT OF THIS BOOK

This book acknowledges that while mining still externalizes social and environmental costs, over the past two decades the mining industry and some mineral-rich jurisdictions have attempted to reposition this industry within a normative framing of 'sustainable development', 'sustainability' or 'responsibility'. It recognizes that mining takes place in developing and developed countries and that resource extraction conflicts arise in both broad contexts. This book shows that in both types of context, the State is vested with an extensive set of roles that revolve around promoting mining *and* protecting society from its impacts. It contends that models of 'sustainable' or 'responsible' mining serve a legitimating function, keeping alive the hope of a socioecologically bounded mining sector. It also argues that it is the tension itself – the push for mining and the pushback against its impacts, a paradox that is felt most strongly in the State mechanism – that holds the current system of unsustainable global mining production in place. This book condemns unsustainable and irresponsible mining, and supports all efforts to chip away at this hard edifice. But it expresses reservation as to whether a 'well thought out transition' to postextractivist mining is possible without a fundamental shift away from the positioning of mining and other extractives within an ideology of progress, and without dismantling an intricate system of narratives, rules and rights in which mining and the hope of its development and sustainability potential are entrenched.

This book draws upon Karl Polanyi's understanding of the 'market society' and the 'double movement' presented in his 1944 work *The Great Transformation*.[32] In this great work, Polanyi outlined his understanding of the transition from traditional societies to the (still prevailing and now global) market society, being a way of life in which an increasing array of social relations is subjected to the demands of the market. Zaman has said that Polanyi's conceptual frame has been little understood, though it is of vital importance for the task befalling the global community.[33] This book contends that it is of

[32] Karl Polanyi, *The Great Transformation* (Beacon 1944).

[33] Asad Zaman, 'The rise and fall of the market economy' (2011) 14(2) *International Association for Islamic Economics* 123, 124.

equally vital importance for understanding and recasting the State's role in relation to mining, development and sustainability.

Polanyi's conceptual frame is presented in section 6 of this introductory chapter. In preparation, and in support of the broad claims made in this introductory section, the chapter now proceeds by outlining globalized demand, globalized supply and globalized impacts relating to the mining of energy and hardrock minerals.

3. GLOBALIZED DEMAND: SOCIETY'S UNEQUAL CONSUMPTION OF MINERALS

The use of minerals, and mining as the correlating activity of supply, is as old as the *Homo* genus. In fact, there is ample proof that even hominids such as species of *Australopithecus* used stone tools more than 2.5 million years ago.[34] Minerals and mining were key to the welfare of ancient societies, from the toolmakers of Olduvai Gorge, who belonged to the *Homo habilis* genus,[35] to the Neolithic miners who dug for flint in southern and western England,[36] to the trading networks that sustained ancient Egyptian, Greek, Roman and African civilizations with construction and energy minerals and precious metals.[37]

Over the course of time, human society's appetite for minerals has become voracious. With the advent of the industrial revolution, mineral commodities were needed to make and power the steam and then diesel and gasoline-fuelled engines that drove unprecedented increases in productivity and forged the path for capital accumulation.[38] From the late 1900s onwards, significant changes in the industries consuming industrial minerals and metals and major historic events further affected mineral production and use.[39] Demand massively increased to meet the technological advances in agriculture, communications, energy generation, construction, health services, transportation and the military.[40] Glover and Morse point out, for example, that over the span of the twentieth century, demand for metals and minerals in the USA increased

---

[34] Henry M McHenry and Katherine Coffing, '*Autralopethicus* to *Homo*: Transformations in body and mind' (2000) 29 *Annual Review of Anthropology* 125, 129.

[35] Cornelius S Hurlbut, *Minerals and Man* (Random House 1970) 26.

[36] Ibid 31.

[37] Ibid 36; IR Phimister, 'Ancient mining near Great Zimbabwe' (1974) 74 *Journal of the South African Institute of Mining and Metallurgy* 233.

[38] David E Morse and Anna N Glover, 'Minerals and materials in the 20th century – A review' (2000) *US Geological Survey Minerals Yearbook* 1.1.

[39] Ibid.

[40] Ibid 1.1–1.3.

from about 160 million tons to 3.3 billion tons per year.[41] Turning to a global figure, total material extraction during the twentieth century increased by a factor of eight,[42] amounting to 59 billion tons per year at the beginning of the twenty-first century.[43] This is an enormous figure – equivalent to the amount of biomass produced annually by green plants using photosynthesis, thus positioning anthropogenic material extraction in the same order of magnitude as global material net primary production.[44]

Along with an exponential increase in global materials use, there has also been a qualitative change in global material metabolism: nonrenewable materials are being used more than ever before. While biomass accounted for three quarters of all extracted materials in 1900, by 2005 its share had declined to a third.[45] In the decades between the end of the Second World War and the oil price peak in the 1970s, the proportion of materials extracted shifted rapidly from renewable biomass to nonrenewable mineral materials, a phenomenon Wrigley describes as a shift from an advanced organic economy to a mineral economy.[46] By the start of the twenty-first century nonrenewable resources accounted for more than 70 per cent of total materials use, a share that is still increasing.[47]

Society's demand for nonrenewable mineral materials is also highly unequal. While growth in the extraction of biomass seems to be linked to population growth, use of nonrenewable minerals is more closely linked to economic growth.[48] Over the course of the twentieth century the developing world's contribution to global materials use has mostly been due to increase in population, which has driven global biomass extraction. In contrast, the growth in the rate of nonrenewable material extraction can largely be attributed to industrialization and postwar prosperity in Europe, North America, Japan and the USSR. As Krausmann *et al* note:

> In the year 2000, fully industrialized countries (inhabited by 15% of the world population) were directly responsible for one third of global resource extraction; this imbalance is even more pronounced for key materials such as fossil energy carriers,

---

41 Ibid 1.1.

42 Comprising agricultural materials, industrial minerals and metallic ores, construction minerals and fossil fuels.

43 F Krausmann *et al*, 'Growth in global materials use, GDP and population in the 20th century' (2009) 68(10) *Ecological Economics* 2696, 2699.

44 Ibid 2707.

45 Ibid 2700.

46 EA Wrigley, *Continuity, Chance and Change: The Character of the Industrial Revolution in England* (Cambridge University Press 1988).

47 Krausmann (n 43) 2707.

48 Ibid 2708.

industrial minerals and metallic ores, where the share of the industrial countries is above 50%.[49]

This trend is shifting with a rapid rise in the social metabolism of China, India and several Latin American countries. In the early 2000s, exceptionally strong demand for minerals and metals in China and India drove metal prices to record nominal highs.[50] China emerged as the largest consumer of total main metals in 2003, and consumes about a quarter of world metal production.[51]

Jébrak divides society's demand for minerals since the late 1800s into three periods of globalization, interspersed with two periods of crisis.[52] From the late 1800s to the outbreak of the First World War (first period of globalization), the demands of industrialization in Europe, the USA and Japan spurred an increase in the use of iron and coal. Despite a colonial structure that supported mineral exploration all over the world, the demand for minerals was still largely filled by local mining suppliers, with limited input from Third World countries.[53] The period from 1918 to 1945 was a time of political turmoil and economic depression and saw the first global mineral commodity downturn. Despite two World Wars that increased the demand for aluminium, nickel and tungsten, the price of copper and other metals fell.[54] Gold was the outstanding exception,[55] and the maintenance of the gold standard led to a boom in gold mine exploration, development and production.[56] The postwar reconstruction period from 1945 to the mid-1970s led to a second period of globalization. The birth of the automotive industry and an explosion in consumer goods reliant on electricity generated enormous demand for construction minerals, base metals (copper, iron and bauxite-aluminium) and rarer metals such as chromium, titanium and platinum.[57] The sources of mineral supply also began shifting to the territories

---

49 Ibid 2710.

50 Shane Streifel, *Impact of China and India on Global Commodity Markets: Focus on Metals and Minerals and Petroleum* (World Bank undated) http://siteresources.worldbank.org/INTCHIINDGLOECO/Resources/ChinaIndiaCommodityImpact.pdf accessed 3 October 2018, 3.

51 Ibid 5.

52 Michel Jébrak, 'Innovations in mineral exploration: Targets, methods and organization since the first globalization period' (June 2012) http://azimut-exploration.com/mining_documents/2012_Jebrak_Innovations_Mineral_Exploration_EN.pdf accessed 9 October 2018.

53 Ibid 14.

54 Ibid 20.

55 For an account of the gold standard and its causal relationship to the Great Depression see Barry Eichengreen and Peter Temin, 'The Gold Standard and the Great Depression' (2000) 9(2) *Contemporary European History* 183.

56 Jébrak (n 52) 20.

57 Ibid 23.

of the nondeveloped world, corresponding with an increase in State control of the mining industry.[58] The oil crisis marked the beginning of the second crisis period, as resource-rich oil-producing States attempted to gain more power on a global scale. The oil crisis, together with expropriations and labour and political unrest, slowed growth in developed countries, reducing demand for metals.[59] A widespread drop in metal prices was accompanied by a marked reduction in mining company activity.[60] By the turn of the century, however, a revolution in communication and renewable energy technologies and the increased involvement of the BRIC States in the world economy led to a surge in the scope and quantity of mineral demand.[61] In some commodities, annual per capita consumption increased tenfold.[62] Some commodities reached record prices, also driven by the low yield of discoveries in the previous period.[63] Between 2003 and 2008 the real prices of energy and metals more than doubled.[64] Since that time, however, and following the 2008 global recession, the outlook for the mining industry has dimmed once again.

Future global mineral demand will be based on (1) uses for mineral commodities; (2) population growth; and (3) standard of living. Based on these variables, Kesler estimates that the combined total increase in global mineral demand will be in the region of 1 per cent per year.[65] Notwithstanding the possibility of recycling certain commodities, and assuming a business as usual approach to current systems of economic production and social reproduction, 'the trend toward gradually increasing global demand has been clear for many decades and is likely to remain in place'.[66]

Mineral commodities are also key to a global sustainability transition. So-called green minor metals such as indium, germanium, tantalum, lithium and rare earths are critical inputs to future sustainable technologies for the generation and conservation of energy which are needed for the existential crisis

---

[58] Ibid.

[59] Ibid 30.

[60] Ibid 37.

[61] Ibid 38.

[62] For example, annual per capita consumption of copper increased from 485 grams in 1990, to 4,343 grams in 2010. See Jébrak (n 52) 38.

[63] Ibid 39.

[64] Bilge Erten and José Antonio Ocampo, 'Super-cycles of commodity prices since the nineteenth century' (January 2012) *Initiatives for Policy Dialogue Working Paper Series* 2.

[65] Stephen E Kesler, 'Mineral supply and demand into the 21st century' in Joseph A Briskey and Klaus J Schulz, *Proceedings for a Workshop on Deposit Modeling, Mineral Resource Assessment, and their role in Sustainable Development* (US Geological Survey 2007) 57.

[66] Ibid.

of our time – climate change.[67] The much-touted 'fourth industrial revolution' (4IR), characterized by a fusion of technologies that blur the line between the physical, digital and biological spheres, will also require major mineral inputs. World Economic Forum executive chairperson Klaus Schwab describes the 4IR as 'a technological revolution and that will fundamentally alter the way we live, work and relate to one another'.[68] And yet, as the World Economic Forum has itself acknowledged, the 4IR will be a nonstarter without the batteries enabling mass storage on a mass scale. Such batteries will in turn require supplies of lithium, nickel, cobalt, manganese and aluminium, among others.[69] As Kesler concludes, 'increases in demand for minerals are almost inevitable for the next 50 years or so unless there is a major breakdown in global economic activity or a catastrophic decrease in world population'.[70]

4. GLOBALIZED SUPPLY: TRENDS IN FORMAL MINING

Over the past 150 years the supply of minerals to meet society's voracious demand has been met by both formal, largescale, industrial mining as well as by the large and burgeoning artisanal and smallscale mining sector (ASM).[71]

ASM is a significant economic sector, constituting a livelihood strategy for millions of people in more than 80 countries, and in sub-Saharan Africa, Asia, Oceania and Central and South America in particular.[72] The exact number of people working in ASM is unknown, but the figure is believed to have increased sixfold over little more than 20 years, reaching an estimated 40.5 million people in 2017.[73] Taking into account relations of dependence on ASM miners, the total number of people dependent on the sector is calculated to

---

[67] Matthias Buchert *et al*, *Critical Metals for Future Sustainable Technologies and Their Recycling Potential* (UNEP 2009) iii–iv.

[68] Klaus Schwab, 'The Fourth Industrial Revolution: What it means, how to respond', www.weforum.org/agenda/2016/01/the-fourth-industrial-revolution-what-it-means-and-how-to-respond/ accessed 3 October 2018.

[69] Benchmark Mineral Intelligence, 'Batteries core to a fourth industrial revolution, World Economic Forum', www.benchmarkminerals.com/batteries-core-to-a-fourth-industrial-revolution-world-economic-forum/ (accessed 21 February 2019).

[70] Kesler (n 65) 58.

[71] Definitions of ASM vary, and may focus on level of mechanization, number of miners, production capacity of the mine, size of capital investments and size and scale of the operation. In some countries, ASM is also reserved for nationals of that jurisdiction.

[72] International Institute for Sustainable Development, *Global Trends in Artisanal and Small-Scale Mining: A Review of Key Numbers and Issues* (2018) 2.

[73] Ibid.

exceed 150 million.[74] ASM operators are believed to work on more than 30 different minerals, although the sector's contribution to global supply differs from commodity to commodity.[75] The problematic environmental, health and safety and social effects of ASM are well documented,[76] but formalization of the sector has proven difficult.

This book is about formal mining only. The governance narratives and issues associated with ASM are distinct and complex, meriting their own coverage in a monograph of this length. In many countries ASM is still an informal and illegal activity, vilified for its associations with social conflict, environmental degradation and human rights violations. Perceptions of ASM vary widely from country to country,[77] as do regulatory frameworks, where these have been set in place. There are nevertheless many linkages between ASM and formal mining. The latter has its roots in ASM and the forms of organization that flowed from early prospecting operations in the nineteenth century. In the mid-1800s, target mineral deposits of iron, copper, nickel and gold were still largely discovered serendipitously in old excavations, and extractive technologies were largely confined to prospecting using handheld instruments and field geology.[78] Early mining regulatory frameworks such as the federal General Mining Law of 1872 in the USA respond more to the needs of ASM than those of industrial mining. In many parts of the world, lowtech, labour intensive mining activities take place in close proximity to the capital intensive operations of formal mining, sometimes even on the same concession.[79] Some have even argued that the same conditions that have facilitated foreign direct investment in largescale mineral exploration and exploitation have also fuelled the explosive growth of the ASM sector.[80]

The focus thus turns to formal mining, and the manner in which the industry has responded, and developed in response to, society's mineral demand. The following sections explore formal mining as an integrated production system, the extent of private and public investment in formal mining, the geographical extent of formal mining and the profitability of the mining industry.

---

74 Ibid.

75 Ibid 3. High levels of contribution include global sapphire supply (80 per cent), and gold (up to 20 per cent).

76 See for example Gavin Hilson, '"Creating" rural informality: The case of artisanal gold mining in sub-Saharan Africa' (2013) 33(1) *SAIS Review of International Affairs* 51; Agnes G Mwakaje, 'Environmental degradation under artisanal and small-scale mining in Tanzania: Can innovations in institutional framework help?' (2012) 2(9) *International Journal of Environmental Protection* 7.

77 International Institute for Sustainable Development (n 72) 3.

78 Jébrak (n 52) 17–19.

79 International Institute for Sustainable Development (n 72) iv.

80 See Hilson (n 76).

4.1 An Integrated, Globalized Production System

By the turn of the twenty-first century, the formal mining industry exhibited the features of an integrated production system aligned with the mining cycle.[81] The mining cycle commences with a specific demand for minerals, which spurs investment in exploring or prospecting, and then mine construction and development if an economically viable reserve is proved. After a period of mine operation – the only phase during which a mine can expect to make profits – the cycle moves to decommissioning and rehabilitation once an ore reserve becomes depleted. Depending on the socioecological features of the mine site, the cycle then moves to a period of managing residual and latent impacts.

Companies of different sizes and scales of operation constitute an integrated production system by occupying identifiable niches within this cycle. As *Breaking New Ground*, the final report of the MMSD project, explains: 'Junior companies find new ore bodies and sell them to larger companies. Intermediaries offer growth potential through merger among themselves or by being taken over by the largest operations. Miners feed product to smelters and refiners, who in turn provide metals or mineral products to fabricators, and so on.'[82]

The corporate landscape of the mining industry can thus be visualized according to a simple distinction between juniors or explorers, which are nonproducing entities; 'majors' (large producing companies, frequently with transnational operations); and 'intermediaries' (all other producing companies, at times formed to exploit only a single deposit).[83] Many of the companies that are now majors were established in the mid-1800s: Broken Hill Proprietary in 1863, Rio Tinto in 1873, and Anglo-American in 1917, for example. Through their association with international finance houses and development of 'world class' deposits, these companies gained a headstart in the business of minerals extraction.[84]

Various commentators have noted a trend of consolidation or concentration in the mining industry over the past 50 years. Based on data sourced by the

---

[81] International Institute for Environment and Development and World Business Council for Sustainable Development, *Breaking New Ground: Mining, Minerals and Sustainable Development* (Earthscan 2002) xiv (henceforth *Breaking New Ground*).

[82] Ibid 60. This patterning is nevertheless not homogenous across commodities, and for some, operations tend to be more vertically integrated.

[83] Magnus Ericsson, 'Mining industry corporate actors analysis' (March 2012) Polinares (EU Policy on Natural Resources) 3. More elaborate typologies exist: see for example Figure 3.3, *Breaking New Ground* (n 81) 60.

[84] Jébrak (n 52) 15.

Raw Materials Group, Mitchell highlighted an increase in corporate concentration for most major minerals for the years spanning 1975–2005. During this period, for example, the percentage of platinum production controlled by the top five producers shifted from 63 per cent to 86 per cent. Copper, iron ore and aluminium exhibited similar trends.[85] Ericsson's corporate actor analysis for the mining industry affirms continuing consolidation post-2005, with an increasingly diminishing number of intermediaries. In 2005, the intermediary level of production included some 957 companies, but by 2009 this figure had been reduced to 305.[86] In 2012, HSBC observed that six large companies controlled the mining of industrial minerals,[87] and about eight companies constituted 'seniors' in the gold mining sector.[88] The conclusion to which this analysis points is that globally, a limited number of companies control an increasing share of the mining industry.[89]

Counterintuitively, the number of mines actually producing metal ores using mechanized methods is quite small: some 2500, based on a 2012 analysis.[90] The spread between the largest and smallest mines is also large. In 2012, just 13 open pit mines were responsible for 20 per cent of the volume of metal ore hoisted annually in the world. The production rate at these mines exceeded 50 Mt of ore annually. A further hundred mines produce more than 10Mt of ore per year, with the remaining 2400 producing considerably less than that.[91] Even smaller mines, however, can have significant socioecological impacts.

Metals and mining has been called 'the oldest truly global sector' because all mining producers are disciplined by global commodity prices, and cross-border investment is common.[92] While there are national, regional and commodity-specific mining associations, in the early 2000s the mining industry also mounted a global institutional and advocacy response to mounting crit-

---

85 Paul Mitchell, 'The structure of the global mining sector' in Christopher Eads, Paul Mitchell and Francisco Paris (eds) *Advancing the EITI in the Mining Sector: A Consultation with Stakeholders* (EITI 2009) 21, 24.

86 Ericsson (n 83) 3. Post 2012 the mining industry saw a sharp dip in mergers and acquisitions. However, by the end of 2017 industry analysts were already highlighting an equity market rally for major firms, and a return to an agenda of growth. See Rebecca Campbell and John Tivey, 'Mining & Metals 2017: A tentative return to form', www.whitecase.com/publications/insight/mining-metals-2017-tentative-return-form, accessed 21 February 2019.

87 BHP Billiton, Rio Tinto, Anglo American, Xstrata, Glencore and Vale.

88 EMA Equity Research, HSBC 'Metals & Mining' (June 2012).

89 Ibid.

90 This figure excludes Chinese mines, which are on average comparatively small (Ericsson (n 83) 4).

91 Ibid.

92 EMA Equity Research (n 88) 5.

icism of its economic, social and environmental impacts, as will be explained in Chapter 2. And, as outlined in Chapter 3, the industry faces increasingly globalized forces of resistance.

4.2 Public and Private Investment in Formal Mining

Over the past 150 years, both the public and private sectors have invested extensively in the production of mineral commodities along the mining cycle. At present, private ownership of the factors of mining production – distinct from ownership of the minerals in the ground – is higher than ever before.[93] But this has not always been the case.[94] Recalling Jébrak's categories of globalization and crisis outlined in section 3 of this chapter, State intervention in hardrock mining production tended to increase in the intervening periods of crisis. During the 1960s, for example, a swathe of nationalizations in the developing world resulted in the expropriation of several foreign mining companies.[95] These nationalizations rode on the momentum of calls for a New International Economic Order, and the developing doctrine of permanent sovereignty over natural resources. Upon gaining independence from European powers, many countries in the developing global South were determined to use mineral extraction to leverage economic and social development. By this stage, though, the supply of raw mineral materials from the global South had already become entrenched in the global North's industrialization processes.[96] While the hope was that nationalized mining industries would serve as engines of economic growth and rapid industrialization, many of these Statist policies failed. In countries where nationalization had taken place, the industry often stagnated, and even declined.[97] Many internal and external factors contributed to this state of affairs, including a fall in the global price of mineral commodities, the inability of State-owned mining industries to access capital and low reinvestment in mining assets.[98]

---

93 *Breaking New Ground* (n 81) 64; Mitchell (n 85) 24.

94 The World Bank has documented State involvement in the mining industry on numerous occasions. See for example World Bank and the International Finance Corporation, *Mining Reform and the World Bank: Providing a Policy Framework for Development* (2003); World Bank (Raw Materials Group), *Overview of State Ownership in the Global Minerals Industry: Long Term Trends and Future* (World Bank 2011).

95 Jébrak (n 52) 24.

96 For an account of these dynamics see, for example, Boni Campbell (ed.), 'Regulating mining in Africa: For whose benefit?' Discussion Paper No. 26 (Nordika Africa Institutet 2004).

97 African Union, *Africa Mining Vision* (February 2009) 11.

98 Ibid.

In the 1980s there was a fundamental paradigm shift and redefinition of the role of the State which centred on almost complete withdrawal from the process of mining production (the minimalist State). Instead of actively engaging in mining, the minimalist State was responsible for promoting and facilitating mining through, among others, favourable institutions of property and taxation. At the same time, the State was burdened with regulating private mining proponents to ensure that the worst economic, social and environmental impacts associated with mining did not materialize. This is the model of the State associated with the sustainable mineral development consensus, and the extractivist critique outlined in section 1 above. Bretton Woods institutions played an important role in this paradigm shift. Rather than simply financing public or private sector projects during the 1980s, the World Bank began to focus on mining as a driver of development, providing financial and technical support to mineral-rich jurisdictions to reform their mining codes and practices.[99] By the early 2000s more than 90 States had adopted new mining laws or revised their mining codes to increase foreign direct investment in the mining sector.[100] The mining reforms giving effect to a reduced State were embedded within a broader package of economic reforms focused on liberalization of imports and export promotion, liberalization of exchange controls, fiscal reform, State-owned enterprise reform, privatization, reduction of public expenditure and reform of public sector management.

More recently, in certain regions (Latin America and, to a lesser extent, Africa), States have reasserted a role in mining production to better position mineral extraction within a national development project. Positively framed as resource nationalism and critiqued as neoextractivism, in this role the more assertive State steps in to force a free carried interest in private mining enterprises, raises taxes, revises contracts or forms State-owned mining companies. The State's responsibility to protect environment and society in this paradigm is still asserted, but comes into conflict with calls to use natural resources for national development projects.

The public sector has also invested in the supply of mineral commodities throughout the modern history of formal mining in less obvious, less visible ways. In the late nineteenth century, huge public investments were made in education, to develop institutions equipped to develop and impart the high-level skills necessary for a competitive edge in mining production. In the USA, the Columbia School of Mines was established in 1964, and more than

---

[99] Kato Lambrechts (ed.), *Breaking the Curse: How Transparent Taxation and Fair Taxes Can Turn Africa's Mineral Wealth into Development* (Christian Aid 2009) 7.

[100] Gavin Bridge, 'Mapping the bonanza: Geographies of mining investment in an era of neoliberal reform' (2004) 56(3) *The Professional Geographer* 406, 407.

20 universities across that country quickly followed suit.[101] Mining schools were also set up in other developed and developing jurisdictions.[102] Further, a number of States invested in developing national geological surveys. The oldest and most respected among these, the British Geological Survey and the United States Geological Survey (USGS), were set up in 1835 and 1879 respectively.[103] But again, such initiatives were not confined to the developed world. In 1896, Khedive Ismail, the Khedive of Egypt from 1863 to 1879, established the Egyptian Geological Survey,[104] and in South Africa the Geological Commission of the Cape of Good Hope was founded in 1895.[105] In addition to the major public investments in transport infrastructure required to move mining ore from sites of extraction to sites of processing, the public sector has also consistently borne the cost of mining externalities, absorbing the healthcare costs of miners sickened by occupational diseases and the high costs of the atmospheric, soil and water pollution associated with mining. Given the State's absorption of the costs of these externalities, the geography of formal mining is pertinent.

4.3 The Geographical Extent of Formal Mining

A popular narrative suggests a geographical restructuring of mining investment as mineral-rich jurisdictions in the developing world have instituted neoliberal reforms and opened their mineral resources to foreign direct investment. This process is frequently interpreted 'as a process of globalization through which mineral rich (but otherwise very poor economies) in the developing world are experiencing an investment bonanza'.[106] The narrative concomitantly assumes a withdrawal of mining investment from established targets in the global North.[107] Bridge affirms a geographic shift in investment following on the heels of extensive neoliberal reforms of law and policy in several mineral-rich

---

101 Jébrak (n 52) 16. The famous Colorado School of Mines was established in 1874.

102 Some of the earliest mining schools were established in Australia (Bendigo School of Mines, 1883), Brazil (Ouro Prêto Mining School, Brazil, 1876), Canada (Department of Mining Engineering at McGill University, 1870), China (Jiaozuo School of Railroad and Mines, 1909, later the Chinese Institute of Mining and Technology, 1909), and South Africa (SA School of Mines, Kimberley, 1896, later the School of Mines at the University of the Witwatersrand).

103 See further section 1.1.2 of Chapter 4.

104 Wikipedia, 'Egyptian Geological Museum', https://en.wikipedia.org/wiki/Egyptian_Geological_Museum accessed 21 February 2019.

105 Council for Geoscience (South Africa), 'About Us', http://www.geoscience.org.za/index.php/about-us accessed 21 February 2019.

106 Bridge (n 100) 417.

107 Ibid.

jurisdictions. His research shows, however, that, contrary to popular belief, a largescale and even shift in private investment has been confined to a few 'rising' stars in the developing world (Chile, Peru, Indonesia), and that mature destinations have continued to attract investment.[108] In the boom years of the mid-1990s, for example, neoliberal reforms opened up new jurisdictions to exploration and mine development, but not all liberalizing mineral-rich countries saw investment inflows.[109] Bridge concludes that neoliberal reforms did not erase existing uneven patterns of mining investment, although they increased the extensity of investment targets. At the same time they contributed to new patterns of differentiation, as some countries attracted the lion's share of new investment, and then mainly during the boom years.[110]

4.4 The Profitability of the Mining Industry

On average, the mining industry has not been profitable over the past 40 years. Profitability is a social construct, a variable dependent upon input costs, financing costs, inflationary trends, taxes and the extent to which externalized costs are internalized, among others. Nevertheless, according to standard measures of profitability – market capitalization, return on capital, return on shareholder equity – the performance of the mining industry relative to other sectors has been poor, even as aggregate data is 'surprisingly sparse'.[111] In the early 2000s, the financial performance of nonferrous metals, steel and gold was falling increasingly below the global price equity index.[112] And the outlook for return on capital and return on shareholder equity also looked bleak. Between 1977 and 1999 the average return on capital was 6.9 per cent, with a lower 5.7 per cent return on shareholder's equity.[113]

However, even as some prophesied that the sector had lost traction and would never regain lost ground,[114] between 2003 and 2007 mining indices rose spectacularly, responding to strong commodity demand from China, India and other developing countries.[115] Between 2006 and 2007, record high commodity prices sent the indices of mining companies soaring above the world

---

108 Ibid 406.
109 Ibid 417.
110 Ibid 419.
111 P. Crowson, 'Mining industry profitability?' (2001) 27 *Resources Policy* 33, 35.
112 *Breaking New Ground* (n 81) 114.
113 Crowson (n 111) 35.
114 Ibid 33.
115 PriceWaterhouseCoopers (PwC), *Mine 2016: Slower, Lower, Weaker . . . But Not Defeated – Review of Global Trends in the Mining Industry* (PwC 2016) 15.

share index.[116] When the financial crisis hit in 2008, the industry was partially insulated by expectations that Chinese growth would support a mining recovery, and mining companies rebounded between 2009 and 2011.[117] Awash with cash, mining management ploughed the money into bigger and more marginal assets, rather than paying out dividends to shareholders.[118] However, from 2011 the value of mining share prices again began to erode relative to broader market indices, reaching a point in 2015 lower than that in the 2008 financial crisis. In 2015, the top 40 mining companies reached lows that were 'stark and irrefutable': their first collective net loss, the lowest return on capital employed, unprecedented restrictions on capital expenditure and debt and impairment levels that sent leverage to new heights.[119] At the height of the 2003–7 boom the market capitalization of the top 40 mining companies exceeded combined book values by US $1 trillion; by 2015 this had shrunk to just US $18 billion.[120] 'All gains made during the commodity super-cycle were effectively wiped out.'[121] However, a mere two years later the pundits were applauding a 'stellar financial performance' and cautiously predicting a positive outlook for the industry.[122]

While the first truism of the mining industry's profitability is therefore that on a long run average, and relative to other industries, the mining industry's performance is disappointing, the second is that the industry is volatile and exhibits boom and bust cycles. This means that in some years, mining companies and their investors can make windfall profits. So while the average return on capital between 1977 and 1999 was a mere 5.7 per cent, in some years the return rocketed to more than 20 per cent.[123] This variability, and the potential for a windfall investment, points to one of the reasons investors continue to put their money into mining stocks. As Crowson puts it:

> [N]either investors nor mining companies invest in the expectation of achieving the industry's average rate of return. The lure has been the pursuit of riches beyond the dreams of avarice. They have always sought the glittering prizes, those deposits that, for one reason or another, offer prospective returns well above both their own cost of capital, and the relatively low average.[124]

---

116 EMA Equity Research (n 88) 3.
117 PwC (n 115) 15.
118 Ibid 17.
119 Ibid 3.
120 Ibid 16.
121 Ibid 13.
122 PwC, *Mine 2018: Tempting Times* (PwC 2018).
123 Crowson (n 111) 35. See chart 8.
124 Ibid 37.

Various reasons have been put forward for these two truisms of mining industry profitability: there are long lead times between the decision to invest and project startup, and the demand for a particular commodity may change significantly before a project comes on stream. Since a large portion of the cost of setting up a project is fixed, project proponents may be forced to proceed, in turn flooding supply when the mine becomes operational and putting downward pressure on commodity prices.[125] There are different market structures for different mineral commodities, and some are more oligopolistic than others. But in other cases there are low barriers to entry and/or competition from ASM mining, making efforts at restricting supply difficult.[126]

The cyclicality of commodity pricing is often posited as the primary cause of the boom and bust nature of the industry.[127] Further, some researchers argue that the pronounced cycles in commodity pricing exhibit a declining trend.[128] According to the Prebisch–Singer hypothesis, for example, there is a tendency for primary commodity prices to deteriorate relative to manufactured goods over longrun cycles.[129] Recently, Erten and Ocampo tested and found support for the Prebisch–Singer hypothesis: for minerals (as for agriculture) the mean of each cycle in prices was significantly lower than the previous one, inclusive of the 2003–7 boom. This supports the view that real commodity prices exhibited a stepwise deterioration over the past century.[130]

There is a fair degree of consensus that the cyclicality of commodity pricing is driven by demand shocks rather than supply shocks. In one of the first papers to examine demand and supply shocks over more than a century (1840–2010),

---

[125] Ibid 41.

[126] Martin Stürmer, '150 years of boom and bust – what drives mineral commodity prices?' (2013) Discussion Paper 5/2013, German Development Institute.

[127] EMA Equity Research (n 88) 10.

[128] Crowson (n 111) 38.

[129] Building on the work of Kondratiev and Schumpeter, Prebisch and Singer studied the longrun cycles of commodity prices in the 1950s. They concluded that in terms of the international division of labour of the time, an improvement for Britain's terms of trade could be understood as a deterioriation for the terms of trade of countries exporting primary commodities. Singer further showed that the terms of trade between innovative products and standardized products also tends to deterioriate. Thus, while developing countries may pursue policies of industrialization and produce manufactured goods, they would be producing standardized products which would not reap the same level of economic rents arising from innovative products. A key dimension of the Singer–Prebisch hypothesis is that the prices of primary commodities rise faster than manufactured goods during the upswing of a supercycle, but then excess capacity and supply pushes those prices down relative to final manufactured goods. See Bilge Erten and José Antonio Ocampo, 'Super-cycles of commodity prices since the nineteenth century' (January 2012) *Initiatives for Policy Dialogue Working Paper Series* 5–6.

[130] Ibid 17, 28.

Stürmer found that price fluctuations in copper, lead, tin and zinc were generally driven by shocks in demand rather than supply.[131] Demand shocks are forms of unexpected strong growth of world output leading to supply shortages, and supply shocks include physical disruptions in supply, such as labour strikes, and cartel action, such as restricting production and stockpiling. For mineral-rich jurisdictions, one of the most interesting results of Stürmer's study is that over the long run self-imposed restrictions on supply by exporting countries are at best only temporarily effective in increasing prices.[132]

During boom times the mining industry has tended to respond by expanding production capacity, and during bust times by cost cutting.[133] Both tendencies affect the intensity and gravity of mining's economic, social and environmental impacts. Extending production capacity and cost cutting are even linked, as 'all too often, a reduction in cash costs has only been achieved through the investment of additional capital'. As Crowson writes:

> [T]he easiest way of lowering unit costs is to spread the fixed element across a larger output . . . Management has pursued the maximum possible technical economies of scale in mine and metal production. New projects have been brought on stream at ever-larger initial throughput rates in order to exploit such economies to the full.[134]

One corollary of reinvesting capital in increased production to cut costs is that dividend payments are withheld, affecting shareholder appetite for the mining industry.[135] Another corollary of the cost cutting mentality is that mines have to operate at full or near full capacity in order to achieve their cost targets.[136] But this means that negative social and environmental impacts associated with the industry are also maximized. And while the cyclicality of commodity pricing has been used as an 'alibi' for low profitability,[137] it has also been put forward as an impediment to adopting the values of sustainable development.[138] The mining industry (so the argument goes) is already stressed by low commodity prices and low average rates of return on investment, and cannot afford the increased environmental and social costs that do not also lead to increased pro-

---

131 Stürmer (n 126) 2.

132 Ibid 2–3.

133 Crowson (n 111) 39. See for example praise for the latest costcutting measures of global seniors in PwC (n 122) 11.

134 Crowson (n 111) 39.

135 PwC (n 115) 17.

136 Ibid.

137 Ibid 38.

138 D. Humphreys, 'Sustainable development: Can the mining industry afford it?' (2001) 27 *Resources Policy* 1.

ductivity, such as costs associated with community programmes, reinforcing a tailings dam or sterilizing an ore body for environmental reasons.[139]

Rather than placing the blame for lacklustre industry profitability on exogenous factors such as project lead times, low barriers to market entry or commodity pricing, the question arises whether responsibility should not be laid at the door of industry players themselves, particularly for poor decisions to develop and acquire additional mineral-producing assets. In this regard, the strong cautionary tone of the 2018 PriceWaterhouseCoopers (PWC) review of the mining industry is interesting:

> Perhaps the most significant risk currently facing the world's top miners is the temptation to acquire mineral-producing assets at any price in order to meet rising demand. In the previous cycle, many miners eschewed capital discipline in the pursuit of higher production levels, which set them up to suffer when the downturn came. While we expect capital expenditure to increase next year as companies implement their longterm growth strategies, miners must be careful to maintain discipline and transparency in the allocation of capital. They need to resist the urge to pursue projects or acquisitions at any price, and instead, focus on mining for profit, not for tonnes.[140]

These cautionary words from a mainstream, conservative organization fly in the face of older, entrenched views that mining is good for development and that mineral-rich developing countries must promote mining investment, as the narratives constructed in Chapter 2 demonstrate. They also fly in the face of the loud voices of recently elected, right leaning populist governments, such as those led by Trump in the USA and Bolsonaro in Brazil, who are riding a wave of nationalist sentiment with promises of increased support for the mining industry.[141]

The caution against acquiring mining assets 'at any price' recognizes that short-run decisions in this vein are damaging to the industry itself. Of far greater importance is that in acquiring assets, mining companies impose costs on third parties – communities, Indigenous Peoples and the environment – where the 'price' involved may be survival itself. This places an even greater responsibility on the mining industry and host governments.

---

139 Ibid 2.

140 PwC (n 122) 2.

141 This trend is further discussed in section 6.2 below.

4.5 Peak Minerals

Since the mid-2000s there has been interest in 'peak minerals', a metaphor that draws on the notion of 'peak oil'.[142] Some researchers have modelled peaks in resource production to determine when resource availability may decline.[143] For example, in a recent contribution, Rustad applied Hubbert-style analysis used in the production history of oil to other raw materials.[144] Relying on histories of production statistics, he found that many resources commonly thought of as being close to peaking (such as copper, the rare earth elements, lithium and helium) actually exhibited exponential growth in production.[145] This research supports the position that while lithographic stocks of minerals are undoubtedly finite, technology (allowing for increasingly efficient extraction of mineral commodities from lower grade ores) and prices (allowing for the extraction of increasingly remote and difficult to access reserves) can prolong resource accessibility.[146] Some mineral-dependent jurisdictions have also prepared tables of the number of extractive years remaining for particular commodities, given known mineral reserves and current rates of production.[147]

However, as Prior and others have pointed out, the 'peak' in peak minerals is unlikely to be associated with mineral stocks, at least viewed from a global perspective. Rather, peak production limits are more likely to be associated with social and environmental constraints.[148] The key driver in this regard is the trend towards declining ore grade and quality.[149] Research conducted in

[142] The work on peak oil stems from Hubbert's modelling of oil production in 48 states in the USA (MK Hubbert, *Nuclear Energy and the Fossil Fuels* (Shell Development Co., Exploration and Research Division 1956). Hubbert predicted an oncoming oil production peak and coined the term 'energy services' as a means to conceptualize how such services could be met using alternative energy sources. See T Prior *et al*, 'Resource depletion, peak minerals and the implications for sustainable resource management' (2012) 22 *Global Environmental Change* 577, 578.

[143] Prior (n 142) 578.

[144] James R Rustad, 'Peak nothing: Recent trends in mineral resource production' (2012) 46 *Environmental Science and Technology* 1903.

[145] Ibid.

[146] Prior (n 142) 577.

[147] See for example GM Mudd, *The Sustainability of Mining in Australia: Key Production Trends and their Environmental Implications for the Future* (Research Report 2009); African National Congress, *Maximizing the Developmental Impact of the People's Mineral Assets* (Policy Discussion Document 2012).

[148] Ibid 578. See also Leah Mason *et al*, 'Availability, addiction and alternatives: three criteria for assessing the impact of peak minerals on society' (2011) 19 *Journal of Cleaner Production* 958.

[149] Ore grades signify both the concentration of a particular mineral or metal being mined, as well as the quality of the ore with respect of processing, such as whether it is

Australia, for example, has shown that the longterm trends for copper, nickel, gold, lead, silver and zinc ore grades are all declining.[150] In the case of iron ore, Australia's known reserves are increasingly composed of magnetite (which has 24 per cent iron in its natural formation), which requires more water and energy to extract and process as an export product than haematite (55–66 per cent iron in natural formation).[151] Similarly, Australia has fairly large reserves of rare earth oxides, but these are locked away in the monazite component of heavy mineral sand deposits, which also contain thorium and uranium. The treatment costs associated with these byproducts currently make these reserves subeconomic to exploit.[152] Internationally, gold ore grades have also constantly declined over the past 80 years.[153] South Africa, for example, is estimated to have at least 30 years of gold production left (having been the world leader in gold production until 2009). However, most of the remaining gold is found in low grade or deep lying deposits.[154]

Declining ore grades substantially increase the energy required for extraction and significantly heighten the pollution burden.[155] The Australian Productivity Commission has also found that capital and labour inputs into the mining industry have risen as ore grades have declined.[156] Pollution increases because as the ore grade declines, miners are forced to exploit economies of scale to meet demand and maintain the same unit costs of production.[157] Social

---

fine or coarse, or contains impurities such as pyrite (see Prior n 142, 579). For a contrasting view see James West, 'Decreasing metal ore grades: Are they really being driven by the depletion of high-grade deposits?' (2011) 15(2) *Journal of Industrial Ecology* 165.

[150] Prior (n 142) 580.

[151] Mason (n 148) 963.

[152] Prior (n 142) 579.

[153] PN Neingo and T Tholana, 'Trends in productivity in the South African gold mining industry' (2016) 116 *Journal of the South African Institute of Mining and Metallurgy* 283, 284; J Müller and HE Frimmel, 'Numerical analysis of historic gold production cycles and implications for future sub-cycles' (2010) 4 *The Open Geology Journal* 29.

[154] Neingo and Tholana (n 153) 284.

[155] Prior (n 142) 580. Determining whether water usage also increases with decreasing ore grades is difficult. While water scarcity is certainly a production limitation for some commodities, water use varies at the mine level, across commodities and across companies, and reporting mechanisms are still too rudimentary to make largescale claims about the relationship between water use and declining ore grades (ibid). Nevertheless, there is some research that establishes this relationship (see GM Mudd, 'Gold mining in Australia: Linking historical trends and environmental and resources sustainability' (2007) 10 *Environmental Science & Policy* 629).

[156] V Topp *et al*, *Productivity in the Mining Industry: Measurement and Interpretation* (Commission Staff Working Paper 2008).

[157] Prior (n 142) 581.

conflict arises not only due to increasing environmental awareness and public concern, but also because exploiting new mineral deposits takes miners into more remote areas that impact high value agricultural, conservation or heritage-associated land.[158]

While the concept of peak minerals has thus been squarely situated within a broader social and environmental context, the governance implications of this awareness have only been vaguely sketched. Prior *et al*, for example, urge that addressing these constraints will require 'innovative and proactive' responses on the part of government and industry.[159] From a government perspective, such innovative resource governance measures could include sovereign wealth funds or resource rent taxes.[160] Emphasis is also placed on a proactive State, engaged in longterm planning that complements primary metal production with the development of secondary production capacity and investment in recycling and recovery technology, facilities and policy.[161]

While global stocks of a particular mineral might be such that global supply will never be significantly threatened, for the State in which such reserve is situated the nonrenewability of the resource is of crucial importance, as mineral reserves can only be exploited once.

The focus of this section has been on the supply of mineral commodities. The following section draws attention to the 'externalities' of mining: impacts on environment, society and economy that would vastly reduce the profitability of mining for mining companies, their shareholders and mineral-rich jurisdictions, were there to be proper accounting of such.

5. GLOBALIZED IMPACT: THE UNEQUAL EFFECTS OF FORMAL MINING ON ENVIRONMENT, SOCIETY AND ECONOMY

Mining has far reaching, and oftentimes irreversible, impacts on the environment, society and economy of localities, regions, the nation State and even the globe. As the chains of mineral commodity production have become increasingly integrated and global in their reach, more and more communities and organizations have voiced resistance to mining on the basis that the industry's externalities are unsustainable and unequally distributed.

The extractives industry itself has acknowledged that it is one of the primary causes of environmental degradation and human-induced climate change

[158] Ibid 581–2.
[159] Ibid 583.
[160] Ibid 585.
[161] Mason (n 148) 964.

worldwide.[162] *Breaking New Ground* was frank in this regard: 'It is hard to argue that mineral extraction, processing, and use generally benefits the local ecosystems concerned or makes them more productive. Overall the ability of local ecosystems to provide biological benefits has often been seriously impaired by mining and mineral processing.'[163]

Environmental concerns relating to mining include mechanical damage of the landscape, loss of biodiversity, acid mine drainage (AMD), extensive mine wastes and tailings, gaseous (CO_2, NO_x, SO_2) and particulate matter emissions and metal contamination of soils and waters.[164] The World Economic Forum estimates that the mining and metals industry is responsible for between 40 and 55 per cent of permanent waste generated annually – some 10 billion tonnes per year. The industry is therefore among the world's 'great generators of waste'.[165] Societal impacts include a range of occupational and community health impacts, relocations, loss of livelihoods, gravesite relocations, social conflict and social decay. Proliferating forms of environmental and social assessment (canvassed in Chapter 6) have been developed to identity, avoid and/or mitigate these intersecting and cumulative impacts. Precautionary assessment of economic impacts is comparatively undeveloped, notwithstanding accepted explanations for 'Dutch Disease' and the resource curse.[166]

The distribution of environmental and social impacts is unequal, as illustrated by initiatives such as the European Commission-funded Environmental Justice, Liabilities and Trade (EJOLT) project.[167] The EJOLT project produced a database of resource conflicts along global production chains for a variety of commodities, including minerals. The Environmental Justice (EJ) Atlas includes hundreds of case studies where Indigenous Peoples and grassroots community-based organizations are resisting mining, often over a number of years. The 'Mineral Ores and Building Materials Extraction' category in the EJ Atlas shows a preponderance of these conflicts in South America, middle America, Africa, Eastern Europe, and South-East Asia. Other networking platforms, such as 'Mines and Communities' (MAC),[168] allow hundreds of indigenous and solidarity NGOs to recount the stories of individuals and

---

[162] Extractives Hub, 'Environmental management: Overview' https://beta.extractiveshub.org/topic/view/ID/7 accessed 11 October 2017.

[163] *Breaking New Ground* (n 81) 232.

[164] Stanislaw Dudka and Domy C Adriano, 'Environmental impacts of metal ore mining and processing: A review' (1997) 26 *Journal of Environmental Quality* 590.

[165] World Economic Forum, *Mining and Metals in a Sustainable World 2050* (September 2015) 22.

[166] These concepts are discussed in section 2 of Chapter 3.

[167] See www.ejolt.org. The project ended in 2015 and more recent information is located at www.envjustice.org accessed 21 February 2019.

[168] See www.minesandcommunities.org accessed 21 February 2019.

organizations battling against mining-related ventures. The MAC website specifically intends to expose the social, economic and environmental impacts of mining.[169]

How can these impacts be measured? Moving beyond conventional measures of economic performance, in natural resource accounting, Adjusted Net Saving (ANS) has been developed as a broader, longrun indicator of the economic, ecological and educational wealth of nations. ANS is a measure that subtracts from national income the consumption of fixed capital (wear and tear of machines), adds educational expenditure, subtracts the depletion of nonhuman capital and adds the costs of pollution.[170] Published under the auspices of the World Bank Group, a report on *The Changing Wealth of Nations* is the most recent global review of ANS.[171] The findings of this report highlight that the level of a country's economic development is strongly correlated to the composition of its national wealth. Natural capital, inclusive of mineral resources, is one form of national wealth; however, it is the largest component of wealth in low income countries, whereas in lower middle income countries it accounts for a quarter of wealth.[172] 'Getting rich', the report emphasizes, 'is not about liquidating natural capital to build other assets'.[173] Growth that leads to wealth rather than spikes in current income (as measured by GDP) 'is in part about more efficient use of natural capital and investing the earnings from natural capital sources, such as minerals, into infrastructure and education'.[174] The extraction of nonrenewable natural capital such as minerals offers a 'one-time chance' to finance development. The report continues:

> Nearly two-thirds of countries that have remained low income since 1995 are classified as resource-rich, or fragile and conflict states, or both. This shows that resources alone cannot guarantee development: strong institutions and good governance are needed to ensure that rents are invested and not used entirely for consumption.[175]

Applied to Africa, even the most rudimentary analysis of ANS is devastating. *The Changing Wealth of Nations* observes that sub-Saharan Africa

---

[169] Mines and Communities, 'About Mines and Communities', www.minesandcommunities.org/list.php?f=14 (accessed 21 February 2019).

[170] Patrick Bond, 'Economic narratives for resisting extractive industries in Africa' (2018) 33 *Research in Political Economy* 4.

[171] Glenn-Marie Lange, Quentin Wodon and Kevin Carey (eds), *The Changing Wealth of Nations: Building a Sustainable Future* (World Bank Group 2018) (henceforth *The Changing Wealth of Nations*).

[172] Ibid 2.

[173] Ibid.

[174] Ibid.

[175] Ibid.

loses roughly US$100 billion of ANS annually (excluding the platinum and diamond sectors). Averaging negative 3 per cent of gross national income over the period 1995–2014, it is the only region of the world with negative levels of ANS, with natural resource depletion being one of the key drivers.[176]

As noted in section 1 above, extractivist and neoextractivist approaches alike have rejected ecological limits to extractives-fuelled economic growth, minimized the impacts of the extractive industries or argued that losses can be compensated for economically. Specifically, the pro-mining discourses outlined in Chapter 2 either explicitly hold or assume that environmental, social and economic externalities are local, temporary or reversible; or argue that impacts can be managed or mitigated through good governance, strong State regulation and better technology; or accept the damage inflicted upon people and planet as a necessary sacrifice. Mining advocates have faith in proliferating forms of environmental and social assessment as instruments of precaution and environmental managerialism that can be used to identify, avoid or mitigate 'impacts'. Purveyors of the discourses of mining dissent outlined in Chapter 3, however, dispute the effectiveness of these tools and argue that mining and mineral processing inflict longterm and potentially irreversible changes to ecological, social, economic and cultural systems.[177]

The recognition of ecological and social limits to growth is integral to the nascent paradigm of postextractivism. Recognition of such limits is not new. In the early 1970s, the Club of Rome's *Limits to Growth* report sparked controversy by suggesting that the limits to growth would be reached sometime within the ensuing 100 years, and that the probable result would be a 'rather sudden and uncontrollable decline in both population and industrial capacity'.[178] The report considered the exploitation of nonrenewable resources in the context of global growth trends, and attempted to determine when the world would run out of major minerals given exponentially increasing rates of use and known reserves.[179] The *Limits to Growth* report was attacked from all sides of the political spectrum, including by scholars and activists in developing countries who took the position that the consumption of material goods and economic growth could be made compatible with the environment.[180]

---

[176] Ibid 63.

[177] An updated mapping on the EJOLT Environmental Justice Atlas features instances of ecocide, potential ecocide and cultural ecocide. See http://ejatlas.org/featured/ecocide (accessed 21 February 2019).

[178] Donella H Meadows *et al*, *The Limits to Growth: A Report for the Club of Rome's Project on the Predicament of Mankind* (Potomac Associates 1972) 23.

[179] Ibid. See the analysis at 54–69.

[180] Gudynas (n 23) 18–19.

More recent work on socioecological limits focuses on the integrity of Earth system processes ('planetary boundaries') rather than global growth trends, and on determining a 'safe operating space for humanity' rather than points of ultimate collapse. As laid out in a groundbreaking 2009 paper by Rockström and 28 colleagues, planetary boundaries index key, interlinked Earth system processes and their associated thresholds, which if exceeded could generate unacceptable environmental change.[181] Planetary boundaries are essentially values for control variables associated with each of these processes, such as atmospheric carbon concentration and change in radiative forcing as control variables for climate change, or the consumption of freshwater by humans (measured in km^3 per year) for global freshwater use. In this first presentation of the planetary boundaries concept, Rockström *et al* suggested that the thresholds for three of the Earth system processes – climate change, biodiversity loss, and interference with the nitrogen cycle – had already been breached, while the boundaries for freshwater use, change in land use, ocean acidification and interference with the global phosphorous cycle were fast approaching.[182] If allowed to continue, the authors warned, these trends and rates of change would significantly erode the resilience of major components of Earth system functioning,[183] with dire consequences for our capacity to pursue longterm social and economic development. In an update to the planetary boundaries framework published in January 2015, the authors suggested subglobal boundaries for those Earth system processes with strong regional operating scales, and identified two core boundaries, namely climate change and biosphere integrity (or rate of biodiversity loss).[184] They also recognized that different human societies and social groups had unevenly contributed to the current levels of control variables and transgression of boundaries, and that the notion of a 'safe operating space for humanity' and the definition of the thresholds was not in itself helpful to determine how to move within the safe operating space, where pressure on the boundaries needs to be released, by whom and how quickly.[185]

---

[181] Johan Rockström *et al*, 'A safe operating space for humanity' (2009) 461 *Nature* 472. Nine such Earth system processes were identified: climate change; rate of biodiversity loss (terrestrial and marine); interference with the nitrogen and phosphorous cycles; stratospheric ozone depletion; ocean acidification; global freshwater use; change in land use; chemical pollution; and atmospheric aerosol loading.

[182] Ibid 473.

[183] Ibid.

[184] Will Steffen *et al*, 'Planetary boundaries: Guiding human development on a changing planet' (2015) 347(6223) *Science*.

[185] Ibid.

The planetary boundaries framework has also been criticized on the basis that it affords insufficient attention to social boundaries. In an Oxfam discussion paper entitled 'A safe and just operating space for humanity', Raworth took up the challenge of complementing planetary boundaries with the concept of 'social boundaries'.[186] This leads to a graphic conceptualization of a safe and just operating space as a ring-shaped doughnut, with an environmental 'ceiling' and a social 'floor'. The social floor is not a given but captures those needs and claims to goods which a broad spectrum of people in society agree should be satisfied. There are various sources of such consensus. International human rights have long supported the fundamental moral claim to 'essentials' such as food, water, healthcare, education, political participation and personal security.[187] Bills of Rights, at the national or subnational level, provide a further indication of a particular society's priorities in setting the social floor. Internationally, the 2000 Millennium Development Goals (MDGs) expand upon the list of potential deprivations that would cause individuals and groups to drop below the social floor.[188] Further, since the Rio+12 conference in 2012, extensive effort is now being put into implementing the Sustainable Development Goals (SDGs) that address emerging concerns around social protection schemes, the need to provide decent work for a rapidly growing global workforce, electrification, combating extreme inequality and ensuring people's empowerment in the political and economic processes that affect their lives. To a certain extent, recognition of these rights and goals allows the social floor to be quantified and for progress to be chartered over time.

Apart from the mining of phosphorous (implicated in one of the recognized Earth system processes), a comprehensive analysis of the impact of mining on planetary or social boundaries has not yet been attempted. Superficially, and given the scale of contemporary mining, it is reasonable to assume that mining is at least contributing to climate change, biodiversity loss, freshwater use, change in land use, chemical pollution and atmospheric aerosol loading. A systematic analysis of the relationship between mining and social boundaries is also largely lacking, notwithstanding numerous reports on the impact of mining on Indigenous Peoples, environmental justice and human rights.[189]

---

[186] Kate Raworth, *A Safe and Just Operating Space for Humanity* (2012) Oxfam Discussion Paper www.oxfam.org/en/research/safe-and-just-space-humanity accessed 21 February 2019.

[187] Ibid 9.

[188] These include eradicating hunger and extreme poverty; achieving universal primary education; promoting gender equality and women's empowerment; reducing child mortality; improving maternal health; combating HIV/AIDS, malaria and other diseases; and extending access to water and sanitation.

[189] See the indepth analyses in Chapter 3.

6. BRINGING THE STATE INTO VIEW: MARKET SOCIETY AND THE 'DOUBLE MOVEMENT' FROM POLANYI TO THE PRESENT DAY

Taking all elements of the foregoing discussion into account – trends in demand, the dynamics of formal mining and the extent and distribution of environmental, social and economic impacts – the central questions are: What are the dynamics that keep the current system in place? Who influences the ways in which the costs and benefits of the mining industry are constituted and distributed? What are the forms and extent of their powers? Is the current system sustainable? What are the alternatives? These questions can be answered from numerous vantage points – those of consumers of mineral commodities, consuming countries, mining companies, investors, financing institutions, international financial organizations, Indigenous Peoples' organizations, community-based organizations and national and international NGOs.

The focus of this book, however falls on the State. This focus is justified because a range of pro- and anti-mining discourses vest the State with agency to promote and facilitate mining production *and* ensure that its worst environmental, social and economic impacts do not materialize. As is evident from the detailed exposition of mining discourses in Chapters 2 and 3, a range of actors make extensive and diverse demands on the State in relation to mining, development and sustainability, either couched positively in terms of what the State should be doing, or negatively in terms of what the State is failing to do. This positions the State as a mediator of conflicting interests, a key actor in distributing the costs and benefits of mining in a manner that advances the greater good.

This framing of the State is not new and was not formed in the crucible of mining-related conflict. In his 1944 work *The Great Transformation*, Polanyi was already able to apprehend the State as a site of paradox, steering multiple, conflicting social forces in a manner that locked the hegemony of market society into place. The thesis of the current book is that the contemporary State constituted by multiple mining narratives plays the same role.

6.1 Polanyi's Market Society and the 'Double Movement'

In *The Great Transformation*, Polanyi meticulously outlined the tumultuous changes that were necessary to effect the shift from a traditional to a market society. Polanyi challenged the idea that markets, based on a 'natural' economic psychology of barter and trade, were central to the functioning of society. On the basis of extensive historical evidence, Polanyi argued that while the institution of the market had been fairly common since the Stone

Age, no economy controlled by markets had existed before the nineteenth century:[190]

> No society could, naturally, live for any length of time unless it possessed an economy of some sort; but previously to our time no economy has ever existed that, even in principle, was controlled by markets. In spite of the chorus of academic incantations so persistent in the nineteenth century, gain and profit made on exchange never played an important part in human economy.[191]

Polanyi's second thesis was that extensive State intervention was needed to maintain the market economy and market society. By market economy he meant 'an economic system controlled, regulated, and directed by market prices',[192] to which the production and distribution of goods was thereby also entrusted; by market society he meant the embedding of social relations within the market rather than the other way around, 'the running of society as an adjunct to the market'.[193] The 'gearing of markets into a self-regulating system of tremendous power', Polanyi argued, 'was not the result of any inherent tendency of markets towards excrescence, but rather the effect of highly artificial stimulants administered to the body social'.[194] These stimulants were applied by newly constituted, centralized nation States in Western Europe and England.[195] Rather than the idea that markets are somehow natural, or stable, Polanyi showed that they were fragile and disaster prone, lurching from one crisis to another, as amply demonstrated in our time through the 2008 financial crisis.[196]

Market economies and market society required the imposition of rules (on enclosures – protectionism) backed by State-imposed violence.[197] They also required the fictitious commoditization of labour, land and money. The market mechanism needed to apply not only to the products of industry, but also to its chief elements. This had further implications for the State and its policy, as Polanyi pointed out, as the State had to assume the additional role of ensuring that no measure or policy countenanced the operation of market mechanisms for labour, land and money. In contemporary mining conflicts, the State's role

---

190 Polanyi (n 32) 45.
191 Ibid.
192 Ibid 71.
193 Ibid 60.
194 Ibid.
195 Ibid 69.
196 Zaman (n 33) 125.
197 Asad Zaman, 'Summary of the Great Transformation by Polanyi' (28 August 2013) https://weapedagogy.wordpress.com/2013/08/28/summary-of-the-great-transformation-by-polanyi/ accessed 21 February 2019.

in 'modernizing' indigenous land title, or failing to protect customary title to land, illustrates the continuing relevance of this insight.

However, the commoditization of land, labour and money necessary for the functioning of the market economy presaged the demolition of society. As Polanyi insisted:

> But labor, land and money are obviously *not* commodities; the postulate that anything that is bought and sold must have been produced for sale is emphatically untrue in regard to them . . . Labor is only another name for human activity, which goes with life itself, which in its turn is not produced for sale but for entirely different reasons, nor can that activity be detached from the rest of life, be stored or mobilized; land is another name for nature, which is not produced by man (*sic*); actual money, finally, is merely a token of purchasing power which, as a rule, is not produced at all, but comes into being through the mechanism of banking or state finance. None of the them is produced for sale. The commodity description of land, labor and money is entirely fictitious.

The fictitious commoditization of land, labour and money causes tremendous damage to society, which continues to this day.[198] Poignantly, commenting on the commoditization of land, Polanyi prognosticated that nature would be 'reduced to its elements, neighbourhoods and landscapes defiled, rivers polluted . . . the power to produce food and raw materials destroyed'.[199] Equally poignantly, in regard to human beings, he said: 'Robbed of the protected covering of cultural institutions, human beings would perish from the effects of social exposure; they would die as the victims of acute social dislocation through vice, perversion, crime and starvation.'[200]

The next element of Polanyi's thesis was that people would dismiss market mechanisms if they had full rein. Because no society could stand the 'ravages of this satanic mill' for the shortest time, contending social forces fought against the imposition of market mechanisms, to protect both the business organization of society and its human and natural elements.[201] Ultimately, however, the balance of contending forces needed to play out in a manner that still secured the supremacy of the market economy.

Polanyi illustrated eighteenth century society's 'unconscious resistance' to being an appendage of the market through his discussion of the 'Speenhamland law', an enactment that suspended the creation of a market for labour in England for a brief time at the turn of the nineteenth century.[202] The popular

---

[198] Zaman (n 33) 124.
[199] Polanyi (n 32) 76.
[200] Ibid.
[201] Ibid 77.
[202] Ibid.

Speenhamland law was supposed to guarantee a basic income to the poor without conditions. But since the market system had already become fairly entrenched, and land enclosures prevented a return to premarket ways of life, it contributed to their pauperization instead.[203] The failure of the Speenhamland episode framed the sensibilities of many of the nineteenth century Western thinkers who laid the ideological groundwork for the market society, convincing them that no alternative could exist to the wholesale commodization of labour in service of the market.[204] It also set the tone for the paradox that continues well into the twenty-first century: the side-by-side existence of extreme plenty and extreme poverty, and with that, forces that seek to continue, deepen and extend market society and forces that fight for society's self-protection.[205] The tension between these forces has not yet reached its apex, and each holds the other in place.

For Polanyi, the State was the site of paradox through which both 'organizing principles of society could be expressed'. He termed this the 'double movement' and described it thus:

> [T]he action of two organizing principles in society, each of them setting itself specific institutional aims, having the support of definite social forces, and using its own distinctive methods. The one was the principle of economic liberalism, aiming at the establishment of a self-regulating market, relying on the support of the trading classes, and using largely *laissez-faire* and free trade as its methods; the other was the principle of social protection aiming at the conservation of man and nature as well as productive organization, relying on the varying support of those most immediately affected by the deleterious action of the market . . . and using protective legislation, restrictive associations, and other instruments of intervention as its methods.[206]

Essential to the idea of the double movement is that it is the contention between these principles that assures the hegemony of the market economy and market society, albeit in milder forms than would otherwise hold sway if market mechanisms were allowed free rein.

6.2 Polanyi's Ideas in Our Time

Are Polanyi's ideas regarding the market economy, market society, State violence in the service of upholding economic systems, commoditization of the factors of production and the double movement still pertinent in our time?

---

203 Zaman (n 33) 139.
204 Polanyi (n 32) 84, 88.
205 Ibid 87.
206 Ibid 132.

Polanyi believed that the Second World War predicated the demise of market society.[207] What transpired instead in some of the most developed countries of the world was 30 years of Keynesian economics, which took labour out of the sphere of self-regulation. According to Zaman, '[m]any analysts have said that Keynes saved the market economy by making the smallest possible alteration that would make it possible to live with'.[208] During those same 30 years, communist, socialist and nationalist sentiments in developing countries fuelled the nationalization of foreign and privately owned industries, including a number of mines.[209]

Polanyi's warnings regarding the market economy and market society are still clearly relevant in contexts where free markets are unabashedly being promoted. Even while Keynesianism reigned, free market ideologues collaborated with State agencies and corporations to intentionally transfer free market ideas from one nation to another. In the USA, the most extreme form of free market capitalism was associated with Milton Friedman and the Chicago School of Economics, and the first intentional and violent transfer of these ideas occurred in Chile.[210] International aid organizations,[211] as well as large corporations, funded the training of intellectuals to believe in free markets as the solution to all social problems.[212] For example, army leaders from South America were trained at the 'notorious' School of the Americas to believe in both capitalism and the violence and ruthlessness required to impose capitalistic policies on a resistant population.[213] General Pinochet was among these leaders and he used force to impose Chicago School economics in Chile, pursuing a 'revolutionary project' that 'propounded economic and market solutions for practically all problems in society'[214] – this notwithstanding that the economic costs would be borne by the poorest and least sheltered sectors of Chilean society.[215] Under Pinochet's rule, Chile became the poster child for liberal reforms in the mining sector, ostensibly necessary to promote investment and stem poverty. As detailed in Chapter 2, IFIs and the mining industry subsequently used the Chilean model to advocate for similar mining policy and law reforms all over

---

207 Zaman (n 33) 124.
208 Ibid 143.
209 See section 4.2 above.
210 Friedman's ideas and the intentional transfer of Chicago School economics to Chile are documented in Naomi Klein, *The Shock Doctrine* (Picador 2008) 59.
211 An example would be the United States Agency for International Development's 'Chile Project'. See Juan Gabriel Valdés, *Pinochet's Economists: The Chicago School in Chile* (Cambridge University Press 1995) x.
212 Zaman (n 33) 143.
213 Ibid.
214 Valdés (n 211) xi.
215 Ibid.

the developing world. However, even at the height of its experiment with free market fundamentalism, Chile did not privatize the State-owned copper mining company Codelco, which had previously been nationalized by Allende. This was the 'only thing' that saved Chile from complete economic collapse in the early 1980s and ensured the State had a steady flow of funds.[216] Codelco remains a State-owned mining company to this day and is amongst the largest copper companies in the world, producing roughly 1.8 million metric tonnes of refined copper in 2017 – 11 per cent of the global total.[217]

At the time of writing, a virile form of free market ideology is on the rise again. Two figures represent this form of free market fundamentalism in the developed and developing worlds, respectively: Donald Trump in the USA, and Jair Bolsonaro in Brazil. Both leaders have been elected to office on the basis of a populist wave of economic and social discontent centred on job insecurity, debt vulnerability, deindustrialization and fear of migration and crime.[218] Both leaders are also advancing a nationalist form of economic liberalism – the first arm of Polanyi's double movement. Trumponomics, for example, has been described as a '21st-century version of Reaganomics' which aims to lower individual and corporate taxes, increase spending on military and physical infrastructure, further deregulate private activity and reduce protections for labour and the environment.[219] Bolsonaro is a far right politician who has appointed a rightwing, University of Chicago-trained banker as his chief economic adviser. This has been taken as a sign that the Brazilian President 'will embrace the neoliberal consensus that investors have been pressurizing Brazil to execute'.[220] On issues of environmental concern, both leaders have caused alarm. Trump is a climate change denialist who has withdrawn the USA from the Paris Agreement. A key element of his 'America First' campaign is to 'reorient' American environmental and energy policy and do away with 'job-killing' environmental regulations.[221] Bolsonaro has

---

[216] Klein (n 210) 104.

[217] Terence Bell, 'The world's 10 largest copper producers' *The Balance* (14 August 2018) www.thebalance.com/the-10-biggest-copper-producers-2010-2340291 accessed 21 February 2019.

[218] Jamie Morgan, 'Trumponomics: Everything to fear including fear itself?' (2017) Issue No. 78 *Real World Economics Review* 3, 7. Both leaders are also notorious for their misogynistic, racist, pro-gun and homophobic attitudes.

[219] Jayati Ghosh, 'Trumponomics and the developing world' (2017) 79 *Real World Economics Review* 29; Morgan (n 218) 3.

[220] Zaid Jilani and Lee Fang, 'American executives: Election of far-right Jair Bolsonaro in Brazil is a "bullish opportunity for US"' *The Intercept*, 25 October 2018 https://theintercept.com/2018/10/25/brazil-election-jair-bolsonaro-us-investors/ (accessed 21 February 2019).

[221] Morgan (n 218) 12.

been described as having a 'love affair' with mining and a desire to unleash the mining potential of the 1.7 billion-acre Amazon rainforest.[222] In line with the play of social forces under a global market economy, one can expect contending social forces to push back strongly against the dynamics that Trump, Bolsonaro and others are unleashing.

Polanyi's model, however, is also relevant in contexts where free market reforms aimed at stimulating the extractive industries have been seriously questioned. This is the case where States are more assertive and interventionist under the banner of neoextractivism. The thinking of Keynes and his compatriots fuelled 'development thinking' for the 'underdeveloped' regions of the world in the postwar period, and it was believed that conventional growth models would solve the problems of poverty and inequality.[223] Beginning with the dependency theorists in the 1960s, critique of the relationship between development and extractive-led economic growth has waxed and waned. In Latin America, periods in which neoliberalism has held sway have alternated with periods in which neoliberal reforms have been halted, and the onward march of the market checked.[224] But as Gudynas has argued, in a number of respects the assumptions underlying a neoextractivist approach are no different from extractivism. These include the belief in progress, development, the importance of exports and investments in extractives and the appropriation of nature.[225] While they may tinker with the detail, neoextractivist governments do not fundamentally eschew the market economy or market society, because they remain embedded in a global system of production organized along these lines.

The voices of the 1960s and 1970s that argued for natural resource use to fuel development in the underdeveloped regions echo through a figure such as Tanzania's president, John Magafuli. Magafuli came to power in November 2015 and almost immediately attracted attention for his strong stance against corruption. He also gained fame/notoriety for an extended confrontation with multinational mining companies, after it was discovered that a subsidiary of a Canadian multinational had allegedly been underreporting mineral exports and thus depriving the Tanzanian State of mineral revenues.[226] This altercation has led to some of the most far-reaching taxation reforms ever pursued in

---

[222] Bloomberg News, 'Amazon's mining treasure at stake as Bolsonaro leads Brazil vote', www.mining.com/web/amazons-mining-treasure-stake-bolsonaro-leads-brazil-vote-2/ accessed 21 February 2019.

[223] Gudynas (n 23) 16.

[224] Ibid 17ff.

[225] Ibid 24.

[226] Dan Paget, 'Magafuli has been president for two years: How he's changing Tanzania' *The Conversation*, 2 November 2017.

a developing country. Magafuli's economic policies rest on enabling intraregional trade, facilitating increased industrialization and – most significantly – capitalizing on the country's natural resources. As a commentator observes, Magafuli 'appears keen to distinguish his presidency by harnessing Tanzania's resources to fuel economic growth'.[227] Magafuli is no different to Trump or Bolsonaro in using the State mechanism to promote mining, commoditize nature and deliver mineral commodities to a global system of mineral production where the market determines the price.

Polanyi restricted his conception of the double movement to a State apparatus that promoted economic liberalism. He also insisted that, contrary to conceptions of *laissez-faire*, market economies and market society require significant State intervention to guarantee sustainability. This form of State intervention differs from that required by neoextractivism, but the end goal (promoting mineral extraction) and even some of the means (commoditizing nature, allowing social relations to be determined by the dictates of the market) are the same.

The Second World War was the crisis Polanyi invested with the potential to break market society. The existential crisis of this time is climate change, and the potential it holds to trigger broadscale, far-reaching and irreversible shifts in social and ecological systems. The latest report of the Intergovernmental Panel on Climate Change (IPCC) warns that limiting greenhouse gas emissions pathways to 1.5°C would require 'unprecedented' systems transitions that lead to deep emissions reductions in all sectors.[228] The IPCC also warned that currently stated national mitigation ambitions would not lead to the emissions cuts necessary to avoid overshooting global warming of 1.5°C by 2030, and that global emissions reductions would need to start declining well before this time.[229] Whether the current generation will be able to rise to this challenge, and whether the current crisis will fundamentally transform market economies, market society and the double movement in mineral production, are matters worthy of serious consideration.

7. AIM AND STRUCTURE OF THIS BOOK

This book uses the conceptual framing of Polanyi's 'double movement' to explicate the paradoxical role of the State in energy and hardrock mining in the

---

[227] Michelle DeFreese, 'Is Magafuli the region's next Kagame?' *HuffPost*, 16 May 2017 www.huffingtonpost.com/young-professionals-in-foreign-policy/is-magufuli-the-regions-n_b_9982846.html. accessed 21 February 2019.

[228] IPCC, *Global Warming of 1.5°C: An IPCC Special Report – Summary for Policy Makers* (October 2018) 17.

[229] Ibid 20.

era of the Anthropocene. It aims to demonstrate the patterning of State roles that orbit around promoting mining on the one hand, and protecting society from the industry's worst environmental, social and economic effects on the other. It adds meat to understanding *how* the State advances extractivism and neoextractivism as governance paradigms that continue to externalize these costs. It gestures towards a postextractivist world, but largely in the sense of identifying what needs to be undone.

To illustrate the State's double movement, the book focuses on four areas of policy, law and governance: property, taxation, environmental assessment, and mine closure. These areas of policy, law and governance constitute the double movement, but in different ways, as subsequent chapters elaborate. For each of these four areas, this book presents the patterning of State roles that give effect to the double movement. The analysis is based on the policies and laws of mineral-rich jurisdictions and the advocacy of IFIs, global and national mining industry associations, Indigenous Peoples' movements, national and international NGOs and academia. These analyses are set out in Chapters 4 (The State, Mining and Property Institutions), 5 (The State, Taxation and Mining), 6 (The State, Mining and Environmental Assessment) and 7 (The State and Mine Closure), respectively.

To frame these analyses, the book also delineates the key narratives or 'discourses' reflecting and constituting current understandings of the relationship between mining, development and sustainability. The 'pro-mining' discourses outlined in Chapter 2 provide an enriched understanding of extractivism and neoextractivism by distinguishing four narratives (the sustainable mineral development consensus, responsible mining, neoextractivism and critical and strategic minerals) and demonstrating the differentiated demands made of the State under each. Chapter 3, on 'discourses of dissent', does the same in respect of the resource curse theory, Indigenous Peoples' rights, human rights theories, environmental justice and feminist theories of mining.

An attempt has been made to refer to mineral policies and laws from mineral-rich jurisdictions the world over. Mining takes place in many places but States are differentiated by their dependence on mineral commodities for export earnings, foreign direct investment and national income. For the most part, the examples in this book are drawn from countries ranked highly on the ICMM's 'Mining Contribution Index' (MCI), that is, jurisdictions in which mining makes a significant contribution to the national (or subnational) economy.[230] Two limitations must nevertheless be acknowledged. As the author is

[230] The ICMM has investigated the role of mining in national economies which revolves around the idea of a Mining Contribution Index (MCI). For the latest explanation of the MCI see International Council of Mining and Metals, *Role of Mining in*

not literate in the languages of Spanish or Portuguese, examples from South American jurisdictions are limited, reliant upon where the author could source legislation or case studies in English. Second, examples from the author's home jurisdiction of South Africa may be over-represented.

The book opts for a discursive theory of the State. There are many theories of the State, spanning Marxist, Statist, feminist and Foucauldian accounts.[231] Discourse-analytic work challenges the idea that the State is a distinct material entity or agent capable of independently intervening in society.[232] Rather than a single 'State', there are only ideas of the State, produced by particular interest groups at particular times (a 'stateless' theory of the State). Discourse refers to the relatively durable social structuring of language, which is in turn one element of the relatively durable structuring and networking of social practices.[233] Discourses are powerful because inasmuch as they reflect how we understand the world, they also reconstitute that world, reproducing perceptions of persons, social relations, action and interaction and our grasp of the material world in a particular way. While any one particular discourse may represent the State as a distinct, material entity responsible for particular roles, or capable of certain misdemeanours, the plurality of State discourses exposes this as an illusion. The plurality of discourses relating to the State, mining, development and sustainability emerges not only at the level of macro level policy debates, as canvassed in Chapters 2 and 3, but also at the level of meso level policy debates on property, taxation, environmental assessment and mine closure, as presented in Chapters 4–7. The argument of the book nevertheless remains that the apparently confusing plurality of State roles gives effect to an overarching 'State': that of the double movement, which locks mining in the Anthropocene into a mould that continues to externalize mining's environmental, social and economic impacts.

National Economies (3rd edn 2016) 18ff. The MCI is a measure of the significance of mining in a national economy and is derived from a number of indicators: the total contribution of mining to export earnings, the extent to which mining's contribution to export earnings changed in the preceding five years, the value of mineral production expressed as a percentage of GDP and mineral rents as a percentage of GDP.

[231] For a fairly recent account of West European and North American developments in theorizing the State, see Bob Jessop, 'Bringing the State back in (yet again): Reviews, revisions, rejections, and redirections' (2001) 11(2) *International Review of Sociology* 149.

[232] Ibid 161.

[233] Norman Fairclough, *Analysing Discourse: Textual Analysis for Social Research* (Routledge 2003) 3.

2. The State, mining, development and sustainability: pro-mining discourses

1. INTRODUCTION

This chapter is the first of two outlining discourses on mining, development, sustainability and the role of the State. The purpose of this chapter and of Chapter 3 is to show the variety in discourses on the State's development and sustainability role that have crystallized around the globalized mining industry since the early 1970s. These discourses are both in favour of and critical of mining. This chapter deals with pro-mining discourses, which include the sustainable mineral development consensus, responsible mining, neoextractivism and critical and strategic minerals. Pro-mining discourses assume a robust, positive connection between progress, development, economic growth and the promotion of the mineral extractives industry. Discourses of dissent are set out in Chapter 3. Discourses in favour of and critical of the mining industry have influences that extend far beyond the State, shaping the role and actions of all parties with a stake in the global and national mining industries.

These chapters show that there is not a single or uniform understanding of the role a State should play in the quest for sustainable, mining-led development. The State emerges as a 'polyvalent, poly-contextual phenomenon which changes shape and appearance with the political forces acting towards it and the circumstances in which they do so'.[1] These political forces include international finance institutions (IFIs), the globally organized mining industry, national mining associations, international and national nongovernmental organizations (NGOs), mining-affected communities, indigenous communities and, not least of all, the State itself.

Chapters 2 and 3 illuminate the variety of expectations placed on the State to promote a 'developmental' mining industry that is also sustainable. The double movement – State promotion of mining and social protection against its impacts – echoes through the discourses canvassed in this chapter, but with varying degrees of emphasis. It is most readily discernible in the policy

---

[1] Bob Jessop, 'Bringing the State back in (yet again): Reviews, revisions, rejections and redirections' (2001) 11(2) *International Review of Sociology* 149, 161.

prescriptions of the sustainable mineral development consensus. Here the hope of mining's contribution to development legitimizes a rigorous push to establish a free market in mineral commodities, extending to the markets for mineral exploration and exploitation and not just the commodities *per se*. Comprehensive State regulation of (at least) environmental impacts is encouraged alongside appropriate environmental management. The discourse of responsible mining does not dispute these basic approaches, but tends to assume an incapable State, thus parsing out space for mining proponents to assume a greater degree of responsibility for social and environmental impacts. Under neoextractivism, States promote mining through contract renegotiations, State-owned mining companies, and State equity participation. Social protection tends to take the form of advancing the short term economic well-being of the nation as a whole or of a politically connected elite, rather than dealing with the immediate and longer term protection of particular communities or the environment. Emphasis on the economic well-being of developed nations emerges strongly in the discourse of critical and strategic minerals, and the forced neoliberal reforms in support of security of supply to the world's economic centres become apparent. Here, interestingly, the State's protective role over society and environment is used to disparage mining investment and trading partners that are not deemed to promote comparably rigorous standards.

2. THE SUSTAINABLE MINERAL DEVELOPMENT CONSENSUS

The sustainable mineral development consensus references a mainstream narrative that rests upon the economic fundamentals of neoliberalism.[2] It is a narrative that underscores the importance of minerals and mining for society, and the possibility of sustainably managing its social, economic and environmental impacts. Advanced by the leading lights in the global mining industry with the support of IFIs, it has tracked the emergence of the sustainable development movement. Within a Polanyian frame,[3] the sustainable mineral development consensus can be viewed as a massive countermovement, a response to trenchant critique of earlier neoliberal reforms in the mining industry and their socio-economic and environmental costs. The sections below outline the emergence of this discourse, before delving into its key claims.

---

[2] Sara L Seck, 'Transnational corporations and extractive industries' in Shawkat Alam *et al* (eds), *International Environmental Law and the Global South* (Cambridge University Press 2015) 380.

[3] See section 6 of Chapter 1.

2.1 Emergence of the Sustainable Mineral Development Consensus

The contours of the sustainable mineral development consensus emerged most sharply in the late 1990s and early 2000s, and were cemented with the Mining, Minerals and Sustainable Development (MMSD) Project in the early 2000s.[4] The bedrock for this discourse, however, was already being laid in the late 1970s and early 1980s, as neoliberal reforms were applied to the mining sector. Following the lead provided by Chile, the World Bank and International Monetary Fund (IMF) actively promoted neoliberal reforms in the mining industry and rapidly assimilated the developing discourse of sustainable development. Industry initiatives concentrated the sustainable mineral development consensus, including through the newly formed International Council on Mining and Metals (ICMM) and the Intergovernmental Forum on Mining, Minerals, Metals and Sustainable Development (IGF). Some mineral-rich jurisdictions also appropriated the discourse of sustainable development in their constitutions, mining policies and laws.

2.1.1 Early role of the World Bank

During the 1980s, the World Bank Group (WBG) and the IMF intentionally shifted their role in the nonfuel minerals sector from financing particular mining projects to promoting economic liberalism through private sector-led development.[5] Initially, however, the raft of legal reforms and best practices recommended by IFIs did not incorporate the language of sustainable development. When the International Bank for Reconstruction and Development (IBRD) or the International Development Association (IDA) provided infrastructure or project finance for major mining projects in the 1980s, sustainability considerations were limited to environmental and social covenants set forth in operational directives.[6] Sustainable development also failed to receive a single mention in the Bank's first comprehensive revised policy position vis-à-vis mining, the 1992 *Strategy for African Mining*.[7]

A noticeable shift, however, soon became evident. In 1994, for example, the IBRD sponsored a conference titled 'Development, Environment and

---

[4] Elizabeth Bastida, 'Integrating sustainability into legal frameworks for mining in some selected Latin American countries' (2002) Report commissioned by the MMSD project of the IIED 7.

[5] See the overview provided in Chapter 1.

[6] World Bank Group and International Finance Corporation, *Mining Reform and the World Bank: Providing a Policy Framework for Development* (Oil, Gas, Mining and Chemicals Department, World Bank Group 2003) 6.

[7] World Bank, *Strategy for African Mining* (1992) World Bank Technical Paper No. 181 (henceforth *Strategy for African Mining*).

Mining: Enhancing the Contribution of the Mineral Industry to Sustainable Development'.[8] And the executive summary of the 1996 *Mining Strategy for Latin America and the Caribbean (Strategy for LAC Mining)* led with the statement: 'This report looks at specific policies that could result in the sustainable development of the mining industries in the countries of the Latin American and Caribbean [LAC] region.'[9] The *Strategy for LAC Mining* insisted that the exploration boom occurring in the LAC countries during the early 1990s could be converted into 'sustainable mining development'.[10] Admitting that mining had at times left 'an unsightly and sometimes dangerous environmental legacy', the World Bank highlighted environmental concerns, suggesting that countries with modern regulations and competent environmental regulatory agencies had a competitive advantage in attracting private sector investment.[11]

By 1998, the World Bank's policy guidance on mining was saturated with references to sustainable mineral development. A Technical Paper on the WBG's involvement in the nonfuel minerals sector underlined the linkages between mining and development. It noted that in some countries in transition, minerals sector development could accelerate broader development programmes by providing immediate economic gains. It cautioned, however, that in some poorer countries (and especially in sub-Saharan Africa), stimulating investment in the minerals sector was necessary 'for the alleviation of poverty and its consequences'.[12] By the time the Extractives Industries Review was undertaken in mid-2001, poverty alleviation through sustainable development was positioned as axiomatic to the Bank's further involvement in the extractives industries.[13]

2.1.2 Mining in the early stages of the sustainable development discourse

A global debate on the relationship between development and environment started in the 1970s. People began to question the assumption of unlimited economic growth and the purpose of such growth; for example, was it meeting basic needs? In 1972, nations of the world convened in Stockholm at the UN Conference on the Human Environment, documenting their concerns in the

---

[8] World Bank, *World Bank Group Assistance for Minerals Sector Development and Reform in Member Countries* (1998) World Bank Technical Paper No. 405, 13 (henceforth *WBG Technical Paper No. 405*).

[9] World Bank, *A Mining Strategy for Latin America and the Caribbean* (1996) World Bank Technical Paper No. 345 xiii (henceforth *Strategy for LAC Mining*).

[10] Ibid.

[11] Ibid xvii.

[12] *WBG Technical Paper No. 405* (n 8) 13.

[13] The Extractives Industries Review is further considered in section 2.1.6 below.

1972 Stockholm Declaration. In the same year the Club of Rome issued a contentious report – *The Limits to Growth* – which suggested that limits to growth would be reached sometime within the ensuing 100 years.[14]

The concept of sustainable development can be traced to the 1980 World Conservation Strategy, formulated by the International Union for the Conservation of Nature (IUCN) in partnership with the United Nations Environment Programme (UNEP) and the World Wildlife Fund (WWF). In the late 1980s the World Commission on Environment and Development popularized the idea of sustainable development in *Our Common Future* (the Brundtland Report).[15] The Brundtland Report defined sustainable development as 'development that meets the needs of the present without compromising the ability of future generations to meet their own needs'.[16] The elaboration and largescale dissemination of sustainable development subsequently unfolded, punctuated by major United Nations meetings on environment and development.[17] The Sustainable Development Goals (SDGs), adopted by the United Nations in 2015, confirm the enduring relevance of sustainable development.[18]

The nonrenewability of nonfuel mineral resources was not a major focus in the Stockholm Declaration, the World Conservation Strategy, the Brundtland Report, the Rio Declaration or Agenda 21. Principle 5 of the Stockholm Declaration simply sounded two cautions: that nonrenewable resources should be employed in a manner that guards against their future exhaustion, and that benefits from such employment should be shared by all mankind. The World Conservation Strategy did not consider the longrun sustainable use of mineral resources, but identified the chemical, nutrient and solid waste pollution emanating from mining and other activities as a cause of habitat destruction

---

14 Donella H Meadows *et al*, *The Limits to Growth: A Report for the Club of Rome's Project on the Predicament of Mankind* (Potomac Associates 1972) 23.

15 World Commission on Environment and Development, *Our Common Future* (1988), www.un-documents.net/our-common-future.pdf accessed 21 February 2019 (henceforth *Our Common Future*). For an account of how *Our Common Future* served as an important preparatory document for UNCED see Iris Boroway, *Defining Sustainable Development for Our Common Future: A History of the World Commission on Environment and Development* (Routledge 2014).

16 Ibid 43.

17 UN Conference on Environment and Development (UNCED) held in Rio, 1992, with the Rio Declaration and Agenda 21 as outcome policy statements; World Summit on Sustainable Development (WSSD) held in Johannesburg, 2002, with the World Strategy on Sustainable Development and Plan of Implementation (PoI) as outcomes; and UN Conference on Sustainable Development held in Rio, 2012, with the report *The Future We Want* as outcome.

18 United Nations General Assembly, *Transforming Our World: The 2030 Agenda for Sustainable Development* A/RES/70/1, 2 (henceforth *Transforming Our World*). The SDGs replace the eight Millenium Development Goals adopted in 2000.

that threatened wild species of plants and animals.[19] In contrast to its greater concern with the rate of use of oil, gas and coal, the Brundtland Report observed that while nonrenewable resources were by definition exhaustible, 'recent assessments' had suggested that few minerals were likely to run out in the near future.[20] Unsurprisingly, given the importance of the Brundtland Report as a preparatory document to the United Nations Conference on Environment and Development (UNCED), the Rio Declaration and Agenda 21 do not raise the nonrenewability or development potential of nonfuel minerals as an issue at all.

The Brundtland Report nevertheless highlighted the sharp uptick in mining growth,[21] and observed that many developing countries were still heavily dependent on mineral exports, usually in unprocessed forms.[22] The political economy of the global production of mining was clear to the members of the Brundtland Commission, for they noted that much of the competition between colonial powers and the subjugation of their holdings had been driven by the quest for raw materials.[23] They also warned that competition for nonrenewable raw materials could intersect with poverty, injustice and environmental stress to threaten peace, security and development.[24]

Calls for international action and cooperation to improve information gathering on the environmental impacts of mining were made as early as 1972, in line with the increasing use of environmental assessment in the mining sector.[25] Recommendations for international action appended to the 1972 Stockholm Declaration, for example, called upon the UN Secretary-General to provide an appropriate vehicle for the exchange of information on mining and mineral processing. According to Recommendation 56, the possible categories for accumulated information included: (1) the environmental conditions of mine sites; (2) action taken in respect of the environment; and (3) positive and negative environmental repercussions.[26] This body of information could be useful for prediction, the Recommendation observed, continuing: 'Criteria for the planning and management of mineral production would emerge and would

---

19 IUCN, *World Conservation Strategy* (1980) chapter 3, para. 11. The *Strategy* nevertheless highlighted a variety of concerns relating to deep seabed mining.

20 *Our Common Future* (n 15), Chapter 8, para. 13.

21 Ibid, Chapter 8, para. 4.

22 Ibid, Chapter 8, para. 30.

23 Ibid, Chapter 11, para. 11.

24 Ibid.

25 The use of environmental assessment in the mining sector is discussed in Chapter 6.

26 United Nations, *Report of the United Nations Conference on the Human Environment, Stockholm, 5–16 June 1972* A/CONF.48/14/Rev.1, 18.

indicate where certain kinds of mining should be limited, where reclamation costs would be particularly high, or where other problems would arise.'[27]

The Recommendation also called upon 'appropriate' UN bodies to make efforts to assist developing countries in exploiting their minerals, including by providing adequate information on technology for preventing present or future environmentally adverse effects of mining and the adverse health and safety effects associated with the mineral industry.

The Rio Declaration amplified the focus on information gathering. Principle 40 called upon governments to ensure that local communities and resource users were provided with the information and skills needed to manage their environment and resources sustainably, including the internalization of environmental costs in national accounting. This principle stated that '[i]nternalization of such costs, the amortization of non-renewable resources, and the development of indicators of sustainability all require not only new data but new thinking'. At this time, the framework for national income accounts did not provide the information necessary to monitor natural capital, or its transformation into other capital forms. However, by the early 2000s there were significant improvements in the System of Economic Environmental Accounting,[28] including through work conducted by the World Bank itself around Adjusted Net Saving.[29]

There is little in these early documents on the ethics and longterm sustainability of the end use of minerals. The Brundtland Report nevertheless pointed out the wastefulness of the use of minerals for arms. The Report pointed out that the 'true cost' of the arms race was the opportunity cost of scarce capital, labour skills and raw materials, and continued: 'The plants that manufacture weapons, the transport of those weapons, and the mining of minerals for their production all place enormous demands on energy and mineral resources and are a major contributor to pollution and environmental deterioration.'[30]

The question of the ethics of the end use of minerals has been taken further in the sustainable mineral development consensus to some extent, for example, through the MMSD's consideration of need, demand, basic needs and over-consumption in relation to minerals,[31] and through the ICMM's development

---

[27] Ibid.

[28] Richard M Auty, 'Natural resources, capital accumulation and the resource curse' (2007) 61 *Ecological Economics* 627, 628.

[29] See section 5 of Chapter 1.

[30] *Our Common Future* (n 15) Chapter 11, para. 27.

[31] International Institute for Environment and Development and World Business Council for Sustainable Development, *Breaking New Ground: Mining, Minerals and Sustainable Development* (Earthscan 2002) xiv (henceforth *Breaking New Ground*) 74–7.

of a knowledge base and systems for the design, use, reuse, recycling and disposal of products containing minerals and metals.[32] Minerals ethics end use has also been addressed in State and activist initiatives to phase out the use of lead in gasoline,[33] as well as the use of cadmium,[34] and, in recent international initiatives, to end mercury mining and use.[35] These efforts all address highly toxic heavy metals that are known to have severe environmental health impacts. However, the ethics of the opportunity cost of metals and minerals use hinted at in the Brundtland Report regarding arms have not received further attention in minerals and sustainability discourses.

In conclusion, while suggesting some avenues for State protection, the early stages of the sustainable development discourse did not foreground mining or mineral processing as a sustainable development focus. International cooperation in this area was (and remains) limited. This left the door open for the mining industry itself to take the initiative.

2.1.3 Early industry initiatives: the Whitehorse Mining Initiative

By the early 1990s, some national mining industries were already taking the lead to develop a mining-specific sustainability discourse. The Canadian Whitehorse Mining Initiative (WMI) was one of the first government–industry partnerships to integrate sustainable development into the operational ethos of mining. George Miller, then President of the Mining Association of Canada, initiated the WMI in 1993 in response to increasingly strident criticism of the impact the Canadian mining industry was having on the environment and communities.[36] Funded by industry and the federal and provincial governments of Canada, the WMI took the form of a comprehensive national roundtable of diverse stakeholder groups, including labour unions, the environmental community and Aboriginal Peoples. The aim was to achieve consensus on how environmental and social issues could be dealt with in a cooperative and col-

---

[32] International Council of Mining and Metals, 'ICMM 10 Principles: Principle 8' www.icmm.com/en-gb/members/member-commitments/icmm-10-principles/icmm-principle-8, accessed 22 February 2019.

[33] Herbert L Needleman, 'The removal of lead from gasoline: Historical and personal reflections' (2000) 84 *Environmental Research Section A* 20.

[34] Nordic Council of Ministers, *Cadmium Review* (November 2003).

[35] The Minamata Convention on Mercury was adopted in January 2013 to consolidate a global effort to reduce anthropogenic emissions of mercury. The Convention entered into force on 16 August 2017. See UNEP Minamata Convention on Mercury, www.mercuryconvention.org/Home/tabid/3360/language/en-US/Default.aspx accessed 22 February 2019.

[36] P Fitzpatrick, A Fonseca and ML McAllister, 'From the Whitehorse Mining Initiative towards sustainable mining: Lessons learned' (2011) 19(4) *Journal of Cleaner Production* 376, 377.

laborative fashion. The industry hoped that it would 'foster a broader and more sympathetic understanding of its activities and role in Canada as well as a more hospitable regulatory environment'.[37] Following the WMI, many provinces in Canada initiated similar consultative processes.[38]

The roundtable concluded in 1994 with the formulation of the Whitehorse Leadership Council Accord.[39] The Accord envisioned 'a socially, economically, and environmentally sustainable, and prosperous mining industry, underpinned by political and community consensus' that continued to be an important contributor to Canada's national and regional well-being within the context of sustainable development.[40] Many of the directive principles for federal and provincial governments set out in the Accord prefigure the model of State engagement articulated in the MMSD project. Governments were tasked, for example, to promote the key tenets of neoliberalism: a private sector-led mining industry; measures to ensure that Canada remained competitive in terms of attracting investment capital;[41] a 'simple, pragmatic and fair' tax regime;[42] elimination of unnecessary duplication and overlap in environmental regulation of mineral exploration and development;[43] clear policies on mineral tenure, revocation and compensation;[44] and a more certain climate for mineral exploration and development in areas subject to unresolved Aboriginal land claims.

Governments were also urged to 'provide services essential to a healthy mining industry' such as geological surveys, exploration data management, the consistent administration of rules for mineral tenure and mine reclamation, investment attraction and facilitation, export promotion and incentivizing research.[45] The Accord encouraged governments to rely on mandatory and voluntary regulatory tools for environmental protection and to adopt 'balanced' regulatory frameworks for mine reclamation that were stable over time, harmonized across jurisdictions and based on standards that met the needs of a sustainable society.[46]

The mechanisms for implementation and accountability for the Accord, however, were not clearly defined. Signatories, for example, simply committed

---

[37] Ibid 377.
[38] Ibid 378.
[39] Whitehorse Leadership Council, *Whitehorse Mining Initiative: Leadership Council Accord (Final Report)* (October 1994).
[40] Ibid 7.
[41] Ibid 10.
[42] Ibid 11.
[43] Ibid 12.
[44] Ibid 21.
[45] Ibid 13.
[46] Ibid 14.

to promoting the Accord among their respective constituencies and advancing its principles and goals.[47] Following the conclusion of the Accord, the monitoring and enforcement of its recommendations were virtually nonexistent.[48] Nevertheless, the partnerships formed during the course of the roundtable led to subsequent agreements in provincial governments, and nationally, among various stakeholders, entrenched the discourse of sustainability.

2.1.4 The Mining, Minerals and Sustainable Development (MMSD) Project and the World Summit on Sustainable Development (WSSD)

By the late 1990s, the mining industry began to act with greater global reach in its quest to entrench the language of sustainability in the sector. This occurred by way of the Global Mining Initiative (GMI), the subsequent undertaking of the MMSD and the formation of the ICMM and IGF.

Mining industry leaders formulated the GMI to respond to a number of converging, negative trends that were 'exposing them to growing reputational risk, threatening the market acceptance of their products, and jeopardizing their social license to operate in many places they wanted to do business'.[49] In 1998, a handful of mining executives came together during the London Metal Exchange week to share their deep concern regarding these negative forces: host States expected minerals development to kickstart and sustain economic growth, local communities had high expectations of job creation and infrastructure provisioning, investors wanted higher returns to counter the industry's high risk, consumers were paying attention to ethically produced products, employees were demanding safer and healthier working conditions and organizations advancing social and environmental concerns expected higher levels of social and environmental performance and compliance with human rights.[50] More stringent environmental and social regulatory requirements, increasing public antipathy towards the dirtiness of the industry, lack of profitability, opposition from local communities, and improvements in communication technology that allowed antimining NGOs to spread their message far more effectively were symptomatic of the industry's failure to meet these expectations.[51] In short, mining industry executives themselves recognized that

---

[47] Ibid 2.

[48] Fitzpatrick (n 36) 380.

[49] Luke Danielson, *Architecture for Change: An Account of the Mining, Minerals and Sustainable Development Project History* (Global Public Policy Institute 2006) 18. The section of the report in question was authored by Caroline Digby, with contributions by Luke Danielson.

[50] *Breaking New Ground* (n 31) xiv.

[51] Danielson (n 49) 17–18.

the State was either not doing enough to protect society against the externalities of mineral production placing the double movement out of kilter, or that in some cases States were acting to protect society in a manner that threatened the fundamentals of economic liberalism.

In January 1999, during the annual meeting of the World Economic Forum, nine mining CEOs formally consolidated the GMI as a multitrack process, incorporating (1) an independent study of the role of the mining sector in the transition to sustainable development (the seed of which became the MMSD), and (2) the establishment of an industry association that could provide a global voice on issues of sustainable development in the mining, metals and minerals industry (later constituted as the ICMM).[52] Through the World Business Council for Sustainable Development, the proponents of the GMI engaged the International Institute for Environment and Development (IIED) to undertake a scoping study, and subsequently the broadranging and collaborative MMSD.[53]

The MMSD unfolded as an extraordinary process of private, global policymaking. Never before had such an extensive survey of the sustainable development implications for a particular sector been conducted.[54] While it was not among the project's objectives to build consensus on how the mineral sector could contribute to sustainable development,[55] the depth and rigour of the research process undoubtedly contributed to the hegemony of a minerals, mining and sustainable development discourse, particularly among industry proponents.

In 2002, on the eve of the World Summit on Sustainable Development, the IIED released the main report for the MMSD project, *Breaking New Ground*. The report situated the minerals sector within the framework of sustainable development, tracked current trends and actors, outlined the sec-

---

52 *Breaking New Ground* (n 31) 4.

53 *Breaking New Ground* (n 31) 4.

54 Over a two year period, the IIED entered into four regional partnerships each with its own governance structure (based in Southern Africa, South America, Australia and North America respectively), organized research and consultation processes in approximately 20 countries, convened 23 global workshops attended by 700 people from diverse backgrounds, and commissioned approximately 175 individual pieces of research. An independent Assurance Group of 25 representatives of different perspectives and regions supervised the project and met eight times to review and advise on the work (see ibid iv–v).

55 The mining 'sector' was understood holistically to include all the key stakeholders associated with mineral extraction, including all the players associated with the mining industry (from explorationists to processors), governments, international organizations, NGOs, academia, civil society, communities and labour. See ibid 5.

tor's key sustainable development challenges and put forward responses and recommendations.

The WSSD was accordingly a watershed for the sustainable development framing of the mining sector. The WSSD's Plan of Implementation affirmed that mining, minerals and metals are important to the economic and social development of many countries, and that minerals are essential for modern living.[56] To enhance the mining sector's contribution to sustainable development, the Plan called for (1) efforts to address the environmental, economic, health and social impacts and benefits of mining, minerals and metals throughout their life cycle; (2) partnerships among interested governments, intergovernmental organizations, mining companies, workers and other stakeholders; (3) the promotion of transparency and accountability for sustainable mining and minerals development; and (4) enhanced participation of stakeholders (including local and indigenous communities and women) in mining development, including after closure.[57] These aspirations echo the key claims of the sustainable mineral development consensus outlined in section 2.2 of this chapter.

2.1.5 The Intergovernmental Forum on Mining, Minerals, Metals and Sustainable Development and the International Council on Mining and Metals

Proceeding directly from the WSSD's call for partnerships, the Intergovernmental Forum on Mining, Minerals, Metals and Sustainable Development (IGF) was set up in 2005 as a voluntary platform for member governments to enhance capacity to achieve sustainable development objectives through good governance.[58] The IGF is open to member countries,[59] along with mining companies, industry associations and civil society organizations.

The work of the IGF has extended and deepened the policy prescriptions set out in *Breaking New Ground.* A Mining Policy Framework – titled *Mining and Sustainable Development* – was endorsed by the UN Commission on Sustainable Development in 2011, and subsequently revised by the IGF in

[56] World Summit on Sustainable Development, *Plan of Implementation of the World Summit on Sustainable Development* para. 46(a).

[57] Ibid.

[58] Intergovernmental Forum on Mining, Minerals, Metals and Sustainable Development, 'Introduction', www.igfmining.org/about/introduction/, accessed 22 February 2019.

[59] There are currently 69 member countries of the IGF: www.igfmining.org/member/ http://igfmining.org/members/, accessed 22 February 2019.

2013.[60] Although initially established to advance the priorities set out in the WSSD Plan of Implementation, the mandate of the IGF has since been extended to promoting the UN SDGs and Agenda 2030 in the mining sector.[61]

As noted above, the ICMM – a global voice for the mining industry – was originally mooted as part of the GMI. Sustainable development has been a guiding frame of conduct for this organization from the start. Following the conclusion of the MMSD, the ICMM Council committed its member companies to implement and measure their performance against ten sustainable development principles.[62] Although these principles are ostensibly squarely focused on mining companies themselves, the broader advocacy work of the ICMM aggressively articulates the sustainable development role of the State, in line with the neoliberal positioning of *Breaking New Ground.* This approach is carried through in a variety of other position statements the ICMM has developed over time, discussed in the ensuing chapters of this book.

2.1.6 The Extractives Industries Review

Response to critique levelled against the mining industry was not confined to the industry. In 2001, while the MMSD was being conducted, the World

---

[60] Intergovernmental Forum on Mining, Minerals, Metals and Sustainable Development, *IGF Mining Policy Framework: Mining and Sustainable Development* (rev. 2013) www.igfmining.org/mining-policy-framework/framework/, accessed 22 February 2019.

[61] Intergovernmental Forum on Mining, Minerals, Metals and Sustainable Development, 'Introduction', www.igfmining.org/about/introduction/, accessed 22 February 2019.

[62] The latest revision of these principles dates from 2015, see www.icmm.com/en-gb/members/member-commitments/icmm-10-principles/the-principles, accessed 22 February 2019. The ten sustainable principles are: (1) to apply ethical business practices and sound systems of corporate governance and transparency to support sustainable development; (2) to implement sustainable development in corporate strategy and decisionmaking processes; (3) to respect human rights and the interests, cultures, customs and values of employees and communities affected by mining activities; (4) to implement effective risk management strategies and systems based on sound science and which account for stakeholder perceptions of risk; (5) to pursue continual performance in health and safety performance with the ultimate goal of zero harm; (6) to pursue continual performance in environmental performance issues, such as water stewardship, energy use and climate change; (7) to contribute to the conservation of biodiversity and integrated approaches to land use planning; (8) to facilitate and support the knowledge base and systems for responsible design, use, reuse, recycling and disposal of products containing metals and minerals; (9) to pursue continual improvement in social performance and contribute to the social, economic and institutional development of host countries and communities; and (10) to proactively engage key stakeholders on sustainable development challenges and opportunities in an open and transparent manner, and to effectively report and independently verify progress and performance.

Bank and IFC initiated the Extractive Industries Review (EIR), a project intended to respond to increasingly strident civil society criticism of the World Bank's support for private sector-led mining reforms.[63] The EIR sought to independently determine whether extractive industries could be a vehicle for poverty alleviation through sustainable development, and, if so, whether there was a role for the WBG to play in achieving this aim. The project was headed by Dr Emil Salim, who had served as a minister responsible for the environment in Indonesia from the late 1970s to the early 1980s. Writing of his experience, Dr Salim stated that he accepted the task 'with full confidence that the World Bank Group is genuinely willing to move away from a "business as usual approach" into sustainable development' which meant 'mainstreaming economic, social and environmental considerations into sustainable development [*sic*] – with the alleviation of poverty as the economic goal, the enhancement of human rights as the social goal, and the conservation of the ecological life-support system as the environmental goal'.[64]

The EIR unfolded over a two year period and was designed to engage all stakeholders in an effective dialogue.[65] The findings and conclusion of the review were published in a 2003 Final Report. The overarching message of this report was clear: there was still a role for the WBG in the oil, gas and mining sectors, and for this intervention to contribute to poverty alleviation through sustainable development, *but only if* the right conditions were in place.

These conditions entailed sensitivity to the existing adequacy of governance in resource-rich countries, far more effective social and environmental policies and respect for human rights.[66] The EIR's elaboration of these conditions pointed to specific policy reforms that resonate more loudly with the discourses of mining dissent outlined in Chapter 3. For example, the EIR recommended that the WBG apply the principle of free, prior and informed consent in its projects – a key claim of the Indigenous Peoples' movements[67] – and stated that the WBG's Natural Habitat Policy should adopt clear 'no go' zones for oil, gas and mining projects.[68] The EIR also found that the WBG was not

---

[63] World Bank, *Striking a Better Balance Volume I: The World Bank Group and Extractive Industries* (December 2003) iv (henceforth *Striking a Better Balance*).

[64] Ibid v.

[65] Listed stakeholders included governments, civil society (represented by nongovernmental organizations, Indigenous Peoples' organizations, affected communities and community-based organizations and labour unions), industry (oil, gas and mining companies), academia, international organizations and the WBG itself (see *Striking a Better Balance*, *Vol. III*, Annexes, 3).

[66] *Striking a Better Balance* (n 63) vii.

[67] Ibid ix.

[68] Ibid x.

set up to effectively facilitate and promote poverty alleviation in its countries of assistance, and detailed a number of institutional reforms.[69]

In a strong reframing that glossed over many of the finer details of the EIR findings, WBG Management stated that it agreed with the 'majority' of the findings and endorsed its two fundamental messages: 'Extractive industries can contribute to sustainable development, when projects are implemented well and preserve the rights of affected people, and if the benefits they generate are well-used' and '[t]here is a continuing role for the Bank Group in supporting [Extractive Industries] provided its involvement supports poverty alleviation and sustainable development.'[70]

Bebbington *et al* describe the Bank Management's response as 'relatively guarded' against the quite critical findings of the EIR.[71] They point out that post the finalization of the EIR, IFIs' investment in extractive industries has proceeded apace: the WBG has continued to support programmes reforming mining and investment codes, reducing and fixing royalty and taxation rates and supporting basic geological surveys; the IFC had invested in several very large mines; and the Multilateral Investment Guarantee Agency had also become involved in large mining investments.[72]

The WBG's discursive washing away of the finer details of the EIR could be attributed to an inherent political bias favouring the mining industry. However, Bebbington *et al* suggest that the WBG's pro-extractives stance lies in a fundamentally different view on the real politics of State formation, that is, the manner in which competent State institutions develop over time.[73] As noted in the discussion above, for example, the EIR stipulated that the 'right' conditions for mining investment included sensitivity to the existing adequacy of governance in resource-rich countries. This condition relates to what Bebbington *et al* describe as 'the consolidation of democratizing institutions', which 'historical experience' suggests 'is more likely to be a product of conflict and shifts in the balance of social power than an outcome of technocratic design, corporate philanthropy or the sorts of public sector management loans than the IFIs are wont to offer'.[74] There is a determination on the part of IFIs, mining companies and host governments, Bebbington *et al* suggest, that good governance

---

[69] Ibid xii.

[70] World Bank Group Management, 'Striking a better balance – The World Bank Group and Extractive Industries: The Final Report of the Extractive Industries Review – World Bank Management Response' (17 September 2004).

[71] Anthony Bebbington *et al*, 'Contention and ambiguity: Mining and the possibilities of development' (2008) 39(6) *Development and Change* 965, 974.

[72] Ibid.

[73] Ibid 973.

[74] Ibid.

is a technical, capacity building issue; a problem that can be solved in project time.[75] They note that, tellingly, '[i]n interviews, IFI staff working in the sector will argue, almost mantra-like, that even if in-country governance conditions are not ideal, it is better for the bank in question to be involved in extractive industry investment because from the inside they will be able to make things better'.[76]

This is hardly a claim that has been empirically proven, however, and the extent and the vehemence of some discourses of mining dissent suggests otherwise.

2.1.7 UN Regional Economic Commissions

The Regional Commissions of the United Nations have also actively promoted extractivist-based developmental models. In 2011, the UN Economic Commission for Latin America and the Caribbean published *Latin America and the Caribbean in the World Economy*, which argued that the trend towards 'reprimarization' in the region (based on increased extraction of minerals, oil, gas and agricultural products) could serve as an opportunity for successful development – this based on a new vision of the developmental State now associated with neoextractivism.[77]

The UN Regional Economic Commission for Africa has also actively advanced a sustainable development agenda, but one that is more aligned with the sustainable mineral development consensus.[78] For example, building on the work of the African Mining Partnership's *Sustainable Development Charter for the Minerals and Mining Sector*,[79] in 2008 this Commission convened a technical task force to draft a new *Africa Mining Vision (AMV)*, which was subsequently finalized in February 2009.[80] The overarching high level ideal of the *AMV*, which acknowledges the formative influence of the WSSD,[81] is the 'transparent, equitable and optimal exploitation of mineral resources to underpin broad-based sustainable growth and socio-economic development'.[82]

---

75 Ibid 974.

76 Ibid.

77 See the discussion in section 3 below.

78 See for example the United Nations Economic Commission for Africa, *Africa Review Report on Mining* (29 September 2009) E/ECA/CFSSD/6/7.

79 The African Mining Partnership was an initiative launched in 2004 under the auspices of the New Partnership for Africa's Development (NEPAD). See South African Government, 'African mining partnership' www.gov.za/african-mining-partnership, accessed 22 February 2019. The AMV was subsequently brought under the wings of the African Union.

80 See www.africaminingvision.org/, accessed 22 February 2019.

81 African Union, *Africa Mining Vision* (February 2009) 1.

82 Ibid 6.

A variety of other claims in the *AMV* are aligned with the key tenets of the sustainable mineral development consensus, while at the same time giving the nod to the discourses of resource nationalism and environmental justice.

2.1.8 Mining in later sustainable development discourse: *The Future We Want* and the Sustainable Development Goals

The outcome document of the 2012 UN Conference on Sustainable Development describes the linkages between mining and development more tentatively than the WSSD of a decade prior.[83] It is also more explicit in outlining the conditions necessary for mining to lead to social and economic benefits. *The Future We Want* notes that minerals and metals make a 'major' contribution to the world economy and modern societies, that mining is important to all countries with mineral resources and that it offers opportunities to catalyze broad-based economic development, reduce poverty and assist countries in meeting internationally-agreed development goals. However, in order for this to occur, mining must be managed 'effectively and properly'. The outcome document therefore underlines the need for 'strong and effective legal and regulatory frameworks, policies and practices' that deliver social and economic benefits while setting safeguards in place to reduce social and environmental impacts, conserve biodiversity and ecosystems and deal with postmining closure.[84] The importance of continuous improvement in the areas of accountability and transparency is emphasized.[85] Reflecting a more realistic view of revenue flows in the mining sector, *The Future We Want* also highlights the effective use of existing mechanisms to deal with illicit financial flows arising from mining activities.[86]

On 25 September 2015, the UN adopted a new set of development targets to replace the eight Millennium Development Goals of 2000.[87] The SDGs comprise 17 goals and 169 targets,[88] which are expressly characterized as inte-

---

[83] United Nations, *The Future We Want*, https://sustainabledevelopment.un.org/content/documents/733FutureWeWant.pdf accessed 22 February 2019.

[84] Ibid, paras 227–8.

[85] Ibid.

[86] Ibid. The topic of IFFs is dealt with in section 2.4 of Chapter 5.

[87] *Transforming Our World* (n 18).

[88] The goals relate to poverty eradication; zero hunger; good health and wellbeing; quality education; gender equality; clean water and sanitation; affordable and clean energy; decent work and economic growth; industry, innovation and infrastructure; reduced inequalities; sustainable cities and communities; responsible consumption and production; climate action; life below water; life on land; peace, justice and strong institutions; and partnerships for the goals.

grated and interlinked.[89] The watchwords of the SDGs are people, planet, prosperity, peace and partnership, and these index a greater focus on safeguarding Earth from degradation driven by unsustainable consumption, production and resource use, and ensuring that economic, social and technological progress occurs in harmony with nature.[90]

Interestingly, the SDGs make no reference to mining. However, a consortium of research institutions recently prepared an 'Atlas' mapping mining to the SDGs.[91] The Atlas opts for a discourse of acknowledgement and strategic positioning, that is, it acknowledges that historically, mining has contributed to many of the challenges the SDGs are trying to address: land degradation, population displacement, human rights violations, corruption, armed conflict, gender-based violence and worsening socioeconomic inequality.[92] But it also goes on to claim that the mining industry has 'an unprecedented opportunity to mobilize significant human, physical, technological and financial resources to advance the SDGs'.[93] Such opportunities include positive externalities such as increased fiscal revenues; the provision of strategic infrastructure for logistics, energy and water; and employment and business creation.[94] The report also notes that many of the commodities produced by mining are essential building blocks for technology, infrastructure, energy and agriculture.[95]

2.1.9 National discourses

Uptake of an industry and IFI-driven discourse of sustainable development in the constitutions, mining policies and laws of mineral-rich jurisdictions has been uneven. References to sustainable development in the constitutions, mining laws and mining policies of mineral-rich jurisdictions are common, but not universal.

---

[89] The Preamble to the Agenda states: '[The SDG goals and targets] are integrated and indivisible and balance the three dimensions of sustainable development: the economic, social and environmental.'

[90] *Transforming Our World* (n 18) 2. The Organization for Economic Cooperation and Development has also weighed in on the theme of mining and sustainable development. For example, it established a Policy Dialogue on Natural Resource-based Development that feeds into the SDGs: www.oecd.org/dev/natural-resources.htm, accessed 22 February 2019.

[91] Columbia Centre on Sustainable Investment, Sustainable Development Solutions Network, United Nations Development Program & World Economic Forum, *White Paper – Mapping Mining to the Sustainable Development Goals: An Atlas* (July 2016).

[92] Ibid 3.

[93] Ibid 2.

[94] Ibid 3.

[95] Ibid.

Many countries of the world enshrine a right to environment in their national constitutions or identify environmental protection as a directive of State policy. Express constitutional references to sustainable development occur but are less common than one might anticipate. The South African Constitution enshrines a right to have the environment protected for the benefit of present and future generations through reasonable legislative and other measures that, among others, 'secure ecologically sustainable development and use of natural resources while promoting justifiable economic and social development'.[96] The Zambian Constitution identifies sustainable development as a foundational national value, which applies to the interpretation of the Constitution, enactment and interpretation of the law and development and implementation of State policy.[97] And the Basic Principles on the Form of Government in the Swedish Constitution include the obligation that '[t]he public institutions shall promote sustainable development leading to a good environment for present and future generations'.[98]

Other States formulate their environmental rights without an express sustainable development reference. The Constitution of Mongolia, for instance, includes a right to a healthy and safe environment, and to be protected against environmental pollution and ecological imbalance.[99] In Indonesia, the Constitution provides that '[e]very person shall have the right to live in physical and spiritual prosperity, to have a home and to enjoy a good and healthy environment'.[100]

In their national constitutions some States specifically relate mining to environmental, economic and social concerns. These pronouncements differ according to their alignment with the neoliberal prescriptions of the sustainable mineral development consensus or the prescriptions of neoextractivism. The environmental managerialism of the sustainable mineral development consensus, for example, is evident in the unusual direct reference to mining in Chapter VI of the Constitution of Brazil. Chapter VI establishes the right to an ecologically balanced environment, and continues as follows: '[T]hose who exploit mineral resources are obligated to restore any environmental degradation, in accordance with technical solutions required by the proper governmental agencies, as provided by law.'[101]

In some States the explicit framing of sustainable development is carried through to mineral and mining policies and laws. This is apparent in South

---

[96] Constitution of the Republic of South Africa, 1996, section 24.
[97] Constitution of Zambia (as amended by Act 2 of 2016), sections 8(f) and 9.
[98] Constitution of Sweden, 1974 (as amended), Article 2.
[99] Constitution of Mongolia, 1992, Article 16.2.
[100] Constitution of the Republic of Indonesia, 1945 (as amended), Article 28H.
[101] Constitution of Brazil, 1988, Article 225.2.

Africa and Zambia. The 1998 Minerals and Mining Policy in South Africa states that sustainable development is an 'overarching goal' of the government, and that the 'essential development'[102] of the country's mineral resources would take place 'within a framework of sustainable development and in accordance with environmental policy, norms and standards'.[103] The Mineral and Petroleum Resources Development Act 28 of 2002 (MPRDA), in turn, affirms the constitutional environmental right,[104] states that one of the objects of the Act is to give effect to this right,[105] and expressly instructs the minister of mineral resources to ensure the sustainable development of South Africa's mineral and petroleum resources.[106] In Zambia, the 2013 Mineral Resources Development Policy articulates the government's vision for the sector as 'a vibrant, well-organised private sector and private-public partnership-led mining sector contributing in excess of 20 per cent towards GDP and sustainable economic development in the country by 2030'.[107] The mining law further affirms that mineral resources must be explored and developed in a manner that 'promotes and contributes to socio-economic development',[108] and that wasteful mining practices must be avoided so as to promote sustainable development and prevent adverse environmental effects.[109]

In other mineral-rich States, however, either the mineral and mining policies and laws are silent on the broader conceptual framing of the sustainability provisions that are nevertheless present in their policies or laws,[110] or sustainable development is mentioned in the mining policy but not taken up further in terms of a statement of objectives in the mining law.[111]

---

[102] Department of Minerals, *White Paper: A Minerals and Mining Policy for South Africa* (October 1998) 55.

[103] Ibid 56, para. 4.2.

[104] See the preamble to the Act.

[105] MPRDA (South Africa), section 2(h).

[106] MPRDA (South Africa), section 3(3).

[107] Ministry of Mines, Energy and Water Development (Republic of Zambia). *Mineral Resources Development Policy* (July 2013) 5.

[108] Mines and Minerals Act, 2015 (Zambia), section 4(b).

[109] Mines and Minerals Act, 2015 (Zambia), section 4(d).

[110] Such sustainability provisions include, for example, environmental impact assessments, (more limited) tools for the assessment of social impacts and enhanced mechanisms for public participation. For example, the mineral laws of Western Australia, Botswana, British Columbia, Chile, the Democratic Republic of Congo, Mongolia, Sweden, Arizona and Uzbekistan make no mention of sustainable development.

[111] The National Mining Policy of Ghana, for example, states that the policy 'seeks to establish a comprehensive and forward looking framework for mining that catalyses sustainable development' (p.9). However, there is no express statement of objectives and no express reference to sustainable development in the Ghanaian Minerals and Mining Act, 2006.

2.2 Key Claims of the Sustainable Mineral Development Consensus

The previous section has outlined the remarkable range of institutions that have formulated and disseminated the sustainable mineral development consensus over the past few decades. The following section outlines the key claims of this consensus, insofar as they relate to the role of the State.

The core claims of the sustainable mineral development consensus are that: sustainable development can transform mining industry practices; mining can catalyze development that leads to poverty alleviation; the State must play a facilitative and regulatory role to support mining's contribution to sustainable development; and environmental impacts are best managed through private investment in technology alongside comprehensive State regulation.

2.2.1 Sustainable development can transform mining industry practices

The architects of the MMSD process positioned sustainable development as a solution to the unique challenges of the mining industry at the turn of the twenty-first century. Echoing the Brundtland Report, the MMSD stated that '[i]n the context of the minerals sector, the goal should be to maximize the contribution to the well-being of the current generation in a way that ensures the equitable distribution of its costs and benefits, without reducing the potential for future generations to meet their own needs'.[112] Breaking this down, the MMSD articulated guiding principles for four sustainable development 'spheres': economic, social, environmental and governance:

- Rather than mere profit maximization, economic considerations would be qualified by a concern for maximizing human well-being, ensuring the efficient use of all resources, and internalizing environmental and social costs.[113]
- Sustainable development principles for the social sphere would entail respecting and reinforcing all fundamental human rights, ensuring a fair distribution of the costs and benefits of mineral development among present generations, and replacing depleted natural resources with other capital and sustained improvements so that future generations would not be deprived.[114]
- Guiding principles for the environmental sphere involved promoting 'responsible stewardship' of natural resources and the environment, including the remediation of past damage; minimizing waste and ecolog-

---

[112] *Breaking New Ground* (n 31) xvi.
[113] Ibid.
[114] Ibid.

ical degradation along the entire mineral values chain; applying the precautionary principle ('exercising prudence' where impacts were unknown or uncertain); operating within ecological limits; and protecting critical natural capital.[115]

- Guiding principles for the governance sphere emphasized free market, democratic neoliberalism: support for representative democracy and participatory decision making, encouraging free enterprise and a 'fair' playing field; avoiding excessive concentration of power through appropriate checks and balances; ensuring transparency through providing stakeholders with timely access to relevant information; ensuring accountability for decisions and actions; building trust and cooperation based on shared goals and values; and respecting the principle of subsidiarity.[116]

These principles are remarkable for their acknowledgement of social and environmental limits (human rights, ecological limits) and recognition that human well-being should 'qualify' economic considerations. By applying and working towards the implementation of these principles in partnership with States, labour unions, indigenous and local communities and NGO, the industry hoped to transform its practices. [117]

2.2.2 Mining can catalyze development that leads to poverty alleviation

Whether sustainable development can transform the practices of the mining industry is distinguishable from the question whether the industry can catalyze development that leads to poverty alleviation. The WBG has rigorously promoted mining's contribution to development and poverty alleviation since the early 1990s.[118] The mining industry itself has been more cautious, as is evident from a series of publications dealing with the Role of Mining in National Economies (RoMine). The first of the RoMine reports was published in 2012;[119] a further edition was released in 2014,[120] and another in 2018.[121]

---

[115] Ibid.

[116] Ibid.

[117] Ibid.

[118] See section 2.1.1 above.

[119] ICMM, *The Role of Mining in National Economies: Mining's Contribution to Sustainable Development* (ICMM 2012) (henceforth *RoMine 2012*). The Romine series was preceded by a conceptual document entitled *Mining's Contribution to Sustainable Development*, which is no longer available online.

[120] ICMM, *The Role of Mining in National Economies: Mining's Contribution to Sustainable Development* (2nd edn ICMM October 2014) (henceforth *RoMine 2014*).

[121] ICMM, *Role of Mining in National Economies* (3rd edn ICMM 2018) (henceforth *RoMine 2018*).

The RoMine reports argue that mining makes a significant contribution to the economies of low and middle income countries. 'Typical' contributions (and their scope) include foreign direct investment (60–90 per cent), exports (30–60 per cent), government revenue (3–20 per cent), national income (GDP or GNI) (3–10 per cent) and employment (1–2 per cent).[122] However, not all of these contributions feature in the Mining Contribution Index (MCI), the instrument developed in the RoMine reports to compare the contribution of the nonfuel mineral sector.[123] The MCI is based on indicators such as mineral exports, expenditure on mineral exploration, mineral production and production value. In the span of RoMine reporting, the MCI comparison of more than 200 countries shows that many low and middle income countries have become more reliant upon mining.[124]

The RoMine reports also emphasize that the relationship between mining, economic development and poverty alleviation is complex and often contentious. The 'economic impulses' that reverberate from commercial mining across society can have direct, indirect and induced effects that *may* lead to sustainable development. The ICMM has been at pains to emphasize that such economic impulses derive both from the spending of the mine and from the government's spending of royalties and taxes, over which the industry has little control.[125] Whether such spending can catalyze sustainable development depends critically on local institutions, regulations and norms varying greatly from one country context to another.[126] Whether mining can contribute to poverty alleviation also depends on the discretion of mining companies, which can choose to develop a mine as an enclave or address high levels of poverty in all its various guises (inadequate access to healthcare, education, housing, employment), alongside the government.[127] Responsible mining companies, the RoMine reports nevertheless assert, aim to develop a mine in an integrated fashion, although given that needs in local communities are often enormous, the industry 'cannot be expected to address the totality of the local problems of poverty and deprivation'.[128] The industry was thus keen to limit expectations on its capacity to alleviate poverty.

---

[122] *RoMine 2014* (n 120) 18.

[123] *RoMine 2012* (n 119) 9. The development of the MCI is also intended to stimulate debate on the data challenges involved in compiling such an index.

[124] Ibid 19; *RoMine 2014* (n 120) 19; *RoMine 2018* (n 121) 3.

[125] Ibid 36. *RoMine 2018* (n 121) 5.

[126] *RoMine 2014* (n 120) 36.

[127] Ibid 39.

[128] Ibid 40.

2.2.3 The State plays a facilitative and regulatory role to support mining's contribution to sustainable development

Under the sustainable mineral development consensus, the State must play a facilitative and regulatory role to assist the mining industry's sustainable development transformation. Over time, the expectations placed on the State have expanded and deepened, from establishing level playing fields for competitive private investment, to whole of government solutions that situate the State as a collaborative partner in transforming mining industry practices and catalyzing its potential socioeconomic benefits.

In the 1980s and early 1990s, development agencies urged States to facilitate private investment by reforming mining legal and regulatory frameworks.[129] Particular emphasis was placed on security of mineral tenure and adopting a 'long run' approach to mineral taxation.[130] *Breaking New Ground* affirmed this facilitative function, arguing that the State's role in transitioning the mining sector to sustainable development should largely be exercised through establishing a clearcut and enforceable policy and legal framework for mining investments and mining regulation.[131]

However, in most 'successful' economies, the State's role as facilitator of investment would be balanced by its role as regulator.[132] This involved establishing the conditions for 'good governance'. Government had a 'central and unavoidable role in improving good governance for sustainable development',[133] that is, establishing the rule of law and effective State institutions, transparency, access to information, public participation in decision making, respect for human rights, official accountability and the control of corruption.[134] If effectively implemented, *Breaking New Ground* said, law could be a leveller by generating consistent incentives for responsible behaviour irrespective of company size, implementing the will of the majority and protecting the interests of minorities.[135]

While *Breaking New Ground* acknowledged the role of subnational governments in federal systems and the increasingly important role of local governments in jurisdictions where authority has been decentralized, its focus fell on national governments: 'National governments play a pivotal role in the minerals sector and will be one of the most significant actors in managing

---

129 *WBG Technical Paper No. 405* (n 8) 13.

130 See, for example, the 'key issues which determine success' in the 1992 World Bank *Strategy for African Mining* (n 7) 20.

131 *Breaking New Ground* (n 31) 337.

132 Ibid 336.

133 Ibid.

134 Ibid 66.

135 Ibid 337.

the transition to sustainable development.'[136] As a 'central enabler' however, national governments were also expected to formulate optimal regulatory frameworks for the economic, social and environmental dimensions of sustainable development, and not merely its good governance aspects. Governments needed to integrate mining into national economic and social development planning, to grant licences and permits for permissible environmental impacts and the usage of natural resources, to set environmental and health and safety standards and to invest and distribute the revenues from mineral extraction.[137]

A 'whole of government' approach to the State's facilitative and regulatory emerges from the *SDG Mining Atlas*. The *Atlas* reiterates the State's responsibility to establish the background policy and legislative framework for mining and to manage the industry, put in place capable institutions, enforce regulations and invest in basic services.[138] However, there is now an added obligation to align mining policies with the SDGs and to ensure 'harmonization and policy coherence across the different branches, agencies and levels of government'.[139] National governments 'across all relevant ministries' (mining, finance, environment, infrastructure and others) must ensure that national development plans are aligned with mining policies and engage more systematically with local government and industry to ensure that mining investments are leveraged for sustainable development.[140]

2.2.4 Environmental impacts are best managed through private investment in technology alongside comprehensive State regulation

The final key claim of the sustainable mineral development consensus is that environmental impacts are best managed through a combination of private sector-led investment and innovation, alongside comprehensive State regulation. This narrative emerged strongly in the 1992 and 1996 World Bank Strategy papers for Africa and the LAC region, respectively.

In these sources, environmental impacts are presented as resolvable, technological and localized problems.[141] The 1992 *Strategy for African Mining*, for instance, states that '[i]t frequently pays companies to acquire new technology as this often reduces environmental damage and production costs',[142] and predicts that '[b]est practice technology is what international mining compa-

---

[136] Ibid 66.
[137] Ibid.
[138] *SDG Mining Atlas* (n 91) 12.
[139] Ibid.
[140] Ibid 2.
[141] Ibid 47.
[142] *Strategy for African Mining* (n 7) 48.

nies can be expected to bring to exploration and development in developing countries'.[143] Major international mining companies are thus depicted as the bastions of progress. The Strategies hold that due to pressure from shareholders, lenders and the evolution of standards of corporate responsibility, mining companies are likely to adopt environmental protection standards superior to that of the State.[144] Because their actions are under the scrutiny of environmentalists and the international public, they cannot afford the reputational risk.[145]

In the Strategies, the poor technology and management of State-owned mining companies is used as a scapegoat for an already existing detrimental ecological legacy. 'The major immediate problem is tackling the worst environmental impacts of existing mining operations',[146] the *Strategy for African Mining* held. Commenting on State-owned mining companies in the LAC region, the *Strategy for LAC Mining* insisted: 'SOEs are generally less well environmentally managed than private companies due to having old mines with obsolete technology, poor economic fundamentals, political protection against demands from environmental authorities or the public, and little exposure to international pressure and stimuli.'[147] The MMSD continued this theme: 'It is hard to contest that past mining methods have led to environmental damage that will take a very long time, if ever, for nature to repair.'[148] Notwithstanding that many mining ventures had been established by the colonial powers prior to the wave of nationalizations in the mid-twentieth century, the World Bank proposed a strict allocation of liability for cleanup to the State.[149] Baseline environmental studies and audits were recommended to establish the degree of environmental degradation, and to ensure that new private investors were not saddled with liability for past damage.[150] Linked to this concern for the sharp division of environmental responsibility, there was support for some level of stabilization of environmental regulation, akin to fiscal stability contracts;[151] or, at the very least, for 'clear and permanent guidelines' formulated at the start of the project that were 'consistent, well-adapted to their purpose, cost-effective and not unnecessarily delaying of development'.[152]

---

143 Ibid.
144 Ibid; *Strategy for LAC Mining* (n 9) 63.
145 *Strategy for LAC Mining* (n 9) 63.
146 *Strategy for African Mining* (n 7) 51.
147 *Strategy for LAC Mining* (n 9) 73.
148 *Breaking New Ground* (n 31) 232.
149 *Strategy for LAC Mining* (n 9) 63, 69.
150 *Strategy for African Mining* (n 7) 49; *Strategy for LAC Mining* (n 9) 73.
151 *Strategy for African Mining* (n 7) 50.
152 *Strategy for LAC Mining* (n 9) 68.

Lack of information on mining-induced environmental damage is a prominent theme in the sustainable mineral development consensus. The MMSD stated, for instance, that while the environmental performance of some mining companies had improved, in absolute terms the damage function could be increasing. This was not known, however, the Report continues, because it had never been measured for a nation, let alone the world.[153] But environmental economists had been developing conceptual and methodological resources for environmental and natural resource accounting from the 1970s.[154] Not only did the authors of the MMSD apparently ignore this work, but they seemed to be suggesting that if national level statistics could not be collected and normalized, nothing could be done.[155]

According to the sustainable mineral development consensus, the progressive technological contribution of multinationals would not obviate the need for State environmental regulation. 'Responsibility' for transforming the vision of an environmentally sound mining industry into practical action vests in governments, the *Strategy for LAC Mining* held.[156] In the early 2000s the World Bank urged that in many developing countries a comprehensive environmental reform package was needed, inclusive of an environmental policy making process, an environmental action plan, an 'umbrella' environmental law allowing for sector specific regulations, environmental quality standards and goals, public institutions responsible for environmental management and environmental management training programmes.[157]

Rigorous environmental regulation was deemed good for both business and investment. The 1992 *Strategy for African Mining*, for example, opined:

> Improved physical environments are conducive to improved productivity in the mines and plants, and in the community at large. Concern for the environment also raises the international standing of the company. It becomes more readily seen as a reliable joint-venture partner by both governments and other companies. This gives it a competitive edge.[158]

The 'competitive edge' argument is extended to States. The *Strategy for LAC Mining*, for instance, proclaimed: 'Countries with competent environmental management have an advantage in the attraction of new investment'.[159] The

---

[153] Ibid 232.

[154] The work on natural resource accounting, emphasized by Auty in his development of the resource curse theory, is discussed in Chapter 3.

[155] I am grateful to Professor Gabrielle Hecht for this insight.

[156] *Strategy for LAC Mining* (n 9) 64.

[157] World Bank (n 6) 17.

[158] *Strategy for African Mining* (n 7) 48.

[159] *Strategy for LAC Mining* (n 9) 63.

World Bank's 2003 Paper on Mining Reform goes even further, stating that companies 'prefer to enter countries with known environmental policies and established environmental management, as those are likely to be the first countries to establish clear, sensible, and non-discretionary policies and standards on the social issues'.[160] Tempering these optimistic claims, however, the MMSD acknowledged that companies resisted taking on greater environmental costs when they perceived that others were not doing the same, and that, when selling commodities on the global market, cost internalization was a daunting task for everyone.[161] Some governments, fearing they would drive the industry away, were also not ready to insist upon improved environmental management in the industry.[162]

Lack of any detailed discussion of technological and institutional capacity to monitor and enforce environmental regulations is a significant gap in sources constituting the sustainable mineral development consensus. The IGF's updated *Mining Policy Framework* is a case in point. Under the heading 'Legal and Policy Environment', it urges States to ensure the ongoing generation of, and access to, geological information; the revision and periodic updating of mining codes and standards; and an efficient mining permitting process,[163] but then goes on to simply state that 'institutional capacity needs to be in place' for ongoing monitoring and enforcement.[164] The *Framework* mentions the need for governmental monitoring, inspection and enforcement activities once more, but this recommendation is confined to the issue of occupational health and safety.[165] The underlying assumption appears to be that regulation and the building of State capacity in project time will be sufficient. However, States need monitoring instruments and infrastructures for regulation to have any effect – resources that in turn require capital and expertise.[166]

Resting on a bed of neoliberal economic reforms, the sustainable mineral development consensus acknowledges social and environmental limits and recognizes that human well-being should 'qualify' economic considerations. The State is a key actor, centrally positioned to facilitate a private-led mining sector, to regulate mining-related impacts and to align the mineral extractive industry with processes of national planning. Environmental 'impacts' are also minimized, presented as technological, localized and manageable, although a legacy of ecological degradation is placed firmly at the door of former colo-

---

160 World Bank (n 6) 16.
161 *Breaking New Ground* (n 31) 265.
162 Ibid.
163 IGF (n 60) 6–7.
164 Ibid 23.
165 Ibid 10.
166 I am indebted to Professor Gabrielle Hecht for this insight.

nial States. Overall, the conception of the State's role under the sustainable mineral development consensus aligns well with Polanyi's concept of the double movement.

3. RESPONSIBLE MINING

As a discourse on mining, development and sustainability, responsible mining overlaps with, but is distinguishable from, the sustainable mineral development consensus. It has gained increasing ground since 2000, although the central meaning of 'responsible mining' is still contested.[167] It is a term closely associated with neoliberalism, corporate social responsibility (CSR) and voluntary initiatives.

In the 1990s responsible mining was largely viewed as a matter of legal compliance with national mining and environmental laws and regulations, the mining contract or concession, labour laws and collective bargaining agreements.[168] The meaning of the term has shifted decisively since then, however, and has become associated with procedural, voluntary schemes and assurance or certification-based schemes that are viewed as going beyond the basic standards set forth in State regulation.

Procedural voluntary schemes include aspirational or dialogue-based initiatives such as the Canadian WMI, the SDGs, the OECD Due Diligence Guidance for Responsible Supply Chains of Minerals from Conflict-Affected and High-Risk Areas and the Responsible Mineral Development Initiative.[169] Such initiatives are characterized by multistakeholder engagement focused on common issue identification, development of mutual understanding, formulation of best practices and the like. They potentially shape governance of mining and sustainability by (1) chipping away at the hierarchy of the State and positioning it as only one among many 'stakeholder voices' and (2) implying State incapacity to engage in 'constructive' dialogue.

Assurance/certification-based schemes include the Extractive Industries Transparency Initiative (EITI),[170] the Kimberley Process (KP), the International Cyanide Management Code, the Business and Biodiversity Offsets Programme, the Initiative for Responsible Mining Assurance and the Alliance for Responsible Mining, among others.[171] A number of these

---

[167] Robin Broad, 'Responsible mining: moving from a buzzword to real responsibility' (2014) 1(1) *The Extractive Industries and Society* 4.

[168] RESOLVE Solutions Network, *Voluntary Responsible Mining Initiatives: A Review* (August 2015) White Paper prepared for the World Economic Forum 7.

[169] Ibid 9.

[170] The EITI is discussed more comprehensively in section 2.6 of Chapter 5.

[171] Ibid.

initiatives have their roots in high level engagement between and among mining companies and civil society organizations following the creation of the GMI and subsequently the ICMM, the MMSD, and the WSSD. For example, the KP certification emerged in the late 1990s and early 2000s after downstream jewellery manufacturers and retailers joined forces with civil society organizations to promote the idea of responsible sourcing of diamonds (and subsequently gold).[172] This led to the establishment of the Responsible Jewelry Council in 2005, which focuses on supply chain assurance of minerals used in jewellery.[173] Miranda *et al* position these initiatives within broader civil society advocacy efforts to campaign for more responsible corporate behaviour, including promoting sustainable forestry and upholding the rights of workers in the apparel industry.[174]

The Mining Association of Canada's 'Towards Sustainable Mining' (TSM) initiative exemplifies an industry developed, national certification scheme based on the discourse of responsible mining. It calls upon Association members to 'responsibly meet society's need for minerals, metals and energy products',[175] and to 'demonstrate a responsible approach to social, economic and environmental performance that is aligned with the evolving priorities of our communities of interest'.[176] The focus of the TSM programme is on member companies' commitment to the TSM Guiding Principles and integration of the indicators associated with six TSM Assessment Protocols into facility-level management systems.[177] The State features, first, in establishing baseline conditions of compliance. The 'base assumption' of the Assessment Protocols is that all member companies are in compliance with all legal and regulatory requirements.[178] But the State is not involved in the layers of accountability and verification that the TSM programme establishes.[179] None of the four forms of accountability or verification – even the final stage of postverification review by the Association's Community of Interest Advisory

---

[172] RESOLVE (n 168) 7.

[173] Ibid.

[174] Marta Miranda, David Chambers and Catherine Coumans, *Framework for Responsible Mining: A Guide to Evolving Standards* (October 2005) xi.

[175] Mining Association of Canada, 'TSM Guiding Principles', http://mining.ca/sites/default/files/documents/TSMGuidingPrinciples_0.pdf, accessed 22 February 2019.

[176] Ibid.

[177] Mining Association of Canada 'Protocols and Frameworks', http://mining.ca/towards-sustainable-mining/protocols-frameworks, accessed 22 February 2019.

[178] Mining Association of Canada, 'TSM Assessment Protocol: A tool for assessing tailings management', http://mining.ca/sites/default/files/documents/TSMTailingsManagementProtocol.pdf accessed 22 February 2019.

[179] Mining Association of Canada, 'TSM Verification', http://mining.ca/towards-sustainable-mining/how-tsm-works/tsm-verification accessed 22 February 2019.

Panel – directly involve the federal or provincial governments or their officials. Governments are simply part of a broader 'community of interest'.[180] Member companies commit to involving communities of interest in the design of the TSM initiative, and working with such communities to address legacy issues.[181]

In the discourse of responsible mining, State legal regulation is often characterized as baseline or inefficient, particularly in developing countries. Miranda *et al* state: 'Many have come to realize that compliance of the law of the countries in which [corporations] operate may not be sufficient to protect the environment or vulnerable communities.'[182] Industry-run certification schemes therefore eclipse the State as the site for certification of responsible behaviour. Corporations seek to distinguish themselves from their peers by participating in certification and assurance schemes, and by submitting their operations to 'independent' scrutiny they are able to verify responsible conduct.[183] There are nevertheless contradictions: while State law is presented as insufficient to protect the environment and vulnerable communities, the 'leading edge' norms established by responsible mining certificate schemes require a 'functioning government context, including strong regulations and the will and capacity to enforce laws'.[184] Governments are also urged to be at the table in future stakeholder engagement processes, to be engaged in formulating 'appropriate' legislative and governance frameworks.[185] One of the central features of self-regulation and voluntary initiatives is the avoidance of civil, administrative or criminal sanctions undergirding State law. The broader shift to a responsible mining discourse therefore tends to diminish the State's governance of the mining sector, and to disempower it from using strongarm tactics.

Responsible mining does not fundamentally depart from the double movement: the State is still expected to furnish legal frameworks that promote private investment, and to establish the baseline conditions for compliance. However, shifting closer towards economic *laissez-faire*, companies are

---

180 'Communities of interest' are defined in the TSM Guiding Principles as including 'all of the individuals and groups who have or believe they have an interest in the management of decisions about our operations that may affect them. This includes: employees, contractors, Aboriginal or indigenous peoples, mining community members, suppliers, customers, environmental organizations, governments, the financial community, and shareholders.'

181 'TSM Guiding Principles' (n 175).

182 Miranda (n 174) xi.

183 Ibid.

184 Ibid xiv.

185 Ibid.

presented as responsible agents capable of regulating their environmental and social impacts through multistakeholder initiatives.

4. NEOEXTRACTIVISM

Neoextractivism (inclusive here of policy approaches supporting 'resource nationalism') signals 'the desire of the people of resource-rich countries to derive more economic benefit from their natural resources and the resolution of their governments to concomitantly exercise greater control over the country's natural resource sectors'.[186] Contrasted with advocacy for a limited State role in the discourses of the sustainable mineral development consensus and responsible mining, under State-led extractivism the State is active and assertive, extending its reach to ownership and control of mining factors of production to secure broader social and economic policy objectives.

In the regions of the world where State-led extractivism now finds traction, there is a long and varied history of engagement with ideas about 'development' that emerged in the post-Second World War period. In his 1949 inaugural address, for example, President Harry Truman urged the USA to embark on a 'bold new program' to make the benefits of scientific advances and industrial progress available 'for the improvement and growth of underdeveloped areas'.[187] These sentiments, backed by the thinking of development economics, supported a 'catchup' model: underdeveloped areas would follow in the footsteps of their industrialised counterparts, through economic growth, industrialization and the embrace of Western technology.[188] In many States of the global South, this catchup model arguably still holds true, whether achieved through radical experiments in free market fundamentalism (as in Chile during the 1970s and 1980s),[189] more tempered neoliberal reforms or State-led extractivism under 'progressive' socialist governments. However, the culture, tradition and scholarly thinking in these regions has also produced alternative conceptions of development that recognize strong limits on eco-

[186] Michael Solomon (compl.), *The Rise of Resource Nationalism: A Resurgence of State Control in an Era of Free Markets, or the Legitimate Search for a New Equilibrium* (South African Institute of Mining and Metallurgy 2012) 73.

[187] Harry S Truman, 'Inaugural address' (20 January 1949), https://trumanlibrary.org/whistlestop/50yr_archive/inagural20jan1949.htm, accessed 11 January 2018.

[188] Eduardo Gudynas, 'Debates on development and its alternatives in Latin America: A brief heterodox guide' in M Lang and D Mokrani, *Beyond Development: Alternative Visions from Latin America* Permanent Working Group on Alternatives to Development (Rosa Luxemburg Foundation transl. 2013) 15.

[189] See the discussion on Chile in section 6.2 of Chapter 1.

nomic growth. This diverse range of intellectual resources accounts for some of the contradictions now apparent in States pursuing a neoextractivist path.

4.1 Tensions and Contradictions in the Emergence of Narratives of Neoextractivism

In the 1950s and 1960s the UN grasped the mantle of promoting and financing economic development in 'underdeveloped' countries, at the same time as the right of all peoples to self-determination was being affirmed in the developing framework for international human rights.[190] The General Assembly's 1962 Resolution on Permanent Sovereignty over Natural Resources declared the right of all peoples and nations to permanent sovereignty 'over their natural wealth and resources', a right which needed to be exercised 'in the interest of their national development and of the well-being of the people of the State concerned'.[191] Although notionally undergirded by the conviction that affirming the State's inalienable sovereignty over their natural wealth would reinforce their economic dependence, the rest of the Resolution reads like an early manifesto of investor rights, with guarded protections for foreign capital. Resolution 1803 therefore affirmed underdeveloped States' mandates to exploit their natural wealth in the service of national development and well-being. But it only thinly veiled the contradictions inherent in asserting the economic dependence of resource-rich countries in a context where power over the flows of material production and wealth had already been determined by colonial relations.

This dynamic of dependency was not lost on scholars of developing regions. In the mid-1970s Brazilian economist Celso Furtado commented on development as a 'myth'. The idea that economic development would one day allow the poor to enjoy the same lifestyles as those of the rich was 'simply unrealisable' and had been used on the peoples of the periphery 'to accept enormous sacrifices, to legitimize the destruction of ancient cultures, to explain and make people understand the need to destroy the environment and to justify forms of dependence that reinforce the predatory nature of the system of production'.[192] A conception of asymmetrical international relations, with the industrialized countries at the core and various resource-rich nations at the periphery, came into focus through various theories of dependency. A base assumption of dependency theory was that underdevelopment was the outcome of capitalist,

---

190 See further the discussion in section 3.4.2 of Chapter 3 in the context of the rights of Indigenous Peoples.

191 General Assembly Resolution 1803 (XVII) of 14 December 1962.

192 Celso Furtado, quoted in Gudynas (n 188) 15.

colonialist and imperialist forces, rather than being a phase preceding capitalist development.

While remaining wary of capitalism, intellectuals, policymakers and diplomats in nations of the global South insisted on the right to benefit from natural resource wealth. The left-leaning report *Catastrophe or New Society? A Latin American World Model* presented an alternative growth model for a socialist, democratic world order in which basic needs would be satisfied.[193] But in similar fashion to conventional notions of development, it defended economic growth, postponed environmental preservation to the point of reaching an acceptable standard of living and supported technological solutions for negative impacts.[194] The scarcity of natural resources was basically rejected.[195] Based on the factors of low population density and the unknown ecological potential of the region, 'the general conviction was that Latin American natural resources were abundant and that it was necessary to exploit them in order to develop the region'.[196] In more recent times, the United Nations Economic Commission for Latin America and the Caribbean has argued that the tendency towards 're-primarization' of the region may offer opportunities for successful development, notwithstanding longstanding critique of extractivist-led development paths.[197]

Martinez-Alier *et al* therefore observe that in Latin America, assumptions of resource abundance have held an economic, resource-driven growth model of development in place for decades:

> From Stockholm in 1972 until Rio+20 in 2012, Latin American governments have emphasized that the solution to the environmental problem does not consist of halting economic growth (*sic*), but rather that the main and ultimate solution resides in changing the unequal distribution of power and wealth in the world, and by stimulating distinct styles of development in accordance with each ecological and social reality at national and continental levels.[198]

Similar sentiments have been expressed in an African context. A flurry of initiatives coinciding with the launch of the African Union in 2002 affirm

---

[193] AO Herrera *et al*, *Catastrophe or New society? A Latin American World Model* (Bariloche Foundation 1976). The report was conceived in response to the Club of Rome's *Limits to Growth* report.

[194] Gudynas (n 188) 19.

[195] Joan Martinez-Alier, Michiel Baud and Héctor Sejenovich, 'Origins and perspectives of Latin American environmentalism' in F de Castro *et al* (eds) *Environmental Governance in Latin America* (Palgrave 2016) 29, 43, 39.

[196] Ibid 40.

[197] UN Economic Commission for Latin America (ECLAC) and the Caribbean, *Latin America and the Caribbean in the World Economy* (ECLAC 2011).

[198] Martinez-Alier (n 195) 43.

the abundance of Africa's natural resource wealth, and the need for a developmental state to harness these resources to address poverty and underdevelopment.[199] For example, the Addis Ababa Declaration on Development and Management of Africa's Mineral Resources (adopted by the first AU Conference of Ministers responsible for mineral resources development in 2008) notes 'deep concern for the continued incidence of poverty and underdevelopment in Africa' despite an 'abundant endowment of mineral resources'. It further highlights the importance of a 'pro-active development state' to maximize the benefits derivable from mineral resources, including through fair and equitable fiscal and investment regimes. The *AMV*, developed under the auspices of the United Nations Economic Commission for Africa, leads with the idea that harnessing natural resources endowments is 'key to Africa's development', and that while Africa is the top producer of numerous mineral commodities, its 'dire need' to industrialize is universally acknowledged.'[200] The *AMV* envisions a mining sector that will become 'a key component of a diversified, vibrant and globally competitive industrialising African economy',[201] helping to establish a 'competitive African infrastructure platform'.[202] This can be achieved through 'propulsive' local and regional downstream, upstream and sidestream economic linkages and a better knowledge of the States' mineral endowment.[203]

Critics argue that rather than leading to broadranging sustainable development, the policies of neoextractivism incubate extractivist enclaves with severe social and environmental impacts. Gudynas' 'ten urgent theses' relating to twenty-first century extractivism in Latin America, for example, include the thesis that neoextractivism has perpetuated, and in some instances even exacerbated, negative social and environmental impacts, and that actions to deal with such impacts are still ineffective, and have even become weaker.[204] 'Progressive' governments have denied or minimized environmental impacts in the region, or presented them as sacrifices for the greater benefit of the whole nation.[205]

And yet Latin American, African and other 'developing region' scholars, activists and Indigenous Peoples have also advanced alternative conceptions

---

199 For an overview of these resources see Annex I of the *AMV* (n 81).

200 *AMV* (n 81) 2–3.

201 Ibid.

202 Ibid.

203 Ibid v.

204 Eduardo Gudynas, 'The new extractivism of the 21st century: Ten urgent theses about extractivism in relation to current South American progressivism' (2010) *Americas Program Report* 7.

205 Ibid.

of development that recognize strong social and environmental limits and the possibility of a postdevelopment era. The Cocoyoc Declaration,[206] the outcome statement of a joint UNEP/UNCTAD symposium convened in 1974 to address north–south tensions around patterns of resource use, environment and development, embodies such an alternative conception of development. Most of the participants at this meeting were from developing countries and the broader context of the meeting was the perceived failure around the establishment of a New International Economic Order. A key theme in the Declaration is that the world economic system must better meet the 'inner limits' of basic human needs, without violating the 'outer limits' of the planet's resources and environment. Like *Catastrophe or New Society?* the signatories to the Declaration locate the breach of these 'inner' and 'outer' limits in political relationships, not in 'unchangeable physical circumstance'. This offers hope because political relationships 'can undergo profound reversals and transformations'. According to the Declaration, the economic and social structures that account for the maldistribution and misuse of natural resources can be located in 'five centuries of colonial control that had concentrated economic power so overwhelmingly in the hands of a small group of nations' and the 'automatic operation of market mechanisms'. The solution to humankind's predicament lay not in harnessing natural resources for development in a manner that articulated with market mechanisms at a higher level (the strategy of contemporary neoextractivists and resource nationalists). It required, instead, redefining the whole purpose of development as satisfying basic needs, particularly of the poorest 40 per cent of the population, and supporting more abstract needs, goals and values such as freedom of expression, democracy and the right to work. A universal and linear conception of development as 'catching up' to the industrialized countries needed to be rejected, in favour of recognition that there were very many different roads of development. Rather than greater integration into world markets, one basic strategy of development, the Declaration suggested, would be self-reliance: a complex concept incorporating primary reliance on one's own human and natural resources, mutual benefits from trade and cooperation, transfer of technology that encouraged adaptation and the generation of local technology, a decentralized world economy, and so on. These recommendations resonate with more recent conceptions of postextractivism.[207]

In some instances, alternative conceptions of development have been incorporated into constitutional frameworks, laws and policies in States pursuing

---

[206] Cocoyoc Declaration (23 December 1974), https://helsinki.at/projekte/cocoyoc/COCOYOC_DECLARATION_1974.pdf, accessed 22 February 2019.

[207] See further the discussion in Chapter 8.

a neoextractivist path. Like the sustainable mineral development consensus, therefore, this suggests a pull towards the contradictory double movement, positioning the State as protector and custodian of mining-impacted interests at the same time as it aggressively promotes mining.

In Ecuador and Bolivia, indigenous ethical–philosophical principles of *Buen Vivir* (the Good Life, collective well-being; *sumak kawsay* in Quechua; *Suma Quamana* in Aymara) have been incorporated into the constitution and legal statutes alongside economic principles that mandate extractive-led development. Advocates of *Buen Vivir* emphasize a life in harmony with the environment and other human beings, unburdened by capitalism and consumption.[208]

In Ecuador, for example, the 2008 Constitution includes among the State's prime duties the duty of 'planning national development, eliminating poverty, and promoting sustainable development and the equitable redistribution of resources and wealth to enable access to the "good way of living"'.[209] The good way of living is *sumak kawsay* and is expressly mentioned in the Preamble, along with the celebration of *Pacha Mama* (Mother Earth). *Sumak kawsay* is further elaborated in Title VI (Development Structure) and Title VII (The Good Way of Living System). These provisions envision a development structure composed of interconnected economic, political, sociocultural and environmental systems. The State oversees this development structure to ensure the social inclusion, equity and integral protection of Ecuador's inhabitants throughout their lives.[210] At the same time, the State must guarantee a sustainable model of development that is environmentally balanced and respectful of cultural diversity, biodiversity, the natural regeneration of ecosystems and the needs of present and future generations.[211] Chapter 7 of Title II (Rights) recognizes the Rights of Nature, which include the right to integral respect for its existence and for the maintenance and regeneration of its life cycles, structure, functions and evolutionary processes; and the right to be restored, which applies an over-and-above State/private duty to compensate individuals/communities that depend on affected natural systems.[212] Other interesting limits are imposed. All extractive activities are forbidden on the territories of the peoples living in voluntary isolation.[213] The Constitution also recognizes the right of indigenous communities, peoples and nations to ownership of their land, and to free, prior and informed consultation on the plans and programmes

---

[208] R Lalander, 'Ethnic rights and the dilemma of extractive development in plurinational Bolivia' (2017) 21(4) *International Journal of Human Rights* 464, 469.

[209] Constitution of Ecuador, 2008, Article 3.5.

[210] Constitution of Ecuador, 2008, Articles 340, 341.

[211] Constitution of Ecuador, 2008, Article 395.1.

[212] Constitution of Ecuador, 2008, Articles 71–74.

[213] Constitution of Ecuador, 2008, Article 57.

for prospecting, producing and marketing nonrenewable resources located on such lands where these activities have an environmental or cultural impact.[214] Herein lies the pivot of the State's roles, however, because while the right of indigenous communities, peoples and nations to keep ownership of their land is constitutionally guaranteed, this does not extend to ownership of nonrenewable resources. Nonrenewables (including products coming from the ground and mineral and petroleum deposits) are instead framed as the 'inalienable property of the State'.[215] The exploitation of nonrenewable resources is a 'strategic sector', which comes under the decision making and 'exclusive control' of the State.[216] The State must participate in profits earned from the tapping of these resources, in an amount that is no less than the profits earned by the company producing them.[217] Even though the State is bound to constitutionally impose socioecological limits in exploiting such resources (for example, minimizing impacts of an environmental, cultural, social and economic nature; restoring the cycles of nature[218]), the Constitution also clearly binds this State to an extractivist path. A similar dynamic is evident in Bolivia, where the 2009 'plurinational Constitution' instructs the State to assume control and direction of the exploration, exploitation, industrialization, transport and sale of 'strategic natural resources', which includes minerals in all their states.[219] Natural resources are of 'strategic character' and of 'public importance' for the development of the country.[220] These overarching directions to the State frame the 'extractive dilemma' in countries such as Ecuador and Bolivia, in which rights around limitations on extractive development in pursuance of *Buen Vivir* clash with State-sponsored extractive projects promoted under the banner of redistributive justice, general welfare and the common good.[221]

4.2 Forms of State-Led Extractivism

Contemporary neoextractivism and resource nationalism may proceed through nationalization or indigenization of mining factors of production, or through

[214] Constitution of Ecuador, 2008, Article 57.7.
[215] Constitution of Ecuador, 2008, Article 408.
[216] Constitution of Ecuador, 2008, Article 303.
[217] Constitution of Ecuador, 2008, Article 408.
[218] Constitution of Ecuador, 2008, Article 317.
[219] Plurinational Constitution of Bolivia, 2009, Article 350.I.
[220] Plurinational Constitution of Bolivia, 2009, Article 348.
[221] See further Lalander (n 208); Radoslaw Poweska, 'State-led extractivism and the frustration of indigenous self-determined development: lessons from Bolivia' (2017) 21(4) *International Journal of Human Rights* 442; and Joanna Morley, '"Beggars sitting on a sack of gold": Oil exploration in the Ecadorian Amazon as *buen vivir* and sustainable development' (2017) 21(4) *International Journal of Human Rights* 405.

various other forms of developmental State participation.[222] The most extreme form of resource nationalism – nationalization – involves a State directive to private foreign firms to sell or transfer all their equity to the government.[223] Many mineral-rich jurisdictions have experienced two or three cyclical processes of nationalization and privatization of their mining assets over a number of decades.[224] More recently, States have provided for a compulsory 'free carried interest' in mining ventures. The 2006 Minerals Law in Mongolia, for instance, initially provided for a 50 per cent State stake when nonstate entities conducted major exploration activities. This was later amended to 34 per cent at around the same time that the government negotiated an agreement with foreign investors for the development of the Oyu Tolgoi mine.[225] In Tanzania, the mining law allows the Minister of Mining to enter into a development agreement with the holder or applicant for a mining right that may provide for a government free carried interest in the venture.[226] A 'free carried interest' is defined in the law as 'the interest derived from holding shares of which the holder enjoys all the rights of a shareholder but has no obligation to subscribe or contribute equity capital for the shares'.[227]

Indigenization occurs when government requires private foreign firms to sell their equity to citizens of the country.[228] In a mining context, recent and industry-contested indigenization processes include the multipronged strategy to promote black economic empowerment under South Africa's mining law and Mining Charter,[229] and Zimbabwe's indigenization and economic empowerment law, which requires compulsory local equity ownership in certain sectors, including mining.[230]

Other than nationalization and indigenization, States may draw upon a variety of coercive and noncoercive institutions to participate in mining.

---

222 Solomon (n 186) 68.

223 Ernest J Wilson III, 'Strategies of State control of the economy: Nationalization and Indigenization in Africa' (1990) 22(4) *Comparative Politics* 401, 402.

224 R Chang and C Hevia, 'Privatization and Nationalisation Cycles' (2010) NBER working paper, no. 16126, www.nber.org/papers/w16126.pdf, accessed 22 February 2019.

225 Sara L Jackson, 'Imagining the mineral nation: Contested nation-building in Mongolia' (2015) 43(3) *Nationalities Papers* 437, 447.

226 Mining Act, 2010 (Tanzania), section 10.

227 Mining Act, 2010 (Tanzania), section 4.

228 Wilson (n 223) 402.

229 Tumai Murombo, 'Regulating mining in South Africa and Zimbabwe: Communities, the environment, and perpetual exploitation' (2013) 9 *Law, Environment and Development Journal* 33.

230 Indigenisation and Economic Empowerment (General) Regulations Statutory Instrument of 2010 (Zimbabwe).

These include establishment of a State-owned mining company, with or without monopoly powers of exploration and exploitation over particular commodities;[231] taxation measures to secure a greater proportion of the mineral resources rent, including windfall taxes;[232] and measures to secure the in-country beneficiation of mineral ores.

Recent mining reforms in Tanzania have extended the envelope of measures designed to increase State and indigenous participation in the mining sector. Laws enacted under a certificate of urgency in July 2017 vest sweeping powers in the national assembly to review and instruct government to renegotiate mining contracts;[233] require at least 16 per cent State free carried interest in all mining companies – a figure that may be increased to 50 per cent to match the value of historical tax benefits granted to the company; and institute an immediate blanket ban on the export of unprocessed minerals, with a view that they will in future be beneficiated domestically.[234] In 2018, indigenization requirements were extended to the procurement of mining services inclusive of the professional services of finance, insurance and legal advice. Regulations enacted under the Mining Act 2010 require, for example, that a mining company shall only retain the services of a Tanzanian financial institution or organization in the event that they require financial services in relation to a mining activity. Approval of the mining commission is required to engage the services of a foreign financial institution.[235] Similarly, in the field of legal services a mining company engaged in a mining activity in Tanzania requiring legal services may only retain a Tanzanian legal practitioner, or a firm of Tanzanian legal practitioners whose principal office is located in Tanzania.[236] These interesting statutory enactments underscore the importance of the sources of policy and legal advice that frame the activities of mining proponents.

---

231 Historical and current examples include the state owned Zambia Consolidated Copper Mines (state equity of 60.3 per cent) and Corporación Nacional del Cobre de Chile (Codelco), the state owned mining company of Chile.

232 Taxation of minerals and mining is comprehensively discussed in Chapter 5.

233 Natural Wealth and Resources (Permanent Sovereignty) Act, 2017 (Tanzania); the Natural Wealth and Resources (Review and Re-negotiation of Unconscionable Terms) Act, 2017 (Tanzania); and the Written Laws (Miscellaneous Amendments) Act, 2017, which amends the Mining Act, 2010.

234 Peter Leon, 'Tanzania's rigid system of mining quotas risks making compliance impossible', *Business Day*, 24 April 2018, www.businesslive.co.za/bd/opinion/2018-04-24-tanzanias-rigid-system-of-mining-quotas-risks-making-compliance-impossible/, accessed 22 February 2019.

235 Ibid.

236 Ibid.

Unsurprisingly, neoextractivism and resource nationalism raise alarm among the community of private mining investors and their institutional supporters. Typical metaphorical imagery includes references to a 'rising tide'[237] or a 'fire'[238] of resource nationalism. Well rehearsed critiques leveraged against the various forms of resource nationalism include lack of institutional capacity to drive State participation in mining; bureaucratic inefficiency; and State corruption[239] – all factors deemed responsible for a dampening of investor confidence and willingness to invest.

In conclusion, the State looms large in neoextractivism and resource nationalism as a promoter of the mining industry. Rather than incubating a private-led mining industry as the 'engine of growth', the State takes direct responsibility for positioning mining as a means towards development. A belief in natural resource abundance undergirds a tendency to minimize environmental impacts or to postpone remedial measures, or to accept environmental degradation as a necessary sacrifice. Notwithstanding official environmental policies that appear to lend little weight to the need for inner and outer socioecological limits, there has been engagement with these ideas in the 'underdeveloped' regions in which neoextractivism and resource nationalism now flourish. In some States, such limits have even been recognized in constitutional and legislative frameworks. This lends weight to the existence of a persistent double movement in State policy towards the mining sector.

5. CRITICAL AND STRATEGIC MINERALS

The final discourse considered in this chapter – critical and strategic minerals – arose from fears around security of mineral supply in the contexts of colonization, decolonization and the Cold War. Unlike the discourses of the sustainable mineral development consensus, responsible mining or neoextractivism, the narrative on critical and strategic minerals has not been framed as official development policy. It presents, rather, the *realpolitik* driving international relations in the field of mining that lies beneath these more foregrounded developmental discourses. A trend towards identifying critical or strategic minerals accelerated in the 1970s, after publication of the Club of Rome's *Limits to Growth* report. In analysing global growth trends, *Limits to Growth*

---

[237] Jenny Wagler, 'Rising tide of resource nationalism threatens Vancouver miners', *Business Vancouver*, 23 July 2012, https://biv.com/article/2012/07/rising-tide-of-resource-nationalism-threatens-vanc, accessed 22 February 2019.

[238] Chris Mayer, 'The rising tide of resource nationalism', *The Daily Reckoning*, 2 May 2011, https://dailyreckoning.com/the-rising-tide-of-resource-nationalism/, accessed 22 February 2019.

[239] Solomon (n 186) 26.

alerted Western powers to the growing deficit in their minerals balance of payments.[240] Following a respite in reporting on critical and strategic minerals, the discourse emerged again in the early 2000s, coincident with the resource boom associated with the rapid economic growth of China and India.[241]

Initially, Western powers' concern with the flow of strategic minerals centred on denying as many strategic minerals as possible to the USSR.[242] In the 1970s the root of this concern was that the supply of metals and minerals was still largely met by primary production tied to particular geological formations unevenly distributed throughout the globe.[243] The decolonization movements that gained momentum in the post-Second World War period threatened the security of the Allies' supply over mineral resources. This led to some 'novel' forms of political cooperation. On 13 June 1944, for example, US President Franklin D. Roosevelt and British Prime Minister Winston S. Churchill reached an agreement on cooperation in respect of uranium and thorium. While the policy of both the United States and Britain was to monopolize the worldwide supply of uranium, their policy on thorium (a potential alternative fissionable material) was to establish control 'by means of options and political agreement'.[244] This led to a clandestine political agreement between the United States, Britain and the Netherlands for export of thorium from the Dutch East Indies. In terms of this 1945 agreement (which was never subjected to processes of parliamentary scrutiny), the Netherlands agreed that thorium and monazite sand from the Dutch East Indies could only be exported with the permission of the United States and Britain.[245] In this fashion the USA and Britain gained control over a part of the global supply of thorium, albeit for a limited period of time.[246]

A more systematic approach to monitoring nonenergy raw materials emerged under the Nixon administration in the United States and intensified under the Reagan administration.[247] Between 1974 and 1983, State offices in both the United States and Britain produced three major reports on critical

---

[240] See the discussion in section 6.2 of Chapter 1.

[241] Bram Buijs, Henrike Sievers, Luis A Tercero Espinoza, 'Limits to the critical raw materials approach' (2012) 165(4) *Waste and Resource Management* 201.

[242] Jacob M van Splunter, 'Strategic minerals and decolonization: The United States and Great Britain versus the Netherlands, 1945–1951' (1995) 17(3) *International History Review* 485.

[243] Ibid.

[244] Ibid 487.

[245] Ibid 493.

[246] Ibid 485. The clandestine agreement only lasted six years.

[247] Buijs (n 241) 201.

raw materials.[248] While the critical raw materials in these reports vary, the concerns, as well as the analysis and proposed solutions, were largely the same.[249] The key risks centred on security of supply (not geological scarcity) as a result of import dependence, coupled with concentration of production in 'unstable' countries, a tendency for increased processing in producer countries and the nationalization of mining companies.[250] Proposed solutions included exploiting domestic resources, setting longterm supply contracts in place and stockpiling raw materials.[251] These solutions are also very similar to solutions proposed in more recent reports on mineral criticality.[252]

The early approach to critical and strategic minerals did not consider social or environmental limits to mineral supply, and subverted political principles relating to social and economic justice. For example, the USA's Comprehensive Anti-Apartheid Act 1986 imposed sanctions on South Africa for its apartheid policies by prohibiting the export and import of a number of products.[253] However, Title III, section 303 of the Act exempted strategic minerals from the import ban, 'for which the President has certified to congress that the quantities essential for the economy or defense of the US are unavailable from reliable and secure suppliers'.[254] At that time South Africa was one of the two major suppliers of chromium (the other being the USSR), producing about 35 per cent of world supply.[255] Chromium was one of the minerals exempted under Title III as it was considered highly critical and highly strategic, particularly for its use in the production of US defence equipment.[256] The

---

[248] In 1974 the US Department of State produced the report *Critical Imported Materials*, which examined the risks of price gouging and supply interruption for 19 major industrial raw nonenergy minerals. The report found that bauxite, platinum and chromium could be considered critical. In 1975, the Commission of the European Communities qualitatively examined the criticality of a number of minerals with reference to supply and demand trends, producer concentration, substitutability and estimated political risk. Tungsten, manganese, chromium, phosphate and platinum were earmarked as being of concern. And in 1983, the US Congressional Budget Office identified chromium, cobalt, manganese and platinum group metals as being of primary concern applying a similar risk profile (Buijs (n 241) 201).

[249] Ibid 202.

[250] Ibid.

[251] Ibid.

[252] Ibid.

[253] LD Anderson, 'Geopolitics and the cold war environment: The case of chromium' (1995) 37(2) *GeoJournal* 209.

[254] Ibid.

[255] Ibid 210.

[256] Ibid 209–10.

exemption was nevertheless secured on the basis of inaccurate and irrelevant information on the importance of South African chromium to the USA.[257]

The critical and strategic minerals discourse underwent a lull in the 1980s and 1990s. The buoyant sentiment in that time was that market mechanisms would ensure availability of supply.[258] This changed at the start of the 2000s, when the demand for raw materials from India and China sent prices soaring. In 1990 China consumed 8 per cent of worldwide steel, a figure that had jumped to nearly 45 per cent by 2012.[259] In response to price increases and a greater awareness of competition for, and the vulnerability of, raw materials supplies, a number of governments and supranational organizations commissioned a new wave of mineral criticality studies.[260] In comparison to the minerals identified in reports of the 1970s, many point to the criticality of minerals needed in green technology applications.[261]

Buijs *et al* maintain that the way of looking at the problem of mineral criticality has remained the same. But in order to measure political stability and the potential for supply disruptions, the most recent reports draw upon a broader range of risk criteria.[262] For example, in addition to looking at import dependence, the ratio of production to reserves, producer concentration and substitutability, recent reports also consider technology demand, the recycling rate and climate change variability.[263] They also use 'established' governance indicators (such as the Human Development Index or the World Bank's world-

---

[257] Ibid 211–13.

[258] Friedrich-W Wellmer and Manfred Dalheimer, 'The feedback control cycle as regulator of past and future mineral supply' (2012) 47 *Miner Deposita* 713.

[259] Ibid.

[260] Ibid. See also Buijs (n 241) 203. The reports, with the identified raw critical materials in parentheses, have included the following: Committee on Critical Mineral Impacts on the US Economy, *Minerals, Critical Minerals and the US Economy* (2008) (indium, manganese, niobium, PGMs, rare earths); Resource Efficiency Knowledge Transfer Network, *Material Security: Ensuring Resource Availability for the UK Economy* (2008) (gold, rhodium, platinum, strontium, silver, antinomy, tin); US Department of Energy, *Critical Minerals Strategy* (2010) (dysprosium, neodymium, terbium, europium, yttrium, indium); European Commission, *Critical Law Materials for the EU* (2010) (antinomy, beryllium, cobalt, fluorspar, gallium, germanium, graphite, indium, magnesium, niobium, PGMs, rare earths, tantalum, tungsten); IZT and Adelphi, *Kritische Rohstoffe fur Deutschland* (2011) (germanium, rhenium, antinomy, tungsten, rare earths, gallium, palladium, silver, indium, tin, niobium, chromium, bismuth). See also UNEP (2009) *Critical Metals for Future Sustainable Technologies and Their Recycling Potential*. For a general overview of the criticality discourse see Jo Dewulf *et al*, 'Criticality on the international scene: Quo vadis?' (2016) 50 *Resources Policy* 169.

[261] Buijs (n 241) 201.

[262] Ibid 202.

[263] See the list of risk criteria set out in ibid 203.

wide governance indicators) to divide the world into 'stable' and 'unstable' countries.

In the most recent mineral criticality reports, environmental and sustainability considerations feature in ambiguous ways. In the 1970s, the reasons put forward for denying the USSR strategic minerals centred on anti-Communism. But in the most recent reports, the threat is the lack of good environmental governance. As Sprance argues: 'China's noninterventionist policy does not demand good governance, democracy, human rights or governmental transparency. As one African official put it: "The US will talk to you about governance, efficiency, about security, about the environment. The Chinese just ask: How do we procure this licence?"'[264]

And yet Beijing's reasons for seeking access to sub-Saharan African resources are no different to those of the United States,[265] as Burgess candidly admits: 'Southern Africa contains strategic minerals, which the United States and its allies require for industrial purposes and that militaries need for the production and sustainment of weapons systems.'[266] The older and newer versions of the discourse of critical and strategic minerals generally display little concern for questions of social, economic and environmental justice. They arguably expose the dark underbelly of the concerns underlying the industry: the race to secure access to resources for industrialization, but also for militarization. This discourse assumes a muscular State – capable of securing supply or development through a range of strong regulatory interventions. It simultaneously assumes a climate of inter-State distrust and clandestine cooperation in a global terrain categorized by stable and unstable countries.

6. CONCLUSION

This review of four pro-mining discourses on mining, development and sustainability shows there is no uniform conception of the role of the State: the sustainable mineral development consensus advocates for a facilitative and regulatory State supporting a private-led mining industry; responsible mining backgrounds and subtly critiques the State's importance and capacity even as the discourse holds that minimum State standards are necessary to promote private investment and ensure baseline conditions of compliance; neoextrac-

264 William R Sprance, 'The new tournament of shadows: The strategic implications of China's activity in Sub-Saharan Africa and Africom's role in the US response' (2008) 10(3) *Journal of Military and Strategic Studies* 1, 2.

265 Ibid 1.

266 Stephen Burgess, 'Sustainability of strategic minerals in Southern Africa and potential conflicts and partnerships' (Occasional Paper 2010), www.dtic.mil/get-tr-doc/pdf?AD=ADA535875, accessed 22 February 2019.

tivism assumes a State prepared to intervene directly and robustly in the industry to secure mining's developmental gains; and the discourse of critical and strategic minerals reveals the strategic State of the developed world, engaging the realm of 'undeveloped' States to secure security of mineral supply.

In all of these discourses, the State is expected to promote mining, though for different reasons. The centrality of economic growth is unchallenged. Under the sustainable mineral development consensus, the State promotes a private-led mining industry to stimulate investment and economic development in the hope that benefits will trickle down, contributing to economic growth and poverty alleviation. These objectives are assumed in the discourse of responsible mining. Under neoextractivism and resource nationalism the State positions mining as a strategic industry in the quest for national development. In the discourse of critical and strategic minerals, developed country States must secure their mineral supplies; States of mineral supply, conversely, are divided into 'stable and unstable' countries, but the expectation that they exist to meet this supply is unchallenged.

All of the pro-mining discourses assume mining's contribution to development. Proponents of neoextractivism arguably present the most insistent vision of the mining sector's development potential. The IFIs have also rigorously promoted the idea of mining as a 'development industry'. The mining industry has guardedly echoed this framing, but its own sponsored research through the *RoMine* reports shows that mining's contribution to development is often precarious. Mining contributes to exports, foreign direct investment, GDP, revenue generation and employment, but these contributions are difficult to measure, or the measurements that are made obscure mining's proclivity towards enclave development.

Social and environmental limits are acknowledged in these discourses, though with different underlying assumptions that service particular political agendas. The environment is a key concern of the sustainable mineral development consensus, which it largely positions as a resolvable, technological concern. It acknowledges historical environmental degradation for the purpose of carving out a historical State liability. This discourse incorporates interesting calls for the recognition of limits, such as the Stockholm Declaration on collaboration in aggregating information on mining and the environment; the Brundtland Commission's stern warning that competition for nonrenewable raw materials could intersect with poverty, injustice and environmental stress to threaten peace, security and development; the EIR's formulation of the 'right' conditions for mining investment; and the MMSD's 'guiding principles' for sustainable development, which include the need to 'qualify' economic considerations by a concern for maximizing human well-being and by operating within ecological limits. Responsible mining uses 'beyond compliance', self-regulatory action on social and environmental impacts to justify multistakeholder initiatives that go beyond the minimum regulations laid down by the State. Neoextractivism rides on the assumption of natural resource abundance and promotes an approach to environmental regulation that some argue exacerbates ecological degradation and weakens environmental regulation. At the same time, in the 'undeveloped' and 'developing' regions of the world, sources have emerged for alternative conceptions of development and ecological and social limits.

The double movement is evident within some of these resources – most notably in the policy prescriptions of the sustainable mineral development consensus. Remarkably, here, it is the mining industry itself that prompted a recalibration of the State's role. Through the MMSD and other initiatives, the industry attempted to address worrying social discontent over its operations and its social licence to operate. The MMSD highlighted the State's protective role and firmly positioned mining within the stream of sustainable development thinking that had gained momentum since the early 1990s. But the State's protective function would also be amplified and deepened through the discourses of mining dissent that flourished over the same period of time.

3. The State, mining, development and sustainability: discourses of dissent

1. INTRODUCTION

This is the second of two chapters outlining discourses on mining, development, sustainability and the role of the State. This chapter focuses on discourses of mining dissent: discourses on the State's sustainability role that dissent from or refute central claims of pro-mining discourses, highlight the harms flowing from mining to a far greater extent or offer alternative conceptions of how mining can contribute to the well-being of people and planet. Over the course of the past half century, these discourses have emerged from the work of academics, intergovernmental organizations, mining-affected communities, Indigenous Peoples' movements, international and national NGOs and community organizations. The discourses of dissent surveyed in this chapter are the resource curse thesis, Indigenous Peoples' rights, environmental justice, human rights and feminist critiques of mining.

Recalling the double movement, discourses of dissent place more emphasis on the State's protective role compared to the State's promotion of mining. But they differ in terms of who or what the State is called upon to protect, and how the State is expected to act. In similar fashion to some of the pro-mining discourses, at times both arms of the double movement are evident: discourses of dissent are not necessarily anti-mining – they may still expect the State to promote mining, albeit under different political, economic, social or environmental conditions. As a result, discourses of dissent present different conceptions of the acceptable limits States should impose upon the mining industry. Taken together, however, these discourses pull an unbridled dash for mineral extraction back to a more socially acceptable equilibrium.

In discourses of dissent, an added layer of complexity is that mining proponents have at times recognized and in some instances even appropriated these discourses. In this chapter, this is illustrated by the mining industry's engagement with Indigenous Peoples' rights and human rights in particular. By adopting the patterned language of its opponents, the globally organized mining industry conveys the impression it is addressing their major concerns.

2. THE RESOURCE CURSE THESIS

The resource curse thesis, initially formulated by Auty in the early 1990s,[1] has functioned as an enduring frame to challenge the mining industry's development claims. Auty investigated how natural resources contribute to economic growth, and how a dominant mineral-exporting sector affected the economies of host States. Inspired by the economists that had studied 'Dutch disease',[2] and building on the pioneering work of Gelb on the effect of Dutch disease in oil-producing countries,[3] Auty's work highlighted the macroeconomic policies needed to deal with mining sector-induced economic distortions, the measurement of mineral reserve depletion and the role of natural resource degradation and protection in sustainable development.[4]

The resource curse thesis challenged the conventional economic wisdom undergirding the policy reform proposals of international financial institutions (IFIs) in the early 1990s: that natural resource endowments can enable developing countries to transition from underdevelopment, develop an industrial base and diversify their economies.[5] The essence of the resource curse thesis is that the economic performance of countries with a significant natural resource endowment tends to lag behind countries that are resource poor.[6] For the hard

---

1 RM Auty, *Sustaining Development in Mineral Economies: The Resource Curse Thesis* (Routledge 1993).

2 Developed in the early 1980s, Dutch disease is a theory explaining the negative effect of extractive industries on nonresource sectors such as agriculture and manufacturing. The theory was initially formulated in response to the decline in manufacturing in the Netherlands after the discovery of natural gas at Groningen. It holds that natural resource booms lead to an increase in domestic consumption that causes inflation and appreciation in the real exchange rate. The mineral sector attracts labour and materials, causing the cost of these inputs for nonresource sectors to increase. The relative prices of nonresource commodities increase and exports become noncompetitive. When the price of mining commodities falls as a result of familiar commodity boom and bust cycles, the mineral producing economy struggles to adjust (see Rameez Badeeb *et al*, 'The evolution of the natural resource curse thesis: A critical literature survey' (2016) Working Paper No. 5/2016, Department of Economics and Finance, University of Canterbury, New Zealand, 8). Dutch disease manifests in the premature shrinkage of the agricultural sector (relative to nonextractive economies) and the underdevelopment or extreme protection of the manufacturing sector.

3 Alan Gelb (ed.), *Oil Windfalls: Blessing or Curse?* (Oxford University Press 1988).

4 Richard M Auty and Raymond F Mikesell, *Sustainable Development in Mineral Economies* (Clarendon 1998) 7.

5 Bedeeb (n 2) 5.

6 Auty (n 1) 5.

mineral economies,[7] Auty located the cause of this underperformance in the capital intensive nature of mineral production (creating comparatively few jobs per unit of investment), domestic linkages (fiscal linkages predominate, predisposing this sector to enclave development) and the deployment of mineral rents (developing country governments promoting too rapid domestic absorption of mineral rents, leading to economic distortions).[8] Inability to manage the macroeconomic risk associated with these features of the mineral sector, coupled with the volatility of mineral commodity pricing, rendered developing States vulnerable to growth collapse.

Sustainable development loomed large in Auty's work. The 'sustainability question' in mineral-rich countries was how mineral resources could best be employed for achieving and maintaining the maximum rate of economic growth consistent with the country's social objectives.[9] Sustainability involved more than substituting the depleted natural capital with other forms of capital (manufactured, human, social or financial), or sustaining mineral production itself.[10] Rather, it required harnessing mining's catalytic effect on an economy and maintaining the economic and social conditions necessary for economic growth, notwithstanding reduction in, or the ultimate winding down of, mining production.[11] Auty pointed out that sustainable development literature had ignored the central importance of minimizing Dutch disease in mineral economies. Addressing the more 'conventional' requirements of sustainable development – providing for depletion of the mineral asset and reducing environmental degradation – was difficult to achieve in an economy afflicted by Dutch disease.[12] Consequently, most mineral economies needed to *first* mute the corrosive impact of the mining sector on agriculture and trade, and *then* direct attention to conventional sustainable development requirements.[13]

In a later paper, Auty underscored that macroeconomic failures in resource-rich developing countries undermined microeconomic policies, including those aimed at environmental improvement.[14] He also ventured that environmental policymakers needed to be more supportive of the efforts of

---

7 Defined as developing countries that generate more than 8 per cent of their GDP and 40 per cent of their export earnings from the mineral sector.

8 Auty (n 1) 3.

9 Auty and Mikesell (n 4) 3.

10 Ibid.

11 Ibid.

12 Auty (n 1) 15.

13 Ibid 16.

14 Richard M Auty, 'Natural resources, development models and sustainable development' (June 2003) Environmental Economics Programme, Discussion Paper 03-01, 1.

IFIs 'to ease the constraint of maladroit macroeconomic management'.[15] The 'basic economic policies for sustainable development' were well known,[16] Auty insisted, namely the foundational policy measures of the 'unjustly, much-maligned' Washington consensus,[17] centring on fiscal discipline, the protection of property rights and maintaining competitive markets. An inability to secure these conditions connoted an inability to implement environmental policies on nonrenewable resources and pollution as well.[18]

In Auty's work, resource-rich developing States present as predatory and incompetent, incapable of steering efficient capital accumulation from natural resources. He states, for instance, that 'natural resource abundance has been associated with predatory political states that distort their economies so that the development trajectory is one that becomes locked in a staple trap of increasing dependence on a primary sector with diminishing competitiveness'.[19]

And yet the State, working together with other roleplayers, is also the locus of policy change that can avert the resource curse. On the face of it, Auty's resource curse-addressing State resembles the facilitative and regulatory State of the sustainable mineral development consensus. But the policy substance differs, with Auty emphasizing the need for (1) a system of environmental and natural resource accounting and (2) institutional measures to sterilize the mineral resource rent, increase the transparency of rent flows and enable rigorous evaluation of alternative uses of mineral rents.

In a 2003 paper, Auty argued that environmental and natural resource accounting (EANRA) could improve the quality of extractives governance. Resting on the work of environmental economists stretching back to the 1970s, EANRA provided the conceptual and methodological resources for correcting the overstatement of investment and output in such indicators as gross national product (GNP) and net national product (NNP). For example, NNP only subtracted the annual depreciation of produced (manmade) capital, whereas EANRA provided measures to account for the depletion of finite resources (such as minerals) and the depletion of environmental assets.[20] Auty cited World Bank data from the early 1970s showing that newly industrializing countries had high and rising genuine saving coefficients of between 20 and 30 per cent, whereas most oil-exporting countries and the hard mineral economies tended to record low or negative genuine saving rates, suggesting that their

15 Ibid.

16 Auty (n 1) 1.

17 Ibid 3.

18 Ibid 1.

19 Ibid. Noted exceptions to this trend include Chile, Botswana, Malaysia and Indonesia.

20 Auty (n 14) 9–10.

trajectories of development were not sustainable.[21] Later still, Auty put his weight behind the System of Environmental Economic Accounting (SEEA) developed by the London School of Environmental Accounting under the auspices of the United Nations Statistical Division.[22] The measure of adjusted net savings under the 2003 version of the SEEA takes into account the depletion of minerals and whether compensatory investments have been made in other forms of capital.[23] According to Auty, one of the most significant tasks of mineral-rich States is to institutionalize a set of national environmental accounts that enables the government to monitor whether there has in fact been any saving from mineral exploitation.[24]

Implementation of SEEA would ground further institutional reforms aimed at countering the deleterious effects of the resource curse. First, the State would need to host a capital fund in its central bank to receive that part of mineral revenue identified by the SEEA as the rent.[25] The role of the capital fund would be to isolate or sterilize the mineral rent, cementing its character as a form of capital, rather than a source of recurrent expenditure. In this fashion, the prudent State would be protected from the prodigality of inefficient domestic absorption of the rent, one of the key risk factors for Dutch disease. Second, prudent States would adopt codes of practice promoting transparency in the flow and allocation of mineral rents, such as the Extractive Industries Transparency Initiative (EITI).[26] Third, States needed to establish a public investment valuation unit. Such a unit would improve mineral rent deployment by evaluating the relative capital returns of investing the rent in offshore assets as opposed to domestic investments in human capital, economic infrastructure or directly productive activities.[27] Without such an institution, Auty warned, 'governments have shown themselves to favor large public sector investments that enhance scope for servicing patronage networks by padding construction contracts and providing employment to favoured groups'.[28] The predatory characterization of the State therefore lingers, even as the State drives institutional reform to guard against its tendency for avarice and incompetence.

---

21 Ibid.

22 Robert Smith, 'Development of the SEEA 2003 and its implementation' (2007) 61(4) *Ecological Economics* 592, 593; see also United Nations, 'System of Environmental Economic Accounting', https://seea.un.org, accessed 23 February 2019.

23 Richard M Auty, 'Natural resources, capital accumulation and the resource curse' (2007) *Ecological Economics* 627, 628. See further the discussion of ANS in section 5 of Chapter 1.

24 Ibid 631.

25 The concept of mineral resource rents is discussed further in Chapter 5.

26 Auty (n 23) 632.

27 Ibid.

28 Ibid.

The resource curse thesis has spawned a massive literature, both contesting and expanding upon the theory.[29] Bebbington points out that debates over the resource curse have dominated much social science output on mining.[30] The very existence of the resource curse has been challenged, and the methodologies used to measure it.[31]

Proponents of the sustainable mineral development consensus have belatedly engaged with the resource curse thesis and attempted to reframe it as an issue of resource endowment, or highlighted the converse possibility of 'resource blessing'. Stunningly, *Breaking New Ground*, the final report of the Mining, Mineral and Sustainable Development (MMSD) project,[32] did not mention the resource curse thesis once, and Auty's work is not referenced in the report's bibliography. Perhaps as a gesture to the resource curse literature, *Breaking New Ground* includes the anodyne observation that '[i]n some countries . . . mineral activities have not brought sustained economic development. Sudden wealth may have detrimental effects on social and political life, leading to or supporting corruption, authoritarian government, human rights abuse, or armed conflict.'[33]

Nevertheless, in 2004, the International Council of Mining and Metals (ICMM) collaborated with UNCTAD and the World Bank on the Resource Endowment Initiative,[34] a project aimed at developing a substantial body of research examining and explaining how and why some countries have managed to evade the 'resource curse' while others have succumbed to it. Illustrative of the technocratization and stripping down of the debate, a 'Resource Endowment Toolkit' was developed in 2006 and applied to Chile, Ghana, Peru and Tanzania. One of the major findings of this work was that the resource curse is not inevitable and that mining investments can drive growth

---

29 See Andrew Rosser, *The Political Economy of the Resource Curse: A Literature Survey* (IDS Working Paper, 2006); JA Frankel, *The Natural Resource Curse: A Survey* (National Bureau of Economic Research, 2010), https://dash.harvard.edu/bitstream/handle/1/8694932/rwp12-014_frankel.pdf?sequence=1, accessed 23 February 2019; and F Van der Ploeg, 'Natural resources: Curse or blessing?' (2011) *Journal of Economic Literature* 366. For critics of the resource curse see GA Davis, 'Learning to love the Dutch disease: Evidence from the mineral economies' (1995) 23(10) *World Development* 1765.

30 Anthony Bebbington *et al*, 'Contention and ambiguity: Mining and the possibilities of development' (2008) 39(6) *Development and Change* 965, 968.

31 See in particular C Brunnschweiler and E Bulte, 'Linking natural resources to slow growth and more conflict' (2008) 320 *Science* 616.

32 See the discussion of this project in section 2.1.4 of Chapter 2.

33 International Institute for Environment and Development and World Business Council for Sustainable Development, *Breaking New Ground: Mining, Minerals and Sustainable Development* (Earthscan 2002) xix (henceforth *Breaking New Ground*).

34 ICMM, *Mining: Partnerships for Development: Toolkit* (ICMM 2011) 8.

and reduce poverty at both an international and a national level. However, mining companies alone cannot 'unlock' the benefits of development, and much depends on the quality of governance.[35]

An emphasis on governance is also evident in a 2006 World Bank feature titled 'From curse to blessing: Natural resources and institutional quality', which engages with Gelb and Auty's work and acknowledges the 'robust empirical evidence for a negative relationship between natural resource wealth and economic growth'.[36] The article nevertheless insists that 'no comprehensive theory exists', and that the resource curse thesis is unable to explain a number of exceptions.[37] Attention is thereupon immediately directed to the problem of 'good governance', which the authors present as 'crucial to transform natural resource wealth into good economic performance'.[38] The 'sustainability rule of thumb' here is 'invest the rents from the exploitation of natural resources', and the key policy issue is how resource rents can be invested effectively and how fiscal stability can be maintained.[39] The institutional 'recipe' in this regard includes avoiding external debt, diversifying the economy and using public expenditures to counter the boom and bust characteristics of commodity markets.[40] Interestingly, this article makes no mention of the natural resource accounting or capital sterilization funds Auty had already canvassed in his work. A recent IMF-sponsored publication on the resource curse/endowment similarly does focus on capital stabilization funds, but devotes scant attention to other dimensions of Auty's policy proposals.[41]

Context and institutions mark the points of convergence between proponents and critics of the resource curse thesis, as Bebbington has observed. 'Increasingly one senses an "it all depends" tone in much analysis.'[42] Karl points out that the focus on institutions positions the resource curse as a *political* rather than an economic problem or a governance issue.[43] A key political issue, for example, is the scale of time and the causal factors triggering the emergence of the necessary resource management institutions, with IFI-aligned

---

35 Ibid.

36 Kirk Hamilton and Giovanni Ruta, 'From curse to blessing: Natural resources and institutional quality' in *World Bank Group Environment Matters* (2006) 24.

37 Ibid.

38 Ibid.

39 Ibid 25.

40 Ibid.

41 Rabah Arezki, Thorvaldur Gylfason and Amadou Sy (eds), *Beyond the Curse: Policies to Harness the Power of Natural Resources* (IMF 2011).

42 Bebbington (n 30) 973.

43 TL Karl, 'Ensuring fairness: The case for a transparent fiscal contract' in M Humphreys, J Sachs and J Stiglitz *Escaping the Resource Curse* (Columbia University Press 2007) 256–285. Cited in Bebbington (n 30) 973.

parties maintaining that these can be successfully instituted in project time and detractors arguing that these would rather emerge as a 'product of conflict and shifts in the balance of social power than an outcome of technocratic design, corporate philanthropy or the sorts of public sector management loans that the IFIs are wont to offer'.[44] Another political issue is the question of the *realpolitik* of the mining sector, which is intent on continuing to expand investment in extractives.[45]

The resource curse thesis warns the State to protect itself from the unintended negative economic impacts of mining on other sectors. These impacts arise from spending mineral resource rents too quickly and wastefully. Resource curse theory alludes to the predatory State, unable to constrain itself from spending mineral resource rents in a manner that does not give effect to Dutch disease. The worrying message of the resource curse theory is that without a rigorous SEEA, a mineral resource rent capital fund, extractives transparency and a public investment evaluation unit, the hard mineral economies are on an inherently unsustainable development path. While the mining industry and the IFIs have belatedly engaged with the resource curse thesis, their advocacy has watered down the hardnosed and longterm political choices that are arguably needed.

3. INDIGENOUS PEOPLES' RIGHTS

The second discourse of mining dissent posits 'Indigenous Peoples' rights' as the object of State protection. This is a complex discourse that necessitates delving into the history and scope of the Indigenous Peoples' rights movement, their relationship to land and mining and the principle of free, prior and informed consent.

3.1 Introduction

In 1987 *The Gulliver File* documented 'the experience of environmental, anti-nuclear, pro-green – *and above all indigenous* – groups, concerned about the negative impact of huge mineral extraction projects'.[46] The publication was a clear and early example of the alignment of Indigenous Peoples movements with antimining activism. Since then, an extensive academic and activist literature has documented conflict and collaboration between Indigenous

---

[44] Bebbington (n 30) 973.

[45] Ibid 974.

[46] Roger Moody, *The Gulliver File: Mines, People & Land: A Global Battleground* (Pluto 1987), my emphasis.

Peoples and mining enterprises.[47] Various dimensions of the relationship between Indigenous People and mining were also canvassed in three working papers produced for the MMSD project in the early 2000s.[48] The ICMM has weighed in on this topic extensively, commencing with a review of mining and Indigenous Peoples in 2004.[49] It subsequently produced a position statement on mining and Indigenous Peoples in 2008 (revised in 2013),[50] and an *Indigenous People and Mining Good Practice Guide* in 2011 (updated in 2015). The impact of extractive projects on Indigenous Peoples has also been a regular feature in reports submitted to the Permanent Forum on Indigenous Issues under the UN Economic and Social Council.[51]

Indigenous peoples' movements, environmental justice advocates, environmentalists and communities have worked within structures of counterglobalization driven by transnational action networks, the information revolution and globalized flows of funding and resources, even as emphasis is placed on grassroots and local impacts.[52] If the pro-mining discourses are global in their

---

[47] Brett Clark, 'The indigenous environmental movement in the United States: Transcending borders in struggles against mining, manufacturing and the capitalist state' (2002) 15(4) *Organization & Environment* 410; Saleem H Ali, *Mining, the Environment and Indigenous Development Conflicts* (University of Arizona Press 2003); Saleem H Ali and Andrew Singh Grewal, 'The ecology and economy of indigenous resistance: Divergent perspectives on mining in New Caledonia' (2006) 18(2) *The Contemporary Pacific* 361; Stuart Kirsch, 'Indigenous movements and the risks of counter-globalization: Tracking the campaign of Papua New Guinea's OK Tedi mine' (2007) 34(2) *American Ethnologist* 303; Anthony Bebbington *et al*, 'Mining and social movements: Struggles over livelihood and rural territorial development in the Andes' (2008) 36(12) *World Development* 2888; Roland G Simbulan, 'Indigenous communities' resistance to corporate mining in the Philippines' (2016) 28(1) *Peace Review* 29.

[48] Marcos A Orellana, 'Indigenous peoples, mining and international law' Report No. 2 commissioned by the MMSD project of IIED (January 2002); Theodore Downing *et al*, 'Indigenous Peoples and mining encounters: Strategies and tactics' Report No. 57 commissioned by the MMSD project of IIED (April 2002); Janeth Warden-Fernandez, 'Indigenous communities and mineral development' Report No. 59 commissioned by the MMSD project of the IIED (April 2001).

[49] Jo M Render, *Mining and Indigenous Peoples Issues Review* (ICMM 2004).

[50] ICMM, 'Indigenous peoples and mining position statement', www.icmm.com/en-gb/members/member-commitments/position-statements/indigenous-peoples-and-mining-position-statement, accessed 23 February 2019.

[51] See for example UN Permanent Forum on Indigenous Issues, 'Consolidated report on extractive industries and their impact on indigenous peoples' (20 February 2013), E/C. 19/2013/16 (henceforth PFIP Report on Extractive Industries); 'Study on the impact of the mining boom on indigenous communities in Australia' (5 March 2013), E/C. 19/2013/20 (henceforth PFIP Report on Australian Indigenous Communities).

[52] The nature and the political efficacy of counterglobalization have been described by authors such as Appadurai, Castells and Escobar. See Arjun Appadurai, 'Grassroots

reach, mining dissent has also become transnational and multiscalar in scope,[53] with claims enunciated by individuals, groups and smaller organizations in a local context articulating with the more systemic work undertaken by larger organizations working from a national or transnational perspective.[54] It is within this context that social movements have emerged. As Kirsch observes, 'social movements bridge the gap between the local and the global as international campaigns piggyback on specific struggles and local struggles hitchhike on global initiatives'.[55] Indigenous Peoples' movements and the emergence of the 'indigenous' as an object of international law are a 'prime example' of this process.[56]

While Indigenous Peoples' movements have enunciated counterglobalization claims that sit alongside environmentalists and environmental justice advocates, a deeper dive into the literature reveals the complexity of Indigenous Peoples' movements, debunking an essentialist alignment with antimining activism, or even environmentalism.

3.2 Scope and Meaning of 'Indigenous Peoples'

The claims in this section must be qualified by the scope and meaning of the term 'Indigenous Peoples'. The only definition of Indigenous Peoples that is legally binding on a somewhat small group of ratifying States is set forth in Article 1.1 of the Indigenous and Tribal Peoples' Convention (ILO Convention, No. 169),[57] which identifies Indigenous Peoples as (1) 'tribal peoples in independent countries whose social, cultural and economic conditions distinguish them from other sections of the national community,

globalization and the research imagination' (2000) 12(1) *Public Culture* 1; Manuel Castells, *The Information Age: Economy, Society & Culture, vol. 2, The Power of Identity* (Blackwell 1997); Arturo Escobar, 'Culture sits in places: Reflections on globalism and subaltern strategies of localization' (2001) 20 *Political Geography* 139.

53 Sara L Seck, 'Transnational corporations and extractive industries' in Shawkat Alam *et al* (eds) *International Environmental Law and the Global South* (Cambridge University Press 2015) 388–9.

54 See Leire Urkidi and Mariana Walter, 'Dimensions of environmental justice in anti-mining movements in Latin America' (2011) 46(2) *Geoforum* 683.

55 Kirsch (n 47) 303.

56 Ibid.

57 ILO Convention No. 169 entered into force on 5 September 1991 and has been ratified by 22 countries, largely in South America and the European Union. See International Labour Organization 'C-169 Indigenous and Tribal Peoples Convention, 1989 (No 169)', www.ilo.org/dyn/normlex/en/f?p=NORMLEXPUB:12100:0::NO::P12100_ILO_CODE:C169, accessed 23 February 2019. ILO Convention 169 replaced the formerly applicable Indigenous and Tribal Populations Convention and Recommendation No. 107 of 1957.

and whose status is regulated wholly or partially by their own customs and traditions' or (2) people in independent countries regarded as indigenous on account of their descent from populations that inhabited the country (or geographical region) at the time of conquest, colonization or establishment of present State boundaries, and who retain some or all of their social, economic, cultural and political institutions. The 'fundamental criterion' for determining such groups is self-identification.[58] The more recent, and nonbinding, United Nations Declaration on the Rights of Indigenous Peoples (UNDRIP)[59] does not provide a definition of Indigenous Peoples or individuals.

Rodríguez-Piñero writes that indigenous rights discourse is a recent construct in modern international law.[60] Over the course of the twentieth century, the understanding of 'Indigenous People' underwent distinct shifts, linked to the formal dismantling of colonialism and the establishment of independent States.[61] Fuelled by Eurocentric assumptions and doctrines of social evolution, colonial understandings of indigeneity positioned such peoples on the lowest rung of the civilized order, allowing the colonizers 'to bridge the moral gap existing between the idealistic principles of "civilization" and the brutish practice of colonial conquest'.[62] This understanding was still present in ILO Convention No. 107 (1957), the predecessor to ILO Convention 169. The former Convention articulated assimilationist goals and characterized Indigenous Peoples as less advanced than their colonial counterparts.[63] By the turn of the twentieth century, however, and following extensive transnational organizing, coalition building and social struggle,[64] Indigenous People had come to be recognized, and even celebrated, as culturally distinct groups, with aspirations of sovereignty *within* the framework of nation States in which they were resident. As nondominant groups, with claims of historical continuity to preinvasion and precolonial societies that developed on their territories, Indigenous Peoples sought rights 'to preserve, develop and transmit to future

---

[58] ILO Convention 169, Article 1.2.

[59] United Nations General Assembly A/61/53 (2007).

[60] Luis Rodríguez-Piñero, *Indigenous Peoples, Postcolonialism and International Law: The ILO Regime* (Oxford University Press 2005) 5.

[61] Ibid 4–8.

[62] Ibid 5.

[63] First Nations and Indigenous Studies, University of British Columbia, 'ILO Convention 107', http://indigenousfoundations.arts.ubc.ca/ilo_convention_107/, accessed 23 February 2019.

[64] Jean E Jackson and Kay B Warren, 'Indigenous movements in Latin America, 1992–2004: Controversies, ironies, new directions' (2005) 34 *Annual Review of Anthropology* 549, 551.

generations their ancestral territories, and their ethnic identity, as the basis of their continued existence as peoples'.[65]

Igoe points out that the 'global Indigenous Peoples' movement' emerged primarily in contexts where such peoples were nondominant, that is, residing in independent countries dominated by settler populations of European descent.[66] In Africa and Asia, where the concept only gained traction in the early 1990s, it did not represent 'miraculously preserved pre-colonial conditions', but rather reflected a convergence of existing identity categories with those emerging from global structures of governance for purposes of social and political mobilization.[67] While Indigenous Peoples' movements in different regions are characterized by different histories, dynamics and agendas, the counterglobalization narrative of indigeneity nevertheless draws upon similar narratives of conquest, assimilation and existential threat.

3.3 Indigenous Peoples, Land and the Complicit State

The theme of land, with its inherent associations to minerals *and* environment, looms large in relation to claims of existential threat and the desire for indigenous sovereignty. Indigenous Peoples' special relationship to land, extending to both cultural and spiritual values, is an entrenched motif in the indigenous rights discourse. For example, ILO Convention 169 devotes an entire chapter to rights and obligations associated with land,[68] with Article 13 insisting that governments respect 'the special importance for the cultures and spiritual values of the peoples concerned of their relationship with the lands or territories' and, in particular, the 'collective aspects' of this relationship. The concept of lands extends to the 'total environment' of areas that Indigenous Peoples occupy or otherwise use.[69] Article 25 of the UNDRIP recognizes the right of Indigenous Peoples to maintain and strengthen their 'distinctive spiritual relationship with traditionally owned or otherwise occupied land, territories, waters and coastal seas'. This right is coupled with responsibilities to uphold this spiritual relationship for future generations.

Indigenous Peoples' relationship to land is tightly bound up with their claims to sovereignty, identity and survival. The right to free determination is of paramount importance to Indigenous Peoples. But in order to freely determine their political status and pursue their self-directed economic, social and

---

65 José Martinez Cobo, 'The Study of the Problem of Discrimination against Indigenous Populations', United Nations E/CN.4/Sub.2/1986/7, para. 5.

66 James Igoe, 'Becoming indigenous peoples' (2006) *African Affairs* 399, 402.

67 Ibid.

68 ILO Convention 169, Part II.

69 ILO Convention 169, Article 13.2.

cultural development, it is regarded as critical for Indigenous Peoples to own, use, develop and control their lands, territories and resources.[70]

The increasing expansion of the extractive industries into the territories of Indigenous Peoples has been associated with dispossession, expulsion and displacement.[71] The 'extractive industries' are posited as a wide church of industrial activity, inclusive of mining, hydrocarbon extraction, dam construction and large infrastructure projects, the tourist industry and so on.[72] Mining and hydrocarbon extraction nevertheless tend to be singled out as particularly problematic.[73] In addition to displacement of Indigenous Peoples, examples highlight the degradation of indigenous lands through depletion of groundwater resources, air pollution, deposition of mining waste and the depredation of cultural sites.[74]

The complicit State emerges from these accounts. Fuelled by a 'disparaging and discriminatory attitude' towards indigenous lifestyles, and protected by an 'invisible veil of complicity' – 'development' and its associated objectives of job creation, poverty reduction and (at times) conservation – States allegedly continually violate the human rights of Indigenous Peoples.[75] The most recent reports to the Permanent Forum on Indigenous Peoples highlight this trend in the context of 'undeveloped areas'.[76]

Considering the more developed jurisdictions of the United States and Canada, Ali opts for a more balanced tone, pointing to the abiding tension in the government's role 'as a trustee for Indians and the land in general on the one hand and as an agent of economic development and prosperity on the other'.[77] In the 'daunting task' of balancing economic issues, environmental concerns and native interests, States may aspire to be 'neutral overarching authorities', he remarks, but they are inevitably stakeholders in conflict ridden mineral development.[78] Important to underscore, however, is that the State remains an 'embedded stakeholder'[79] with integral responsibilities to work through social conflict in the public interest, at least in States where democracy prevails.

---

70 PFIP Report on Extractive Industries (n 51), paras 19–21.

71 Ibid para. 8.

72 Ibid para. 6.

73 Ibid, see the examples cited in paras 10, 12–13.

74 Ibid.

75 Ibid paras 5–6; Permanent Forum on Indigenous Issues: Secretariat 'Indigenous peoples' collective rights to lands, territories and resources' (8 February 2018), E/C. 19/2018/5, para. 4.

76 Ibid para. 5.

77 Ali (n 47) 72.

78 Ibid.

79 Ibid.

3.4 The State's Role to Protect the Relationship Between Indigenous People and Their Lands and the Principle of Free, Prior and Informed Consent

In response to the conflict among Indigenous Peoples, land and pressures for 'development', international law emphasizes the State's duty to protect Indigenous Peoples' relationship to their lands, and extractive companies' duty to respect indigenous rights. This paradigm emerges clearly from the ICMM's most recent position statement on Indigenous Peoples, which reads: 'Indigenous peoples have individual and collective rights and interests and it is internationally recognized that their rights should be protected by governments and respected by companies.'[80]

The State's duty to protect the lands of Indigenous Peoples has been concentrated in debates on the recognition of indigenous title to land, on the one hand, and in the protracted discussions on the principle of free, prior and informed consent, on the other.

3.4.1 State protection of indigenous land title

The international legal framework for Indigenous Peoples' rights recognizes their rights to lands, territories and resources that they have either traditionally owned and occupied, or otherwise used and acquired.[81] Indigenous Peoples' land rights thus extend over both territories of occupation and territories of use, both of which may be affected by extractive operations. Under ILO Convention 169, States are duty bound to identify the lands which Indigenous Peoples traditionally occupy, and guarantee effective protection of their rights of ownership and possession.[82] The UNDRIP requires States to give 'legal recognition and protection' to the lands, territories and resources of Indigenous Peoples, having due regard to the 'customs, traditions and land tenure systems of the indigenous peoples concerned'.[83]

In developed mineral-rich jurisdictions, national case law recognizing indigenous title has been laid down since the early 1900s,[84] while in Latin

---

[80] ICMM (n 50).

[81] ILO Convention 169, Article 26.1; UNDRIP, Article 14.1.

[82] ILO Convention 169, Article 14.2.

[83] UNDRIP, Article 26.3.

[84] In the United States see the 1905 Supreme Court decision in *United States v. Winans* (198 Sup. Ct. 662) (recognition of the concept of 'reserved sovereignty'); in Canada, in the Supreme Court rulings in *Calder v. Attorney-General of British Columbia* [1973] SCR 313 (recognition that indigenous title had existed at the time of the Royal Proclamation 1973) and in *Delgamuukw v. British Columbia* [1997] 3 SCR 1010 (dealing with the content and extent of Aboriginal title, extinguishment of

America recognition has largely proceeded through high level commitments such as ratification of ILO Convention 169, constitutional commitments and the development of detailed regulatory frameworks.[85] In Africa, the recognition of customary land rights has also proceeded by way of constitutional or statutory recognition.[86] Landmark decisions in the Inter-American Court on Human Rights,[87] as well as in the African Commission on Human and Peoples' Rights,[88] have elaborated on the State's role to protect indigenous property rights, frequently in the context of protecting indigenous lands from extractive concessions.

The international normative framework for indigenous rights also requires States to resolve land claims,[89] impose penalties for intrusion upon indigenous lands,[90] and afford Indigenous Peoples a right of redress where their lands, territories or resources have been confiscated, taken, occupied, used or damaged without their free, prior and informed consent.[91] In cooperation with the peoples concerned, governments must protect and preserve the environment of territories they inhabit,[92] and establish nondiscriminatory conservation and environmental assistance programmes for Indigenous Peoples.[93] Finally, States should institute 'effective measures' to ensure that no storage or disposal

---

Aboriginal title and the use of oral history in testimony); and in Australia, in the High Court case of *Mabo v. Queensland (No 2)* [1992] HCA 23.

85 Roque Roldán Ortega, *Models for Recognizing Indigenous Land Rights in Latin America* (World Bank 2004).

86 RS Knight, 'Statutory recognition of customary land rights in Africa: An investigation into best practices for law-making and implementation' (2010) FAO Legislative Study No. 105.

87 *Mayagna (Sumo) Awas Tingni Community v. Nicaragua* IACtHR, Judgment of 31 August 2001 (Merits, reparations and costs); *Yakye Axa Indigenous Community v. Paraguay* IACtHR, Judgment of 17 June 2005 (Merits, reparations and costs) (highlighting importance of land to indigenous communities, and identifying the four cumulative conditions that must be met by the State when placing restrictions on indigenous land rights); and *Case of the Saramaka People v. Suriname* IACtHR, Judgment of 28 November 2007 (Merits, reparations and costs) (establishing as an additional condition that the restriction on indigenous land rights should not amount to the denial of the traditions and customs of the group in a manner that endangers the very survival of the group and its members).

88 *Centre for Minority Rights Development (Kenya) and Minority Rights Group International obo Enderois Welfare Council v. Kenyan Africa Commission on Human Rights* 276/03.

89 ILO Convention 169, Article 14.3; UNDRIP, Article 27.

90 UNDRIP, Article 8.2(b).

91 UNDRIP, Article 28.1.

92 ILO Convention 169, Article 7.4.

93 UNDRIP, Article 29.1.

of hazardous materials takes place on the lands or territories of Indigenous Peoples without their free, prior and informed consent.[94]

Notwithstanding the recognition of these State duties, substantive protection of indigenous property rights tends to be the exception rather than the rule, especially in the face of valuable extractive projects. The Permanent Forum on Indigenous Issues, for example, has recently underlined the 'innumerable examples' of State action denying Indigenous Peoples' rights to their lands, territories and resources, relegating them to 'squatters on their own lands'.[95]

Even where Indigenous Peoples are recognized and their rights to land legally protected, Indigenous People face political, legal and administrative challenges around the substantive enjoyment of such rights. States frequently have a greater power to extinguish Aboriginal title in comparison to the legal protection afforded nonindigenous rights;[96] State allotment of land rights to individuals and groups, rather than to the collective, undermines the character of indigenous rights in some instances;[97] States frequently fail to demarcate indigenous lands;[98] and legal consequences for the infringement of indigenous land rights are inadequately enforced.[99] The Secretariat of the Permanent Forum expressly noted that Indigenous Peoples have been, and continue to be, removed from their territories when valuable resources are discovered on or beneath such lands, and/or when exploitation of the land is associated with national development priorities or interests. Natural resource extraction projects inclusive of mining constitute typical examples of this phenomenon.[100] That such activities are frequently public–private partnerships impairs the State's capacity to protect indigenous land rights and feeds the perception of State complicity.[101]

3.4.2 States and the principle of free, prior and informed consent

In two recent decisions, South African courts have afforded communities a right to consent to mining projects on their lands. In the *Maledu* case, the Constitutional Court overturned a High Court order evicting members of a community from their land to make way for a mining project. The court

---

94 UNDRIP, Article 29.2.

95 UN Permanent Forum on Indigenous Issues 'Indigenous peoples' collective rights to lands, territories and resources: Note by the Secretariat' (8 February 2018), E/C. 19/2018/5 (henceforth 2018 Secretariat Note) para. 18.

96 Ibid para. 21.

97 Ibid para. 20.

98 Ibid para. 22.

99 Ibid para. 23.

100 Ibid paras 25, 35.

101 Ibid para. 36.

found that mining would result in a deprivation of their statutorily protected informal rights, and that the necessary consent had not been obtained.[102] A month later, a High Court confirmed that consent was also required in the longstanding dispute over the right to exploit mineral sands on South Africa's so-called Wild Coast – a project that impacted the Amapondo people.[103]

These cases bring the second aspect of the State duty to protect Indigenous Peoples into focus – upholding the principle of principle of free, prior and informed consent (FPIC). As the ensuing discussion shows, FPIC sits uncomfortably beside the indigenous right to self-determination – specifically when mining projects do not align with Indigenous Peoples' developmental vision and the 'right to veto' is raised.

On the face of it, the FPIC principle includes the right of veto. Rumler, for instance, defines FPIC as '[t]he right to consent or withhold consent to development which is realized through processes consistent with consultation and participation'.[104] The rationale for FPIC stretches back in time to the International Covenant on Civil and Political Rights (ICCPR),[105] which affirmed that all peoples have the right to self-determination and to the free pursuit of their economic, social and cultural development.[106] Any mining-affected community could potentially assert the right to FPIC, but the principle is 'most apparent' in the case of Indigenous Peoples, arising from the affirmation of FPIC under ILO Convention 169 and the UNDRIP.[107]

The international legal framework for Indigenous Peoples rights stops short of affirming the sovereignty of Indigenous Peoples independent from the States in which they reside.[108] Nevertheless, there is support for an indigenous right to self-determination. Article 7.1 of ILO Convention 169, for instance, states that Indigenous Peoples have 'the right to decide their own priorities for the process of development as it affects their lives, beliefs, institutions and spiritual well-being and the lands they occupy or otherwise use'. Indigenous Peoples have rights 'to the extent possible' over their own economic, social

---

[102] *Maledu v. Itereleng Bakgatla Mineral Resources (Pty) Ltd* [2018] ZACC 41, 2019 (1) BCLR 53 (CC). The Constitutional Court is the highest court in South Africa.

[103] *Baleni v. Minister of Mineral Resources* [2018] ZAGPPHC 829, [2019] 1 All SA 358 (GP).

[104] Mark Rumler, *Free, Prior and Informed Consent: A Review of Free, Prior and Informed Consent in Australia* (Oxfam 2011) 5.

[105] UN Doc. A/6316 (1966); 993 UNTS 3; ILM 368 (1967).

[106] ICCPR, Article 1.

[107] Rumler (n 104) 5.

[108] See Article 46 of the UNDRIP, for example, which states that nothing in the Declaration should be construed 'as authorizing or encouraging any action which would dismember or impair, totally or in part, the territorial integrity or political unity of sovereign and independent States'.

and cultural development.[109] They must also participate in the formulation, implementation and evaluation of plans and programmes for national and regional development that may affect them directly.[110]

But this right to self-determination is not absolute. ILO Convention 169 states that for 'planned development activities' (ambiguous whether initiated by Indigenous Peoples themselves, State organs or third parties), the duty of governments is one of assessment only: 'Whenever appropriate', governments must ensure that studies are carried out to assess the social, spiritual, cultural and environmental impact of planned development activities on Indigenous Peoples.[111] The UNDRIP is less ambiguous, clearly stating that '[i]ndigenous peoples have the right to self-determination' by virtue of which they may 'freely pursue their economic, social and cultural development'.[112] Article 10 of the UNDRIP, however, goes on to state that Indigenous People may not be forcibly removed from their lands and territories, which suggests that the right to self-determination coexists with other development priorities that may cause Indigenous Peoples to have to abandon their lands or territories. In circumstances where this must occur, '[n]o relocation shall take place without the free, prior and informed consent of the indigenous people concerned and after agreement on just and fair compensation'.[113]

Mineral exploration and exploitation is the context most likely to trigger the sacrifice of an indigenous right to self-determination. In this vein, Article 15.2 of ILO Convention 169 provides:

> In cases in which the State retains the ownership of mineral or sub-surface resources or rights to other resources pertaining to lands, governments shall establish or maintain procedures through which they shall consult these peoples, with a view to ascertaining whether and to what degree their interests would be prejudiced, before undertaking or permitting any programmes for the exploration or exploitation of such resources pertaining to their lands. The peoples concerned shall wherever possible participate in the benefits of such activities, and shall receive fair compensation for any damages which they may sustain as a result of such activities.

Willingness to support the protection of indigenous title does not, therefore, extend to land containing minerals or subsurface resources. As discussed in Chapter 4, centralized State ownership of minerals and subsurface resources is the rule in mineral-rich jurisdictions.[114] In situations where indigenous

---

[109] ILO Convention 169, Article 7.1.
[110] Ibid.
[111] ILO Convention 169, Article 7.3.
[112] UNDRIP, Article 3.
[113] UNDRIP, Article 10.
[114] See the discussion in section 2.1 of Chapter 4.

self-determination conflicts with the development of mineral lands the State is therefore positioned as ultimate decisionmaker. Under the ILO Convention, the State's role towards Indigenous Peoples in these circumstances is simply to accommodate and facilitate, ensuring consultation prior to permitting mineral development, and encouraging participation and the payment of fair compensation.

The UNDRIP's scope of protection is similar, albeit with more express emphasis on the need for Indigenous Peoples to consent to extractive projects on their lands. The indigenous right of self-determination over the development and use of their lands, territories and other resources extends only to the right 'to determine and develop priorities and strategies'.[115] In this regard, Article 32.2 states:

> States shall consult and cooperate in good faith with the indigenous peoples concerned through their own representative institutions in order to obtain their free and informed consent prior to the approval of any project affecting their lands or territories and other resources, particularly in connection with the development, utilization or exploitation of mineral, water or other resources.

This provision does not clearly include a right of veto. It focuses on the State's duty to consult and cooperate, rather than the substantive outcome of these processes. There is no guidance on the State's duties when Indigenous People say 'no' to projects affecting their lands, territories and resources. The sovereign State is still positioned as ultimate decisionmaker, legally capacitated to proceed in the face of resistance.

The ICMM's position is that FPIC does not support the right of veto. The ICMM position statement presents FPIC as a vehicle for procuring support to allow a project to proceed: 'Consent processes should focus on reaching agreement on the basis for which a project (or changes to existing projects) should proceed. These processes should neither confer veto rights to individuals or sub-groups nor require unanimous support from potentially impacted indigenous peoples (unless legally mandated).'[116]

Some actors in the sustainable mineral development consensus have resisted FPIC altogether. For example, in its Extractive Industries Review conducted in 2000 (and on other occasions), World Bank Group management opposed FPIC.[117] The World Bank Group finally admitted FPIC as an environmental

---

115 UNDRIP, Article 32.1.

116 ICMM (n 50).

117 Fergus MacKay, 'Indigenous peoples' right to free, prior and informed consent and the World Bank's Extractive Industries Review' (2004) 4 *Sustainable Development Law and Policy* 43.

and social standard for investment project financing in the third revision of its Environmental and Social Framework, finalized in August 2016.[118] Even then, its application is limited to three circumstances: where the project (1) adversely impacts on land and natural resources subject to traditional ownership or under customary use or occupation; (2) would cause relocation of affected peoples or communities from such land; and (3) has significant impacts on peoples' or communities' cultural heritage that is material to the identity and/or cultural, ceremonial or spiritual aspects of their lives.[119]

As a vehicle through which mining dissent can be expressed, FPIC is therefore precarious, vested with uncertain outcomes and the possibility of wasted effort on the part of dissenters. There is ample research on FPIC showing that the implementation of the right is difficult in resource extraction contexts,[120] even as some jurisdictions are now boldly upholding a right to consent as the South African examples above demonstrate.

In a compelling article, Rodríguez-Garavito argues that legal disputes over FPIC are part of a broader juridification of ethnic claims, which he calls ethnicity.gov.[121] He presents ethnicity.gov as a sociolegal process reproduced through the overlapping claims and actions of seemingly diametrically opposed actors – from the World Bank Group and the ICMM, to State entities, companies, communities, NGOs and civil society organizations. It is a 'third way' of regulation that is neither top down State regulation, nor market regulation.[122] The divergence of claims made by a diverse set of actors for 'participation', 'empowerment', 'consultation' enforce the broader hegemony of the neoliberal 'governance' paradigm,[123] and the procedural logic of

---

[118] See World Bank, Environmental and Social Framework: Setting Environmental and Social Standards for Investment Project Financing (4 August 2016). ESS7 of the new Environmental and Social Framework deals with Indigenous Peoples as well as 'Sub-Saharan African underserved traditional local communities'. Inclusion of the latter was novel and in opposition to many African governments' resistance to the inclusion of the FPIC principle on the basis that the concept of Indigenous Peoples did not find application on the African continent. The Standard includes criteria for the identification of such underserved traditional local communities.

[119] Ibid para. 24.

[120] See César Rodríguez-Garavito, 'Ethnicity.gov: Global governance, indigenous peoples, and the right to prior consultation in social minefields' (2011) 18(1) *Indiana Journal of Global Legal Studies* 1; Sango Mahanty and Constance L McDermott, 'How does "Free, Prior and Informed Consent" impact social equity? Lessons from mining and forestry and their implications for REDD+' (2013) 35 *Land Use Policy* 406.

[121] Rodríguez-Garavito (n 120) 1.

[122] Ibid 15.

[123] Ibid 10.

FPIC undermines the substantive legality that could derive from the right to self-determination.[124]

This proceduralization produces a variety of effects that facilitate extractivism and neoextractivism: displacement, miscommunication, and domination. Displacement effects occur whenever the substantive conflict over the actual resource use is displaced, replaced or postponed.[125] For example, Rodríguez-Garavito points out that a large part of consultation projects in Latin America consist in calculating the economic and social harm associated with the project and the manner in which such harms can be ameliorated through compensation payouts, rather than whether the project should proceed at all.[126] The FPIC paradigm also contributes to a miscommunication effect, that is, the tendency for consultation processes to take on a nonlinear character where delays, repetition and misunderstanding appear to be endemic.[127] Excluding consultation processes that are imposed by deception or coercion, Rodríguez-Garavito attributes this to the radically different ontological and epistemological positions held by the different groups engaging in consultation processes.[128] The procedural logic of FPIC also fails to capture what is really at stake – life itself: 'The life of the people involved; the physical survival of its members; the extractive companies' survival in the market; the biodiversity at stake; the plans for life and death executed by the illegal, armed groups that swarm the minefields.'[129]

The effect that most clearly implicates the role of the State, however, is the domination effect. The process of FPIC, Rodríguez-Garavito claims, reinforces the dominant relations between companies, the State and Indigenous Peoples.[130] Debunking the neoliberal myth of equality among interlocutors, the greatest power imbalance is between companies and Indigenous Peoples at the coalface of mining developments.[131] But the State also stands in a subservient position to companies, detached and disempowered from taking action in the face of the demands to institute a fair playing field. Consultation processes tend to be privatized operations. As Rodríguez-Garavito notes:

> Within the enclave economies where many consultations occur, the company, for practical purposes, *is* the state: access to the locale depends on the company, local authorities coordinate and interact with the company, and a large sector of the

---

124 Ibid 18.
125 Ibid 30.
126 Ibid 31.
127 Ibid 33.
128 Ibid 34.
129 Ibid 35.
130 Ibid 36.
131 Ibid.

> population is subordinated to it, either through labor relations or indirect economic dependence.[132]

Rather than serving as the guarantor or regulator of consultation processes, the State tends to function as an 'official witness', as Rodríguez-Garavito concludes: '[T]he state apparatus rarely mitigates, or even mediates, the company's dominance over the community.'[133] In light of the protections that the State should afford the land and environment of Indigenous Peoples as set out in ILO Convention 169 and the UNDRIP, one may thus add to this observation the figure of the 'abdicating State'.

3.5 Indigenous Peoples, Mining–Environment Conflicts and the Abdicating State

The international normative framework for Indigenous Peoples' rights affirms their special spiritual and cultural attachments to land. It would be wrong-headed, however to assume that attachment to land translates into an irrevocable attachment to environmentalism.[134] Ali highlights that mineral development can be the locus of 'immense environmental dissent within communities'.[135] As the following account shows, indigenous, tribal, traditional and rural communities also support mining on their lands. Institutions have developed to accommodate collaboration between such communities and mining companies in a manner that some claim increasingly bypasses the State and its fiduciary responsibilities, inclusive of responsibilities towards the environment.

The assumption of congruence between the interests of Indigenous Peoples and environmentalists is fuelled by a stereotyped understanding of indigenous environmentalism as a form of ecological nobility.[136] In a narrative that goes back to at least the late 1970s, environmentalists have looked to Indigenous People for inspiration, invoking native traditions and philosophies to articulate their ideas of an ecologically ideal society.[137] This view has been deconstructed by academics,[138] and disputed by Indigenous Peoples themselves. As the Cherokee writer and scholar Jace Weaver has stated: 'Indians have been stere-

---

[132] Ibid.

[133] Ibid 38.

[134] Ali (n 47) 32.

[135] Ibid xix.

[136] See Kent Redford, 'The Ecologically Noble Savage' (1991) 15 *Cultural Survival Quarterly* 46.

[137] Paul Nadasdy, 'Transcending the debate over the Ecologically Noble Indian: Indigenous Peoples and Environmentalism' (2005) 52(2) *Ethnohistory* 291.

[138] Shepard Krech (ed.), *The Ecological Indian: Myth and History* (W.W. Norton 1999).

otyped far too long by the environmental movement as those with the mystical, ancient wisdom that alone can save the planet. Rather we presented and represented the honest and extremely difficult struggles of indigenous peoples to meet ecological challenges confronting them.'[139] Nadasdy goes a step further. Arguing on the basis of his study of the Kluane, a Yukon First Nation People, he argues that the debate over the ecological nobility of Indigenous Peoples is spurious, as it is irremediably tainted by Euro-American cultural assumptions of indigenousness *and* environmentalism.[140]

The relationship between Indigenous People and environmentalists is therefore ambivalent. According to Ali, there have been moments of confluence and congruence between the indigenous rights and environmental movements, but there have also been many points of disagreement, and 'alliances that form are often opportunistic and may even be mutually destructive'.[141] In his groundbreaking study on the causes of environmental resistance in indigenous communities in the developed world, Ali found that a sense of sovereignty was the key factor driving cooperation with environmentalists. Environmental conservation would only be preferred if it is more likely than the development of a mine to advance indigenous self-determination.[142]

A variety of institutions exist throughout the world to procure the involvement and cooperation of Indigenous Peoples in mining ventures. The best known of these are arguably Impact Benefit Agreements (IBAs)[143] in Canada, and agreement-making between mining companies and indigenous communities in Australia under the Aboriginal Land Rights (Northern Territory) Act, 1976; the Native Title Act, 1993; Queensland's Mineral Resources Act 1989; and Australian corporate social responsibility initiatives.[144] O'Faircheallaigh holds that based on the Canadian and Australian experiences, 'community

---

[139] Jace Weaver (ed.), *Defending Mother Earth: Native Perspectives on Environmental Justice* (Orbis 1996), xvi.

[140] Nadasdy (n 137) 321.

[141] Ali (n 47) xxi; Saleem H Ali, 'Green alliances: Anti-mining activism and indigenous communities in the New World' (1999) 15(3) *Cultural Survival Quarterly*.

[142] Ali (n 47) 161.

[143] There is an extensive literature on IBAs and whether they provide substantive benefits to indigenous communities. See, for example, Ken J Caine and Naomi Krogman, 'Powerful or just plain power-full? A power analysis of impact and benefit agreements in Canada's North' (2010) 23(1) *Organization and Environment* 76; Sandra Gogal, Richard Riegert and Joann Jamieson, 'Aboriginal impact and benefit agreements: Practical considerations' (2005–2006) 43 *Alberta Law Review* 129.

[144] Ciaran O'Faircheallaigh, 'Negotiating cultural heritage? Aboriginal-mining company agreements in Australia' (2008) 39(1) *Development and Change* 25; Ciaran O' Faircheallaigh, 'Aboriginal-mining company contractual agreements in Australia and Canada: Implications for political autonomy and community development' (2010) 30(1–2) *Canadian Journal of Development Studies* 69.

development agreements' are becoming more common in virtually all parts of the world.[145]

Apart from contractual agreements such as IBAs and community development agreements, other mechanisms for involving Indigenous People in mining include preferential treatment in licensing applications. South Africa offers an example here in the form of a preferential prospecting or mining right for communities who own or have won a land claim to their traditional lands.[146] South Africa also requires mining rights holders to compile Social and Labour Plans as a mechanism for socioeconomic transformation in mining and labour-sending areas.[147] Other forms of institutional support for Indigenous People in mining include the programmes of the Bureau of Indian Affairs for mineral assessments on tribal land in the United States of America,[148] and more traditional avenues for participation, such as indigenous and tribal communities taking equity in mining ventures.[149]

Agreement-making between indigenous communities and mining companies, as modelled on the Canadian and Australian experiences, can carve out a role for Indigenous Peoples in environmental management on their lands and ancestral territories.[150] Hitch *et al*, for example, point out that IBAs generally provide opportunities for indigenous communities to benefit from mineral resource development, at the same time as allowing them to participate in management, monitoring and mitigation of social, cultural and environmental impacts.[151] At the same time, such agreements give rise to concerns around a disappearing or absent State, as matters formerly within the State's purview

---

[145] Ciaran O'Faircheallaigh, 'Community development agreements in the mining industry: An emerging global phenomenon' (2013) 44(2) *Community Development* 222.

[146] Mineral and Petroleum Resources Development Act, 2002 (South Africa) s 104.

[147] Centre for Applied Legal Studies, *The Social and Labour Plan Series – Phase 1: System Design Trends Analysis Report* (CALS 2016).

[148] Ali (n 47) xx.

[149] For a case study of this avenue for participation see the discussion of the Bafokeng, the so-called richest tribe in Africa, in A Manson and B Mbenga, '"The richest tribe in Africa": Platinum mining and the Bafokeng in South Africa's North-West Province, 1965–1999' (2003) 21(1) *Journal of Southern African Studies* 25.

[150] Ciaran O'Faircheallaigh, 'Indigenous participation in environmental management of mining projects: The role of negotiated agreements' (2005) 14(5) *Environmental Politics*, 629, 634.

[151] Michael Hitch *et al*, 'Emergence of differential social license: A case of impact and benefit agreements in Nunavut, Canada' in ZX Li *et al*, *Proceedings of the 8th International Conference on Sustainable Development in the Minerals Industry* (SDIMI 2017) 242.

are superseded by the terms of a bilateral, contractual arrangement concluded between mining companies and Indigenous Peoples directly.[152]

The perception of an abdicating, disappearing or absent State emerges from a number of problematic features of IBAs and Aboriginal land agreements. Such agreements frequently require corporations to comply with environmental legislation, including environmental assessment (EA) regulations,[153] but may also require corporations to go above and beyond the letter of the law. In jurisdictions where EA laws are weak, IBAs may be a First Nation's only hope to ensure that environmental impacts of a project are minimized.[154] More rarely, agreements may entrench consultation mechanisms, or provide for indigenous participation in, or even joint decisionmaking on certain environmental matters.[155] This may lead to overlapping objectives, blurred boundaries and conflicts with EA processes.[156]

However, very little is in fact known about the environmental provisions of indigenous agreements, due to controversial confidentiality clauses bolstered by the protections of contract law – a situation States, as the guardians of the bastions of private law, are seemingly unwilling or powerless to change.[157] Lack of transparency, in turn, fuels scepticism relating to the equitable distribution of risks and benefits in mining-affected indigenous communities, especially affecting women.[158]

3.6 Conclusion

As a discourse of mining dissent, Indigenous Peoples' rights are therefore complex and multidimensional. 'Indigenous Peoples' are the object of protection, but this concept is a social construct that has had different meanings in different times and regions. States are required to protect Indigenous Peoples' special relationship to their lands and territories. This encompasses duties to identify, recognize and enforce their rights, and to uphold FPIC when extractive projects are mooted. The practical outworking of these roles, however, falls far from the ideal. Some argue that FPIC proceduralizes substantive claims, leading to displacement, miscommunication and domination effects.

---

[152] Courtney Fidler and Michael Hitch, 'Impact and benefit agreements: A contentious issue for environmental and aboriginal justice' (2007) 35(2) *Environments* 49.
[153] Ibid 61; O'Faircheallaigh (n 150) 637.
[154] Fidler and Hitch (n 152) 63.
[155] O'Faircheallaigh (n 150) 637.
[156] Fidler and Hitch (n 152) 49.
[157] Ibid; O'Faircheallaigh (n 150) 631.
[158] Fidler and Hitch (n 152) 63.

The Indigenous Peoples' rights movement has enabled self-identified Indigenous Peoples to call attention to how mining projects have dispossessed, expelled and displaced them. In these accounts the State emerges as complicit with 'development agents' in depriving Indigenous Peoples of the right to access, use and enjoy their lands. This is not a benign or facile complicity but one that concerns the question of life itself. However, indigenous groups' support for mining projects debunks the notion that Indigenous Peoples inevitably support environmentalism. The emergence of a range of institutional measures to capture agreements between mining companies and indigenous groups is in turn fuelling perceptions of the abdicating, disappearing or absent State.

4. ENVIRONMENTAL JUSTICE

Environmental justice is a popular framing for discourses of mining dissent, and overlaps with the discourse of Indigenous Peoples' rights.[159] Tribal groups, for example, participated in the First National People of Color Leadership Summit in 1991, and supported the landmark Principles of Environmental Justice endorsed there.[160] Indigenous groups the world over have used the concept of environmental justice to capture the pluralistic sense of justice underlying their claims for sovereignty and self-determination. Environmental justice is nevertheless a discourse with a distinctive history, developmental path and sphere of application, which extends beyond Indigenous Peoples and defines an additional set of State roles. Discursive sources for environmental justice include the aforementioned Principles of Environmental Justice,[161] as well as the London Declaration, the founding document of a network of indigenous and solidarity organizations representing mining-affected individuals and communities.[162]

---

[159] See the case studies reported on the EJOLT network (Environmental Justice Organizations, Liabilities and Trade), available at http://www.ejolt.org/, accessed 23 February 2019.

[160] David Schlosburg and David Carruthers, 'Indigenous struggles, environmental justice, and community capabilities' (2010) 10(4) *Global Environmental Politics* 12. The United States Environmental Protection Agency has a Policy on Environmental Justice for working with Federally Recognized Tribes and Indigenous Peoples (July 2014). See also Laura Westra, *Environmental Justice and the Rights of Indigenous Peoples: International and Domestic Legal Perspectives* (Earthscan 2012).

[161] People of Color Environmental Leadership Summit, Principles of Environmental Justice (1991), www.ejnet.org/ej/principles.html, accessed 23 February 2019 (henceforth 'Principles of Environmental Justice'.

[162] Mines and Communities 'London Declaration' (October 2008), www.minesandcommunities.org/article.php?a=9315, accessed 23 February 2019.

'Environmental justice means many things to many people', but in 2000 Kuehn outlined a fourfold typology to capture the essence and breadth of environmental justice concerns experienced at local, national and international levels.[163] This typology, comprising distributive justice, procedural justice, corrective justice and social justice, was intended to identify the common causes of, and solutions to, environmental injustice.[164] Kuehn's framework was developed to respond to the evolution of the environmental justice movement in the United States of America. As late as 2008, Sze and London observed that as a social movement and scholarly field, environmental justice had only recently been expanded to other national contexts.[165] And while the conceptual transfer of environmental justice beyond the initial sites of grassroots activism has been rapid, in some cases this has occurred within political and economic elites and has not necessarily been strongly articulated with forms of civil society resistance to environmental injustices,[166] notwithstanding recognition of the 'environmentalism of the poor'.[167] The environmental justice typology must accordingly be read with this caveat in mind.

Kuehn's typology also sanitizes the emancipatory tone of the first expressions of environmental justice, and its associations with colonialism and oppression. The Preamble to the Principles of Environmental Justice, for instance, calls for people of colour to begin to build a national and international movement of people of colour to ensure environmental justice and to promote economic alternatives that would contribute to environmentally safe livelihoods. Such economic alternatives would also secure the political, economic and cultural liberation denied for more than 500 years through colonization and oppression, resulting in the poisoning of lands and the genocide of peoples.[168]

4.1 Distributive Justice

Distributive justice highlights the fairness of distributed outcomes amongst members of society, that is, the extent to which members of different economic, racial, gender and other social groupings are exposed to environmental

---

[163] Robert R Kuehn, 'A taxonomy of environmental justice' (2000) 30 *Environmental Law Reporter* 10681.

[164] Ibid.

[165] J Sze and JK London, 'Environmental Justice at the Crossroads' (2008) 2(4) *Sociology Compass* 1331, 1334.

[166] G Walker and H Bulkeley, 'Geographies of environmental justice' (2006) 37 *Geoforum* 655.

[167] Rob Nixon, *Slow Violence and the Environmentalism of the Poor* (Harvard University Press 2013).

[168] Principles of Environmental Justice (n 161) Preamble.

risks, for example, air pollution from a mining operation or the siting of tailings facilities.[169] 'Environmental Justice demands that public policy be based on mutual respect and justice for all peoples, free from any form of discrimination or bias', the Principles of Environmental Justice proclaim.[170] In a mining context, distributive justice could also be used to critique the allocation of benefits arising from mining.

Environmental justice claims were first asserted in a context of local distributional injustice: the 1982 protests against the siting of a PCB landfill in a predominantly African American community in Warren County, North Carolina.[171] The focus of the first environmental justice projects was predominantly on race and class as drivers of environmental inequity. For example, in 1982 Benjamin Chavis, head of the United Church of Christ's Commission for Racial Justice, coined the term 'environmental racism' to refer to racial discrimination in environmental policymaking and legal enforcement.[172]

The charge of discriminatory racial intent in environmental policy, law and enforcement, however, proved to be a controversial topic. A series of studies in the late 1980s and 1990s in the USA sought to both prove and disprove the claim that minority communities were disproportionately affected by locally undesirable land uses, and that a causal connection existed between racism and the siting of toxic facilities and polluting industries.[173] Already by the early 1990s, therefore, the terms environmental equity and environmental justice had become preferred over the term environmental racism.[174] This shift represented both a broadening and a dilution of the conceptual purchase of the set of concepts – extending their protective ambit to other vulnerable groupings and also incorporating forms of justice other than the distributive.

The State's role, under a distributive environmental justice lens, involves identifying and addressing disproportionately high adverse human health and environmental effects on minority and lower income populations.[175] This may involve difficult issues of policy and law: Where does the boundary of the affected community lie? Have they been disproportionately impacted? What needs to be done?[176] However, distributive justice in an environmental context

---

[169] Kuehn (n 163) 10684.

[170] Principles of Environmental Justice (n 161) principle 2.

[171] RJ Lazarus, 'The Meaning and Promotion of Environmental Justice' (1994) 5(1) *Maryland Journal of Contemporary Legal Issues* 1.

[172] SL Cutter, 'Race, class and environmental justice' (1995) 19(1) *Progress in Human Geography* 111, 112.

[173] V Been, 'Analyzing evidence of environmental justice' (1995) 11(1) *Land Use and Environmental Law* 1.

[174] Cutter (n 172) 113.

[175] Kuehn (n 163) 10684.

[176] Ibid 10688.

has also been interpreted to mean equal protection for all by lowering the risks of environmental harm, rather than redistributing pollution or risk.[177]

Allegations of local distributive injustice in a mining context are not as clearcut as they might be in contexts where the siting of nuclear facilities or other toxic waste installations are in question, due to the fact that reserves of ore only occur in particular locations. Geological indicators, rather than socioeconomic factors, are thus more likely to determine the site of a mine.[178] However, the rigour of policy, law and enforcement to prevent or ameliorate socioeconomic and ecological harms subsequently arising from mining operations can certainly be viewed from a distributive justice angle.[179]

A distributive justice framing is also conducive to analysing the unequal power relations between developed and developing countries on a global scale. Scholars working in this area have argued that the social dynamics inherent in the constitution of racial and class-based inequalities around pollution and access to natural resources are replicated in relations between the nations of the so-called global North and global South.[180] The study of distributive justice at this scale inevitably draws upon colonial studies, and an understanding of how colonialism established the foundations of resource extraction in minerals and other extractive commodities.[181] Relying on the notion of corrective justice, scholars have argued that the North owes an ecological debt to nations of the global South.[182] Rather than seeing existing ecological degradation as a legacy issue, for example, the concept of ecological debt would vest liability in wealthier countries for their excessive consumption of natural resources and utilization of natural sinks.[183]

4.2 Procedural Justice

A focus on environmental equity – the idea that everybody is affected by deteriorating environmental quality, irrespective of race or class – challenged the underlying assumptions of distributive justice. Academics and activists turned to procedural justice because much of the environment is already

---

177 Ibid 10684.

178 Ali (n 47) 13.

179 Ibid.

180 CG Gonzalez, 'Environmental Justice and International Environmental Law' Seattle University School of Law Paper Series 12-11 4 (2012) Retrieved from http://papers.ssrn.com/abstract=2011081 12.

181 Ibid.

182 Ibid.

183 For further reading see Erik Paredis *et al* (eds), *The Concept of Ecological Debt, Its Meaning and Applicability in International Policy* (Gent Academia Press 2008).

inherently unevenly distributed, burdens and risks cannot sensibly be shared and a focus on distributional effects does not necessarily address the root causes of such effects.[184] However, procedural justice was already a key focus of the Principles of Environmental Justice formulated by the People of Color Environmental Leadership Summit in 1991.[185] Rather than a focus on fair outcomes, procedural justice centres on the right to equal concern and respect in political decisionmaking concerning the distribution of environmental risks and rewards.[186]

To advance procedural justice, the State must entrench democratic environmental decisionmaking – ensuring public participation, access to information, proper representation on decisionmaking structures, procedural fairness, status attached to public inputs – but with a special emphasis on how low income groups are positioned in these processes.[187] One of the main critiques against decisionmaking in an environmental context is that the 'predominant expertise-oriented, interest-group model' favours those with resources and political power over marginalized and low income groups.[188] This debate is especially lively in the use of environmental assessment in the mining industry, as discussed in Chapter 6.

There are obvious overlaps between procedural justice and the principle of FPIC outlined in section 3.4.2 above. Allegations of procedural injustice in an environmental justice context, however, may arise in respect of a broader range of communities and at numerous points in the cycle of a mine – commencing with the decision to explore or exploit, to grant or amend an environmental authorization, to expand the mine, to mothball the mining operations and to close the mine.

One of the most intractable debates surrounding procedural justice is whether a procedurally just process justifies the imposition of an unfair outcome.[189] This unresolved issue lies at the core of dissatisfaction with environmental assessment processes in the mining industry.[190] Tellingly perhaps, the mining industry has enthusiastically embraced procedural justice: the ICMM's 10 Sustainable Development Principles contain no commitment regarding distributional impacts, but are saturated with references to 'consultation' and 'engagement'. Principle 4 commits ICMM members to '[c]onsult with interested and affected parties to identify, assess and manage all significant social,

---

184 Cutter (n 172) 113.
185 See Principles of Environmental Justice (n 161) principle 7.
186 Kuehn (n 163) 10688.
187 Cutter (n 172) 113.
188 Kuehn (n 163) 10689.
189 Ibid 10692.
190 See further sections 2.2 and 2.4 of Chapter 6.

health, safety, environmental and economic impacts associated with [mining] activities'.[191] Principle 10 requires members to 'proactively engage key stakeholders on sustainable development challenges and opportunities in an open and transparent manner'.[192] The ICMM's most far reaching commitments in the arena of procedural justice are set out in Principle 9, relating to the management of social impacts. However, commitments to engage and to respond to issues and conflicts apply only to 'affected parties'.[193]

4.3 Corrective Justice

Corrective justice involves fairness in the administration of punishment and the manner in which damages inflicted upon individuals and communities are addressed.[194] In an environmental context, the 'polluter pays principle' in international law supports the proposition that mining proponents could be strictly liable to repair environmental damage – that is, even in the absence of fault.[195]

Under the banner of corrective justice, the State is duty bound to ensure that mining companies comply with the law and that enforcement efforts are not applied with discriminatory impact. This duty, in turn, assumes a precautionary approach to the forms of environmental and social damage that may arise as a result of the presence of a mining operation in a particular locality. States should ensure that policies and laws are in place to minimize mining's social and environmental impacts, and that processes are followed, particularly at the end of the cycle of the mine, to prevent the perpetuation of negative legacies.[196] Corrective justice could further imply a State duty to ensure the availability of a sufficiently broad range of administrative, civil and criminal legal remedies for State functionaries, individuals, mining-affected communities and interested parties to hold mining companies to account.

---

[191] International Council of Mining and Metals, 'Principle 4', www.icmm.com/en-gb/members/member-commitments/icmm-10-principles/icmm-principle-4, accessed 23 February 2019.

[192] International Council of Mining and Metals, 'Principle 10', www.icmm.com/en-gb/members/member-commitments/icmm-10-principles/icmm-principle-10, accessed 23 February 2019.

[193] International Council of Mining and Metals, 'Principle 9', https://www.icmm.com/en-gb/members/member-commitments/icmm-10-principles/icmm-principle-9, accessed 23 February 2019.

[194] Kuehn (n 163) 10693.

[195] Ibid 10694.

[196] Many of the State's duties in these regards are ostensibly fulfilled through the governance regimes associated with environmental assessment (Chapter 6) and mine closure (Chapter 7) respectively.

There are numerous reported examples of the difficulties individuals and communities face when attempting to hold mining companies to account, either for individual and group compensation and/or to repair and rehabilitate the environment. The most intractable of these cases occur when individuals and communities seek redress against the parent companies of the operators that have inflicted damage in the jurisdiction in which they are incorporated.[197]

Until recently, the mining industry has resisted attempts to uphold a strong interpretation of corrective justice. The industry has instead put its weight behind weaker forms of redress, such as buyouts, relocation and compensation for loss of livelihoods.[198] A shift in the mining industry's stance towards corrective justice is nevertheless detectable in some regions. On 3 May 2018, for example, the South African gold mining industry reached an unprecedented and historical agreement between seven gold mining companies and mineworkers afflicted by the occupational diseases of silicosis and/or tuberculosis.[199] The agreement was reached after years of litigation and negotiation, including historic court victories (1) allowing mineworkers to proceed with claims under the common law, notwithstanding small payouts under a statutory occupational health and safety regime;[200] and (2) certifying that a class action suit against virtually the entire South African gold mining regime could proceed.[201] The affected miners agreed to set aside ZAR 5 billion in the 'Tshiamiso' trust,[202] a title derived from a Setswana word which means 'to make good' or 'to correct'.[203]

---

[197] See for example the case of *Lungowe & others v. Vedanta Resources plc & another* [2017] EWCA Civ 1528, which involved an action instituted by Zambian claimants against the parent company in its home jurisdiction for environmental damage and pollution caused by an operating subsidiary in Zambia.

[198] Kuehn (n 163) 10696 observes that these efforts at corrective justice are increasingly common.

[199] Richard Spoor Inc Attorneys, 'Settlement of the silicosis and TB class action', http://goldminersilicosis.co.za/wp-content/uploads/2018/05/2018-05-03-settlement-statement-final.pdf, accessed 23 February 2019.

[200] *Mankayi v. Anglogold Ashanti 2011* (3) SA 237 (CC).

[201] *Nkala & others v. Harmony Gold Mining Company Limited & others* 2016 (5) SA 240 (GJ).

[202] Staff Reporter, 'Landmark settlement for silicosis sufferers in the gold mining industry', *Huffington Post*, 4 May 2018, www.huffingtonpost.co.za/2018/05/04/landmark-settlement-for-silicosis-sufferers-in-the-gold-mining-industry_a_23426771/, accessed 23 February 2019.

[203] Richard Spoor Inc, Abrahams Kiewitz Inc and the Legal Resources Centre, 'Media Statement: Settlement of the silicosis and TB class action'.

4.4 Social Justice

Social justice has been characterized as the most 'nebulous' and far reaching goal of the environmental justice movement.[204] Essentially, it brings the intersectionality of environmental and other factors of social well-being into view. Social justice demands that 'the members of every class have enough resources and enough power to live as befits human beings, and second, that the privileged classes, whoever they are, be accountable to the wider society for the way they use their advantages'.[205] The strong interrelationship between issues of ecological and social justice comes out strongly in Pope Francis' encyclical on the environment, where he states that 'we have to realize that true ecological approach *always* becomes a social approach: it must integrate questions of justice in debates on the environment so as to hear *both the cry of the earth and the cry of the poor*'.[206] Kuehn points out that social justice influences the work of the environmental justice movement in at least two ways: on the one hand, the same economic, racial and political factors responsible for heightening environmental risks in communities may also be involved in other social problems, such as inadequate housing, poor water, poor infrastructure, and poor schools and health facilities.[207] On the other hand, undesirable land uses, inclusive of mine exploration, exploitation and processing facilities may trigger further social and economic deterioration.[208]

The State's role in advancing the social justice dimension of environmental justice is potentially openended and far reaching. The Principles of Environmental Justice provide some guidance. For example, they call for 'economic alternatives that contribute to the development of environmentally safe livelihoods'.[209] Under this banner, States could be duty bound not only to ensure that mining occurs in a way that does not materially impair livelihoods, but to consider whether mining is the *best* land use option to advance environmentally safest livelihoods, all things considered. States also have a duty to ensure that the assessment of mining as a land use option encompasses an integrated assessment of environmental and socioeconomic linkages, for example,

[204] Kuehn (n 163) 10698.

[205] Robert E Rodes Jr, 'Social justice and liberation' (1996) 71 *Notre Dame Law Review* 619, 626.

[206] The Vatican, 'Encylical letter Laudato Si'of the Holy Father Francis on Care for our Common Home', http://w2.vatican.va/content/francesco/en/encyclicals/documents/papa-francesco_20150524_enciclica-laudato-si.html accessed 23 February 2019, para. 49.

[207] Kuehn (n 163) 10699.

[208] Ibid.

[209] Principles of Environmental Justice (n 161) Preamble.

by providing policy and legislative frameworks for integrated and cumulative environmental assessment.

The Principles of Environmental Justice even extend the ambit of social justice beyond human beings. Principle 1, for example, affirms 'the sacredness of Mother Earth, ecological unity and the interdependence of all species, and the right to be free from ecological destruction',[210] while principle 3 'mandates the right to ethical, balanced and responsible uses of land and renewable resources in the interest of a sustainable planet for humans and other living things'. These principles require the State to extend the scope of its concern to encompass all living things and the value of ecological unity.

In some contexts, the pressure of social justice claims may lead to mining companies functioning as pseudo-States. Whether as a result of corporate social responsibility initiatives, or in some jurisdictions even as the result of statutorily formulated requirements,[211] mining companies may provide basic services to local communities such as the provision of electricity, water and sanitation services and education and healthcare facilities. The globalized mining industry has resisted this role to some extent. Nevertheless, pressure at the coalface of development causes some mining proponents to behave differently, reinforcing perceptions of an absent or abdicating State. The chief difficulty with placing social justice expectations squarely on the shoulders of mining companies is that the presence of mining in a locality is temporary – at some point the mineral reserve will inevitably be depleted and the company will withdraw its presence, causing severe problems of institutional continuity when individuals and groups have become dependent upon a mine's provision of social services, over and above the employment and income generating activities.

4.5 Conclusion

In the discourse of environmental justice, the State's protective role extends beyond Indigenous Peoples to encompass other marginalized communities, often defined on the basis of race and/or class. The four part typology of distributive, procedural, corrective and social justice is useful for distilling the claims of environmental justice advocates, even as it waters down the various strong calls for combating colonization, oppression and environmental racism articulated at the birth of the environmental justice movement. As the advocate of environmental justice, the State is expected to identify and promote substantively just environmental outcomes (distributive justice), entrench democratic

---

[210] Ibid.

[211] For example, the framework for social and labour plans in South Africa.

decisionmaking (procedural justice), address environmental damage and secure redress (corrective justice), and ensure that mining does not oppress affected communities in a socioeconomic-ecological sense while promoting a fair distribution of the industry's benefits (social justice). The mining industry has engaged with some of the claims of environmental justice activists, for example, giving strong support for procedural justice and much weaker support for corrective justice. As a discourse of mining dissent, environmental justice posits a heroic State, constituted by a broadranging set of demands, which include demands for radical economic alternatives that promote environmentally safe livelihoods.

5. MINING AND HUMAN RIGHTS

The fourth discourse of mining dissent – mining and human rights – overlaps with both Indigenous Peoples' rights and environmental justice. According to a recent baseline survey on human rights issues arising throughout the mining cycle, land, environmental issues and Indigenous Peoples issues are the areas of highest risk for largescale and industrial mining.[212] Adverse human rights impacts can arise at any stage of the mining cycle, from licensing and exploration through to construction, operations and closure. The most common rights infringements relate to FPIC; the right to participation and information; freedom of association; the rights to adequate housing, food, water and health; the right to privacy; the right to labour and occupational health and safety; the right to work; the right to life; and the right to remedy. The interdependency of these rights and the environment, and infringement of the right to environment itself, is marked from the period of mine construction onwards, when area clearing may result in resettlement, displacement, forced evictions and conflict. Environmental contamination of soil, water and air and the depletion of water resources becomes a major driver of adverse human rights impacts during the operational and closure phases of mining. Mud and landslides and tailings dam failures can also be fatal during these phases of the cycle. As the

---

[212] M Spohr, *Human Rights Risks in Mining: A Baseline Study* (BGR 2016) 146. The Baseline Survey also examined human rights issues related to Artisanal and Small-Scale Mining (ASM), but for the purposes of this work ASM is not further considered. Human rights analyses in the mining sector are common. See for example Donald M Zillman, Alistair Lucas and George Pring, *Human Rights in Natural Resource Development: Public Participation in the Sustainable Development of Mining and Energy Resources* (Oxford University Press 2002); Deanna Kemp *et al*, 'Mining, water and human rights: Making the connection' (2010) 18(15) *Journal of Cleaner Production* 1553; C Coumans, 'Alternative accountability mechanisms and mining: The problems of effective impunity, human rights and agency' (2010) 30(1–2) *Canadian Journal of Development Studies* 27.

baseline survey notes, 'Large-Scale Mining projects have one of the biggest environmental impacts in the entire industrial world, often only surpassed by gigantic hydropower projects'.[213]

In a study on human rights in the mining sector in Indonesia (commissioned for the MMSD in 2002), Ballard observed that the mining industry's attitude toward human rights only shifted in the late 1990s.[214] Industry support for human rights was nevertheless already entrenched by 2003, with the formulation of the ICMM's ten sustainable development principles. Principle 3 commits ICMM members to 'respect human rights and the interests, cultures, customs and values of employees and communities affected by [mining] activities'.[215] The ICMM published its own review of human rights issues in the mining and metals industry in 2009,[216] and has formally supported the United Nations Guiding Principles on Business and Human Rights (Ruggie Principles), as detailed below.

The language and normative framework of human rights imposes a variety of obligations upon the State. In a mining context, a human rights frame adds to the polyphony of discourses of mining dissent in at least three areas, namely: (1) debates on the content and scope of the environmental dimension of human rights and a substantive human right to the environment; (2) recognition of the precarious and dangerous situation of environmental and human rights defenders; and (3) the rapidly evolving framework for business and human rights. The ensuing discussion focuses primarily on international developments in these areas. Regional human rights frameworks, together with high level constitutional or statutory commitments in the national legal frameworks of mineral-rich jurisdictions, not only add to the normative complexity of the State's human rights obligations relating to mining, but also to the range of institutional mechanisms through which dissent can be channelled and adjudicated. A comprehensive discussion of these mechanisms, and the patterns emerging from their use in regional and national forums of adjudication, is beyond the scope of this work.[217]

---

[213] Spohr (n 212) 49.

[214] Chris Ballard, 'Human rights and the mining sector in Indonesia: A baseline study', Report No. 182 commissioned by the MMSD project of the IIED (October 2001) 7.

[215] ICMM, 'ICMM 10 Principles: Principle 3', www.icmm.com/en-gb/members/member-commitments/icmm-10-principles/icmm-principle-3, accessed 23 February 2019.

[216] International Council on Mining and Metals, Human Rights in the Mining & Metals Industry: Overview, Management Approach and Issues (May 2009) (henceforth 'ICMM Human Rights Guidance').

[217] For a leading work on environmental constitutionalism see James R May and Erin Daly, *Global Environmental Constitutionalism* (Cambridge University Press 2016).

An important point bears emphasizing: the discussion of mining-related human rights below comes across as apolitical, even technical and bland. This arises from the subject matter. As Klein has documented, the 1948 United Nations Declaration of Human Rights – the touchstone of contemporary human rights movements – was very quickly used as a bipartisan battering ram by both sides of the Cold War.[218] To counter this, and to uphold impartiality, independence and the supposed universality of human rights, there is a tendency in human rights discourse to reify rights and rights violations in a manner that obscures broader political and economic ends. Thus human rights violations and abuses may be documented without condemnation of the reasons why such violations are occurring. In a mineral extraction context, for example, organizations may condemn human rights abuses inflicted by State and private actors to quell unrest in communities resisting mining in the areas in which they live and work. But they do not condemn the broader capitalist, globalized system for the production of mineral commodities, or neoextractivist projects that position mineral extraction as crucial to national development, or the consumerism and trajectory of 'development' that drives the demand for mineral commodities. In a similar fashion to critiques of FPIC, therefore, it is important to remember that 'human rights' can have displacement, miscommunication and domination effects.

5.1 Mining, the Environmental Dimension of Human Rights and a Substantive Human Right to the Environment

There is no explicit recognition of a human right to a safe, clean, healthy and sustainable environment in a human rights instrument of global application, although it has been recognized in regional agreements and most national constitutions.[219] Since 2012, with the appointment of a Special Rapporteur on human rights obligations relating to the enjoyment of a safe, clean, healthy and sustainable environment, the UN Human Rights Council has nevertheless led work in this area. John Knox, the first incumbent to this position, was extraordinarily active, and produced a number of reports scoping and mapping the outstanding issues pertaining to the environmental dimension of human rights, identifying good practices and advising on implementation. During the second half of his six year tenure Knox also produced topic-specific reports

---

[218] Naomi Klein, *The Shock Doctrine* (Picador 2008) 147.

[219] United Nations Human Rights Council, Report of the Special Rapporteur on the issue of human rights obligations relating to the enjoyment of a safe, clean, healthy and sustainable environment (24 January 2018), A/HRC/37/59 (henceforth 'Framework Principles').

on climate change, biodiversity and children's rights and the environment.[220] His work culminated in the formulation of 16 Framework Principles on human rights and the environment, which he presented to the Human Rights Council in March 2018.

In his mapping report of 2013 (a review process involving 45 States),[221] Knox noted that mining operations had been identified as a threat to the right to a healthy environment, on a par with climate change and desertification.[222] The Special Rapporteur on hazardous substances and wastes had already indicated that waste from extractive industries could infringe the right to water,[223] and the Special Rapporteur on the rights of Indigenous Peoples had emphasized that extractive industry activities generated effects that often infringed upon Indigenous Peoples' rights.[224]

The 16 Framework Principles on human rights and the environment, however, apply to the full range of environmental harms that may occur, and not expressly to environmental threats arising from the extractive industries. They currently stand as the most comprehensive articulation of the State's basic human rights obligations relating to the environment. In his report, Knox was at pains to emphasize that the principles do not create new obligations, but rather reflect the application of existing human rights obligations in an environmental context, as derived from treaties, binding decisions of human rights tribunals and statements of human rights bodies with authority to interpret human rights law.[225] There has been a 'greening' of human rights law, making explicit recognition of the human right to a healthy environment unnecessary for applying human rights norms relating to environmental issues.[226] Clear advantages would nevertheless flow from the UN's recognition of an explicit human right to a safe, clean, healthy and sustainable environment, not least

---

[220] See the reports accessible from United Nations Office of the High Commissioner, 'Special Rapporteur on human rights and the environment – Annual Reports', www.ohchr.org/EN/Issues/Environment/SREnvironment/Pages/Annualreports.aspx, accessed 19 February 2019. See also the dedicated website of the Special Rapporteur at http://srenvironment.org, accessed 23 February 2019.

[221] United Nations Human Rights Council, Report of the Independent Expert on the issue of human rights obligations relating to the enjoyment of a safe, clean, healthy and sustainable environment A/HRC/25/53.

[222] Ibid para. 18.

[223] A/HRC/21/48 para. 39.

[224] A/HRC/18/35 para. 26.

[225] Framework Principles (n 219) para. 8.

[226] Ibid para. 13.

of which would be raising the profile and importance of environmental protection.[227]

The normative content of the human right to a healthy environment rests upon a bedrock of interdependence: 'Environmental harm interferes with the enjoyment of human rights, and the exercise of human rights helps to protect the environment and to promote sustainable development.'[228] The first two Framework Principles flow directly from this recognition of interdependence: 'States should ensure a safe, clean, healthy and sustainable environment in order to respect, protect and fulfil human rights' and 'States should respect, protect and fulfil human rights in order to ensure a safe, clean, healthy and sustainable environment'.[229] The commentary on these Framework Principles suggests that a right to a healthy environment is necessary for the full enjoyment of *all* human rights, but singles out for specific mention the rights to life, to the highest attainable standard of physical and mental health, to an adequate standard of living, to adequate food, to safe drinking water and sanitation, to housing and to participation in cultural life and development, alongside the right to a healthy environment itself.[230] Conversely, human rights expressly instrumental to achieving a human right to the environment include freedom of expression and association, and the rights to education, information, participation and effective remedies.[231] The State's duty to respect and protect the rights to freedom of expression, association and peaceful assembly in environmental matters is articulated in Framework Principle 5. The commentary on this principle underlines that restrictions on the exercise of these rights must be narrowly tailored, and that blanket prohibitions on protests surrounding the operations of mining, forestry or other resource extraction companies, for example, would be unjustifiable.[232]

There is strong intertextuality between the Framework Principles and the discourses of Indigenous Peoples' rights and environmental justice. Framework Principle 15 concentrates on States' duties towards Indigenous Peoples in an environmental context, and lends support for the indigenous rights discourse across four dimensions: the recognition and protection of lands, territories and resources; entrenching the principle of FPIC; respecting and protecting indigenous knowledge insofar as it relates to the conservation and sustainable use

227 Ibid. Knox therefore urged the Human Rights Council to support recognition of the right to environment in a global instrument (para. 14).

228 Ibid, Annex para. 1. The reference to sustainable development in this key claim also ties the Framework Principles to the mainstream sustainability discourse.

229 Ibid, Annex.

230 Ibid, Annex para. 6.

231 Ibid.

232 Framework Principles (n 219) Annex, para. 13.

of lands, territories and resources; and ensuring that Indigenous Peoples fairly and equitably share in the benefits of activities relating to their lands, territories and resources.[233] This principle therefore undergirds the normative web responding to the vulnerability of Indigenous Peoples and other marginalized groups, particularly as they are affected by extractive projects.

The Framework Principles' nod to the discourse of environmental justice comes through in its strong position against unfair discrimination in an environmental context (that is, distributive justice). The prohibition against discrimination requires that States protect against environmental harm that results from or contributes to discrimination,[234] ensure that their own actions do not lead to discrimination, and provide for an equitable sharing of environmental benefits.[235] Discrimination can be direct or indirect. The Special Rapporteur especially notes that indirect discrimination arises 'when measures that adversely affect ecosystems, such as mining and logging concessions, have disproportionately severe effects on communities that rely on the ecosystems'.[236] Significantly, the prohibition against unfair discrimination extends to a transboundary context, in that States should provide for equal access to information, participation and remedies without discriminating on the basis of nationality or domicile.[237] This norm is pertinent to corrective justice in a mining context, as outlined in section 4.3 above.

States must take additional measures to protect the rights of persons or groups vulnerable to, or at particular risk from, environmental harm, taking into account their needs, risks and capacities.[238] Specifically mentioned groups include children; women; persons living in poverty; persons with disabilities; Indigenous Peoples; ethnic, racial and other minorities; and displaced persons.[239] For example, given the existence of these particular vulnerable groups, it would not be enough for States to simply provide a general right of access to environmental information. Instead, the State should take additional measures to develop disaggregated data on the specific effects of environmental harm on particular segments of the population.[240] This norm could have clear application in a mining context, requiring States to develop disaggregated datasets on effects of a full range of environmental harms on mining-affected communities, for example.

---

233 Ibid, Annex.
234 See Framework Principles (note 219), Framework Principle 3.
235 Ibid, Annex, para. 7.
236 Ibid, Annex, para. 9.
237 Ibid, Annex, para. 8.
238 Ibid, Framework Principle 14.
239 Ibid, Annex, para. 41.
240 Ibid, Annex, para. 43.

Support for procedural justice comes through in Framework Principles 7 (public access to environmental information) and 9 (public participation in decisionmaking relating to the environment, and taking the view of the public into account), while Framework Principle 10 lends support to corrective justice (access to effective remedies for violations of human rights and domestic laws relating to the environment). The Framework Principles weigh in on the debate whether a just procedure can validate an unjust outcome through the principles of openness and accountability. In making their final decisions, States must ensure that the relevant authorities take the expressed views of the public into account, explain the justifications for their decisions and ensure that both decisions and justifications are made public.[241]

Of the remaining Framework Principles, principles 8 (prior assessment of the possible environmental impacts of proposed projects and policies, including their impact on human rights), 10 (establishment and maintenance of substantive environmental standards that are both nondiscriminatory and nonregressive) and 12 (effective enforcement) all have clear application in a mining context. Exhortations to procedural justice and nondiscrimination undergird all these norms and assist in determining the bounds for the limitation of these rights.

The recently formulated Framework Principles accordingly serve as a rich source of norms for the State's protective role, significantly overlapping with the discourses of Indigenous Peoples and environmental justice.

5.2 Mining and Environmental and Human Rights Defenders

The second dimension of the mining and human rights discourse concerns 'environmental and human rights defenders'. Intimidation, killing and murder of grassroots leaders agitating for the rights of Indigenous Peoples and the environment has been documented and is a trend that unfortunately appears to be on the increase.[242] In 2007 the first UN Special Rapporteur on Human

---

[241] Ibid, Annex, para. 26.

[242] The following is a sample of recent cases in the media documenting the death of human rights defenders in the extractives context: San Tun (a 47 year old land and environmental rights defender in Burma; shot and killed in June 2014); Chit Pandaing (22 year old woman who strongly advocated against land confiscation and the negative environmental impacts of mining in Burma; stabbed to death on 19 November 2016 – see ALTSEAN-Burma and International Federation for Human Rights, 'Burma: Investigate murder of lawyer Ko Ni, take measures to protect human rights defenders', http://progressivevoicemyanmar.org/2017/01/29/burma-investigate-murder-of-lawyer-ko-ni-take-measures-to-protect-human-rights-defenders/, accessed 24 February 2019); Fernando Salazar Calvo (human rights defender gunned down on 9 April 2015 – see Forest Peoples International, 'Colombia: Human rights defender opposing

Rights Defenders noted that the second most vulnerable group of human rights defenders were those working on land rights and natural resources.[243] In August 2013, her successor reported that the situation appeared to have worsened since 2007.[244] In *On Dangerous Ground*, Global Witness reported that 2015 was the worst year on record for the killing of land and environmental defenders, and that mining and extractives industries were the sectors most implicated in these killings. In 2015 42 killings in this sector were reported across ten countries, representing a 70 per cent increase over 2014.[245] The hardest hit countries for antimining activists were Colombia, Peru and the Philippines.[246] The overall hardest hit country for natural resource-related killings was Brazil, with 50 people murdered in 2015 alone.[247] The most recent report on the situation of human rights defenders submitted in August 2016 by the third Special Rapporteur raises alarm about the 'shocking rate' of killings, threats, harassment and intimidation experienced by environmental human rights defenders.[248]

In her 2013 report, the second UN Special Rapporteur on Human Rights Defenders noted that human rights defenders trying to protect the rights of local communities, inclusive of Indigenous Peoples, minorities and people living in poverty, face 'extraordinary risks' including threats of physical assault and death, intimidation, criminalization and actual assault and killings.[249] Both State and non-State actors are perpetrating these violations of

---

"illegal mining" is killed', https://business-humanrights.org/en/colombia-human-rights-defender-opposing-%E2%80%9Cillegal-mining%E2%80%9D-is-killed, accessed 24 February 2019); Valsa John (Indian mining activist hacked to death on 15 November 2011); Jeremy Barrios (22 year old human rights activist shedding light on abuses perpetrated by mining companies in Guatemala – see Telesur, 'Guatemalan activists' murder sparks alarm over human rights crisis', www.telesurtv.net/english/news/Guatemalan-Activists-Murder-Sparks-Alarm-over-Rights-Crisis-20161116-0015.html, accessed 24 February 2019). For summative reports see Article 19, *A Deadly Shade of Green: Threats to Environmental Human Rights Defenders in Latin America* (2016); Global Witness, *On Dangerous Ground* (June 2016); Front Line Defenders, *Annual Report 2016: Stop the Killing of Human Rights Defenders* (2016).

243 A/HRC/4/37, para. 45.

244 A/68/262, para. 18.

245 Global Witness (n 242) 16.

246 Ibid.

247 Global Witness, 'Report/June 2016 "On Dangerous Ground"', www.globalwitness.org/en/campaigns/environmental-activists/dangerous-ground/, accessed 24 February 2019.

248 Report of the Special Rapporteur on the Situation of Human Rights Defenders (3 August 2016) A/71/281, para. 2 (henceforth Special Rapporteur Report on Human Rights Defenders).

249 A/68/262 para. 15.

human rights. They include private security companies employed by oil and gas companies, cases in which local authorities collude with the private sector, and situations in which private companies aid and abet violations committed against human rights defenders.[250]

In his 2016 report, the third Special Rapporteur took time to outline the pertinent normative framework for the protection of human rights defenders. Deriving in the first instance from the Universal Declaration on Human Rights, the ICCPR and the International Covenant on Economic, Social and Cultural Rights (ICESCR), States have a primary responsibility to protect the rights to life, liberty and security of the person.[251] Article 2.1 of the UN Declaration on Human Rights Defenders goes further,[252] stating that '[e]ach State has a prime responsibility and duty to protect, promote and implement *all* human rights and fundamental freedoms'. As the third Special Rapporteur notes, the right to self-determination is centrally positioned amongst the constellation of human rights, being affirmed in Article 1 of both the ICCPR and the ICESCR. States must take legislative, administrative and other steps to create 'all conditions necessary in the social, economic, political and other fields' to ensure that all persons under their jurisdiction – individual and in association with others – are able to enjoy these rights and freedoms in practice.[253] The Declaration on Human Rights Defenders also affirms State responsibility to take measures to promote understanding of civil, political, economic, social and cultural rights among people falling within its jurisdiction.[254]

The Framework Principles discussed in section 5.1 above support these normative statements on environmental human rights defenders. States must provide a 'safe and enabling environment' in which individuals, groups and organs of society can work on human rights or environmental issues free from threats, harassment, intimidation and violence (Principle 4),[255] and States must respect and protect the rights to freedom of expression, association and peaceful assembly in relation to environmental matters (Principle 5).[256]

---

[250] Ibid para. 18.

[251] Special Rapporteur Report on Human Rights Defenders (n 248) para. 11.

[252] UN General Assembly Declaration on the Right and Responsibility of Individuals, Groups and Organs of Society to Promote and Protect Universally Recognized Human Rights and Fundamental Freedoms A/RES/53/144 (henceforth Declaration on Human Rights Defenders).

[253] Ibid Articles 2.1, 2.2.

[254] Declaration on Human Rights Defenders (n 252) Article 14.

[255] Framework Principles (n 219) Annex.

[256] Ibid.

5.3 Mining and 'Business and Human Rights'

Similarly to the manner in which the mining industry has appropriated elements of an environmental justice discourse,[257] it has strongly emphasized the State's primary responsibility to *protect* human rights.[258] The industry's duty to *respect* human rights has also been identified as a 'key aspect' of sustainable development,[259] thus bringing a potentially dissenting human right discourse within the fold of the sustainable mineral development consensus.

The mining industry was an active participant in the formulation of the 'Guiding Principles on Business and Human Rights' (Ruggie Principles),[260] the framework developed by special representative John Ruggie unanimously endorsed by the UN Human Rights Council in June 2011.[261] They were also the first industry body to endorse the principles and require implementation on the part of their membership.[262] The international framework is evolving further, however, and following a proposal initiated by Ecuador and South Africa, the Human Rights Council resolved on 26 June 2014 to establish an intergovernmental working group to elaborate an international, legally binding instrument to regulate the activities of transnational corporations and other business enterprises under human rights law.[263] The openended intergovernmental working group was established and its work is continuing.[264]

The Ruggie Principles are not the first voluntary human rights guidance to apply to the mining industry. In 2000, following 'dialogue' between the

[257] See the discussion on procedural justice in section 4.2 above.

[258] ICMM Human Rights Guidance (2012) 1.

[259] Ibid.

[260] United Nations Guiding Principles on Business and Human Rights: Implementing the United Nations Protect, respect and remedy' framework (2011) HR/Pub/11/04 (henceforth Ruggie Principles). The Office of the High Commissioner has issued a number of interpretive guides on the Ruggie Principles for different sectors but, as yet, no specific guide for the extractive industries has been developed.

[261] United Nations Office of the High Commissioner, 'Business and human rights', www.ohchr.org/EN/Issues/Business/Pages/BusinessIndex.aspx accessed 24 February 2019. The ICMM made three submissions: see ICMM Human Rights Guidance (n 258) 3.

[262] ICMM, 'ICMM first industry body to commit to UN Guiding Principles on Business and Human Rights', www.icmm.com/pe-pr, accessed 24 February 2019.

[263] Jens Martens and Karolin Seitz, *The Struggle for a UN Treaty: Towards Global Regulation on Human Rights and Business* (Global Policy Forum and Rosa Luxemborg Stiftung 2016) 1.

[264] See United Nations Office of the High Commissioner, 'Working Group on the issue of human rights and transnational corporations and other business enterprises', http://www.ohchr.org/EN/Issues/Business/Pages/WGHRandtransnationalcorporationsandotherbusiness.aspx, accessed 24 February 2019.

governments of the USA, the United Kingdom and certain extractive companies and NGOs, the Voluntary Principles on Security and Human Rights (VPSHR) were agreed.[265] The VPSHR guide mining companies on an operating framework that respects human rights as they seek to maintain the safety and security of their operations.[266] They promote a discourse of cooperation, recognizing the 'constructive role' that business and civil society can play in promoting and protecting human rights.[267] They also align with the 'Protect, Respect and Remedy' framework subsequently elaborated in the Ruggie Principles, by pointing out that the primary responsibility for promoting and protecting human rights lies with governments, while companies bear the duty of 'respect'.[268] While seemingly promoting empowered States, the VPSHR also hint at the reality of failed, weak and tyrannical States: a company's duty to accurately assess risk in its operating environment must include a risk assessment of the human rights records of public security forces, as well as the capacity of the local prosecuting authority and judiciary to hold human rights offenders accountable.[269] Although the VPSHR refer to 'security risks' and 'potential for environment', they do not deal with the environment or sustainability expressly as a security or human rights issues. Duties incumbent upon companies to support and respect the protection of 'internationally proclaimed human rights' and to avoid complicity in human rights abuses are also part and parcel of the UN Global Compact, touted as the world's largest corporate sustainability initiative.[270]

The Ruggie Principles currently stand as the most authoritative statement on the human rights obligations of businesses and the State–society relationship these obligations assume. The theoretical background to these principles is significant. Ruggie originated the concept of 'embedded liberalism',[271] a term he applied to postwar attempts to ensure the social legitimacy of markets –

---

[265] For the dedicated website of the Voluntary Principles on Security and Human Rights see www.voluntaryprinciples.org, accessed 24 February 2019.

[266] Ibid. In 2011, together with other partners, the ICMM produced a 'first of its kind' Implementation Guidance Tool for the VPSHR: see ICMM, 'Voluntary Principles on Security and Human Rights: Implementation Guidance Tools', www.icmm.com/en-gb/publications/mining-and-communities/voluntary-principles-on-security-and-human-rights-implementation-guidance-tools accessed 24 February 2019.

[267] Voluntary Principles on Security and Human Rights (n 265) 'Introduction'.

[268] Ibid.

[269] Ibid, see 'Risk Assessment'.

[270] United Nations Global Compact, 'The ten principles of the UN Global Compact', www.unglobalcompact.org/what-is-gc/mission/principles, accessed 24 February 2019.

[271] John G Ruggie, 'International regimes, transactions and change: Embedded liberalism in the postwar economic order' (1982) 36(2) *International Organization* 379.

a project essential to their longterm political sustainability.[272] In his earlier work on this concept, Ruggie drew expressly on a Polyanian frame and highlighted the latter's key insight: That society could not bear the social and environmental repercussions of disembedded markets.[273] Just as influential policymakers in the immediate postwar period had grappled with the problem of disciplining classical liberalism without losing the benefits of the free flow of goods and services, so too policymakers in the twenty-first century were needing to recognize that the current era of globalization and its neoliberal paradigm were suffering from a 'profound crisis of legitimacy'.[274] Putting global regulatory frameworks in place to embed and legitimate the activities of transnational corporations was a key pillar to addressing this crisis.[275]

The Ruggie Principles should be positioned within this overarching imperative and that of a 'socially sustainable globalization'.[276] Rather than applying only to transnational corporations, they apply to all States and to all business enterprises, transnational or not, and 'regardless of their size, sector, location, ownership and structure'.[277] They would thus apply to the full spectrum of companies engaged in the mining cycle.

The Ruggie Principles rest on a 'protect, respect, remedy' framework constituted by three foundational principles: States must protect against human rights abuses occurring within their territory and/or jurisdiction;[278] business enterprises must respect human rights by not infringing on the human rights of others, and addressing adverse human rights impacts with which they are involved;[279] and, as part of its duty to protect, the State must provide or facilitate an effective, appropriate and comprehensive system to remedy business-related human rights abuse, inclusive of judicial mechanisms, non-judicial grievance mechanisms and non-State-based grievance mechanisms.[280] So while the Ruggie Principles push the envelope – by contextualizing the application of human rights in a business context – they do not disrupt the

---

[272] Rawi Abdelal and John G Ruggie, 'The principles of embedded liberalism: Social legitimacy and global capitalism' in D Moss and J Cisternino, *New Perspectives on Regulation* (Tobin Project 2009) 151.

[273] Ruggie (n 271) 387.

[274] Abdelal and Ruggie (n 272) 153.

[275] Ibid.

[276] Ruggie Principles (n 260) 2.

[277] Ibid. Principle 14 nevertheless notes that the scale and complexity of the means through which businesses meet their human rights obligations may vary according to size, sector, operational context, ownership and structure, as well as the severity of the enterprise's adverse human rights impacts.

[278] Ruggie Principles (n 260) 4 (Principle 1).

[279] Ibid 14 (Principle 11).

[280] Ibid 28, 31, 32 (Principles 25, 27, 28).

fundamental role of the State in a system of embedded liberalism. '[I]n the end there is no substitute for governments doing what governments exist to do: to govern, and to govern in the public interest.'[281]

The Ruggie Principles conceive of the State's protective role as facilitative, regulatory, punitive, structural and reflective. For example, States must enforce laws aimed at requiring business enterprises to respect human rights, but they must also provide such enterprises with guidance on how they can address human rights throughout their operations, and encourage (and where appropriate require) them to communicate their human rights impacts.[282] States must address the structural conditions for businesses' human rights compliance by ensuring that laws and policies governing the creation and ongoing operation of business enterprises (for example, corporate or company laws) do not constrain, but enable, respect for human rights.[283] States must monitor and periodically assess the adequacy of such laws and also look to the adequacy of their own conduct, for example, by ensuring policy coherence across departments.[284]

In the State–business nexus, relevant to a neoextractivist context, States must take additional steps to protect against abuses by State-owned or State-controlled companies.[285] States must also protect against the human rights abuses of agencies that receive substantial State support and services, such as export credit agencies.[286] When the State pursues business-related policy objectives with business enterprises or other States, it must maintain adequate domestic policy space to meet its international human rights obligations.[287] This principle is of particular relevance to the question of mineral taxation, and whether States, and the international policy guidance framing State conduct, ensure a fair allocation of mineral resource revenues, as discussed in Chapter 5.[288] The extensive tax breaks States have granted mining companies to encourage investment have been the source of much controversy, and in some jurisdictions they are even triggering revisionist policies.[289] Overall, therefore, the Ruggie Principles do not depart from a liberal and statist model.

---

[281] Abdelal and Ruggie (n 274) 156.

[282] Ruggie Principles (n 260) 5 (Principle 3(a), (c) and (d)).

[283] Ibid 5 (Principle 3(b)).

[284] Ibid 11 (Principle 8).

[285] Ibid 7 (Principle 4).

[286] Ibid 7 (Principle 4). As noted in Chapter 6, the MMSD identified such agencies as the 'quiet giants' of mining finance and noted that their actions were generally not subject to public scrutiny (see *Breaking New Ground* (n 33) 135).

[287] Ruggie Principles (n 260) 12 (Principle 9).

[288] See section 2.1 of Chapter 5.

[289] See the discussion of Tanzania in section 2.4 of Chapter 5.

A question of particular relevance to the mining industry is whether the State's duties outlined above apply when a business operates extraterritorially. States and business enterprises have been trenchantly criticized when the social and environmental standards to which companies are held in their home jurisdiction do not extend to their extraterritorial operations. However, the State duties set out in the Ruggie Principles apply only to human rights abuses perpetrated by business enterprises within their territory and/or jurisdiction.[290] International human rights law does not currently require, but neither does it prohibit, States from regulating the extraterritorial activities of business enterprises, provided a recognized jurisdictional base is present.[291] The Ruggie Principles subtly support a more far reaching State expectation of human rights compliance both at home and abroad, because the policy reasons for clearly articulating the human rights expectations of businesses include the State's 'own reputation'.[292] Ruggie was at pains to emphasize that the State duty to protect is a standard of conduct, and that States were not *per se* responsible for the human rights abuses of private actors. However, in certain circumstances private conduct could be attributed to the State, or where States failed to take appropriate steps to prevent, investigate, punish and redress private actors' abuse.[293] Of course, by expressing that it does *not* expect its business enterprises to operate with the same standards abroad as at home, a State would suffer reputational harm.

The Ruggie Principles also flesh out the meaning of the business duty to 'respect' human rights. The duty of respect encompasses both actions of avoidance and precaution, as well as actions of mitigation and prevention for adverse human rights impacts directly linked to a business enterprise's operations, products or services.[294] The inclusion of products and services within the ambit of a business's duty of respect catches the users of mineral commodities within the net of human rights compliance. It lends support, for example, to existing initiatives such as the Kimberly Certification Scheme and the Responsible Jewelry Council, but arguably opens up debate on the human rights impacts of downstream users of bulk precious and industrial mineral commodities as well.

The business duty to respect human rights applies in respect of 'internationally recognized human rights'.[295] As noted above, notwithstanding the recently formulated Framework Principles, there is still no explicit recognition of

---

290 Ruggie Principles (n 260) 4 (Principle 1).
291 Ibid 4–5.
292 Ibid 5.
293 Ibid 4.
294 Ibid 15 (Principle 13).
295 Ibid 14 (Principle 12).

a human right to a safe, clean, healthy and sustainable environment in a human rights instrument of global application. This may in part explain the mining industry's tendency to juxtapose its human rights and environmental performance. For example, in the ICMM's 2009 review of human rights, environmental issues were not discussed under select 'human rights-related issues'. The ICMM explained that though protection of the environment was 'clearly an aspect of upholding human rights', good practice in this area 'had for some time been well understood and documented'.[296] However, this statement misses the strong interdependency between environmental and other human rights, and obfuscates the environment as an issue of human rights concern in and of itself. With the formulation of the Framework Principles, there is a need to revisit such good practices on the basis that the right to a safe and clean environment now forms part of 'internationally recognized human rights'.

To meet their responsibility to respect human rights, business enterprises should have in place: (1) a high level policy commitment to meet their responsibility to respect human rights; (2) a human rights due diligence process to identify, prevent, mitigate and account for how they address their impacts on human rights; and (3) processes to enable remediation of adverse human rights impacts which business enterprises have caused or to which they have contributed.[297] This is a foundational principle, supported by more detailed operational guidance.[298] Although the norms of respect outlined in this second part of the Ruggie Principles apply only to business enterprises, States feature contextually: first, through their lawmaking power to set the parameters for the exercise of a business enterprise's human rights obligations; second, through their capacity, collectively, to determine the scope and content of 'internationally recognized human rights'. Business enterprises must '[c]omply with all applicable laws and respect internationally recognized human rights wherever they operate'.[299] In fact, when faced with 'conflicting requirements', business enterprises must seek ways of honouring the latter, rather than domestic laws.[300]

The Ruggie Principles strongly emphasize the right to remedy. The State's duty to establish effective judicial and nonjudicial mechanisms to remedy business-related human rights abuses undergirds its duty to protect, for without such mechanisms it would be rendered weak, even meaningless.[301] Although this part of the Ruggie Principles directs business enterprises to establish

---

296 ICMM Human Rights Guidance (n 258) 4.
297 Ruggie Principles (n 260) 17 (Principle 15).
298 Ibid 17–27 (Principles 16–24).
299 Ibid 26 (Principle 23(a)).
300 Ibid 26 (Principle 23(b)).
301 Ibid 28.

operational-level grievance mechanisms for individuals and communities to voice allegations of adverse human rights impacts,[302] the focus really falls on the State and the efficacy, fairness and integrity of judicial and nonjudicial processes. In the case of judicial mechanisms, States are specifically directed to reduce legal, practical and other barriers that lead to a denial of access to remedy, for example, the attribution of legal remedy amongst members of a corporate group, or accessing justice in a business enterprise's home State for a human rights abuse perpetrated in a host State.[303] States are also required to guard the integrity of the courts, ensuring that corruption does not impede access to justice.[304]

5.4 Conclusion

The international framework for human rights presents a richly developed set of norms for the State's protective role in relation to mining. Grave human rights abuses can arise throughout the mining cycle. Both 'human rights' and 'the environment' emerge as objects of protection. The State must protect the environment for the sake of upholding human rights, and uphold human rights for better protection of the environment; protect the life, liberty and security of human rights defenders; and protect against human rights abuses through facilitative, regulatory, punitive, structural and reflective roles that enable businesses to respect human rights. The human rights frameworks discussed in this section, however, are all relatively new. Notwithstanding limited work on this issue by the ICMM, States and mining companies have yet to fully protect and respect the constellation of human rights associated with mining.

6. FEMINIST CRITIQUES OF MINING

Feminist critiques of mining constitute a fifth discourse of mining dissent. Feminist critiques have drawn attention to the hypermasculinized image of mining and the failure to acknowledge women's agency in mining. This agency extends to women's productive role in mining activities, their productive role in reproducing labour and caring for the sick and their resistance to mining.[305] The range of women foregrounded by this critique thus includes

302 Ibid 32 (Principle 29).
303 Ibid 30 (Principle 26).
304 Ibid.
305 Kuntala Lahiri-Dutt, 'Digging women: Towards a new agenda for feminist critiques of mining' (2012) 19(2) *Gender, Place and Culture* 195, 196.

women miners, the wives and partners of male miners and women whose bodies and livelihoods are affected by mining.[306]

Lozeva and Marinova, for instance, state that mining is probably 'the best example of an industry that displays traits of masculinity and dominance'.[307] The popular image of the miner as the quintessential masculine icon of the working class grew out of the dangerous, dirty and risky working conditions that existed in early modern mines.[308] Supported by moralistic and religious conceptions of 'true womanhood' in the early twentieth century, the ILO passed Conventions that cemented the notion of separate (and disparate) productive spheres for men and women in mining, even as these Conventions tried to protect women from exploitation.[309] During the course of the twentieth century, protective legislation banning women from underground work contributed to a decline in the proportion of women in productive mining activities, as did technological change. The gigantic machines for which the mining industry is known have become associated with men.[310] The machismo associated with mining plant has in turn extended to popular representations of mining entrepreneurs, corporate actors and shareholders.[311]

The mainstream response to a male dominated industry has been to call for greater integration of women in the mining sector, and a number of 'Women in Mining' associations have grown worldwide.[312] Even so, some of these initiatives are tainted by problematic, essentialist gender assumptions. The World Bank's 'Gender in Extractive Industries' project, for example, calls for women to have equitable access to jobs, education and participation in the mining sector.[313] Highlighting the benefits of including women, the Bank argues that women can make better employees, as they 'are often more reliable, follow rules, obey health and safety regulations, and can be more reliable employ-

---

[306] Silvia Lozeva and Dora Marinova, 'Negotiating gender: Experience from Western Australian mining industry' (2010) 13(2) *Journal of Economic and Social Policy* 2.

[307] Ibid 3.

[308] Lahiri-Dutt (n 305) 197.

[309] These included the ILO's 1919 Convention on Night Work, and the 1935 Underground Work (Women) Convention prohibiting women from being employed underground in a mine in both public and private undertakings. See Lahiri-Dutt (n 305) 204.

[310] Lahiri-Dutt (n 305) 196.

[311] Ibid; Robyn Mayes and Barbara Pini, 'The "feminine revolution in mining": A critique' (2010) 41(2) *Australian Geographer* 233.

[312] See for example the International Women in Mining network, https://internationalwim.org, accessed 24 February 2019.

[313] World Bank, 'Gender in extractive industries', www.worldbank.org/en/topic/extractiveindustries/brief/gender-in-extractive-industries, accessed 24 February 2019.

ees'.[314] This statement clearly justifies the feminist critique of policy advice emanating from IFIs, that is, that the so-called business case for women in mining 'hinges upon the instrumental value of women as cheap and available labour to enhance the efficiency of private sector and economic growth'.[315]

Feminist historians have demonstrated that the hypermasculinity of the mining industry is a twentieth century construction, and that a greater proportion of women used to be actively engaged in mining.[316] There is also an extensive literature documenting the engagement of women in artisanal and smallscale mining, particularly in economies with large informal sectors.[317] In the masculinized imagery of mining, women nevertheless tend to be represented as miners' wives or caregivers,[318] a construct reinforced by the sustainable mineral development consensus. In its report on gender disparities, for example, *Breaking New Ground* noted that '[i]n occupational communities, women are more often spouses of mine employees, and are therefore passive recipients of benefits'.[319]

Feminist critique that challenges this disempowering representation of women and unearths their agency calls attention to the notion of 'unpaid care'. Unpaid care references:

> [T]he processes involved in maintaining and reproducing people, specifically the labouring population, and their labour power on a daily and generational basis. It involves the provision of food, clothing, shelter, basic safety and health care, along with the development and transmission of knowledge, social values and cultural practices and the construction of individual and collective identities.[320]

Unpaid care is a feminist issue because it is poorly measured in formal metrics of economic activity, is regarded as unskilled and is therefore poorly compen-

---

314 Ibid.

315 Lahiri-Dutt (n 305) 195.

316 See for example J Gier and Laurie Mercier (eds), *Mining Women: Gender in the Development of a Global Industry, 1670–2005* (Palgrave 2006); Jane L Parpart, 'Class and gender on the copperbelt: Women in Northern Rhodesian copper mining communities, 1926–1964' in Claire Robertson and Iris Berger, *Women and Class in Africa* (Africana Publishing Company 1986) 141–60.

317 See for example, Kuntala Lahiri-Dutt and Martha Macintyre, *Women Miners in Developing Countries: Pit Women and Others* (Ashgate 2006); Daniele Moretti, 'The gender of the gold: An ethnographic and historical account of women's involvement in artisanal and smallscale mining in Mount Kaindi, Papua New Guinea' (2006) 76(2) *Oceania* 133.

318 Lahiri-Dutt (n 305) 197.

319 *Breaking New Ground* (n 33) 205.

320 K Bezanson and M Luxton, *Social Reproduction: Feminist Political Economy Challenges Neo-Liberalism* (McGill-Queen's University Press 2006) 3.

sated.[321] Through unpaid care, women 'participate in, shape and contribute to the ambitions and profits of the extractivist industries' in myriad and complex ways that are largely also invisible and unremunerated.[322] Feminist research has shown how women take on leadership, social and welfare roles that assist in sustaining mining communities.[323] In contexts where the mining industry relies on migrant labour, women's unpaid care takes the form of sustaining subsistence agriculture in the labour-sending areas. Research on this phenomenon in the South African gold mining industry, for example, has demonstrated how the single sex, migrant hostels on the gold mining fields eliminated the need to pay a 'family wage', and enabled the payment of an even lower wage as the male miners' activities were being subsidised by women's agricultural subsistence work in distant rural villages.[324] Women's caregiving to the sick also subsidises the mining industry, as it is women who tend to take on the role of tending to male miners who have acquired a mining-related occupational disease or sustained an occupational injury.[325] Further, if miners die prior to receiving compensation for occupational injury or disease, their claims are usually not transmissible to their female caregivers and dependents.

Women's nonmining productive role was recognized in the recent South African case of *Nkala & others v. Harmony Gold Mining Company Limited.*[326] The case was an application for the certification of a class action suit against the South African gold mining industry for damages arising from the occupational diseases of silicosis and tuberculosis. One of the legal questions posed to the court was whether the mineworkers' delictual (tort) claims for pain and suffering, loss of amenities of life and disfigurement were transmissible to their dependents. In a resounding victory for the mineworkers and their female counterparts, the court decided that the claims were transmissible, drawing upon a feminist understanding of the role of women in mining production.[327]

---

[321] Womin, 'Women's unseen contribution to the extractives industry: Their unpaid labour' Paper Four: Women, Gender and Extractivism in Africa: A collection of papers (IANRA) 2 (henceforth Womin: Paper Four).

[322] Ibid.

[323] Lahiri-Dutt (n 305) 198.

[324] Womin: Paper Four (n 321) 10.

[325] See the case study on asbestosis in Womin: Paper Four (n 321) 14–15.

[326] 2016 (5) SA 240 (GJ).

[327] For example, at paragraph 192 the court stated: 'The evidence they brought shows that the mineworkers come from rural areas ("labour providing areas") where they are dependent largely upon home-based care to assist them in coping with their illnesses. Such care is ordinarily provided by their wives and daughters. The care-work is demanding and includes efforts such as carrying, lifting and bathing the mineworkers, monitoring their medication, and staying up at night to attend to their needs'. The court further reasoned: 'Often, the care work requires full-time attention, effectively

A further dimension of the feminist critique of mining centres upon the manner in which mining uniquely, and disproportionately, affects women. This phenomenon has also been recognized by the sustainable mineral development consensus. *Breaking New Ground* acknowledged that as subsistence farmers, herders and agriculturalists, women are 'likely to be disproportionately affected by any negative environmental consequences of mining'.[328] The report also notes the increased incidences of family violence and marital breakups that can result from men spending extensive amounts of time away, the risk of women picking up sexually transmissible diseases from partners home on leave and cases of sexual abuse of indigenous women and girls.[329]

Feminist scholars acknowledge these effects but take issue with the underlying representation of women 'as victims, bearers of dislocations, or daughters who have dubious links with Mother Earth'.[330] In feminist scholarship and activist literature on these issues, women are more likely to be represented as having strong agency. For example, in a report on how mining affects the land and food sovereignty of peasant women, Womin highlights how women are affected by actual loss of land for farming and harvesting of natural resources, the impact of mining on water, the impacts of water and environmental pollution and loss of male agricultural labour and other contributions due to migration.[331] In response, women are 'mobilizing' to address the abrupt loss of their partners' mine jobs, 'organizing' to hold mining companies accountable, 'leading' community campaigns and 'reclaiming' land.[332]

These different representations of women and mining and the issues women face manifest in different claims on the State. The sustainable mineral development consensus tends to focus on softer, and more generic interventions. For example, to address gender disparities in mining, *Breaking New Ground* calls on governments to examine legislation restricting women's work in mines

---

compelling many women and girls to forego income-generating, educational, and other opportunities. Should the mineworkers receive compensation for the pain and suffering and loss of amenities of life they endured, (i.e. general damages) these women and girls would benefit therefrom by reducing the care-work they provide. It would also indirectly compensate them for the care-work they have already provided.'

[328] *Breaking New Ground* (n 33) 205.

[329] Ibid.

[330] Lahiri-Dutt (n 305) 194.

[331] Womin, 'Land and food sovereignty undermined: Impacts on peasant women' Paper Three: Women, Gender and Extractivism in Africa: A collection of papers (IANRA) (henceforth Womin: Paper Three).

[332] Ibid iii. For the representation of women in sex work, the transmissibility of HIV/AIDS and violence against women, see Womin, 'Extractivism's impacts on women's bodies, sexuality and autonomy' Paper Five: Women, Gender and Extractivism in Africa: A collection of papers (IANRA) (henceforth Womin: Paper Five).

using 'current scientific evidence', to develop national gender specific policies on access to credit and land ownership for women and to encourage the formation of 'loose associations, cooperatives and savings clubs among women', and so on.[333] The recommendations from overtly feminist organizations highlight more far reaching reforms, such as transforming women's land rights within communal tenure systems, ensuring just and fair compensation for any losses related to land rights or livelihoods, empowering women with legal authority and knowledge to freely influence decisionmaking about mines,[334] and decriminalizing and regulating prostitution.[335]

7. CONCLUSION

This chapter has outlined five discourses of mining dissent that frame the claims of social actors that oppose the claims of pro-mining advocates. They represent a range of State roles: from the predatory State of the resource curse theory, needing to rein itself in through institutional controls designed to sterilize Dutch disease; to the protective and facilitative but also complicit and abdicating State associated with Indigenous Peoples' rights; to the heroic State of environmental justice; to the regulatory, punitive, facilitative, structural and reflective State associated with various dimensions of human rights and feminist critiques. These different roles manifest in a constellation of State responsibilities, but the legal status of the State's expected conduct is not uniform. The discourses of Indigenous Peoples' rights and human rights set forth the most legally entrenched norms of State conduct. In some instances, this overlaps with the concerns of environmental justice advocates. But calls for more radical State action – strong corrective and social justice for instance, or the demands of feminist scholars – have not yet been legally entrenched.

Despite areas of overlap, there is not necessarily a common agenda among discourses of mining dissent. There is support for mining – among some Indigenous Peoples, for example, and in the women in mining movement. While the resource curse theory cautions against the too rapid assimilation of mineral resource rents, it does not dispute that mining can contribute to development. There are also different objects of protection, from the social construct of Indigenous Peoples, to groups marginalized on the basis of colour and race, to more abstract notions of human rights, to the women involved in or affected by mining. To protect these different pockets of society against the economic, social and environmental impacts of mining, the State is expected to institute

333 *Breaking New Ground* (n 33) 213.
334 Womin: Paper Three (n 331) 22.
335 Womin: Paper Five (n 332) 23.

a very wide range of institutional and legal controls. While the discourses of mining dissent may not serve a common agenda, they nevertheless collectively constitute the State's protective role under Polanyi's double movement.

Do discourses of mining dissent expose the hard political choices needed to transition to a postextractivist mining model? At least three of the discourses of dissent – the resource curse thesis, Indigenous Peoples' rights and the entire human rights framework – are firmly positioned within a mainstream neoliberal model that views economic growth, good governance, rights frameworks and upholding the rule of law as sufficient to contain the negative social, economic and environmental effects of mining. With the exception of conceptions of social justice in environmental justice narratives, some strands of the Indigenous Peoples' movements and some strands of feminist critique, there is little engagement on the need for alternative models of development.

The chapter has documented the mining industry's engagement with discourses of dissent, which is also not uniform. From a belated engagement with the resource curse thesis, to position statements on Indigenous Peoples' rights and FPIC, to its contribution to the business and human rights debate and gender disparities, the mining industry has been alive to the claims of its critics. However, the chapter has also demonstrated how agents of the sustainable mineral development consensus – inclusive of IFIs and the ICMM – have used language that reframes discourses of dissent in a manner that technocratizes and waters down claims of discrimination and harm.

4. The State, mining and property institutions

1. INTRODUCTION

The preceding two chapters outlined favourable and dissenting discourses on mining, development, sustainability and the role of the State. They have demonstrated the variety that exists in conceptualizing the State as both promoter of, and protector against, mining. Taken together, these roles give effect to the double movement necessary to establish and sustain a disembedded market in mineral exploration and exploitation and secure its political and social legitimacy.

But the double movement not only exists at the level of broadranging, overarching narratives on mining, development and sustainability. It also operates at the level of more detailed, technical prescriptions relating to property, taxation, environmental assessment and mine closure, among other areas of mining governance. It is through the policies, rules and institutions within each of these areas that the key claims of the dominant favourable and dissenting mining narratives are realized, or not. Accordingly, commencing with mining and property institutions, the following four chapters take the analysis of the double movement to this level. As will become evident, in each of these four areas, there is a dominant patterning of State roles giving effect to the double movement and driving unsustainable mineral extraction.

Property institutions have played a critical role in disembedding the market for mineral exploration and exploitation,[1] and securing a stable supply of mineral raw materials. Property laws, that is, play a particularly important role

---

[1] In most countries mineral extraction is regulated through two main categories of exploitation rights: the exploration permit or licence, and the exploitation concession or licence. References to mining rights in this chapter are intended to include both types of authorization (see Elizabeth Bastida, 'A review of the concept of security of mineral tenure: Issues and challenges' (2001) 19 *Journal of Energy and Natural Resources Law* 31, 33). The distinction between exploration and exploitation rights turns on the distinction between searching for minerals, on the one hand, and 'winning' such minerals, on the other – that is, extracting such minerals from their natural state and disposing of waste substances arising through this process.

in strengthening the first arm of the double movement. This has been achieved through policies that support separate rights to minerals from rights to land, distinguish rights to minerals as such from rights to extract them, institute the State as a centralized authority that acts on behalf of the people, and reinforce a raft of rules that secure the primacy and efficacy of mining as a land use and the security of mining ventures. The separation of mineral and mining rights from other land rights is a construction that is already centuries old, with different permutations in different regions. But crafting such rights to serve the dictates of a globalized market economy is a more recent phenomenon, beginning in the developed regions of the world during the Industrial Revolution. During the latter half of the twentieth century, and particularly from the 1980s onwards as direct State participation in the mining sector began to wane, policy advocacy and legal reforms aimed at establishing disembedded markets for mining in the furthest regions of the Earth have sped up significantly.

This chapter focuses on the dominant model for the State's role in relation to mining and property, a model that centres on (1) differentiating mineral and mining rights from surface rights to land and (2) allocating mining rights to third parties.[2] The dominant model is based on a distinction between the State as centralized, national landlord of minerals, and the State as a concessioning authority for mining rights. Pivoting on these two major roles, the State undertakes a variety of functions – maintaining a mineral rights cadastre, archiving geological knowledge, ensuring the efficacy and primacy of mining, allocating mining rights and providing security of tenure. This current articulation of mineral and mining rights around a centralized, national authority serves as a precondition for, and facilitates mining capital flows in, both private and State-led forms of extractivism.[3]

---

2 As with the discourses outlined in Chapters 2 and 3, the dominant model is reconstructed from a variety of sources, particularly the strategy and policy documents put forward by the international financial institutions (IFIs), the Intergovernmental Forum on Mining (IGF) and the International Council of Mining and Metals (ICMM). The emphasis in this and subsequent chapters, however, shifts to the laws of mineral-rich jurisdictions.

3 Jody Emel *et al*, 'Extracting sovereignty: Capital, territory and gold mining in Tanzania' (2011) 30 *Political Geography* 70.

2. MINING RIGHTS: PRESENTING THE DOMINANT MODEL

Breaking New Ground, the final report of the industry-driven Mining, Minerals and Sustainable Development (MMSD) project, explained the dominant model for mineral property relations as follows:

> [T]he surface rights to land are under either public or private ownership in most countries, whereas the mineral rights are generally owned solely by the state. The state then grants those rights to mining companies through concessions or permits. These are often granted as a matter of right to those who meet criteria specified by law.[4]

This statement highlights (1) a distinction between surface rights to land and rights to minerals as such (which may occur in surface formations or underground) and (2) a distinction between rights to minerals and the right to undertake mining activities. The State's major roles of national landlord and concessioning authority, as detailed below, pivot on these two fundamental conceptual distinctions.

2.1 Mineral Rights: The State as National Landlord

The State's role as national landlord of minerals has ancient origins. In contemporary times, this role has been entrenched in the constitutions and laws of mineral-rich jurisdictions. The tendency towards the State as central, national authority over mineral resources tends to be the same, irrespective of whether policy in a mineral-rich jurisdiction tends more towards private- or State-led extractivism. The State's landlord role is associated with a variety of further functions, namely maintaining a mineral cadastre, securing geological data and entrenching the efficacy and primacy of mining as a land use.

As national landlord of mineral resources, the State is not necessarily the owner of such resources. As discussed below, thinkers in common and civil law jurisdictions have grappled with the 'problem' of mineral ownership and how it relates to State control and public and private ownership of land.[5] Control in this context encompasses the decision to decide whether, and when, mineral resources should be exploited. Initially, common law systems tended

---

[4] International Institute for Environment and Development and World Business Council for Sustainable Development, *Breaking New Ground: Mining, Minerals and Sustainable Development* (Earthscan 2002) 143 (henceforth *Breaking New Ground*).

[5] Nicolas J Campbell, 'Principles of mineral ownership in the civil and common law systems' (1956–7) 31 *Tulane Law Review* 303.

more towards a private conception of mineral ownership/control. In civil law systems the approach has always been more State-centric.[6] Some jurisdictions have vacillated between private and State-centric mineral rights systems over time.[7] Nevertheless, in civil and common law systems alike, and over long spans of time, the authorities tended to consolidate and centralize the right to mine in a manner that advantaged mining, even as the 'ownership' of minerals as such attached to land ownership.[8] The State's role was more often than not justified on the basis of the 'patent national importance of the mining industry'.[9]

In Roman law, the principle of *cuius est solum, eius est usque ad coelum ad inferos* held sway, roughly translated as 'to whomever the soil belongs he owns also to the sky and to the depths' (the *ad coelum* doctrine).[10] Although this phrase was not in fact used by any of the authors of the Roman sources[11] – it is rather attributed to the thirteenth century glossator Accursius[12] – it was nevertheless the pattern according to which the law developed, beginning with a fusion of land and mineral rights in private hands, or the principle of the 'nonseparation' of mineral rights.[13] Minerals were not in themselves capable of ownership prior to the separation from the ore body in which they were located, they were regarded as 'fruits' of the land.[14] Roman governors granted third parties the right to mine on public lands. This was not a departure from the *ad coelum* doctrine, since the 'State' was the owner of the land.[15] The

---

6 Michael O Dale, 'Security of tenure as a key issue facing the international mining company: A South African perspective' (1996) 14 *Journal of Energy and Natural Resources Law* 298, 308.

7 See for example H Mostert, *Mineral Law* (Juta 2012) for a particularly in-depth account of mineral property relations in South Africa over the course of more than a century.

8 MO Dale, *An Historical and Comparative Study of the Concept and Acquisition of Mineral Rights* (1979) Thesis submitted in part fulfilment for the degree of Doctor of Laws, University of South Africa 36.

9 Ibid.

10 Owen L Anderson, 'Lord Coke, the Restatement, and modern subsurface trespass law' (2010) 57 *57th Annual Institute on Mineral Law* Article 6.

11 Roman law on mining and metals has been gleaned from the comments of jurists such as Sabinus, imperial legislation (the *Lex Metalli Vipascensis* and the *Lex Metallis Dicta*, discovered in 1876 and 1906 respectively) and the chapter *De Metallis et Metallariis* in the *Codex Theodosianus* (C.T.10.19).

12 Accursius took it upon himself to systematize the medieval comments on Justinian's *Corpus Iuris Civlis* (see C Lincoln Bouvé, 'Private ownership of airspace' 1 *Air Law Review* 232, 246–8).

13 Dale (n 8) 3.

14 Ibid 4.

15 Ibid 5. The term 'State' is being used here with awareness that public authority in Rome differed considerably from the manner in which the term 'State' is used in a modern, neoliberal context.

authorities' conferment of a right to mine on public lands also entrenched a system of mineral royalties. The imperial legislation of the time stipulated, for example, that the discoverer of a mine on public land obtained a right to mine it, provided he paid a lump sum to the *procurator*, a government representative.[16] The State could also reserve a share of the mine to itself, which could fall away in respect of certain mines if the discoverer or 'occupier' of the mine paid a lump sum.[17] During the time of the late Empire (from the fourth century AD), the Roman authorities extended control over the right to mine on private lands, thus restricting private mineral ownership.[18] This trend is evidenced by legal rules imposing an obligation on the occupier of a mine to pay a royalty in favour of the landowner and/or the State for mining on private land.[19]

Under Germanic law, rights to minerals and the power to authorize mining also attached to land ownership.[20] Germanic law developed to recognize payment of a fee or royalty to the landowner as consideration for the right to mine – the concept of 'regal'.[21] This royalty payment later became payable to the King, who in turn tributed the right to receive such monies, and to grant the right to mine, to members of the nobility.[22] The development of this 'Bergregal' occurred over the course of a few centuries and led to the separation of a right to mine from land ownership. The right to mine, and the power to grant such right to financially able persons, vested exclusively in the king and the nobles.[23] According to German legal historian Heinrich Matteis, the separation of land and mineral rights ownership was justified on the basis that mining required an entirely different technique to that of agriculture.[24]

In England, the *cuius est solum* rule was affirmed in the case of *Bury v. Pope* (1587).[25] From the earliest times, the development of English mineral

---

[16] Ibid 6.
[17] Ibid.
[18] Ibid 3.
[19] Ibid 9.
[20] Ibid 16.
[21] Ibid 17.
[22] Ibid 18.
[23] Ibid 19.
[24] H Mitteis, *Deutsche Privatrecht: Ein Studienbuch* (Beck 1950) 83.
[25] Scholars have suggested that Accursius' son, who held high office under the Crown of Edward I, introduced this principle in England, paving the way for its later affirmation in the case of *Bury v. Pope* (1587) (see Bouvé (n 12) 232, 246–8). In his eighteenth-century *Commentaries* Blackstone also used the phrase, pointing out that land had an 'indefinite extent, upwards as well as downwards' and that downwards 'whatever is in a direct line between the surface of any land, and the center of the earth, belongs to the owner of the surface; as is everyday's experience in the mining countries. And therefore if a man grants all his lands, he grants thereby all his mines of metal and

and mining law was strongly influenced by the nobility's hold over land and thus followed a different development trajectory compared to continental legal systems. This was felt, in particular, through the reservation of certain minerals to the Crown, and reservation of the right to mine on certain types of feudal land.[26] While it is contentious whether Roman law recognized regalian rights to minerals,[27] from the sixteenth century all gold and silver (Royal metals), whether situated on public or private land, vested in the Crown. According to Blackstone, the sovereign's royal prerogative over gold and silver arose to facilitate the availability of metal for coinage.[28] Over and above a separate right to minerals and to mines, English law provided various legal forms for entering upon land and removing minerals. Landowners, or the owner of a separate mineral estate, could grant a separate right to remove minerals by way of a profit à prendre.[29] As a limited, incorporeal right, a profit à prendre granted a holder the right to enter upon and use a servient tenement and to remove some part of the soil or minerals under it.[30]

This brief historical survey shows that even in common law systems where mineral rights initially attached to private land ownership, over time the system drifted towards more State-centric forms of control. This was justified on the basis of the importance of the mining industry, or its special features in relation to other industries. In modern common and civil law systems, however, rights to minerals and to mine have become fully disembedded from land ownership. States the world over have firmly asserted control over mineral resources. It is rare to find this control expressed as ownership.[31] More commonly, State landlordship is articulated in a manner that gives effect to a (1) regalian or (2) domanial mineral resource system.

Under a regalian system, the State assumes a role of custodianship, not ownership. Mineral resources belong to no one until they are discovered, and the State uses its regalian power to grant mining rights.[32] The Indonesian Constitution, for example, provides that '[t]he land, the waters and the natural resources within shall be under the powers of the State and shall be used to the

---

other fossils' (William Blackstone, *Commentaries on the Laws of England* (Clarendon 1765–9) Chapter 2, Book 2, 18).

[26] Dale (n 8) 43.

[27] Ibid 44.

[28] Blackstone (n 25) 264.

[29] Ibid 48.

[30] Ibid 52.

[31] The mining law of Botswana is something of an outlier, stating that 'all rights of ownership in minerals are vested in the Republic', Mines and Minerals Act, 1999 (Botswana) s 3.

[32] Emel (n 3) 72.

greatest benefit of the people'.[33] In Mongolia, the Constitution states that the 'land, its subsoil . . . and other natural assets . . . shall be subject to the people's authority and under the protection of the State'.[34] Similarly, the Constitution of Uzbekistan holds that the 'land, its minerals . . . and other natural resources shall constitute the national wealth and shall be rationally used and protected by the state'.[35] In South Africa, the mining law states that '[m]ineral and petroleum resources are the common heritage of all the people of South Africa and the State is the custodian thereof for the benefit of all South Africans'.[36] In these formulations, references to 'people', 'national wealth', 'heritage' and 'benefit' institute the State as protector or custodian of mineral resources.

Under a domanial system, which tends to be more common in mineral-rich jurisdictions, minerals are the property of the State.[37] Formulations vary in terms of whether property is vested in the State, the Republic or the President, and how the high level meaning and purposes of mining are framed. The Constitution of Ghana, for example, states that '[e]very mineral in its natural state . . . is the property of the Republic of Ghana and shall be vested in the President on behalf of, and in trust for the people of Ghana'.[38] A new, draft Tanzanian Constitution specifies that '[a]ll national resources including mining, gas and oil are public property, and the Government of the United Republic or the Government of Zanzibar shall make provision to ensure it is used for the benefit of present and future generations'.[39] In a more extended version, the Constitution of Ecuador states that '[n]onrenewable natural resources and, in general, products coming from the ground, mineral and petroleum deposits . . . are the unalienable property of the State, immune from seizure and not subject to a statute of limitations'.[40] Nonrenewable natural resources are part of the unalienable heritage of the State and, in managing these sectors, the State must 'give priority to responsibility between generations, the conservation of nature, the charging of royalties or other non-tax contributions and corporate shares' and must 'minimize the negative impacts of an environmental, cultural, social and economic nature'.[41] Notable is that all these formulations emphasize the need to use mineral resources to secure a public benefit.

---

[33] Constitution of the Republic of Indonesia, 1945, Article 33(3).

[34] Constitution of Mongolia, 1992, Article 6.

[35] Constitution of Uzbekistan, 1992, Article 55.

[36] Mineral and Petroleum Resources Development Act, 2002 (South Africa), section 3(1).

[37] Ibid.

[38] Constitution of the Republic of Ghana, Article 257(6).

[39] Proposed Draft Constitution of Tanzania (September 2014), Article 25.

[40] Constitution of Ecuador, 1998, Article 408.

[41] Ibid, Article 317.

Irrespective of the positioning of the State as custodian or as holder of mineral resources as a form of public property, the function of these high level statements is the same: to institute the State as a centralized landlord of mineral resources, usually at a national level of government. Creating a single point of reference for mineral rights plays an important role in facilitating the flow of mining capital and promoting extractivism.[42]

In Australia and Canada, mineral resources are also subject to centralized authority, although high level statements to this effect will not be found in the federal or provincial constitutions. Here the State's assertion of control over mineral resources stretches back into the late nineteenth century, and was often effected through the legal construction of 'reserving' minerals to the State. Following the example set by the United Kingdom, the 1831 land regulations in New South Wales contained a provision that in all grants the Crown would reserve to itself all mines of gold, silver and coal. And by 1884 governors had been given powers to declare mining a 'public purpose', enabling them to effect an absolute reservation of minerals in land.[43] The colonial governments of other Australian states followed suit, leading to a situation today where throughout Australia the Crown, in right of the State, owns nearly all the minerals. The Queensland Mineral Resources Act, 1989, for example, distinguishes between gold, coal and all other minerals. Gold on or below the surface of the land is the property of the Crown.[44] Coal and all other minerals generally vest in the Crown, with the exception of specific historical transactions.[45] Here, the construction of 'reservation' rather than national wealth, heritage, custodianship or public property secured the State's centralized control over mineral resources.[46]

The State's role as national landlord of mineral resources is usually associated with two additional sets of functions: maintaining a mineral rights cadastre, and promoting geological exploration.[47] Through its role as national landlord, the State also specifies legal entitlements and duties that have the

---

[42] This argument is developed in sections 2.2 and 2.3 below.

[43] AC Veatch and Walter Lowrie Fischer, *Mining Laws of Australia and New Zealand* (1911).

[44] Mineral Resources Act, 1989 (Queensland), section 8(1).

[45] Mineral Resources Act, 1989 (Queensland), sections 8(2) and (3).

[46] See section 8(4) which provides that each deed of grant or lease of unallocated State land must contain a reservation of minerals on and below the surface of the land, and the right of access for prospecting, exploring or mining.

[47] EO Girones, A Pugachevsky and G Walser, *Mineral Rights Cadastre: Promoting Transparent Access to Mineral Resources* (World Bank 2009) 12. This World Bank document outlines the functions of so-called Public Mineral Institutions, which comprise the Ministry of Mines, the Mineral Rights Cadastre, the Geological Survey and the Mines Inspectorate.

effect of securing the efficacy and primacy of mining. These additional functions are outlined in the sections that follow. All these additional functions have the effect of promoting mining.

2.1.1 Keeper of the mineral rights cadastre

As national landlord, the State is expected to maintain a mineral rights cadastre, that is, a public institution charged with maintaining a comprehensive public register of mining titles, their geographical coordinates and details of ownership. The mandate of a mineral rights cadastre, according to research sponsored by the World Bank, is to act as a liaison between the State and holders of exploitation titles. To undertake this function, the State must process applications for new licences, deal with changes to the initial grant of exploitation rights and act as a technical referee if disputes arise between different mining title holders. The State must also maintain a public register and cadastral maps.[48] The working of the mineral cadastre, as a State institution, is often set out in the national mining law.[49] The 2002 Mining Code of the Democratic Republic of the Congo, for instance, established a mining registry as the 'guardian' of mineral and quarry exploration rights.[50] The functions of the registry included registering applications for mineral and quarry rights, decisions on the granting of rights, the 'transformation' and lease of such rights, securities on mining assets and so on.[51]

The State's role over a mineral rights cadastre, however, is not ideologically neutral. It contributes to the construction of mineral rights as separate from land, and facilitates the conditions for a functioning global market in mining rights. A properly recorded mining title is aligned with investor protection, buttressing the exclusivity of the entitlement to undertake mining activities and thus advancing the miner's security of tenure.[52] *Breaking New Ground* highlighted mining titles registration as an area of institutional reform,[53] and identified mining companies as the primary beneficiaries: 'Companies rely on constantly evolving databases and enhancements of the mining cadastre.'[54]

At the same time, a mineral rights cadastre potentially undergirds the State's facilitative and regulatory role in respect of taxation, environmental assessment and mine closure. The IGF's *Mining Policy Framework*, for

---

48 Ibid 13.

49 See, for example, Law on Subsoil, Republic of Uzbekistan, 2002, Articles 11–14 as an example.

50 Mining Code, 2002 (DRC), Article 12.

51 Ibid.

52 Girones (n 47) 9–10.

53 *Breaking New Ground* (n 4) 178.

54 Ibid 294.

example, holds that a cadastre system and land tenure rules and regulations are 'not driven by the needs of mining', but are instead 'a national planning and administration necessity'.[55] A sound cadastre system is one in which the population has confidence that it contributes to social satisfaction, reduces recourse to legal action and supports all manner of developmental activity, of which mining is only one.[56]

There is a dearth of in-country and comparative research on the functioning of the mineral rights cadastre, on the one hand as an administrative clearing-house for mining titles and on the other as an institution that could aid in monitoring contributions to development. How mining title registration offices can also serve as a single institutional repository for information on environmental authorizations and compliance, or the provision of security for mine closure, are unexplored areas of research and action.

2.1.2 Repository of geological data

Apart from establishing and maintaining a mineral rights cadastre, States spanning the Western, former Communist, and now developing worlds have also played a critical role in the advancement of geological knowledge. During the Victorian era, Western States invested heavily in training highly qualified people by subsidizing university schools and research centres,[57] and in establishing geological surveys.[58] The oldest of these were founded in the late 1800s. The British Geological Survey, for example, was established in 1835 as an 'essential public service' with a mandate to undertake the geological mapping of Britain.[59] An Act of Congress established the United States Geological Survey in 1879, charging this institution with 'classification of the public lands, and examination of the geological structure, mineral resources and products of the national domain'.[60] During the golden post-Second World

---

55 Intergovernmental Forum on Mining, Minerals, Metals and Sustainable Development, *IGF Mining Policy Framework: Mining and Sustainable Development* (October 2013) 24.

56 Ibid.

57 Michel Jébrak, 'Innovations in mineral exploration: Targets, methods and organization since the first globalization period' (June 2012) Occasional Paper Université de Québec à Montréal 16.

58 Ibid 16.

59 PJ Cook and PM Allen, 'The example of the British Geological Survey: Past, present and future' Technical Report WO/92/16 (National Environment Research Council, 1992) 4. For information on the current British Geological Survey see www.bgs.ac.uk/, accessed 24 February 2019.

60 Mary C Rabbitt, 'The United States Geological Survey: 1879–1989' US Geological Circular 1050, https://pubs.usgs.gov/circ/c1050/index.htm, accessed 24 February 2019.

War phase the activities of these geological surveys expanded considerably,[61] but downsizing took place at the turn of the twenty-first century.[62]

A State-sponsored geological survey is supposed to develop and maintain 'reliable national earth science infrastructure', including geological maps and databases.[63] Although not necessarily instituting a State monopoly of geological services, the mining laws of a number of mineral-rich jurisdictions assign responsibility to the State to investigate the geological potential of the national territory, compile geological data, develop maps and information tools and assist members of the public. In the Philippines, for example, the Mines and Geosciences Bureau must 'undertake geological, mining, metallurgical, chemical and other researches as well as geological and mineral exploration surveys'.[64] In Tanzania, the Executive Agencies Act, 1997 established the Geological Survey of Tanzania as a semiautonomous executive agency. Under the mining law, the Geological Survey (designated the 'Agency' in the mining law) assumes responsibility 'for all matters related to geological activities', including providing the political authority with geological advice, undertaking the geological mapping of Tanzania, providing data on Tanzania's geology and mineral resources and maintaining laboratory, library and records facilities as are deemed necessary to discharge its functions.[65] For the purposes of geological mapping the Agency has the power to enter upon any land, and to carry out any lawful operations.[66]

Public or donor-funded national geological surveys secure a 'better deal' for the State when it negotiates mining concessions with private investors – this is the thinking underlying both private and State-led forms of extractivism. The Natural Resource Charter, an instrument authored by an 'independent' group of practitioners and academics under the auspices of the National Resource Governance Institute, states: 'Pre-licensing investment in geological and geophysical surveys, funded by the government or external donors, can provide a high return on investment for the government if the resulting information increases the attractiveness of the geology to investors, thereby attracting higher bids.'[67]

The Charter hints at other reasons for State investment in geological data. With such data in hand, the State can take more informed decisions on the rate

---

[61] Jébrak (n 57) 25.
[62] Ibid 33.
[63] Girones (n 47) 12.
[64] Mining Act, 1995 (Philippines), section 9.
[65] Mining Act, 2010 (Tanzania), section 21.
[66] Mining Act, 2010 (Tanzania), section 22.
[67] Natural Resources Governance Institute, *Natural Resource Charter* (2nd edn) 13.

of exploitation and potential future revenues, the establishment of property and exploration rights in the country and future social and environmental impacts.[68] What should not be lost from sight, however, is that State-sponsored geological surveys benefit the global mining industry through taxpayers' money – and further, that the trove of geological information increases the rate of extraction. As commentary on the Charter explains: '[T]he presence of one mineral deposit is an indication of further mineralization in the area. Other firms, acting on this piece of information, can now focus their exploratory efforts around the site of the first discovery.'[69]

Many States also increase their geological archive by burdening exploration concessionaires with the obligation to submit their findings to the central State repository. The Natural Resource Charter is unequivocal:

> The government has a duty to collect, store and analyze technical information arising from all exploration operations carried out under its jurisdiction. This information is key to building the government's geological understanding, which will serve to strengthen its negotiating position with investors and better enable it to optimize the licensing regime.[70]

The aforementioned Tanzanian Mining Act, 2010, for example, requires the holder of a prospecting right to maintain detailed information on (among others) boreholes drilled, aerial photographs, strata penetrated and logs thereof, minerals discovered and the results of seismic surveys and geochemical and geophysical analyses.[71] The holder must furnish the State with such reports and information on termination of the right.[72] Acknowledging the fiercely competitive environment in which prospecting can take place, the Tanzanian legislation – similar to that of other mineral-rich jurisdictions – prohibits the disclosure of information in such reports without the consent of the holder while the mineral right is still operative.[73] While this prohibition may understandably be aimed at protecting sensitive commercial information, it inhibits the power of other non-State interested and affected parties, preventing them from fully apprehending the scale and scope of potential mining in an area with mineral potential.

---

68 Ibid.

69 Natural Resource Governance Institute, 'Geological information: Pre-investment to maximize value' (no date) 2.

70 Natural Resource Governance Institute (n 67) 13.

71 Mining Act, 2010 (Tanzania), Schedule 2.

72 Ibid s 100.

73 Ibid s 25.

2.1.3 Guarantor of the primacy and efficacy of mining

As an extension of its role as national landlord over mineral resources, and drawing upon the creative lawmaking power that stems from its sovereignty over the national territory, the State defines entitlements and obligations that secure the efficacy and primacy of mining. It is common for these entitlements and obligations to be defined in the national mining law and/or stated in court precedent. This section considers (1) entitlements ancillary to the activity of mining; (2) cadastral saturation and the 'use it or lose it' principle; and (3) legal provisions that affirm the primacy of mining.

2.1.3.1 Ancillary entitlements

When the State awards a mining concession to a third party, it will usually also allow the holder to conduct activities to search for (explore or prospect) or 'win' (extract or exploit) minerals. In mineral-rich jurisdictions the world over, the law also commonly defines a set of ancillary entitlements, allowing a title holder to carry out all activities incidental to mineral exploration or extraction. These activities vastly expand the miner's licence to use land, water and other natural resources.

The origin of these ancillary entitlements is ancient. For example, in Roman law the right to mine was granted *ius abutendi*.[74] Even though the State retained a form of residuary ownership in the land and minerals, the occupier of the mine was afforded an entitlement to make full use of the property, 'to the point of wasting or destroying it'.[75] In Germanic law, the holder of a right to mine appeared to enjoy a right of perpetual occupation, ancillary rights to wood and water and even rights to certain forms of protection. This was subject to compliance with certain obligations, the most notable being the duty to pay royalties to the holder of the Bergregal.[76]

In modern legal systems, mining title holders are allowed to enter the land where a reserve or potential reserve is located, erect structures and bring vehicles, vessels, machinery and equipment onto the area. The Mines and Minerals Act, 2015 of Zambia, for example, holds that subject to the conditions of a mining (exploitation) licence, the holder has exclusive rights 'to carry on mining, processing and exploration in the mining area and to do all such other acts and things as are necessary for, or incidental to, the carrying on of those

---

74 Ibid.

75 Definition of *ius abutendi*, Merriam-Webster Dictionary.

76 Dale (n 8) 20.

operations'.[77] Without limiting the generality of this entitlement, the holder may (among other entitlements):

> Enter onto the mining area and take all measures on or under the surface for the purpose of the mining operations;
> Erect the necessary equipment, plant and buildings for the purposes of mining, transporting, dressing, or treating the mineral recovered in the course of mining operations; and
> Dispose of any recovered mineral product.[78]

Elaboration on these general entitlements includes, for example, the right to pass through land adjacent to the mining area,[79] or the right to the 'moderate' use of explosives.[80] The effect of these statutory entitlements is to create a bias in favour of legality, making it very difficult for persons affected by such activities to contest their impact.

Frequently, the right to conduct mining also incorporates the right to conduct primary and secondary treatment operations. In New South Wales, for example, the holder of a mining lease is entitled to prospect and mine on land for specified minerals and to 'carry out on that land such primary treatment operations (such as crushing, sizing, grading, washing and leaching) as are necessary to separate the mineral or minerals from the material from which they are recovered'.[81] The mining law in Botswana allows the holder of a mining licence to erect equipment, plant and buildings not only for the purpose of mining, but also for the purposes of 'dressing, treating, smelting, or refining minerals recovered by him (*sic*) during mining operations'.[82] The law of the Democratic Republic of the Congo allows the holder of a mining exploitation right to 'proceed with the concentration, metallurgical or technical treatment operations, as well as the transformation of the mineral substances extracted from the deposit within the exploitation perimeter'.[83] Naturally, the wider the range of primary and secondary activities incorporated into the scope of authorization, the wider the range of socioecological impacts arising from the mining operation, and the more difficult it is to contest the legality of these operations.

---

77 Mines and Minerals Act, 2015 (Zambia), section 32(3).
78 Ibid s 32(4).
79 Law on Minerals, 2006 (Mongolia), Articles 21.1.6 and 27.1.8.
80 Mineral Resources Act, 1989 (Queensland), section 50(1)(c).
81 Mining Act, 1992 (New South Wales), section 73(1)(b).
82 Mines and Minerals Act, 1999 (Botswana), section 44(1)(b).
83 Mining Code, 2002 (Democratic Republic of the Congo), Article 64(e).

In some mineral-rich jurisdictions, mining title expressly allows the holder to stack or dump mineral waste.[84] In others this is extended to the right to exploit tailings in the mining area. In the Democratic Republic of the Congo, for instance, the 2002 Mining Code expressly stated that a mining exploitation licence 'entails the right to exploit artificial deposits located within the mining perimeter covered by the permit'.[85] In line with the ideal of a disembedded market for mineral rights, the holder of an exploitation licence may transfer the right to exploit artificial deposits to a third party.[86] In other jurisdictions, however, these activities are subject to a separate authorization process. For example, in South Africa, recent amendments to the law require the applicant for a mining right to apply for and obtain a waste management licence under the country's waste management legislation, albeit that the authority granting that licence is the agency responsible for mineral resources.[87]

The use of water is one of the most contentious aspects of mining operations. Mining activities not only pollute water resources, but may also reduce the quantity of surface and underground water resources in the mining area and surrounds. In some mineral-rich jurisdictions, the use of water (including how such use is defined) is subject to a separate authorization process, as referenced in the national mining law. In Queensland, for example, the mining law prohibits the holder of a mining claim from diverting or appropriating water unless they hold an authority for doing so under any relevant Act.[88] The law of the Democratic Republic of the Congo used to be more liberal, allowing the holder of a mining exploitation licence to use water and wood within the mining perimeter for conducting exploitation, subject only to the limits articulated as part of the environmental assessment process.[89]

In other jurisdictions the law is more ambiguous. In Mongolia, a mining licence holder has the right to use land and water 'in compliance with applicable laws'.[90] And in South Africa, the holder of a prospecting or mining rights may use water 'subject to' the national legislation governing the use of scarce water resources.[91] In all cases where water use is subject to a separate authorization process, but especially where the law itself is ambiguous, the political

---

[84] Mines and Minerals Act, 1999 (Botswana), section 44(1)(e).

[85] Mining Code, 2002 (Democratic Republic of the Congo), Article 86.

[86] Ibid.

[87] National Environmental Management: Waste Act, 2008 (South Africa), section 43(1A).

[88] Mineral Resources Act, 1989 (Queensland), section 50(4).

[89] Mining Code, 2002 (Democratic Republic of the Congo), Article 64(c).

[90] Law on Minerals, 2006 (Mongolia), Article 27.1.10.

[91] Mineral and Petroleum Resources Development Act, 2002 (South Africa), section 5(3)(d). The language of this provision, however, had led to heated debate on whether this requires that the mining title holder should have the water authorization

and social legitimacy of the miner's use of water is subject to the integrity of such processes. Where such processes are weak, or misaligned with the processes for authorizing mining, there are real risks that the mining sector's use of water will be seen to, and will in fact, cause serious and even irreparable harm to water resources, at great social and ecological cost.

The reforms instituted by Finland's new Mining Act, 2011 take a different approach to ancillary rights. Instead of simply defining a set of statutory entitlements miners are deemed to have by virtue of having a mining concession, the Finnish law establishes an additional layer of State oversight, via the option of a redemption permit. A mining proponent must apply for a redemption permit from the government when they wish to utilize an area in the possession of another party as a mining area.[92] The law lays down principles for the determination of such a mining area: it must be a continuous area of a size and shape that facilitates compliance with requirements concerning safety, location of mining activities and mining technology; it must not be 'larger than necessary for the purposes of mining activity, in view of the quality and extent of the deposit in question'; and the location of the mining area must be planned so as not to cause infringement of public or private interests that are 'reasonably avoidable in view of the overall costs of mining operations'.[93] Further, in granting a redemption permit the authorities must consider whether the mining project is based on 'public need'.[94] The permit authority must inform owners and holders of property affected by the application,[95] and both the applicant and the affected parties must be provided with an opportunity for a hearing.[96] There are rules to ensure that the mining area is coordinated with the land use planning authorities.[97] Importantly, the holder of a redemption permit cannot claim possession of the mining area unless 'advance compensation' as ordained in the proceedings establishing the mining area is paid.[98] And landowners have the right to demand that the real property or part thereof be redeemed if the redemption permit and associated mining area causes 'substantial inconvenience' to the usage of the real property.[99] In this case, the compensation must be 150 per cent of the value of the redeemed area.[100] These

prior to commencing mining, in a context where the issuing of water authorizations has been delayed, at times, for many years.

92 Mining Act, 2011 (Finland), section 20.
93 Ibid s 19.
94 Ibid s 35.
95 Ibid s 41.
96 Ibid s 42.
97 Ibid ss 77–79.
98 Ibid s 82.
99 Ibid s 86.
100 Ibid.

provisions have therefore had the effect of strengthening the position of landholders vis-à-vis mining proponents.[101] However, this is the clear exception to the pattern of granting ancillary rights around mining.

2.1.3.2 Cadastral saturation and the 'use-it-or-lose it' principle

The State's role as national landlord of mineral resources includes attracting investment into mining exploration and exploitation, thereby assuring the longterm development of the mining industry. In addition to levels of exploration and exploitation spending, cadastral saturation can be used as a measure of the State's success in this quest. Cadastral saturation describes the situation where the national territory is substantially occupied by mineral concessions, whether exploration or exploitation rights.[102]

While pro-mining advocates view cadastral saturation as a healthy and positive sign,[103] mining dissenters regard this phenomenon as a threat, and indicative of the priority given to mining as a land use. For example, in a paper on the effect of new mining legislation in South Africa, Hermanus and Watson point out that 61 per cent of the land in the agricultural-rich province of Mpumalanga had come under mining and prospecting rights applications.[104] The 'growing physical footprint of mining', they argue, reduces the amount of land available for agricultural production.[105] The current rate of coal mining, together with areas under prospecting, is putting a quarter of South Africa's high potential arable land in danger of irreversible transformation, with implications for a drop in maize production and food security.[106] The metaphor of a footprint connotes real physical impacts on land, other natural resources and the society. As a number of projects captured in the Environmental Justice Atlas affirm, often the granting of an *exploration* concession fuels a variety

[101] See also Borenius, 'Legal Alert – Amendment of the Finnish Environmental Legislation' (28 June 2011), www.borenius.com/2011/06/28/legal-alert-amendments-of-the-finnish-environmental-legislation/, accessed 24 February 2019.

[102] Girones (n 47) 37.

[103] Girones *et al*, for example, write: '[I]n countries where the mining sector is well developed, a high occupancy level is considered an indicator of good cadastral management and good performance in general – the mining sector is able to attract investment' (ibid, 37).

[104] May Hermanus *et al*, 'Impact of the Mineral and Petroleum Resources Development Act on levels of mining, land utility and people' (2015) 48(1–2) *Labour, Capital and Society* 11.

[105] Ibid 14.

[106] Ibid.

of environmental, health and socioeconomic impacts, in addition to social conflict and (at times violent) resistance.[107]

The mining industry has itself at times voiced disquiet over the level of cadastral saturation, arguing that rather than representing vital new investment in mineral exploitation, the lack of 'space' to undertake mineral exploration signifies speculative practices, that is, titleholders hoarding licences without significant development activity onsite.[108] In order to reduce negative speculative practices – where there is no development of a mining area whatsoever[109] – most mining jurisdictions incorporate measures to incentivize the pace of mining or penalize the late commencement of works. These measures include escalating rental fees,[110] mandatory relinquishment requirements,[111] minimum investment requirements or work obligations,[112] and the 'use it or lose it' principle.

---

[107] Examples include the Minas-Rio Project in Brazil (see https://ejatlas.org/conflict/impacts-of-iron-ore-mining-in-conceicao-do-mato-dentro-mg-brazil), the iron ore mine on the Simandou Mountain Range in Guinea (see https://ejatlas.org/conflict/simandoun-mine) and the copper mine in Piura, Peru (see https://ejatlas.org/conflict/rio-blanco-mine-majaz-peru), among others.

[108] Girones (n 47) 36–7.

[109] Negative speculation is contrasted, in World Bank-produced literature on mineral cadastre, with positive speculation. The latter involves the development of reconnaissance or exploration activities onsite, usually by junior miners, in order to increase the value of a mineral property (see ibid 37).

[110] Escalating rental fees for exploration rights (as opposed to rental fees for mining rights, which are more closely related to the fiscal treatment of the industry) are intended to encourage voluntary relinquishment of unwanted parts of the licensed area. The implementation of annual escalating rental fees is deemed to be easy, direct and transparent, since little interpretation or subjective evaluation is required on the part of the regulator (see ibid 38–9). For example, in terms of Article 34 of the Mining Law of Ecuador, 2009, mining concessionaires must pay an annual maintenance patent fee for each mining hectare. The annual fee increases with each major phase of the project. For example, during the exploration period the maintenance patent fee is 2.5 per cent of the unified base salary per mining concession hectare, increasing to 5 per cent during the advanced exploration period and 10 per cent during the exploitation stage.

[111] A mandatory relinquishment requirement requires the periodic obligation to reduce the size of an exploration licence, which may or may not be associated with the renewal of the licence (see Girones n 47, 40). For example, in the Democratic Republic of the Congo, exploration rights are granted for a period of five years, renewable twice for a period of five years each (Mining Code, Law No. 007/2002, Article 52). However, Article 62 provides that upon each renewal, the holder automatically relinquishes 50 per cent of the perimeter covered by his licence. See also s 38 of the Ghanaian Minerals and Mining Act, 2006 which provides for the compulsory reduction of the area of a prospecting licence.

[112] Mineral-rich jurisdictions commonly require minimum investment or work requirements as a condition of an exploration or exploitation right. Meeting the

Measures to reduce negative speculation also stimulate mineral exploration and exploitation in a particular area. This becomes a concern when mining proponents then undertake exploration or exploitation in haste. For example, under the 'use it or lose it' principle licence holders stand to lose their rights if they do not commence exploration activities within a given time period. This principle, again, has ancient origins. Under Roman law, the right to mine was stated to be *proprietas* (the holder became the owner of the right).[113] However, this right was subject to forfeiture if the holder failed to pay the requisite royalty to the State, or if he failed to diligently work the mine. The State thus retained a 'residuary ownership' over the land and over the right to mine itself.[114] Even at this early stage, therefore, the authorities enforced a form of the 'use it or lose it' principle.

In a modern, globalized world with integrated markets for minerals, the 'use it or lose it' principle can accelerate extraction to the detriment of both mining companies (if the market is flooded and commodity prices fall) and mineral-rich jurisdictions. In a number of African jurisdictions the holder of an exploration right must commence exploring within a set period of time, usually a couple of months.[115] Even when the law does not set a specific time, States may reclaim unused mining tenements under the 'use it or lose it' principle, particularly in times of political or economic stress, or upon a change in the political regime.[116] In 2017, for example, the Zimbabwean government's

---

promised requirements may result in penalties and eventual loss of the concession. For example, in Peru the General Mining Law (approved by Supreme Decree N° 014-92-EM of 4 June 1992), requires a titleholder to maintain a minimum annual level of production or investment. Failure to meet the minimum production period within a ten year term results in the payment of a fine, until the 15th year after the concession was awarded. Thereafter, the loss of the mining concession may only be avoided by paying a fine and demonstrating investments ten times greater than the amount of the fine payable. If the minimum production requirement is not met by the twentieth year, the mining concession will be unfailingly lost (see Ernst & Young, *Peru's Mining and Metals Investment Guide 2014/2015* 40).

[113] Dale (n 8) 6.

[114] Ibid 7.

[115] Mining and Minerals Act, 2006 (Ghana) s 37(2) requires the holder of a prospecting licence to commence operations within three months after the date of the issue of the licence. Section 19(2)(b) of South Africa's Mineral and Petroleum Resources Development Act, 2002 allows for a commencement period of six months.

[116] See for example the comments made by Ian MacFarlane, minister under the Abbott government in Australia from 2013 to 2015, regarding the revocation of offshore oil and gas projects in Australia (Pat McGrath, 'New Industry Minister Ian MacFarlane warns miners to start projects or lose leases', www.abc.net.au/news/2013-09-18/macfarlane-warns-miners-to-use-it-or-lose-it/4966250, accessed 24 February 2019).

desire to ramp up gold and platinum mining production under the banner of 'command mining' incorporated the 'use it or lose it' policy on existing mining claims, a move heavily criticized by the industry.[117]

2.1.3.3 Primacy of mining over surface rights

While not expressly stating so in their national mining laws, States secure the primacy of mining over other surface uses of the land. *Breaking New Ground* acknowledged this candidly: 'The holder of the concession or permit generally has the right to take as much of the surface as is needed to gain access to the minerals, regardless of the preference of the surface owner or occupant.'[118]

The primacy of mining over other surface uses may be secured through judicial precedent. For example, in South Africa, the courts have stated unequivocally that in the event of irreconcilable conflict, the use of surface rights has to be subordinated to mineral exploitation.[119] More often, however, the primacy of mining as a land use is secured more subtly. The following subsections explore this phenomenon from the perspective of (1) land uses excluded or protected from mining and (2) the determination of disputes between holders and surface owners or occupiers, including payment of compensation.

2.1.3.3.1 Land uses excluded or protected from mining Excluded or protected land uses are usually defined restrictively,[120] the unstated assumption being that the rest of the national territory is open for mining. Sometimes this 'open for business' mentality is stated expressly, as in the mining law of the Philippines, which provides that '[s]ubject to any existing rights or reservations and prior agreements of all parties, all mineral resources in public or private lands, including timber or forestlands as defined in existing laws, shall be open to mineral agreements'.[121]

Even if mineral agreements are subjected to existing rights or reservations, the ancillary rights afforded miners, coupled with the incompatibility of mining with other land uses, mean that mining enjoys *de facto* primacy. This sense of primacy comes through clearly in the mining law of Chile, which directs that at the time a mining concession is established, and 'in order to

---

[117] Mthandazo Nyoni, 'Proposed command mining likely to fail', *The Standard*, 23 April 2017, www.thestandard.co.zw/2017/04/23/proposed-command-mining-likely-fail/, accessed 24 February 2019.

[118] *Breaking New Ground* (n 4) 143.

[119] See the decision in *Hudson v. Mann* 1950 (4) SA 485 (T) at 488.

[120] Common restrictions include places of burial, built structures such as railways or aerodromes, established townships or settlements, military installations, heritage sites and protected natural areas.

[121] Philippine Mining Act, 1995 (Philippines), section 18.

contribute to convenient and unconstrained exploration and operation', surface tenements are subjected to the following encumbrances, as the Mining Code of Chile elaborates:

> '[O]re, overburden, tailing and slag piles, ore separating and processing facilities, communication systems, conduits, channels, dams and ponds, pipelines, housing, buildings and other supplementary and ancillary facilities'; as well as 'the right of way and occupancy by roads, railroads, airfields, pipelines [and] tunnels, inclined planes, aerial cable cars, conveyor belts and any other system used to connect the concession to public roads, processing facilities, railroad stations, airfields and inhabited settlements'.[122]

Some States have legal provisions allowing for surface uses to take place simultaneously with mining, but the preeminence of the mining enterprise is usually also expressly stated. For example, the law of Botswana recognizes the right of an owner or lawful occupier of any land within a mineral concession to continue to graze stock or cultivate the surface, but only 'insofar as such grazing or cultivation does not interfere with the proper use of such area for prospecting, retention or mining purposes'.[123] The law of Ghana similarly provides that lawful occupiers of land retain rights of grazing and cultivation, but only insofar as these activities do not 'interfere with the mineral operations in the area'.[124]

Formally protected natural areas are among the categories of land frequently excluded from mining, unless authorization from political or executive authorities is secured.[125] In developed countries, and particularly the European Union, protection of natural sites is robust, and the bar on mineral exploration or exploitation in these areas is real. The mineral law of Sweden, for example, prohibits *exploration* work 'within a national park or an area which a central government authority has requested the Government to designate as a national park'. By prohibiting work that initiates the mining cycle, the Swedish authorities seem to avoid difficult political disputes over the exploitation of minerals, were they to be discovered in these areas.

One also finds provision for a mining 'no go' in protected areas in the laws of some developing countries. For example, the Philippine Mining Code

---

[122] Mining Code (Chile), Article 120.

[123] Mines and Minerals Act, 1999 (Botswana), section 61(1).

[124] Minerals and Mining Act, 2006 (Ghana), section 72(3).

[125] The important and controversial topic of mining in protected areas and areas of high ecological value merits extended treatment, but unfortunately falls beyond the scope of this book. Following the World Summit on Sustainable Development in 2002, the IUCN and the ICMM launched a joint dialogue on mining and biodiversity. At the same time the ICMM developed a position statement on mining and protected areas.

includes among the areas closed to mining operations old growth or virgin forests, wilderness areas, mangrove forests, greenbelts, parks and areas protected under that country's National Integrated Protected Areas System.[126] The Philippine Mining Code does not provide for an executive authority to override this rule. Nevertheless, the implementation of these nature protection provisions is problematic. A 2003 study undertaken by the Environmental Science for Social Change Institute in the Philippines, for example, found that nearly one third of mining concessions overlapped with formally protected areas, notwithstanding this legal protection.[127]

The greater concern, however, is that even as mining and protected areas law provide some level of protection for *formally* protected areas from mining, areas of high ecological value that have no formal protections – including high biodiversity areas and important watersheds – are not protected at all.[128] Further, a significant number of active mines, while not located within the protected area as such, occur within the buffer zone of protected areas.[129] As the socioecological impacts of mining areas are not confined to the mining area, mining activities therefore affect the integrity of the conserved site.

Allowing for executive or political authorities to override the prohibition against mining in protected areas is the more common model. In Ecuador, nonrenewable resources may not be extracted from protected areas. But the law goes on to provide that on an exceptional basis such resources may be mined based on a prior 'declaration of national interest' issued by the National Assembly, and as per the 'grounded petition' of the Presidency of the Republic.[130] The mining law of Tanzania has an interesting construction, stating that without the written consent of the authority having control over an area, the holder of a mining right may not *exercise* any of his rights under a mining licence in a national park, forest reserve, game reserve, and so on.[131]

---

[126] Philippine Mining Act, 1995 (Philippines), section 19(f).

[127] ESSC Institute, 'Mining in environmentally vulnerable areas', http://essc.org.ph/content/wp-content/uploads/2007/02/mining_chapter3.pdf, accessed 24 February 2019.

[128] Centre for Environmental Rights, 'New proceedings launched to protect Mpumalanga strategic water source area from coal mining', https://cer.org.za/news/new-proceedings-launched-to-protect-mpumalanga-strategic-water-source-area-from-coal-mining, accessed 24 February 2019.

[129] For mining in the buffer zone of a protected area see the case study of plans to mine coal in the Mapungubwe Cultural Heritage site (also a UNESCO World Heritage site): Christelle du Toit, 'Mining halted at Mapungubwe heritage site, for now', 10 September 2017, *eNCA*, www.enca.com/south-africa/mining-halted-at-mapungubwe-unesco-world-heritage-site-for-now, accessed 24 February 2019.

[130] Mining Law, 2009 (Ecuador), Article 25.

[131] Mining Act, 2010 (Tanzania), section 95(1)(c).

This implies that the law simply impedes the exercise of rights, but does not place any obstacles in the way of granting rights in the first instance.

The ICMM's position statement on mining is that exploration and exploitation in protected areas are ultimately still permitted. The only strict 'no go' concession on the part of the industry body is to desist from exploring or mining *in* world heritage properties (but not around them).[132] ICMM member companies have further committed to respecting legally designated protected areas, ensuring that any new operations or changes to existing operations 'are not incompatible with the value for which they are designated'.[133] Clearly, there is little in this provision about considering unprotected areas of high ecological value, or proceeding with caution in the buffer zones of protected areas.

The ICMM position statement does not intimate that a conservation use can ever trump mining. But there are isolated provisions in national laws that allow executive authorities to stop mining for environmental reasons. As part of the process of creating a streamlined environmental assessment system for the mining sector, for example, South Africa amended the national framework environmental law. The amendment institutes the minister responsible for mineral resources as a 'competent authority' for the purpose of granting environmental authorizations for mining.[134] At the same time, the national minister of the environment is given the power to prohibit or restrict the granting of an environmental authorization by a competent authority for a specified geographical area for such period and upon such terms and conditions as the environmental minister may determine. This intent of this law is expressly identified as the advancement of the precautionary principle, enshrined as a principle in the national framework environmental act.[135] Using this power, the minister for environment can block mining in certain areas (as mining is unlawful in the absence of an environmental authorization), even if such areas are not formally protected.

2.1.3.3.2 Conflict between rights holders and surface owners or occupiers over access and compensation

Conflict procedures and compensation mechanisms form part of the sustainable mineral development consensus' broader policy advice on implementing a system of 'integrated land use planning' to deal with difficult land use

---

[132] International Council on Mining and Metals, 'Mining and protected areas position statement', www.icmm.com/en-gb/members/member-commitments/position-statements/mining-and-protected-areas-position-statement, accessed 24 February 2019.

[133] Ibid.

[134] National Environmental Management Act, 1998 (South Africa), section 24C(2A).

[135] Ibid, section 24(2A).

disputes throughout the mineral cycle. *Breaking New Ground*, for instance, acknowledged the significance of land use disputes,[136] and called upon stakeholders to establish an integrated approach to land management that 'recognizes competing interests and attempts to negotiate the most appropriate course of action, bearing in mind the ecological and social limits of the area'.[137] In an 'ideal world' an integrated approach to land management would comprise (1) 'a solid database about land use and land use potential'; (2) a way to establish the needs and preferences of those currently based on the land, including through free, prior and informed consent;[138] (3) a 'negotiation or arbitration mechanism to balance local, regional and national priorities', and (4) a compensation mechanism for loss of land or livelihoods and for resettlement.[139]

It bears mentioning that the first of the recommended pillars of an integrated land use management approach has been contentious in the context of Indigenous Peoples' rights. As outlined in Chapter 3, indigenous land rights have been at the fore of demands put forward by the Indigenous Peoples movement. Researchers have noted, however, that the variety of movements and countermovements to recognize and formalize indigenous title can exacerbate conflict amongst Indigenous Peoples themselves.[140] While boundaries remain fluid and unarticulated, differing local imaginaries of rights of access to and use of the same resources can exist side by side – a situation of 'entangled'[141] but nevertheless peaceful landscapes. As soon as these boundaries are formally drawn, conflict between neighbouring units can arise. The boundaries mapped and validated by the State generate 'conflicting images of reality [that] cannot be overlooked any longer and must be addressed'.[142] Further, the processes of mapping indigenous title and mapping reserves of fossil fuels and minerals may play out in parallel, with few or no points of articulation. In their research on the titling of Original Community Lands in Bolivia, for example, Athias

---

136 *Breaking New Ground* (n 4) 143.

137 Ibid 145.

138 This element of an integrated land use management approach is dealt with in section 3.4.2 of Chapter 3 (Indigenous Peoples and the principle of free, prior and informed consent), and in section 2.4 of Chapter 6 (public participation and consultation).

139 *Breaking New Ground* (n 4) 145.

140 Actors in the global environmental movement, and multilateral development agencies have also advanced the recognition of indigenous title.

141 DS Moore, *Suffering for Territory: Race, Place, and Power in Zimbabwe* (Duke University Press 2005).

142 Jefferson Fox, '*Siam Mapped* and mapping in Cambodia: Boundaries, sovereignty and indigenous conceptions of space' (2002) 15 *Society and Natural Resources* 65, 73.

and Radcliffe point out that while World Bank employees, State officials and indigenous leaders laboured over the law recognizing indigenous territorial claims (a law that also commodified land and consolidated private property), other government ministries – and indeed other Bank staff – were busy drawing *other* maps of these territories, zoning them into sites of gas, mineral and timber extraction. 'By 2008, 20 of Bolivia's 84 Original Community Lands were subject to contracts for hydrocarbons exploration or exploitation'.[143] There is also a danger that the criteria for recognizing and maintaining indigenous property rights cements a reified, outmoded notion of subsistence traditional identity, or even a notion of Indigenous Peoples as the 'guardians of nature'.[144] This could trap Indigenous People into a mode of living and being frozen in time that fails to reflect reality.

However, it is in the procedures and compensation mechanisms for land use conflicts – the third and fourth pillars of *Breaking New Ground*'s integrated land use management approach – that the bias towards mining as a primary land use comes to the fore.

Where the law requires the State to oversee conflict between mineral and surface rights holders, bias arises when the authorities responsible for resolving the dispute are also responsible for promoting mineral extraction. The law of Ecuador, for example, states that the land surface is subject to a variety of easements that come into effect upon the constitution of a mining concession. These include easements required for installations and buildings required for mining activities.[145] Conflict between the surface holder and the mining concessionaire can only arise over compensation for the use and enjoyment of the easement, and land damages, as the easement arises *ex lege*. The law recognizes that mining rights holders may enter into agreements with landowners for such easements, but in the absence of an agreement, the Regulation and Mining Oversight Agency must determine the compensable amount.[146] No provision is therefore made for independent assessment. This appears to go against the advice of *Breaking New Ground*, which states: 'Part of the issue of arriving at fair compensation is that there must be some system, some neutral party or institution, that is trusted by those concerned to set compensation.'[147]

A similar bias is evident in the law of some African mineral-rich jurisdictions. In Ghana disputes regarding compensation for the disturbance of an

---

143 Penelop Anthias and Sarah A Radcliffe, 'The ethno-environmental fix and its limits: Indigenous land titling and the production of no-quite liberal natures in Bolivia' (2015) 64 *Geoforum* 257, 264.

144 Ibid 267.

145 Mining Law, 2009 (Ecuador), Article 100.

146 Ibid, Article 100(a).

147 *Breaking New Ground* (n 4) 150.

owner's surface rights are determined by the minister responsible for mineral resources in consultation with the government agency responsible for land valuation;[148] and in Tanzania compensation to a surface holder is determined by the Commissioner for Minerals.[149] South African mining law does not even provide for a right to compensation and the bias towards the mining rights holder is even more apparent. Here, the holder of a mining authorization must notify the regional manager for mineral resources if the owner or lawful occupier of land refuses to allow the holder to enter the land, places 'unreasonable demands' in return for access to the land or cannot be found in order to apply for access.[150] The landowner is allowed to make representations to the regional manager, but does so with the threat of his actions being framed as a 'contravention' of the law.[151] In considering the issue, the regional manager may conclude that the owner/occupier has or is likely to suffer loss or damage as a result of the prospecting or mining operations, and must then request the parties concerned to reach agreement.[152] If they fail to do so, the matter must be determined by arbitration or a competent court.[153] The tone and onerous process of this provision pressurizes owners and occupiers to reach agreement with mining rights holders, without involving State oversight. It also prevents the owner/occupier from escalating any dispute concerning compensation without also allowing the mining rights holder access to the land, unless the regional manager determines this is due to the 'fault' of the holder.[154] The South African law in this regard may have been modelled on the Namibian mining legislation, drafted a decade earlier, which makes provision for a Mining Ancillary Rights Commission to adjudicate disputes where landholders and the holders of mining title cannot agree to the terms of the latter's use of the surface. The Mining Ancillary Rights Commission is composed of a three-member panel consisting of a chairperson and two other members appointed from time to time by the president,[155] who all hold office 'at the President's pleasure'.[156] The broad discretion afforded the president reduces confidence in the independence of the assessment.

---

[148] Minerals and Mining Act, 2006 (Ghana), section 73(3).
[149] Mining Act, 2010 (Tanzania), section 96(4).
[150] Mineral and Petroleum Resources Development Act, 2002 (South Africa), section 54(1)(a).
[151] Ibid, section 54(2).
[152] Ibid, section 54(3).
[153] Ibid, section 54(4).
[154] Ibid, section 54(6).
[155] Mineral Act, 1992 (Namibia), section 108(1).
[156] Ibid, section 108(2).

In some jurisdictions a greater degree of independence in dispute resolution is more apparent. For example, in Zambia disputes regarding compensation payable for damage to the surface of the land must simply be determined by arbitration.[157] In the Philippines, the Mining Code makes provision for a panel of arbitrators who sit in the regional office of the Department of Environment and Natural Resources (DENR). Two of the panel members must be members of the Philippine Bar in good standing, and the third member must be a licensed mining engineer or professional in a related field.[158] The panel has a mandate to hear disputes involving surface owners, occupants and claimholders or concessionaires, among other types of dispute.[159] Their findings are appealable to a Mines Adjudication Board, composed of two officials representing the DENR and the Directors of the Mines and Geosciences Bureau.[160] The involvement of DENR officials appears to balance the influence of the mining authorities, but would depend on the bias towards environmental protection or extraction in the Department. An aggrieved party may however also approach the Supreme Court after the Mines Adjudication Board has handed down an appeal.[161] As noted in the discussion of ancillary entitlements above, reforms to Finnish mining law significantly strengthened the hand of landowners. The effect of these provisions – centring on the granting of a redemption permit and establishment of a mining area – were aimed at both avoiding disputes and providing a vehicle for the interests of landowners and mining proponents to be more evenly balanced.

The bias toward mining as a surface use is also constituted through the principles underlying compensation. Under the dominant model, it is not contentious that landowners, or even at times, lawful occupiers, should be compensated for loss and damage caused by mining.[162] However, perceptions of 'fair' compensation may differ widely among different stakeholder groups. Bias and injustice arises when the frame of reference used to determine compensation does not take such different views into account,[163] when the qualification criteria for compensation exclude particular groups,[164] or when the law affords mining proponents a variety of grounds to contest the amount of compensation payable.

---

157 Mines and Minerals Development Act, 2015 (Zambia), section 57(6).
158 Mining Code, 1995 (Philippines), Article 77.
159 Ibid.
160 Ibid, section 78.
161 Ibid.
162 *Breaking New Ground* (n 4) 148.
163 Ibid 151.
164 Ibid 149.

For example, the mining laws of Botswana and Zambia contain a similar legal provision that ostensibly balances the interests of surface users and mining proponents, but is in fact sharply biased against landholders and occupiers. The general principle is that the holder of a mining concession must pay surface users 'fair and reasonable compensation' for any 'disturbance of rights' or 'damage done to the surface of the land by mining operations'.[165] A claim may include damage done to crops, trees, buildings or works.[166] However, payment of rent under a lease agreement between the mining proponent and surface user is deemed to be adequate compensation for deprivation of the use of the land to which such rent relates.[167] This formulation takes no account of the power dynamics involved in the conclusion of the lease agreement, inclusive of who negotiated the lease and whether this extended to land used by a community. Further, in assessing compensation, there must be consideration of any improvement a mining proponent has effected to the land that will inure to the benefit of an owner or occupier.[168] Again, the question of whose benefit is paramount. This also opens the door for mining proponents to present inflated values of their infrastructural improvements to reduce the amount of compensation payable to owners or occupiers. Finally, the law provides that the basis upon which compensation is payable for damage to the surface is the extent to which the market or saleable value of the land has been reduced by reason of such damage. For purposes of determining market value any enhanced value due to the presence of minerals must not be taken into account.[169] Any reference to market value situates the determination of compensation within the frame of reference of the market (cash) economy and takes little account of livelihood values or values measured in terms of violation done to human rights. The gendered nature of loss and damage is also almost never taken into account.

2.1.4 Summary

Since the early 1980s, States have promoted a global system of formal mining production by disembedding mineral and mining rights from other social relations, chief among these being rights to land. Centralized authority over mineral resources has ancient origins. But in the late twentieth century a global disembedding of mineral rights has taken the legal form of vesting the State with powers to protect or use mineral resources as a national form of

---

[165] Mines and Minerals Act, 1999 (Botswana), section 63(1). The parallel provision in the Zambian mining law is section 57 of the Mines and Minerals Act, 2015.

[166] Mines and Minerals Act, 1999 (Botswana), section 63(1).

[167] Ibid, section 63(1)(i).

[168] Ibid, section 63(1)(ii).

[169] Ibid, section 63(1)(iii).

wealth for the benefit of the people or nation, or even future generations, or defining mineral resources as a form of public property over which the State has custodial functions. This pattern applies in States irrespective of whether extractivist or neoextractivist policies prevail. As national landlord of mineral resources, the State further promotes mining by a set of mutually supportive institutions that include maintaining a public cadastre of mining rights, generating and archiving geological knowledge that often subsidises private exploration, and recognizing widely defined ancillary entitlements that vastly expand the miner's licence to use land, water and other natural resources. In many mineral-rich jurisdictions there are also regulatory tools to reduce speculative practices and promote actual exploitation, including the 'use it or lose it' principle, narrowly defined and ineffective protections for other land uses (particularly conservation), and the wideranging powers of mining authorities to determine mining land use access and compensation conflicts. However, even as many mineral-rich jurisdictions conform to this dominant model for mineral rights, there are examples of alternative approaches and formulations that could effect a more balanced approach to mining as a land use.

2.2 Mining Rights: The Concessioning State

As national landlord of mineral resources, the State must promote mining. The mantra of the sustainable mineral development consensus is that the State must promote mining by playing a facilitative and regulatory role rather than undertaking mining activities directly.[170] In States where neoextractivism prevails, the State's participation in mining ventures may be more direct, but even here the State will often proceed by setting up State-owned mining companies or joint ventures with private entities. The Bolivian Constitution, for instance, directs the State to 'assume control and direction of the exploration, exploitation, industrialization, transport and sale of "strategic natural resources" through public, cooperative or community entities. These entities may in turn contract private enterprises and form mixed enterprises'.[171]

Whether the State engages with mining proponents who are wholly privately owned, or entities that mix public and private capital and forms of control, the laws of mineral-rich jurisdictions tend to institute the State as a concessioning authority. The State must allocate mining rights to prospective miners, either

---

170 See section 3.2.3 of Chapter 2.

171 Constitution of the Plurinational State of Bolivia, 2009, Article 351.

through public auction,[172] judicial confirmation,[173] State contracts,[174] or executive/administrative decisionmaking.[175] The dominant models for this function – possessory or administrative – are explored in the first subsection of this part.

States must not only ensure the 'neutral' allocation of mining rights, but also assure investors of security of tenure, particularly where extractivism is dominant. The assuring role of the State manifests in a variety of rules governing the transition between exploration and exploitation, and the transferability, mortgageability and stability of mining rights.

The dominant patterning of rules governing the allocation of mining rights and the protection of mining investments tends to promote mining without regard for socioecological limits, as the ensuing discussion shows.

2.2.1 Allocating exploration rights

In many mineral-rich jurisdictions, the State is particularly interested in promoting mining *exploration*, that is, the entry point of the mining cycle.[176] Although representing less than 10 per cent of the total budget in the full

---

[172] Recently, for example, the Indian government identified coal and lignite blocks for allocation via public auction, potentially disrupting State-owned Coal India Limited's monopoly on coal exploitation (Ajoy K Das, 'India to review coal blocks identified for allocation', *Mining Weekly*, 16 January 2018, www.miningweekly.com/article/india-to-review-coal-blocks-identified-for-allocation-2018-01-16/rep_id:3650, accessed 24 February 2019).

[173] Article 34 of the Mining Code of Chile, for example, provides that mining concessions shall be established by judicial decree, awarded following a nonadversarial proceeding.

[174] Prior to 2009, for example, Indonesia concluded contracts of work with a number of mining companies, which it has recently attempted to transition to a new system of mining permits (Wilda Asmarini, 'Indonesia amends contracts with 13 coal mining companies', *Thomson Reuters*, 14 November 2017, www.reuters.com/article/us-indonesia-coal/indonesia-amends-contracts-with-13-coal-mining-companies-idUSKBN1DE1C0, accessed 24 February 2019).

[175] Executive/administrative decision making is exercised over a wide variety of mining permits, extending over most of the range of the mining cycle and usually outlined in the national mining law. The Queensland Mineral Resources Act, 1989, for example, provides for the allocation of prospecting permits, mining claims, exploration permits, mineral development licences and mining leases. In South Africa, prior to the entry into force of the Mineral and Petroleum Resources Development Act, 2002, a bewildering array of common law and statutory entitlements to mining exploitation were recognized in law, since replaced by a more streamlined distinction between prospecting rights, mining rights, mining permits and reconnaissance permissions. In Zambia, the newly enacted Mines and Minerals Development Act, 2015 recognizes mineral processing licences and mineral trading permits in addition to licences for exploration and mining proper.

[176] It is remarkable that, as a scientific field, mineral exploration is only about 100 years old. The development of geology as a scientific discipline gained scientific trac-

mining cycle, exploration is the 'fundamental process' initiating the mineral industry.[177] Over the years States have adopted different policy responses to the problem of allocating exploration rights, frequently acting on the advice of international institutions.[178] The principles and procedures adopted can have significant effects on the rate and scale of extraction, as detailed below with reference to the (1) possessory and (2) administrative models of exploration rights allocation.

2.2.1.1 Possessory model of exploration rights allocation

The possessory model of allocation requires a *laissez-faire* State: a withholding of State involvement in determining who should be allowed to conduct exploration and where. The free entry system in use in the USA and Canada relies upon possessory allocation,[179] and has features in common with historical periods during which miners themselves had a stronger hand in formulating the legal rules that governed their operations.[180] The essence of the free entry system is self-initiation.[181] Free entry incorporates the miner's right to enter and explore public lands, a right to stake a claim on such lands and a right to obtain a lease or grant that authorizes mineral extraction.[182] In the USA and Canada, and historically also in Australia and New Zealand, the State has codified the free entry system and plays a continuing role to ensure that the elements of the system keep pace with technological developments. In the USA, the federal government has been unable to significantly amend the 'treasure hunt' model of mineral exploration codified in the General Mining Law of 1872.[183] In Canada, provincial legislatures have been more proactive in improving and modernizing the free entry system, with significant implications for the rate and extent of exploration. In Australia and New Zealand, provincial mining

---

tion in the nineteenth century – Charles Lyell's *Principles of Geology*, for instance, was published in 1833.

177 Jébrak (n 57) 3.

178 The World Bank and United Nations have both played a pivotal role in promoting mineral exploration. After the Second World War the United Nations 'was strongly involved in mineral exploration' and contributed to the discovery of several reserves, particularly in South America (ibid 26).

179 Also known as the 'location system'.

180 See Barry Barton, 'The history of mining law in the US, Canada, New Zealand and Australia, and the right of free entry' in Elizabeth Bastida, Thomas Wälde and Janeth Warden-Fernàndez, *International and Comparative Mineral Law and Policy* (Kluwer 2005) 643, 644.

181 Loren Mall, 'Outline: The General Mining Act of 1872', http://scholar.law.colorado.edu/cgi/viewcontent.cgi?article=1010&context=federal-lands-laws-policies-and-development-of-natural-resources, accessed 24 February 2019, para. 6.

182 Barton (n 180) 644.

183 Mall (n 181) para. 5(b).

jurisdictions have steered the system of mineral rights allocation away from a possessory towards an administrative model.[184]

In the USA the primary sustainability relevance of the free entry system today is arguably the preeminence that it establishes for mining as a land use.[185] The opening provision of the Law declares: 'All valuable mineral deposits in lands belonging to the United States, both surveyed and unsurveyed, are hereby declared to be free and open to exploration and purchase, by citizens of the United States and those who have declared their intention to become such'.[186] As environmental advocates have noted, the General Mining Law positions hardrock mining as the highest and best use of public lands … regardless of other competing land uses or environmental sensitivity. Through the operation of the General Mining Law this principle has been cemented into US public land policy, a result also of the particular design for free entry in this country which is not limited to the right to explore but entails an offer of outright title to the land surface.[187] However, the free entry system is of little practical relevance today. Over time free access has been steadily eroded, through environmental and land use restrictions and replacement with leasing systems for some substances (notably coal).[188] Most areas targeted for sophisticated exploration have already been claimed by someone else, meaning access must be negotiated.[189] Nevertheless, as Barton notes, the General Mining Law, through the free entry system, has symbolic significance, representing 'independence, freedom from bureaucracy, self-reliance, and the gambler's hope of overnight wealth'.[190]

In Canada free entry still forms the basis of the mining law in all provincial jurisdictions, with the exception of Alberta, Nova Scotia and the Prince Edward Islands.[191] Similarly to the USA, companies can acquire exploration rights through ground staking, without the need for prior government approval, although other regulatory requirements may hedge in this primary right. Under s 11(1) of the Mineral Tenure Act in British Columbia,[192] for example, a 'free miner' has a right to enter upon all 'mineral lands' for purposes of exploring for, developing and producing minerals. Various entities qualify for obtaining

---

[184] See Barton (n 180) 653–7.
[185] Ibid 648.
[186] §2319 General Mining Law, 1872.
[187] JD Leshy, *The Mining Law: A Study in Perpetual Motion* (Resources for the Future 1987) 26.
[188] Ibid 28, 348.
[189] Barton (n 180) 647.
[190] Ibid.
[191] Ibid 652.
[192] [RSBC] 1996 Chapter 292.

a free mining certificate, and free miners are required to notify an owner of land before entering private land for any form of mining activity.[193] This does little to detract from the fact that mining, new or historical, is positioned as the preeminent land use,[194] affording mining an extraordinary privilege over all other sectors of the economy.[195] Having staked a valid claim, a mineral claimholder is entitled to a variety of rights, including the right to enter upon the land and explore for minerals.[196]

Canadian provincial jurisdictions have also bullishly promoted online staking of mineral claims, a process that has accelerated exploration. The provinces of British Columbia, Newfoundland and Labrador, Ontario and Québec have replaced the process of physical claim staking with an online map staking process.[197] In these jurisdictions there are online mineral titles systems that enable users to select single or adjoining grid cells and pay the requisite fees via credit card.[198] Online staking changes the gaze of the explorer, eliminating the physicality associated with on the ground staking. Among the concerns raised in connection with online map staking has been the ease with which large areas of claims can be acquired, and the difficulty other interested and affected parties have in monitoring staking activity.[199] Clogg, for example, discusses the case of Pender Island (located in the Gulf of Georgia off British Columbia) where two local prospectors registered more than 20 mineral claims covering large expanses of private property.[200] The local community resisted this process and wrote to the provincial Minister of Mines seeking an exemption from mineral staking for the Island Trust area.[201]

Anecdotal evidence suggests online staking speeds up staking activity. Jébrak, for instance, writes that Québec's introduction of electronic staking sped up the process, 'allowing claims to be taken almost instantaneously, from anywhere in the world, reducing the cost for the administration and mining

---

193 Mineral Tenure Act (BC), §19.

194 Jessica Clogg, *Modernizing BC's Free Entry Mining Laws for a Vibrant, Sustainable Mining Sector* (West Coast Environmental Law, n.d.) 1.

195 Ibid 4.

196 Mineral Tenure Act (BC), §14(1).

197 MiningWatch Canada, 'Introduction to the Legal Framework for Mining in Canada', http://miningwatch.ca/publications/2012/7/18/introduction-legal-framework-mining-canada#Q2, accessed 24 February 2019.

198 See, for example, the explanation of the Mineral Titles Online system in British Columbia at Government of British Columbia, 'Claims: Mineral and Placer Titles', www2.gov.bc.ca/gov/content/industry/mineral-exploration-mining/mineral-titles/mineral-placer-titles/claims-mineral-placer-titles, accessed 24 February 2019.

199 MiningWatch Canada (n 197).

200 Clogg (n 194) 2.

201 Patrick Brown, 'Island Trust: no mining claims', *Island Tides*, 14 February 2013.

companies'.[202] In 2008, the British Columbia Ministry of Energy, Mines and Petroleum Resources observed that the area of land staked in the immediate aftermath of the introduction of online staking increased fourfold – from 1.08 million hectares in 2004 to 4.87 million hectares in 2005.[203] Clogg, however, observes a paradox: while staking and exploration have increased dramatically, between 2001 and 2012 no new mines entered production in British Columbia, with new projects mired in controversy and delayed by protests and court challenges.[204] This leads her to conclude that the costs of the free entry system are borne not only by First Nations and communities, but by the mining companies themselves.[205]

Following the Yukon Appellate Court's decision in the matter of *Ross River Dena Council v. Government of Yukon*,[206] however, the future of the free entry system in Canada has been left in legal limbo. In this case an Aboriginal group challenged the lack of consultation associated with the physical staking of a claim under Yukon's Quartz Mining Act,[207] and the entitlements that flow from this action. Applying the principles laid down by the Supreme Court of Canada in *Haida Nation v. British Columbia (Minister of Forests)*[208] the court held that while the free staking system was historically and economically important to Yukon, it needed to be modified in order for the Crown to act in accordance with its constitutional duties.[209] The Crown is required to act honourably by taking Aboriginal claims into account before divesting itself of the control of land.[210] Rather than being a factor that obviated the need for consultation, the lack of government discretion in the recording of claims under the Quartz Mining Act really constituted the nub of the problem.[211] A system allowing for an appropriate level of consultation before Aboriginal claims were adversely affected accordingly needed to be grafted onto the regime set out in the legislation.[212] In 2013, the Supreme Court of Canada refused to review the decision of the Yukon Court of Appeal.[213]

---

202 Jébrak (n 57) 12.

203 British Columbia Ministry of Energy, Mines and Petroleum Resources, 'Overview of trends in Canadian mineral exploration' (2008), cited in Clogg (n 194) 30.

204 Clogg (n 194) 3.

205 Ibid.

206 2012 YKCA 14 (henceforth *Ross River* case).

207 S.Y. 2003, c. 14.

208 2004 SCC 73, [2004] 3 S.C.R. 511.

209 *Ross River* (n 206) para 43.

210 Ibid para 38.

211 Ibid.

212 Ibid para 44.

213 Drew Hasselback, 'Supreme Court of Canada refuses leave to hear appeal of Yukon mining case', *Financial Post*, 17 September 2013, https://business.financialpost

2.2.1.2 Administrative model of exploration rights allocation

Most mineral-rich jurisdictions, however, have an administrative rather than a possessory model of exploration rights allocation, requiring an active rather than a *laissez-faire* State. Such systems can be further distinguished according to whether they allow for spontaneous applications or systems of public tendering, or both.[214] In practice this is also referred to as a distinction between open mineral access on a first come, first served basis or competitive resource tenders.[215]

In most well developed mining jurisdictions, the first come, first served principle determines the allocation of mineral exploration licences.[216] The tender bid methodology is used far more rarely, unlike the petroleum sector where auctioning is the predominant method of allocation.[217] If a State possesses strong geological knowledge about a deposit then the case for auctioning is strengthened.[218] Bulk commodity minerals such as iron ore, coal, phosphate and construction minerals are also more conducive to tendering processes.[219] Post the 2008 financial crisis, changes in the mining industry piqued State

---

.com/legal-post/scc-to-issue-leave-decision-on-yukon-staking-case-this-thursday, accessed 24 February 2019.

[214] Applications on a first come, first served or first to file basis are provided for in the Australian States, Brazil, Chile, Finland, Ghana, Mongolia, Nigeria, South Africa, Tanzania, Zambia and other countries. By contrast, the allocation systems of Ecuador, Indonesia, Kazakhstan, Mexico and Uzbekistan are based on tenders. A third model – that of direct negotiations – has also been employed in some jurisdictions. Stanley and Mikhayalova note that direct negotiations are employed where the mining investment is a means to secure other investments. Unfortunately, direct negotiations have also resulted in corrupt practices: see Michael Stanley and Ekatarina Mikhaylova, *Mineral Resource Tenders and Mining Infrastructure Projects Guiding Principles* (World Bank 2011) Extractive Industries for Development Series #22, 2.

[215] Stanley and Mikhaylova (n 214) 4.

[216] Girones (n 47) 34.

[217] Indonesia's Mineral and Coal Mining Law (Law No. 4/2009) establishes competitive tendering in designated mining areas as the predominant method of allocation. A surprising number of jurisdictions also allow for tendering in the alternative to first come, first served concessioning. Often this occurs in relation to specially determined mineral areas. For example, sections 14–17 of the New South Wales Mining Act, 1992 provides for a tendering process for allocated minerals in land within a mineral allocated area. Article 29 of the Mining Law of Ecuador, on the other hand, entrenches public auction as the predominant method for allocating mineral concessions. Article 30 goes on to hold that the State may delegate participation in the mining sector through concessions 'on an exceptional basis'. Tanzania's Mining Act, 2010 empowers the State to conclude development agreements, designate areas for competitive tendering and confer prospecting licences on a concession basis.

[218] Girones (n 47) 34.

[219] Stanley and Mikhaylova (n 214) 7.

interest in tendering processes, including higher commodity pricing driven by the economic growth of China, India and Brazil and increased competition to access mineral resources worldwide as a result of new, developing country multinationals.[220] This led some States to believe they could demand better terms, both as regards the fiscal terms of the concession, but also as regards the overall development of the mining area and infrastructural investments.[221] Legal provision for a tender methodology to be employed is also sometimes made in circumstances where rights have been revoked, relinquished, expired or annulled and cadastral and geological information is open to the public.[222]

The State's oversight of a first come, first served system is not radically different to that required in competitive tendering processes. In both systems, the principles of transparency, the reduction of discretion and the minimization of subjectivity are supposed to hold sway,[223] preserving the State's role as a regulator. However, a more recent trend in competitive tendering, which requires applicants to bid on revenue sharing, shifts the role of the State to that of collaborating partner.[224] World Bank Guidelines on mineral resource tenders, for example, assume that bidders will compete on the basis of financial terms and incentives (for example, level of investment in the mining sector), and, more recently, the package of contributions a mining company intends to make to magnify the broader economic impact of the operation.[225] The recent revenue-based coal concessions instituted by the central government of India and the model planned for State concessions of other mineral commodities require bidders to quote bids as a percentage of revenue to be shared with the government.[226] While being lauded as a way to rejuvenate the flagging Indian mining sector and improve transparency,[227] this ties central and provincial governments ever closer to mining production.

In both first come, first served and competitive tendering systems, environmental and sustainability considerations can be integrated as a prior adminis-

---

220 Ibid ix.

221 Ibid.

222 Girones (n 47) 34. For example, the authors mention the legal provisions in the laws of Mozambique and Peru.

223 Ibid 15–18.

224 Anjani K Agrawal, *Mineral Concessions Framework: Imperatives for Success* (September 2015) 1.

225 Stanley and Mikhaylova (n 214) 10.

226 Agrawal (n 224) 5.

227 PTI, 'Government mulls competitive bidding for allocation of mining leases', *The Economic Times*, 17 November 2014, http://economictimes.indiatimes.com/industry/indl-goods/svs/metals-mining/government-mulls-competitive-bidding-for-allocation-of-mining-leases/articleshow/45181030.cms, accessed 24 February 2019.

trative requirement to undertake an environmental impact assessment.[228] For example, in South Africa (a first come, first served jurisdiction) no person may prospect or mine without an environmental authorization,[229] and in Ecuador (competitive tendering) the Ministry of Environment's approval of the Environmental Impact Study and report on impacts in protected areas is a prior administrative act for engaging in mining activities.[230] But this is unusual as exploration rights are usually granted based on an applicant's financial and technical competence and experience, a proposed programme of work and the absence of an overlapping claim with a preexisting exploration or exploitation right.[231]

Botswana, South Africa and Zambia nevertheless specify additional environmental criteria for the issuing of prospecting and mining rights. In Botswana and Zambia, the proposed programme of prospecting operations must be 'adequate' and make 'proper provision for environmental protection'.[232] South African mining law goes substantially further, requiring that prospecting should not result in 'unacceptable pollution, ecological degradation or damage to the environment'.[233] The Minister of Mineral Resources must consider a similar criterion when granting or refusing the application for a mining right.[234]

2.2.2 Providing security of tenure

As part of its concessioning role, the State is also expected to assure mining investors of security of tenure. In the mid-1990s Dale wrote that for at least three decades, the mining industry had regarded security of tenure as a 'critical and non-negotiable factor' in decisions to invest, and that even countries with favourable geological deposits were expected to ensure an acceptable level of security of tenure.[235] The preoccupation with security of tenure remains relevant to this day. In a recent World-Bank sponsored review of mining cadastre, for example, security of tenure was listed as the first of several 'ground rules'

---

[228] See further the discussion in Chapter 6.

[229] Mineral and Petroleum Resources Development Act, 2002 (South Africa), section 5A.

[230] Mining Law (Ecuador), Article 26.

[231] See s 13(5) of the Mining Act, 1992 (New South Wales) for a fairly typical set of requirements.

[232] Mines and Minerals Act, 1999 (Botswana), section 14(b); Mines and Minerals Development Act, 2015 (Zambia), section 22(1)(d).

[233] Mineral and Petroleum Resources Development Act, 2002 (South Africa), section 17(1)(c).

[234] Ibid, section 23(1)(d).

[235] Dale (n 6) 298.

necessary for the proper operation of a mining cadastre.[236] Affirmation that the mining policy and legal framework advances security of tenure can be found in developed and developing mineral-rich jurisdictions alike.[237]

Security of tenure is a complex concept that has evolved over time. Essentially, it references the set of clear, predictable and transparent norms and procedures relating to the nature, transferability, allocation, continuity and stability of mining rights that are deemed necessary to attract mining investment. The deep structure of these assurances, however, is a disembedded market in mining rights, and the norms and procedures function as the preconditions for that market.

Initially, security of tenure concerns centred on a smooth and guaranteed transition from the exploration to the exploitation phase of a project. The 1992 World Bank *Strategy for African Mining*, for example, stated that '[g]iven good geological prospects, a guarantee of mining rights before starting exploration [is] an essential pre-condition'.[238] Bastida presents this as representative of a narrow security of tenure concept: 'A reasonable legal entitlement for extraction rights after successful completion of the exploration phase.'[239]

Security of tenure was subsequently defined more expansively, for example, as the 'stability' of rights granted to implement the different operational phases of mining.[240] This broader interpretation focuses attention on the conditions attached to exploitation, and the bases upon which exploitation rights can

---

[236] Girones (n 47) 2.

[237] See, for example, British Columbia, where the mining strategy states: 'The Province works with communities, First Nations, industry and others to maintain security of tenure and access to land for mineral exploration' (Ministry of Energy and Mines, British Columbia, *British Columbia's Mineral Exploration and Mining Strategy: Seizing Global Demand* (undated) 10); a brochure on *Botswana Mineral Investment Promotion* (undated) prepared by the Republic of Botswana, which states that the 1999 Mines and Minerals Act as a 'modern mining law' 'streamlines licensing and enhances security of tenure' (at 2); and the mineral policy in Tanzania, which asserts that '[t]he legal and regulatory framework of the mineral sector requires transparency, predictability, minimum discretion and security of tenure' (see Ministry of Energy and Minerals, United Republic of Tanzania, *The Mineral Policy of Tanzania* (2009) 13).

[238] World Bank, *Strategy for African Mining* (1992) World Bank Technical Paper No. 181 (henceforth *Strategy for African Mining*) 17.

[239] Bastida (n 1) 35.

[240] J Otto, F Chand and C Foong, 'Guidelines for a National Mineral Policy' in *Mineral Development Policy and Planning Project*, UN, Department of Technical Cooperation for Development (1990).

be revoked or suspended. For example, the World Bank, in its 1996 *Mining Strategy for Latin America and the Caribbean*, stated:

> Security of title is the prime requisite of any investor. The law must ensure that a mineral right, once granted, (a) cannot be suspended or revoked except on specified grounds which are clearly set out in the law and (b) provides reasonable assurances guaranteeing the continuity of operations over the life of the project.[241]

The emphasis on 'specified grounds' in this quotation masks concerns relating to clarity, transparency and foreseeability. In the first wave of mining code legal reforms developing countries were encouraged to eliminate discriminatory eligibility criteria,[242] eliminate discretion in the implementation of the mining law (ostensibly to minimize corruption and processing time'),[243] specify clear timeframes and procedures for obtaining, maintaining and terminating mineral rights and incorporate mechanisms of accountability and review.[244] Developing countries were also directed to allow mineral rightsholders to transfer their title to any eligible third party, along with being able to mortgage the title to raise finance.[245]

Other commentators raised the duration of exploitation rights as an issue,[246] and the problem of 'excessive' regulation,[247] such as the need for a holder to demonstrate financial and technical capacity to conduct a work programme; standardized work, investment or production requirements; and specification of local training requirements, use of local services, provision of infrastructure, and the like. Environmental regulations have also been highlighted as a potential source of regulatory uncertainty affecting security of tenure.[248]

In the discourse of the sustainable mineral development consensus, Chile stands out as a 'lead reformer' in the arena of promoting security of tenure.[249] A 2003 review of mining reforms over the 1980s and 1990s put forward by the World Bank and the International Finance Corporation states baldly, for

---

241 World Bank, *A Mining Strategy for Latin America and the Caribbean* (1996) World Bank Technical Paper No. 345 xiii (henceforth *Strategy for LAC Mining*).

242 Ibid xv.

243 Ibid 14. Indeed, possibly the main mantra emerging from the sustainable mineral development consensus is to limit ministerial discretion as far as possible. See Dale (n 6) 300.

244 Ibid 16.

245 Ibid xv.

246 J Otto, 'The exploration and mine development regulatory time dilemma' (1995) University of Dundee: CEPMLP Professional Paper PP15.

247 Bastida (n 1) 37.

248 *Strategy for LAC Mining* (n 241) 14–15.

249 World Bank and IFC, *Mining Reform and the World Bank: Providing a Policy Framework for Development* (IFC 2003) 2.

example, that the reforms effected to the Chilean Mining Code by the repressive Pinochet regime during the mid-1980s were 'aimed at *creating a market for mineral rights* by providing clear, non-discretionary norms and transparent procedures',[250] and continues:

> To this end [creating a market for mineral rights], the Code included the following major features. Exploration and exploitation concessions are real property rights. Concessions are freely transferable, mortgageable, and inheritable, with no requirement of government approval. Concessions are awarded to the first eligible person who requests an available area, on a first come-first served basis. Restrictions on eligibility are minimal. Only the holder of an exploration concession can apply for an exploitation concession and is not required to demonstrate a discovery to do so. Concessionaires can exploit all concessionable minerals within the property. Exploitation concessions continue in effect for as long as the holder continues paying his concession fee; no minimum work or investment requirement applies.[251]

The World Bank's representations of the Chilean Mining Code in this publication have not been verified for accuracy against the actual provisions of that Code applicable at the time. They nevertheless stand as an idealized vision of an extreme version of security of tenure that requires both proactive and withholding conduct on the part of the State in the service of a disembedded market for mining rights. It bears emphasizing that there is little in the way of systematic, empirical analysis of the longterm socioecological impacts of each of the elements of security of tenure. The institutions advancing security of tenure policy prescriptions do not appear to have deliberated on how the various elements of security of tenure impact upon the rate and quality of extraction, although, as the discussion below intimates, these impacts are definitely present.

A comprehensive, comparative overview of security of tenure in the mineral policy and law of mineral-rich jurisdictions and their sustainability impacts is beyond the scope of this monograph. Nevertheless, in a globalized and competitive arena for attracting funds for mining investment, mineral-rich jurisdictions have taken security of tenure policy prescriptions on board, even if they fall short of the idealized versions presented in some documents advanced by IFIs or the mining industry. For example, according to World Bank advice, exploration and exploitation concessions should be real property rights. Notwithstanding this, the legislatures and courts in many jurisdictions have struggled to characterize the right to exploit minerals in terms of whether it *is* a real right (a corporeal, possessory or residual interest in the land), or whether it is more in the nature of a personal or derivative right, simply allowing for

---

[250] Ibid 24 (my emphasis).
[251] Ibid.

access and rights to remove minerals for a limited period of time. The mining laws of many mineral-rich jurisdictions do not as a matter of course articulate the legal character of mining rights.[252] The Chilean Mining Code is rather exceptional in containing a provision that asserts that mineral concessions are real rights and outlining the implications thereof:

> A mining concession is a real and immovable right, distinctive and independent from property rights over the surface tenements, although owned by the same individual. Said rights may be claimed against the State and any other person and may be mortgaged or subject to other real rights and, in general, all acts and contracts.[253]

The emphasis in this provision falls on the distinctiveness of a mining concession relative to surface rights, and on the security it provides as a real right: enforceability against the State and any other person, and mortgageability.

In the USA, where the character of mineral ownership and exploitation rights developed in response to the needs of the coal industry, the first coal cases heard in the mid-nineteenth century labelled the interest in coal as corporeal, irrespective of whether it flowed from a conveyance of the right to mine coal or the conveyance of the coal as such.[254] The interest in coal was akin, the courts said, to a possessory or residual interest in a buried tract of land.[255] The rationale for doing so stemmed from a desire to afford coal miners the benefit of substantive rules only available to those with corporeal interests, that is, transferability, divisibility, the right to use the mined-out space for continuing mining operations on other lands and immunity from the rules governing aban-

---

[252] Although a number are clear that once severed from the earth, minerals become the property of the holder: see Mineral Resources Act, 1989 (Queensland), section 114.

[253] Mining Code (Chile), Article 2. Similarly, section 5(1) of the South African Mineral and Petroleum Resources Development Act asserts that the range of exploitation rights recognized in the law have the character of a 'limited real right'.

[254] Ronald W Polston, 'Mineral ownership theory: Doctrine in disarray' (1994) 70 *North Dakota Law Review* 541. See the discussion of *Caldwell v. Fulton*, 31 Pa. 475,481 (Pa. 1858) in n 2 (henceforth *Caldwell v. Fulton*).

[255] Ibid 548–9. The one exception to this ownership theory of mineral rights in the USA is the civil law-based state of Louisiana, where the mineral servitude is a secondary right of ownership in property, separate from the principal right of ownership in the land: see Patrick S Ottinger, 'A primer on the mineral servitude' (1997) 44 *Annual Institute on Mineral Law* 68. This nonownership or servitude theory of minerals was adopted in the case of *Frost-Johnson Lumber Co. v. Salling's Heirs* 150 La. 756, 91 So. 207 (1922). A mineral servitude is nevertheless a real right in favour of a third party, burdening a tract of land owned by another.

donment.[256] This example illustrates the significance of a mining right being characterized as 'real'.[257]

Even though mineral-rich jurisdictions do not expressly categorize extractive rights as real, national mining laws commonly allow for direct and indirect transfers of mining rights.[258] Contrary to the advice of IFIs, however, most require some level of State authorization.[259] The following provision from Ghana's Minerals and Mining Act, 2006, for example, illustrates a common way of framing the right of transfer:

> A mineral right shall not in whole or in part be transferred, assigned, mortgaged or otherwise encumbered or dealt in, in a manner without the prior approval in writing of the Minister, which approval shall not be unreasonably withheld or given subject to unreasonable conditions.[260]

Western Australia similarly restricts 'dealing' in mining tenements, which is defined as 'the transfer or mortgage of a legal interest in a mining tenement'.[261] Reflecting the creative power of the State, Article 30 of the Bolivian Constitution states that a mining concession is 'an administrative act that grants a mining title which constitutes a limited *personal* right'.[262] Albeit that the right is a personal one, the law continues to affirm that the right is transferable (based on a previous mandatory qualification of fitness of the concession of the rights, issued by the sectorial ministry), and that pledges, assignments and other forms of security may be made over such rights.[263]

---

256 Polston (n 254) 557.

257 The character of a right as corporeal or noncorporeal could also have material implications for the operation of a jurisdiction's rule on expropriation (eminent domain).

258 Direct transfers occur through the direct sale of a mining asset coupled with transfer of the authorization; indirect transfers occur through changes in control of the company holding the right (through either listed or unlisted securities).

259 In Argentina, exploration and exploitation concessions can be freely transferred to third parties (that is, without State approval), subject only to an obligation to register the transfer with the mining registry: Globalmine, 'Basics of mining law – selected jurisdictions' (2015). Free transfer, however, is the exception rather than the rule in mineral-rich jurisdictions. Some jurisdictions prohibit the transfer of exploitation licences for certain commodities, for example, diamonds (Ghana and Sweden).

260 Minerals and Mining Act, 2006 (Ghana), section 14(1). See also section 1, chapter 6 of the Minerals Act, 1991 (Sweden), which provides that '[a]n exploration permit or exploitation concession may be transferred with the permission of the authority responsible for considering applications'.

261 Mining Act, 1978 (Western Australia), section 8.

262 A mining concession is an exceptional instrument in this jurisdiction, where most mining rights are allocated by way of public auction. My emphasis.

263 Mining Law, 2006 (Ecuador), Article 30.

As outlined in greater detail in Chapter 7, transferability is one of the features of security of tenure that may have very troubling sustainability implications. As case studies in that chapter show, not all mining rights transfers are caught in the net of State approval. Even where approval is required it is often not effective in securing consideration of the broader public interest, and is a mere veil to the free transferability of mining rights. The real effect of transferability is that it allows a State to suffer the socioecological effects of a decrease in the quality of investor: as the attractiveness of the geological resource decreases (for example, through decreasing grades or higher costs), mining rights are transferred to increasingly marginal mining proponents. It is interesting that 'quality of investor' is one of the major themes sustained by mining companies in critiques of neoextractivism.[264] And yet, the gradual shift to more precarious mining investment is almost a built in feature of the transferability of mining rights for which the mining industry vociferously advocates.

2.2.3 Summary

This part has explored State concessioning of mining rights as part of a broader analysis of how mineral and mining rights are disembedded, which is essential to the operation of the double movement in Polanyi's conceptual frame. Sitting secure as the national landlord of mineral rights, the State is expected to neutrally allocate exploitation rights and assure security of tenure. The technical rules giving effect to these functions tend to promote extraction without regard for social and environmental limits. From the principle of free entry and online staking under possessory systems of allocation, to the first come, first served and 'use it or lose it' principles and associated rules under administrative systems of allocation, to the rules that affirm the stability, transferability and mortgageability of mining rights, the State emerges as a robust promoter of mining extraction.

3. CONCLUSION

The 'double movement', as employed in this book, rests on the idea that there are two potentially conflicting organizing principles for the extraction of minerals that resonate through the State apparatus: the State must both promote mining and protect society from its worst environmental, social and economic effects. Property institutions play a particularly important role in strengthening the first arm of the double movement. Minerals are commoditized through rules that allow them to be conceptualized separately from the bedrock and lands that contain them (in isolation from other aspects of nature). Property

[264] See the discussion in section 3 of Chapter 2.

rules position minerals as the object of rights – both in themselves and as the target of rights to explore and exploit. 'Minerals', conceived simply as objects of extraction, are also disembedded from the chains of processing and manufacture and the end uses to which mineral commodities are put. By centring rights to minerals in the State as the national landlord, mining proponents are spared the need to negotiate with endless individual landowners. Instead, a global market for mineral production comes into view, with a more manageable number of traders.

Through their permanent sovereignty over natural resources, and based on ancient precedents, States use their lawmaking and police powers to drive mineral extraction. Institutions governing the mineral rights cadastre, the archiving of geological knowledge, the commencement of mining works and the system for allocation of exploitation rights reinforce a market in mineral extraction rights but frequently have unintended consequences, such as quickening the pace of mineral extraction. Other property rules secure the primacy of mining over other land uses, including rules allowing broad ancillary entitlements to use water or to use land for disposing waste or conducting primary or secondary treatment processes; narrowly defined protections for other land uses, such as conservation; biased procedures for resolving conflict; and unfair rules for calculating compensation for mining-inflicted damage.

Although some institutions could accommodate socioecological protection – for example, using the mineral rights cadastre as a tool for national planning – consideration of social and environmental issues and limits is barely apparent in mining-related property laws.

5. The State, mining and taxation

1. INTRODUCTION

This is the second of four substantive chapters detailing the operation of Polanyi's 'double movement'[1] in the system of global mining production. In similar fashion to the preceding chapter on property institutions, it focuses on the dominant patterning of State roles, now focused on the taxation of minerals and mining.

Tax revenues are likely to be the core benefit of mineral extraction for host States.[2] They are not the only macrolevel contribution mining can make to national economies.[3] However, for the reasons outlined by Boadway and Keen, the fiscal linkage is often the most significant. Mining investments are highly capital intensive, hence employment can be quite modest and relatively low skilled. And although up and downstream industrial linkages can be useful, they too are often quite limited[4] – in developing countries, mining continues to be an 'enclave economic activity'.[5] At various stages, UNCTAD, the United Nations Economic Commission for Africa and the International Monetary Fund (IMF) have agreed that generating public revenue through a transparent tax and budget system is the 'paramount' development potential of mining. But this is a view challenged by the World Bank and mining industry, who advocate for the industry's broader sustainable development potential.[6] The Mining, Mineral and Sustainable Development (MMSD) project was also lukewarm on the importance of mineral tax revenues, positioning them instead

1 See section 6.1, Chapter 1 for an explanation of this concept.

2 Robin Boadway and Michael Keen, 'Theoretical perspectives on resource tax design' in Philip Daniel, Michael Keen and Charles McPherson, *The Taxation of Petroleum and Minerals: Principles, Problems and Practice* (Routledge 2010) 13, 19.

3 See, for example, the 'inverted pyramid' of contributions in International Council on Mining and Metals (ICMM) *The Role of Mining in National Economics* 2nd edn (October 2014) 18. Foreign direct investment, exports and employment can also be significant, particularly in low income countries.

4 Boadway and Keen (n 2) 19.

5 Kato Lambrechts (ed.), *Breaking the Curse: How Transparent Taxation and Fair Taxes Can Turn Africa's Mineral Wealth into Development* (Christian Aid 2009) 15.

6 Ibid.

as a 'more general economic benefit'.[7] The final report noted, however, that the division of resource rents between the host country and foreign investors is a 'basic issue' in capturing mineral wealth, and that many crucial issues centre on taxation.[8]

Viewed through the lens of the double movement, taxation is obviously important as the basis upon which the State subsists. In some mineral-rich jurisdictions, the mining industry is a significant source of annual government revenues.[9] A variety of factors impact on the salience of this revenue stream flow, including the extent to which the State can raise taxes through other bases (income and corporate taxes, capital gains tax, import and export taxes and even targeted environmental taxes).[10] In some mineral-rich jurisdictions, mineral resource taxes have assumed even greater significance as trade liberalization agreements erode import and export taxes and corporate tax rates continue their worldwide decline.[11]

At first sight, the State's power to impose taxes sits with firmly with the arm of the double movement that seeks to protect society from the free rein of markets. Taxation is the mechanism that links the economic and political spheres: governments tax economic activity to service a particular political agenda in order to secure their own reelection. Depending on the needs within a mineral-rich jurisdiction, there may be great pressure on the State to spend taxes on social projects such as roads, clinics, hospitals and schools, free education and social welfare. The State accordingly is a key agent in transforming

---

[7] International Institute for Environment and Development and World Business Council for Sustainable Development, *Breaking New Ground: Mining, Minerals and Sustainable Development* (Earthscan 2002) 174 (henceforth *Breaking New Ground*).

[8] Ibid 179.

[9] Paul Mitchell, 'Taxation and investment issues in mining' in Christopher Eads, Paul Mitchell and Francisco Paris *Advancing the EITI in the Mining Sector: A Consultation with Stakeholders* (EITI 2009) 27, 31. In 2010, Boadway and Keen calculated that the percentage of government revenues derived from mining operations in ten mineral-rich jurisdictions ranged between 1 and 44 per cent, averaging 11 per cent overall (see Boadway and Keen (n 2) 18). Data on the extent to which hardrock mining contributes to government revenues is otherwise hard to access. For example, the 2014 compilers of the 'Mining Contribution Index' wanted to incorporate contribution to government revenues as a variable in the index, but abandoned this plan after 'data limitations' became evident (see ICMM (n 3) 26).

[10] UNCTAD, *Fiscal Space for Stability and Development: Contemporary Challenges*, Trade and Development Report, 2014 (United Nations 2014) 168.

[11] Ibid 169. UNCTAD notes that in developing countries and least developed countries (LDCs) in particular, revenues from import tariffs and export tariffs imposed on metals, minerals and agricultural commodities accounted for a large proportion of public revenues.

the financial wealth arising from mining activity into human, social and built capital.

But the State's fiscal framework for the extractive industries not only serves the objective of securing enough of the mineral resource rent to finance its development goals. According to conventional wisdom, the fiscal framework must also be 'appropriate to attract private investment',[12] and thus please the rich and economically active so they are not discouraged from taking mining investments elsewhere. Taxation, therefore, can equally be used to promote free market principles. Rather than a mechanism that merely protects society from the free market, taxation therefore sits at the crux of the State's management of paradox under the double movement.

The policy directive to design fiscal frameworks attractive to private investors rests, in turn, on the claim that fiscal regimes can distort investment decisions all the way through the mine development and closure chain.[13] A great deal of research has been expended on determining the optimum design of fiscal regimes, and how this objective intersects with the geology of reserves, the economics of their extraction and the optimum investment and development trajectory.[14] The claim is that taxes not only influence *whether* a mine will be developed, but also *how* and *when* exploration and exploitation occur, including 'the scope of exploration and discovery, the timing and scale of initial development, the rate of production and decline, the timing and scale of enhanced recovery operations, the overall resource recovery factor, and the timing of final abandonment'.[15] Whether fiscal regimes influence decisions along the mineral value chain and whether tax benefits incentivize investment in the mining sector are two separate questions. As discussed below, there is little evidence to suggest that tax incentives on their own will attract mining investment. Other factors, such as the general investment climate and the quality of the mineral reserve, are likely to play a larger role in what are essentially 'location based' investment decisions.[16]

Taxes may be designed to influence other forms of behaviour, as well as power relations between actors involved in the production chain. At the time that commoditization of labour was taking place, for example, taxes were

---

[12] UNCTAD (n 10) 180.

[13] Mitchell (n 9) 28.

[14] James L Smith, 'Issues in extractive resource taxation: A review of research methods and models' (2012) IMF Working Paper WP/12/287 3, 5–17.

[15] Ibid 3.

[16] United Nations, 'Secretariat note on agenda item 3(o) of the provisional agenda: Tax competition in corporate tax: Use of tax incentives in attracting foreign direct investment' E/C. 18/2010/CRP.12 (United Nations 2010) 2.

imposed to force people into waged labour.[17] In contemporary times, a great deal of effort is increasingly being expended on the use of tax instruments to encourage virtuous environmental behaviour. In mining, these debates have centred upon the design of the carbon tax.

This chapter focuses on the dominant model underlying the State's taxation of minerals and mining. This is a more complicated task than explicating the dominant model for mineral and mining property relations, for, as Smith asserts, '[n]o two countries tax extractive resources in quite the same way'.[18] Yet for all the variation in surface detail, a dominant model based on six distinct State roles is apparent, namely: (1) capturing a portion of the mineral resource rent; (2) easing mining investment; (3) incentivizing appropriate environmental behaviour; (4) curbing tax avoidance and tax evasion; (5) distributing wealth through fiscal decentralization and natural resource revenue sharing; and (6) promoting tax transparency.

2. THE STATE'S TAXATION OF MINERALS AND MINING: EXPLICATING THE DOMINANT MODEL

Taxing the mining industry is an age old idea. The payment of royalties to the mining procurator in ancient Rome,[19] the development of the *Regal* in German mining law,[20] the considerations payable to the Crown under English law[21] – all show that the idea of binding some form of governmental authority to the mining enterprise through the use of tax instruments is hardly new. Today, taxation is still central to the positioning of mining as a development industry, at least in contexts where private-led extractivism prevails: the State withdraws from direct involvement in the mining enterprise,[22] but through

---

[17] In this regard, see a reference to the hut tax in Karl Polanyi, *The Great Transformation* (Beacon 1944) 172.

[18] Smith (n 14) 3.

[19] For example, the *Lex Metallis Dicta*, an ancient Roman mining law dating from 117–138 AD, stated that the discoverer of a mine on public land obtained a right to mine it, provided he paid a lump sum to the procurator of the mines of Vipasca. The *Lex* further decreed that to safeguard the State's royalty, ore could only be transported from the mine by daylight. See MO Dale, *An Historical and Comparative Study of the Concept and Acquisition of Mineral Rights* (1979), Thesis submitted in part fulfilment for the degree of Doctor of Laws, University of South Africa 6–7.

[20] Ibid 17–19.

[21] Ibid 45.

[22] Government's equity participation in mining projects, to the extent that this falls short of a fully paid up share on commercial terms, can also be viewed as a form of taxation. See Boadway and Keen (n 2) 40.

a variety of taxes reaps part reward, part compensation for the exploitation of nonrenewable mineral resources – a bounty it can put to use for socioeconomic development and the maintenance of political stability.

In most mineral-rich jurisdictions, the rules pertaining to mineral royalties are set out in the national mining law,[23] or in separate mineral royalty legislation.[24] These rules may sit alongside constitutional prescriptions on fiscal matters and national, regional and even local level legislation on general taxation, such as laws establishing the level of corporate taxation, tax incentives, and the imposition of VAT and customs and excise duties. Constitutional rules on fiscal matters may specifically mention the extractive industry or nonrenewable resources.[25]

The diversity and idiosyncrasy of mineral fiscal regimes the world over should not mask the intense discursive construction of risk advanced by stakeholders with different interests. Agents of pro-mining discourses have aggressively advanced ideas about appropriate fiscal regimes, while agents of discourses of mining dissent have largely pointed to the unfairness of preferential tax treatment given to the mining industry.

Bretton Woods and allied institutions have been particularly active participants in mineral taxation debates. The World Bank's influential 1992 *Strategy for African Mining*,[26] as well as its 1996 *Mining Strategy for Latin America and the Caribbean* (*Strategy for LAC Mining*),[27] incorporated policy guidance on economic and fiscal policy and mineral taxation regimes biased towards promoting private investment. Similar policy prescriptions were presented in

---

[23] In Ecuador and in the jurisdictions of New South Wales, Queensland and Western Australia, for example, rules setting out the terms of the mineral royalty can be found in the national mining law.

[24] Latecomers to the imposition of mineral royalties such as Peru and South Africa, for example, have separate mineral royalty legislation. See the Mining Royalties Law (Law N° 28258) in Peru and the Mineral and Petroleum Resources Royalty Act 28 of 2008 and Mineral and Petroleum Resources Royalty (Administration) Act 29 of 2008 in South Africa respectively.

[25] For example, Ecuador's 2008 Constitution provides that nonrenewable natural resources are part of the unalienable heritage of the State, and in managing these resources the State must give priority to 'the charging of royalties or other no-tax contributions and corporate shares' (Constitution of Ecuador, 2008, Article 317).

[26] Mining Unit, Industry and Energy Division, *Strategy for African Mining*, World Bank Technical Paper No. 181 (World Bank 1992) (henceforth *Strategy for African Mining*).

[27] Industry and Mining Division, *A Mining Strategy for Latin America and the Caribbean*, World Bank Technical Paper No. 345 (World Bank 1996) (henceforth *Strategy for LAC Mining*).

a 2002 World Bank report on mineral royalties,[28] and research conducted or commissioned by the International Council of Mining and Metals (ICMM)[29] and the IMF.[30] Accounting, auditing and legal firms have echoed the policy advice emanating from these institutions.[31] More recent contributions include the World Bank's *Extractives Industries Sector: Essentials for Economists, Public Finance Professionals and Policy Makers*,[32] their Mining Investment and Governance Review,[33] and an IMF-sponsored publication on policies to harness the power of natural resources and to break the resource curse.[34] Although more centric in tone, multistakeholder initiatives such as the MMSD, and the Natural Resource Governance Institute's Natural Resources Charter,[35] also promote taxation regimes that strongly promote private investment. Proponents of neoliberalism have also weighed in heavily on the appropriate design of the carbon tax for the mining industry.

Advocates of neoextractivism in South America, and resource nationalism in Africa, on the other, have countered the heavy emphasis on designing fiscal regimes to promote private investment. In South America, various progressive, left-leaning governments have assigned the State a major role in 'development' through the extractive industries, either by way of State equity in

---

[28] James Otto *et al*, *Mining Royalties: A Global Study of Their Impact on Investors, Government and Civil Society* (World Bank 2006).

[29] Evelyn Dietsche, *Minerals Taxation Regimes: A Review of Issues and Challenges in their Design and Implementation* (ICMM 2009). The publication nevertheless includes a disclaimer indicating that the views expressed in this publication are not necessarily those of the ICMM.

[30] Thomas Baunsgaard, 'A primer on mineral taxation', IMF Working Paper No. 01/139 (IMF 2001) 16; Emil M Sunley and Thomas Baunsgaard, 'The tax treatment of the mining sector: An IMF perspective', Background paper prepared for the World Bank workshop on the taxation of the mining sector, 4–5 April 2001.

[31] Notable examples include PricewaterhouseCoopers' (PwC) occasional series on mineral fiscal rates and rules in selected countries (see PwC, *Corporate Income Taxes, Mining Royalties and Other Mining Taxes: A Summary of Rates and Rules in Selected Countries* (June 2012)) and their series on the mining industry's Total Tax Contribution (see PwC, *Total Tax Contribution: A Study of the Economic Contribution Mining Companies Make to Public Finances* (2010)).

[32] Håvard Halland, Martin Lokanc and Arvind Nair (eds) with Sridar Padmanabhan Kannan, *The Extractives Industries Sector: Essentials for Economists, Public Finance Professionals and Policy Makers* (World Bank Group 2015).

[33] World Bank, 'Mining Investment and Governance Review (MInGov), www.worldbank.org/en/programs/mingov, accessed 25 February 2019.

[34] Rabeh Arezki, Thorvaldur Gylfason and Amadou Sy (eds), *Beyond the Curse: Policies to Harness the Power of Natural Resources* (IMF 2011).

[35] Natural Resource Governance Institute, *Natural Resource Charter* 2nd edn (2014).

mining enterprises, or through higher taxes and royalties.[36] In Africa, the *AMV* (2009) highlights the issue of weak tax administration, which it claims has led to African States garnering an inequitable share of mineral resource rents.[37] Links are also made to the State's role as the repository of geological data: Poor geological mapping increases the risk for investors, 'who consequently demand extremely favourable tax regimes that may result from their blue-sky operation'.[38] Like their South American counterparts, the advocates of higher mineral taxes in Africa have in mind securing a higher proportion of mineral rents for development projects.

Nongovernmental organizations, academics and intergovernmental organizations have criticized neoliberal and neoextractivist tax policies, highlighting the inequities of tax incentives given to the mining industry,[39] alongside the problems of tax avoidance and tax evasion. In recent years, the discourses of tax avoidance and evasion have been subsumed into discussions on illicit financial flows (IFFs), which have emerged around resource transfers in developing countries,[40] and the issue of base erosion and profit shifting (BEPS), on which developed countries have taken the lead.[41] The United Nations' recently

---

[36] Eduardo Gudynas, 'Debates on development and its alternatives in Latin America: a brief heterodox guide' in M Lang and D Mokrani, *Beyond Development: Alternative Visions from Latin America* (Transnational Institute/Rosa Luxemburg Foundation 2013) 15, 25.

[37] African Union, *Africa Mining Vision* (February 2009) 14.

[38] Ibid 15.

[39] Lambrechts (n 5); Claire Kumar, *Undermining the Poor: Mineral Taxation Reforms in Latin America* (Christian Aid 2009) 5; JW van Gelder *et al*, *Tax Avoidance by Mining Companies in Developing Countries – An Analysis of Potential Dutch Policy Initiatives* (Profundo 2016).

[40] Work on IFFs was spearheaded by the work of Kar and Freitas, in cooperation with Global Financial Integrity ; see Dev Kar and Devon Cartwright-Smith, *Illicit Financial Flows from Developing Countries, 2002–2006* (Global Financial Integrity 2008); Dev Kar and Sarah Freitas, *Illicit Financial Flows from Developing Countries over the Decade Ending 2009* (Global Financial Integrity 2011); Dev Kar and Sarah Freitas, *Illicit Financial Flows from Developing Countries: 2001–2010* (Ford Foundation 2012). Africa-focused work in this vein was continued by the African Development Bank in cooperation with Global Financial Integrity African Development Bank and Global Financial Integrity: *Illicit Financial Flows and the Problem of Net Resource Transfer from Africa: 1980–2009* (AdB and Global Financial Integrity 2013). Even the World Bank has recently stepped into this arena: see Peter Reuter (ed.), *Draining Development: Controlling Flows of Illicit Funds from Developing Countries* (World Bank 2012).

[41] The BEPS initiative grew out of the 2012 G20 Los Cabos Summit, which mandated the OECD to develop an Action Plan (see OECD, *Action Plan on Base Erosion and Profit-Shifting* (OECD Publishing 2013). A BEPS Package for reform of the international tax system to tackle tax avoidance, comprising 15 reports, was agreed at the

published *Handbook on Extractive Industries Taxation* also contains useful guidance on tax issues arising from tax treaties, transfer pricing and the government's fiscal take.[42]

In the field of tax transparency in the extractives industry, the field is dominated by the Extractives Industry Transparency Initiative (EITI)[43] and the extensive literature since produced on the efficacy of this governance initiative. The EITI has stimulated a variety of other nationally based transparency regimes that establish mandatory country-by-country and project-by-project reporting for companies, using various connecting factors – usually listing on the stock exchange in the jurisdiction implementing the transparency initiative.

It is from these and other sources that the double movement of the State in mining and minerals taxation has been constructed, as constituted by the ensuing overview of State roles.

2.1 Mineral Resource Rents: The Capturing State

The dominant patterning of roles under the current global system of mining production assumes that the State must gain an 'adequate' or a 'fair' share of mineral resource rents. In the discourse of the sustainable mineral development consensus this role is assumed rather than expressly stated, because the emphasis falls instead on the function of *balancing* State capture of rents with the role of promoting private investment. The task of balancing also vests in the State. The MMSD, for example, opined that '[m]any of the crucial decisions rest on taxation – as governments attempt to gain an adequate share of the rents from mining without setting taxes so high that they scare off investors'.[44] The discourses of neoextractivism and resource nationalism, however, place far greater emphasis on the State simply appropriating mineral resource rents in support of the development project.[45]

The fiscal flows arising from mineral resource rents always tie the State to the mining enterprise, and would thus further the first arm of the double

---

G20's 2015 summit in Antalya (for a list of the reports see www.oecd.org/ctp/beps-2015-final-reports.htm). In November 2016 the Multilateral Convention to Implement Tax Treaty Related Measures to Prevent BEPS was adopted. The Convention enables governments to close gaps in bilateral tax treaties by transposing the results of the OECD/G20 BEPS Project into bilateral tax treaties worldwide.

42 United Nations, *Handbook on Extractive Industries Taxation* (2018).

43 See Extractive Industry Transparency Initiative, https://eiti.org accessed 25 February 2019.

44 *Breaking New Ground* (n 7) 179.

45 Hans-Jürgen Burchardt and Kristina Dietz, '(Neo-)extractivism – a new challenge for development theory from Latin America' (2014) 35(3) *Third World Quarterly* 470.

movement. However, resource taxes may be used to protect society, even to shift a State away from reliance on the market-driven exploitation of its natural resources.

The State's resource rent capturing role is difficult and complex for a variety of reasons. The concept of 'mineral resource rents' is itself multifaceted. The neoliberal principles of taxation and investor promotion that restrict the State's rent capturing ambitions are entrenched, well developed and supported by a phalanx of financial, accounting and legal professionals.[46] Implementing taxes to cover rents may require complex administrative measures in a situation of information asymmetry, where mining companies hold the information the State needs to set appropriate levels of taxation.[47] Asymmetric information makes the determination of profit and rent difficult, particularly when coupled with corporate strategies for understating profits, for example through transfer pricing.[48] This is even more the case in low income countries where limited domestic policymaking capacity is pitted against the resources of multinational companies.[49] And, in instances where States have attempted to recover a greater share of the rent, they have faced aggressive advocacy and lobbying on the part of the mining industry.

The ideological battle over the State's capture of the mineral resource rent has been waged at the level of principle – *why* the State should share in mineral resource rents, or even capture all of those rents; and through policy advice on the forms and level of mineral taxation – *how* the State recovers the rents, whether through specially designed resource rent taxes, flat fees and/or production or profit-based royalties. The sections that follow outline the concept of mineral resource rents, the principled basis for State capture of rents and the design of tax instruments to recover rents.

2.1.1 Resource taxes and mineral resource rents

In addition to all the usual taxes that apply to businesses (corporate tax, income tax, VAT, import and export duties and taxes targeted at externalities), States usually require mining companies to pay some form of resource tax. Resource taxes are in turn based on the multilayered concept of mineral resource rents,

---

46 See Leonard Seabrooke and Duncan Wigan, 'Powering ideas through expertise: Professionals in global tax battles' (2016) 23(3) *Journal of European Public Policy* 357.

47 Boadway and Keen (n 2) 23. Generally, mining proponents will be far better informed of the geological and commercial circumstances of particular resource projects at all stages. Mining companies hold the knowledge of the true division between profits and rents, and they have no incentive to share this information with the State.

48 Otto (n 28) 52.

49 Boadway and Keen (n 2) 24.

a concept that reflects different conceptions of the financial returns from mining available for sharing between the agents in control of mining factors of production, and the 'host' of the mineral resources themselves – whether conceived as the State, the nation or citizens. Three features of mineral resource extraction influence thinking about a 'fair share' of the rents: as a factor of production, mineral reserves are always fixed in a particular location; the extraction of mineral resources involves a once-off opportunity to convert natural into financial capital; and the economic rents of mining may be substantive, with the opportunity for 'super normal' profits.[50]

At times the concept of resource rents is used in a wide sense, to refer to the full range of benefits that may arise from the exploitation of a mineral resource. This usage is apparent, for example, in the MMSD quotation above ('governments attempt to gain an adequate share of the *rents* from mining'). 'Rent' in this case simply refers to the payment made for the opportunity of working a mine. But the more technically correct, narrower meaning of rents refers to what a firm receives *in excess* of the return required for it to enter and stay in the market.[51] 'Rent' or 'economic rent' in this case refers to 'surplus operating profit' over and above the fair rate of return necessary to incentivize private investment. The surplus operating profit would refer to the amount remaining after all fixed and variable costs, including the cost of capital and other tax obligations (corporate taxes, mineral royalties and other statutory levies[52]), have been fulfilled.

Taxing economic rents is attractive for two reasons. First, it does not fall foul of the taxation principle of neutrality, because the surplus profits are theoretically not necessary to motivate investors to stay in the market. Second, taxing rents is deemed to be efficient because it evens out competitive advantage gained on the quality of the mineral reserve. Such rents are called Ricardian rents, after British economist David Ricardo's studies on the differing fertility

---

50 Lindsay Hogan and Brenton Goldsworthy, 'International mineral taxation: Experience and issues' in Philip Daniel, Michael Keen and Charles McPherson, *The Taxation of Petroleum and Minerals: Principles, Problems, and Practice* (Routledge 2010) 122, 135; Otto (n 28) 10, 19.

51 Boadway and Keen (n 2) 15. Stiglitz has defined economic rent as 'the difference between the price that is actually paid and the price that would have to be paid in order for the good or service to be produced': Joseph E Stiglitz, *Principles of Micro-Economics* 2nd edn (Norton 1996) 298. Hogan and Goldsworthy (n 50, 138) distinguish between the broader concept of economic rents (which incorporate advantages based on technology, leadership or managerial skill, for example) and resource rents, which relate directly to the quality of the resource deposit.

52 South African Institute of Mining and Metallurgy, *The Rise of Resource Nationalism: A Resurgence of State Control in an Era of Free Markets or the Legitimate Search for a New Equilibrium?* (2012) 146.

of agricultural land.[53] In the case of mining, reserves located near the surface or within easy reach of transportation routes will earn rents to the extent that the price for a particular commodity settles closer to the production costs of more difficult to exploit reserves.[54] Mineral taxation targeting only economic rents would level the playing fields, applying only to those proponents making profits from the comparative natural advantage of their reserves, and then only to the extent of that advantage.

Following the work of Alfred Marshall, however, mining proponents would argue that rents must be even more narrowly construed to exclude 'quasi-rents'. A quasi-rent is a payment to the actors controlling factors of production that provides an inventive over the long term to maintain an economically valuable allocation of resources.[55] Specifically, in a mining context, this means that the surplus operating profits received by mining proponents at any given time must also factor into account investment in exploration and mine development, which might have taken place a long time ago. If mining proponents are not allowed a satisfactory return on their past investment in exploration and mine development, so the argument goes, new exploration will not be undertaken.[56] Research conducted on behalf of the ICMM has argued that quasi-rents include the profits made from short term cyclical commodity price increases.[57] Excluding all quasi-rents allows one to arrive at the 'pure rent' from mineral resource extraction, the mining industry has argued.[58]

From the outset, therefore, the State's role in capturing a share of 'rents' is complex, hamstrung by technical arguments on the true range of benefits arising from mining. It also bears mentioning that the conceptualization of rents outlined above does not take the social and ecological costs of mining into consideration at all. As highlighted elsewhere in this book, these costs are usually borne by the State and local communities.

2.1.2 Principled basis for State capture of rents

The principled arguments for the State sharing in, or indeed taking all, the mineral resource rents differ between the discourses of the sustainable mineral

---

53 To meet the needs of the population, the most fertile land is cultivated first. With population growth, the demand for food and agricultural land increases and less fertile land is brought into production. If the price of food is determined by the cost of production on the *least* fertile land, the owners of more fertile land earn an economic rent proportionate to the fertility of their lands, without further effort or costs.

54 Otto (n 28) 21–3.

55 Ross Garnaut, 'Principles and practice of resource rent taxation' (2010) 43(4) *Australian Economic Review* 347, 348.

56 Ibid.

57 Dietsche (n 29) 21.

58 Ibid.

development consensus and neoextractivism. In the case of the former, arguments tend to centre on the State's ownership of the mineral resource, equity and efficiency. For the latter, greater emphasis is placed on the use of rents as a means to achieve a particular ideal of development.

In 1885 Alfred Marshall described 'rent' as 'that payment for the use of land which the owner can obtain by free competition for lending out the use of it to others'.[59] Following this train of thought, the principled basis for paying mineral resource rents in the broader sense is State ownership of mineral resources. There is a property interest at play, heightened because the resource is nonrenewable. The mining proponent must pay a resource tax for the privilege of access to the nation's mineral reserves, and the financial gains that can be made from their exploitation.[60] Collier has held that since extraction rents belong in their entirety to citizens, as the agent of citizenry the government needs a tax regime that captures them.[61] The State should accordingly tax economic rents for purposes of national development, rather than allowing the rents to end up in the hands of foreigners.[62]

The argument on the basis of efficiency is restricted to the narrower conception of rents. In the mid-1990s, for example, Cordes argued that because resource rents are not a financial return required to motivate economic behaviour, they could be taxed up to 100 per cent without courting the danger of altering decisions on production and consumption.[63] Much of the theoretical literature on mineral taxation dating back to the 1980s emphasizes the need for direct taxation (such as mineral royalties) to encourage and support the economically efficient exploitation of mineral reserves.[64] Of course, this is an industry-biased view that reduces the amount of taxes payable to the State.

'Fairness' also makes an appearance as a principled basis for the State share in mineral resource rents. The 1992 *Strategy for African Mining*, for example, advocated for 'taxation arrangements that are fair to both the government and the investors'.[65] Representing the view of the sustainable mineral development consensus, 'the policy conclusion of the theoretical literature on minerals taxation is that "fair sharing" of revenue between government and companies

---

59 Alfred Marshall, *The Economics of Industry* (MacMillan 1985) 81.

60 Smith (n 14) 18.

61 Paul Collier, 'Principles of resource taxation for low-income countries' in Philip Daniel, Michael Keen and Charles McPherson, *The Taxation of Petroleum and Minerals: Principles, Problems and Practice* (Routledge 2010) 75.

62 Boadway and Keen (n 2) 16.

63 John Cordes, 'An introduction to the taxation of mineral rents' in James Otto (ed.), *The Taxation of Mineral Enterprises* (Graham and Trotman 1995) 26.

64 Dietsche (n 29) 20.

65 *Strategy for African Mining* (n 26) 27.

ought to focus on sharing the [limited] pure rent'.[66] Industry-biased research has gone even further, arguing that even then '[i]f a country is interested in the longterm viability of its mineral sector, it should leave a sufficient share of the pure rent to companies in order to retain their interest in the continued development of the country's mineral sector'.[67]

These claims, however, represent a very particular construction of fairness, skewed towards the interests of the mining industry. The *AMV* brings other interests into view when it concedes:

> While the attention of national policymakers has traditionally focused on the fairness of the allocation of benefits between mining investors and the host country as a whole, increasing attention is now being paid to the benefits derived by the communities where mining operations take place to ensure that local and national level concerns and interests are balanced.[68]

Admitting other interest groups and concerns and interests is critical for longterm sustainability. It is stunning, for example, that discussions on fairness in the split of the resource rent take into account the effect of taxes on exploration expenditures and not the State's loss in natural capital, or the financial burden of dealing with the socioecological effects of irresponsible mining.

The principled arguments for State capture of mineral resource rent under neoextractivism reflect the key tenets of this development orientation, that is, that the State must capture surplus revenue to expand social structures favouring development. The *why* of mineral taxation corresponds with these goods, for example, to reduce poverty, secure national development and sovereignty, diversify the local and energy economy and promote political stability.[69]

2.1.3 Tax instruments to recover resource rents

Under the dominant model for mineral taxation, the State's rent capturing role is exercised through one or more forms of resource tax. Over the years, the following primary forms of resource tax have crystallized out of the work of academics, policy advisers and the practice of States: (1) the 'flat fee', being a one-off upfront cash payment to the State; (2) specific mineral royalties, imposed either on the volume of mineral production (unit-based royalties), the value of such production (*ad valorem* royalties) or profit (various forms of profit-based royalties); and (3) economic rent taxes such as the Resource Rent

---

66 Dietsche (n 29) 21.
67 Ibid.
68 African Union (n 37) 23.
69 Burchardt and Dietz (n 45) 470.

Tax or the Brown Tax, which are designed to tax the narrower conception of economic rents.[70]

The choice among these differing forms of resource tax is significant, affecting how much rent the State will receive, when the revenues will start to flow and the demands made on systems of tax administration. They pose different kinds of risk for the State. Flat fees are easy to administer, for example, and revenues are received prior to any mine exploration or development, but the State may miss out on the rents at a later stage if the reserve proves to be very rich. Both unit and value-based royalties also assure a flow of mineral taxation revenues from the outset of production, and are payable irrespective of whether the mine makes a profit or a loss.[71] Unit-based royalties are easy to administer because the calculation of the royalty only requires knowledge of the amount of mineral produced.[72] *Ad valorem* royalties require knowledge of both the amount produced and the value of the mineral. Unlike unit-based royalties, therefore, they fluctuate according to commodity price.[73] Profit-based royalties allow for a broader range of costs to be deducted, including capital costs.[74] However, they are complex to administer and are affected by the problem of information asymmetry.

2.1.3.1 Mineral royalties

Historically royalties have been the most important instrument for taxing the mineral industry,[75] and most nations impose some form of mineral royalty.[76] Even States that have historically opened their mineral reserves to foreign investment on extremely favourable terms have eventually imposed some form of royalty. In Chile, a mineral royalty was instituted after ExxonMobil Mineral attempted to sell the Disputada de Las Condes mine. The sale of the mine was planned through the sale of companies incorporated in tax havens, which circumvented taxation in Chile. The Chilean government became aware of the transaction and initiated a campaign to address the perceived low level of taxes paid by mining companies. A Specific Tax on Mining Activities came into effect on 1 January 2006 but was modified in 2010.[77] The Chilean mineral

---

70 Ian Murray, 'The minerals resource rent tax is dead, long live resource rent taxes?' (2015) 40 *University of Western Australia Law Review* 111, 115; Garnaut (n 55) 347, 349).

71 Otto (n 28) 268.

72 Ibid 269.

73 Ibid 268.

74 Ibid 53.

75 Baunsgaard (n 30) 10.

76 Otto (n 28) 267.

77 Pablo Mir, 'Mining royalties and taxation, the Chilean experience' (June 2010) www.ibram.org.br/sites/1300/1382/00000615.pdf accessed 26 February 2019.

royalty is progressive and profit-based, and small firms (with a yearly output of less than 12,000 tonnes in sales) are exempted.[78] In South Africa, after more than a century of mining, the Mineral and Petroleum Resources Royalty (Administration) Act, 2008 finally introduced a progressive, *ad valorem* royalty, differentiating between refined and unrefined mineral resources.[79]

In 2006 Otto *et al* undertook a detailed study on mineral royalties and found a wide variety of approaches, with 'no clear trend for global convergence',[80] although some regional patterning emerged.[81] Most royalty methods were either unit-based or value-based (*ad valorem* royalties), with a smaller but increasing group of States charging royalties based on profit. Value-based royalties were the most common.[82] Royalties could also be progressive and differentiated on the basis of mineral commodity, state of processing and mine size. Otto also found that many States had moved from a 'unique assessment model', with royalties differentiated on the basis of mineral commodity and even type of mine, to systems of greater uniformity – either a royalty that applied uniformly to all minerals, or an assessment method applying uniformly to a class of minerals, for example, a unit-based royalty for homogenous bulk or construction minerals and an *ad valorem* royalty for precious metals.[83] The unique assessment model is increasingly only found in States with many mines and a mature and competent tax administration, such as in the USA or Australia, where these royalties can also be found in negotiated State agreement acts.[84]

Mineral royalties can significantly affect extraction, exploration and development decisions.[85] For example, it has been argued that since royalties apply only at the extraction stage, and take no account of the sunk costs of exploration and site development, they discourage risky exploration projects.[86] Unit-based royalties, Boadway and Keen claim, tend to defer extraction, since the present value of the charge is lower the later extraction occurs.[87] *Ad valorem* royalties, on the other hand, will tend to accelerate extraction if the

---

[78] Kura Mineral Resources, 'Chile fiscal regime: Considerations for the mining industry', http://kuraminerals.com/documentation/2016/8/1/chile-fiscal-regime-considerations-for-the-mining-industry, accessed 26 February 2019.

[79] FT Cawood, 'The South African mineral and petroleum resources royalty act – Background and fundamental principles' (2010) 35(3) *Resources Policy* 199–209.

[80] Otto (n 28) 267.

[81] Ibid 270–1.

[82] Ibid 51.

[83] Ibid 48.

[84] Ibid 44.

[85] Boadway and Keen (n 2) 28.

[86] Ibid.

[87] Ibid.

resource price increases at a rate above the interest rate used to calculate net present value (NPV).[88] One of the more commonly expressed concerns is that royalties can contribute to premature mine closure, particularly if their imposition is unexpected.[89] Otto *et al* broaden this claim, noting that the discussions between mining companies and governments frequently canvas the impact of royalties on interrelated production parameters such as the cutoff grade, reserves and mine life.[90] Mineral royalties, in whatever form, impact upon the cost scenarios used to optimize profits and will thus have an influence on these production parameters.

The mining industry and IFIs have rigorously promoted a model of mineral taxation focused on taxing profits rather than production. Governments, these institutions have argued, should take a longterm view, encouraging investment in the industry rather than the short term recovery of rents. The World Bank's 1992 and 1996 *Strategies*, for example, urged governments to maximize tax returns over the long term by focusing on profit-related taxes,[91] doing away with unit-based or *ad valorem* royalties altogether and keeping royalties at very low rates. The *African Mining Strategy* advised governments to keep royalties in the 1–2 per cent range to avoid significant distortions, such as raising the cutoff grade and shortening the life of the mine.[92] The *Strategy for LAC Mining* praised Chile, Mexico and Peru for eliminating royalties on production, thereby greatly advancing their attractiveness to private investors.[93] While emphasizing profit-related taxes, the *Strategies* strongly cautioned against a too high tax rate – as this was likely to disincentivize exploration and mine development[94] – and consistently highlighted the need for rates to be comparable with those of other countries. 'Common-sense suggests', the *Strategy for African Mining* held, 'that a country's mining tax regime cannot move too far out of line with those prevailing in countries with close substitute deposits, or investment will be diverted'.[95]

Over the course of the past 20–25 years, these policy positions have been only slightly modified by the World Bank and industry bodies such as the ICMM, even as staff from these organizations have cooperated in initiatives such as the MMSD and the Natural Resource Charter. An ICMM report, for instance, advises governments to maximize their revenues from mining over

---

88 Ibid.
89 Otto (n 28) 168.
90 Ibid 164.
91 *Strategy for African Mining* (n 26) 27.
92 Ibid 32. See also Otto (n 28) and Baunsgaard (n 30) 10.
93 *Strategy for LAC Mining* (n 27) 23.
94 Ibid 9.
95 *Strategy for African Mining* (n 26) 30.

the long run,[96] even as it acknowledges that this quest 'is sometimes difficult to attain in a developing country context'.[97] Their review of mineral taxation regimes urges host countries to reduce reliance on 'indirect' taxes such as unit- or value-based royalties (*in rem* taxes), and increase reliance on profits-based taxes (*in personam* taxes),[98] while conceding that the policy-oriented mining taxation literature does not provide a sufficiently grounded theoretical basis for developing countries to make the switch from *in rem* to *in personam* taxes, and while strongly urging host countries to simplify their tax administration systems.[99] Without stating so explicitly, the MMSD also supported profits-based royalties, claiming that over the course of the twentieth century governments had seemed to move away from royalties towards profits-based taxes.[100] However, as Otto's review of mineral taxation trends showed, profit-based mineral royalties are still only implemented in a handful of countries.

This advocacy sits alongside research showing that profit-based taxes have been ineffective in securing a reasonable government share of mineral resource rents. An analysis of low government revenue from mining in Zambia and Tanzania for the period 1998–2011 showed, for example, that revenue from profit-based taxes had been virtually nonexistent.[101] The main sources of government revenue from mining during this time were the employee tax, a production-based royalty and VAT. Employee taxes contributed either more or the same as corporate taxes to overall mining payments in Zambia and Tanzania for a period that included a boom in mineral commodity pricing. This led the authors to conclude: 'Considering that mining uses a non-renewable resource with considerable economic rent, this situation is clearly unsustainable and represents ineffective revenue-sharing between the companies and the government.'[102]

2.1.3.2 Economic rent taxes

Economic rent taxes differ from mineral royalties in being specifically targeted to supernormal profits. The best known of these economic rent taxation types are the Brown Tax and the Resource Rent Tax (RRT). The Brown Tax is

---

96 Dietsche (n 29) 11.

97 Ibid 8.

98 Ibid 12.

99 Ibid.

100 Ibid.

101 Olva Lundstøl, Gaël Raballand and Fuvya Nyirongo, 'Low government revenue from the mining sector in Zambia and Tanzania: Fiscal design, technical capacity, or political will' (April 2013) International Centre for Tax and Development, Working Paper 9, 31.

102 Ibid.

charged on revenue from the sale of all output less all cash outlays for purchases of all capital and current inputs (with no deduction allowed for interest or other financial costs). Allowing for immediate expensing of investment expenditure, however, gives rise to refundable negative tax liabilities.[103] This tax essentially positions the State as a silent partner in resource projects, because during the years in which cash flow is negative (for example, during exploration or development or a downturn in commodity pricing), the government pays out a sum to mining companies equivalent to the Brown tax rate multiplied by the losses. But during years in which cash flow is positive the government receives the same proportion of profits in return.[104] In theory this tax is risk neutral, as it reduces both losses and profits and does not result in any switching between economic and uneconomic projects.[105] The opinion from the literature is that because the Brown Tax shares the risk of resource projects between risk averse private investors and governments, extraction may increase.[106]

The RRT, proposed by Garnaut and Clunies Ross in 1975,[107] is regarded as a practical alternative to the Brown Tax as it obviates the need for government to refund investors during years of negative cash flow.[108] RRT tax only becomes payable once the private investor has achieved the threshold rate of return in the project. Losses are allowed to be carried forward, or transferred between projects within a company or between companies.[109] Determining the threshold rate of return is a delicate matter, and will depend on the level of risk an investor is prepared to tolerate. If an investor is risk averse, for instance, the threshold rate of return must be set at the risk free interest rate plus an appropriate risk premium. Hogan and Goldsworthy observe that the remaining cash flows can be regarded as the *economic* rent of the project, which incorporates the resource rent but is not necessarily conflated with it. For example, the rents from a project may be due to superior managerial skill or new technology.[110] They advise, accordingly, that governments should not target 100 per cent of the economic rent since it can be ascribed to non-resource related factors, and because taking the full rental pie could encourage 'rent dissipating activities'

---

[103] Boadway and Keen (n 2) 33.

[104] Hogan and Goldsworthy (n 50) 137.

[105] Ibid.

[106] Ibid.

[107] Ross Garnaut and Anthony Clunies Ross, 'Uncertainty, risk aversion and the taxing of natural resource projects' (1975) 85 *Economic Journal* 272–87; 'The neutrality of the Resource Rent Tax' (1979) 55 *Economic Journal* 193–201; *Taxation of Mineral Rents* (Clarendon 1983).

[108] Hogan and Goldsworthy (n 50) 138.

[109] Ibid.

[110] Ibid.

such as early mine closure, transfer pricing or lobbying the government for tax breaks.[111]

States have relied far less on economic rent taxes than mineral royalties, but this in a context where the mining industry has vociferously opposed attempts to tax supernormal profits. Otto's 2006 review of mineral royalties noted that no government had implemented a mining taxation system based solely on the concept of economic rent.[112] Since then a few governments have experimented with economic rent taxes, the most notable example arguably being the Australian Commonwealth government's attempts to impose first a Resource Super Profits Tax (RSPT) and then a Mineral Resources Rent Tax (MRRT) in the period 2010–14. In Australia, mining is largely regulated at state level and most resource taxes are unit-based or *ad valorem* royalties on coal and iron ore extraction. The revenues from these state-based royalties amounted to around AUD 11.1 billion in 2011–12, with the vast majority flowing to Western Australia, Queensland and New South Wales.[113] In 2009, the 'Henry Review' on Australia's future tax system recommended the adoption of a uniform resource rent tax imposed and administered by the Commonwealth.[114] On the strength of this recommendation, the Rudd/Gillard government proposed a RSPT in May 2010. The RSPT was envisaged as a Commonwealth, profit-based tax levied against the whole of the mining industry at the rate of 40 per cent. Revenues of AUD 3 billion were envisaged for the first year of implementation, increasing to AUD 9 billion by 2013–14.[115] Resonating in design with the Brown tax,[116] it was sold on the basis that very profitable projects would pay more tax, thus ensuring that taxation arrangements were responsive to changes in profits.[117] The Australian mining industry vehemently opposed the RSPT in a campaign that contributed to the downfall of Prime Minister Kevin Rudd. The Australian Electoral Commission's report on political spending over 2009–10 showed that the mining industry spent more than AUD 22.2 million on a six-week ad campaign against the RSPT. This added to a slump in the Labor Party's standing that led to Rudd's replacement

---

[111] Ibid.

[112] Otto (n 28) 266.

[113] Murray (n 70) 116.

[114] Australia's Future Tax System Review Panel, *Australia's Future Tax System: Report to the Treasurer* (2009), Part Two 231.

[115] Parliament of Australia, 'Taxation – Resource super profits tax' www.aph.gov.au/About_Parliament/Parliamentary_Departments/Parliamentary_Library/pubs/rp/BudgetReview201011/TaxationRSPTax, accessed 26 February 2019.

[116] The RSPT allowed for upliftment and carry forward of annual negative cash flows, rather than refunds.

[117] Parliament of Australia (n 115).

by Julia Gillard.[118] The new Prime Minister, Gillard, made it a priority of her tenure to introduce the redesigned MRRT. Rather than the whole of the mining industry, this tax applied only to new and existing coal and iron ore projects, affecting around 320 companies.[119] After much negotiation it was pegged at 30 per cent of annual profits above AUD 75 million. This was further reduced to 22.5 per cent taking into account an extraction allowance. The new levy was narrowly squeezed through the lower house of the Federal Parliament with the passage of the Mineral Resource Rent Tax Act 2012 (Cth) on 19 March 2012, and commenced on 1 July 2012. The MRRT was shortlived, however, and in September 2014 the new Coalition Government succeeded in its third attempt at repeal. The revenues raised by the tax during its short existence were far below projections. In 2013, for example, the Finance and Treasury Departments forecast receipts of AUD 6 billion, AUD 16.5 billion below original projections.[120] The tax was also expensive and complex to administer, reportedly costing more than AUD 50 million to set up, with running costs of AUD 20 million a year.[121]

While States may ostensibly choose from among a wide variety of tax instruments to capture a ‘fair’ or ‘effective’ share of mineral resource rents, in practice their options have therefore been restricted. International development agencies and the mining industry have argued strenuously for profit-based taxes, or taxation of the ‘pure’ economic rent. But as the case study of the RSPT/MRRT shows, when this advice is followed even a developed State such as Australia has faced enormous hurdles in implementation as a result of the formal mining industry’s intense political lobbying against their plans.

2.2 Easing Mining Investment: The Investment-Promoting State

Under the dominant model of mineral taxation, States must impose taxes in a manner that also promotes private investment. This role was firmly rooted in the policy reforms of the 1980s and 1990s and is still dominant in a context

---

[118] Mark Davis, ‘A snip at $22 million to get rid of PM’, *Sydney Morning Herald*, 2 February 2011, www.smh.com.au/business/a-snip-at-22m-to-get-rid-of-pm-20110201-1acgj.html, accessed 26 February 2019.

[119] Phil Mercer, ‘Can Australia’s new mining tax achieve its objective?’ *BBC News*, 23 November 2011, www.bbc.com/news/business-15850019 accessed 26 February 2019.

[120] Glenda Kwek, ‘Forecast bumps up mining tax intake’, *The Age*, 13 August 2013, www.theage.com.au/business/the-economy/forecast-bumps-up-mining-tax-intake-20130813-2ru78.html#ixzz2cf3AQF1B, accessed 26 February 2019.

[121] ‘Labour leads economy in the wrong direction’, *The Australian*, 16 August 2013.

where foreign ownership of formal mining production prevails.[122] This role is underpinned by an important yet unstated assumption: that States are competing for mining investment. Guidance on mineral fiscal policy from the recently launched 'Extractives Hub', for instance, points out that the type of fiscal regime a State designs and implements also determines its 'competitive position' within the global mining investment arena.[123] The notion of a global 'investment arena' in which all jurisdictions compete invokes the idea of a 'mining bonanza' in the developing world. As noted in Chapter 1, contrary to popular belief, investment in new mining jurisdictions has not been a bonanza, but has rather been concentrated in a few 'rising stars'.[124] Investor surveys carried out over the past decade have also confirmed that tax motivations rank relatively low among the factors influencing a decision on where to invest.[125]

In similar fashion to the capture of mineral resource rents, ideological contestation over the State's private investment role takes place at the level of principle, and through policy advice on the fiscal measures to promote private investment.

2.2.1 Principled basis for State promotion of private investment through fiscal measures

The principled basis for State promotion of investment through fiscal measures has been framed against a particular construction of risk informed by generic features of mineral extraction that make it both risky and distinct from other economic activities. These features include citizen or State ownership (thus rendering a project vulnerable to political risks), production as asset depletion rather than the creation of new goods and services, high sunk costs and long periods of payback and volatile commodity pricing and input costs.[126]

---

[122] The World Bank's *Strategy for African Mining* identified the need to attract private investors 'to reverse a massive underinvestment in exploration' (see n 26, 11). The *Strategy for LAC Mining* called upon States to deepen and sustain the policy, legal and regulatory reforms that had been successful in attracting billions of dollars in private investment in 'reformed' countries such as Chile (see n 27, viii).

[123] Extractives Hub, 'Mineral Policy – 8. Fiscal policy', https://beta.extractiveshub.org/topic/view/ID/16, accessed 26 February 2019.

[124] See section 4.3, Chapter 1.

[125] UNCTAD (n 10) 182; M Keen and M Mansour, 'Revenue mobilization in sub-Saharan Africa: Challenges from globalization' (2009) IMF Working Paper 157; Vale Columbia Center on Sustainable Investment, 'Background Paper for the eighth Columbia International Investment Conference on the Good, the Bad and the Ugly: Assessing the costs, benefits and options for policy reform', Columbia University, New York, NY, 13–14 November 2013.

[126] Collier (n 61) 75.

The 'obsolescing bargain' references the power struggle between the State and industry that frequently transpires as a result of these risks. The obsolescing bargain indicates a shift in bargaining power between the State and mining investors as a project progresses. Because the policy mantra is that taxes influence a company's decision to invest, companies may be reluctant to proceed without promises of favourable tax treatment. As noted in the *AMV*, lack of geological data also strengthens the hand of mining companies. The State, desiring investment, is in a weaker bargaining position.[127] However, once the investments are made they are immobile and have little, if any, alternative use. The State's bargaining hand is strengthened and the company becomes vulnerable to fiscal changes instigated either by the negotiating or future governments.

Two features of the obsolescing bargain impact upon socioecological sustainability. The phenomenon may lead to what investors term the 'hold up' problem: recognizing the shift in bargaining power and the incentive for the State to change its fiscal tune, the forward looking investor may be reluctant to invest even if offered generous tax treatment.[128] If the investment was planned for socially or ecologically sensitive areas, the deferment of the mining investment would be welcomed by those seeking to protect the socio-ecological integrity of such areas. More importantly, however, the obsolescing bargain does not recognize a *second* shift in bargaining power as the project nears a close. The ecological, social and economic costs of a project increase and accumulate as a project nears completion. The company, having recovered a return on investment, can withdraw from the investment in a number of ways, either selling the mining venture on to another operator, selling shares in the company holding the mine asset or utilizing various options for dealing with corporate distress under the jurisdiction's corporate laws. The State is once again in a weaker bargaining position and may be persuaded to apply various fiscal concessions to keep the company invested.[129]

The State's investment promotion role is supported by an entrenched and well developed set of principles for the design of mineral fiscal regimes, namely neutrality, stability and flexibility. According to conventional wisdom, a fiscal instrument is neutral if the investor would have made the same decision

---

[127] Otto (n 28) 12.

[128] Boadway and Keen (n 2) 15.

[129] For example, a media report of 2015 describes calls from the mature, ailing South African gold mining industry for various forms of tax relief, including a 'royalty holiday'. These calls were made over and above existing legal provisions to cushion this industry, facing its 'sunset phase'. See Dineo Faku, 'Ailing mines clamour for tax relief', *Business Report*, 27 August 2015, www.iol.co.za/business-report/companies/ailing-mines-clamour-for-tax-relief-1906367, accessed 26 February 2019.

regardless of the instrument chosen, or, put another way, if the action or project assessed to be economically profitable remains viable after the fiscal instrument is applied.[130] The stability of a regime reflects investors' desire for time consistency in a fiscal regime and is integrally connected to sovereign risk.[131] Perceptions of instability raise the supply side of investment.[132] Flexibility is related to stability in that States may palliate investors' fears regarding time consistency by making fiscal instruments responsive to changes in future market conditions and/or allowing flexibility in the operation of the market, such as by liberalizing foreign exchange requirements or allowing mining proponents to access foreign currency to import mining inputs and to repatriate profits.[133]

These principles can be discerned in earlier and more recent literature promoting investor-friendly fiscal regimes in the mining industry. The *Strategy for LAC Mining*, for example, advised that 'investors are receptive to contractual regimes where they provide . . . fiscal and foreign exchange stability'.[134] And Dietsche, reporting for the ICMM, opined that '[t]he literature agrees that ideally the overall effect of a tax system should be neutral with respect to production decisions and that the tax base should be taxed progressively'.[135]

The ideological character of these private investment principles, however, is well reflected in debates on fiscal stability contracts. The use of fiscal stability contracts in the mining industry is highly contentious. Their use has led to situations where mining companies pay very little taxes at all, which is then frequently contrasted with the extensive social and environmental damage that has been incurred. The World Bank's *Mining Strategies* came out in favour of fiscal stability contracts. In the *Strategy for African Mining*, for instance, the World Bank urged that '[a]ssurance of the stability of contract terms will lower the risk perceived by investors that the terms may subsequently be altered if a project turns out to be especially profitable'.[136] The policy advice in the *Strategy for LAC Mining* was more aggressive. In particular, the World Bank argued that the 'lock-in' of tax, customs and foreign exchange provisions in Chilean and Peruvian law had 'played a major role in attracting new investment capital'.[137] This *Strategy* even went so far as to suggest that investors in Latin America seek stability in *environmental* requirements, while conceding

130 Hogan and Goldsworthy (n 50) 132.
131 Ibid.
132 Garnaut (n 55) 350.
133 Boadway and Keen (n 2) 15.
134 *Strategy for LAC Mining* (n 27) 13.
135 Dietsche (n 29) 10.
136 *Strategy for African Mining* (n 26) 30.
137 *Strategy for LAC Mining* (n 27) 15.

that most LAC countries had not yet reached the stage in environmental management where they were in a position to accede to such requests.[138] Baungaard's IMF-sponsored Primer on Mineral Taxation was more cautious, suggesting that while fiscal stability contracts were ostensibly an inexpensive and attractive means for government to reduce investor risk, over the long term such agreements could not only lead to revenue loss, but could also restrict the government's capacity to set tax policy.[139] In a departure from the World Bank's 1990s position, the ICCM 2009 *Review* did not expressly support fiscal stability contracts, arguing instead that the sector-specific characteristics of the mining industry do not *per se* justify special mining tax regimes, and that subjecting the mining industry to a country's general taxation regime (with a few special characteristics, such as capturing the resource rent element) would provide for greater assurance of stability over the long term.[140]

Viewed through the lens of the double movement, the ideological debate on the principled basis for mineral taxation has a distracting function. The set of principles that comes most clearly into view shift the focus of the State from protecting/enhancing society through resource rent capture to promoting the conditions necessary to oil the global market for mineral commodities. A preoccupation with operationalizing neutrality, stability and flexibility can also obscure risk of fiscal loss, where the government obtains a lower than expected return for the exploitation of the resource. Coupled with the feature of resource exhaustibility, this signals an opportunity foregone forever.

2.2.2 Fiscal measures to promote private investment

The dominant model for mineral taxation assumes that States promote private investment by (1) keeping mineral resource taxes as low as possible and (2) offering tax incentives. As discussed above, policy contestation on mineral resource rents tries to limit the rents arising from mineral extraction. The mining industry and its supporters have advocated strongly for profit-based taxes or economic rent taxes that only target the 'pure rent'. States, on the other hand, have been more inclined to favour production-based taxes calculated on the basis of units of production or value. The focus in this section, however, falls on the incentives deemed necessary to promote investment in the mining industry, especially in developing countries. Tax incentives could apply to any one of the normal business taxes: corporate income tax, VAT and import and export duties.

---

138 Ibid 16.

139 Baunsgaard (n 30) 18.

140 Dietsche (n 29) 62.

The policy advocacy of the sustainable mineral development consensus in the 1990s pushed for reductions in all these forms of business tax. The World Bank *Strategies* called for a variety of measures to reduce 'investor risk', such as accelerated depreciation;[141] the rapid amortization of exploration and development expenditures;[142] the reduction or exemption of mining from import duties and related taxes on capital equipment and supplies; exemption from capital gains taxes, withholding taxes and payments for services;[143] and the elimination of exchange controls.[144] They strongly discouraged States from forcing the mining industry to undertake social and economic projects directly, or forcing companies into downstream processing;[145] from instituting an additional profits tax;[146] from having an ownership stake in mining companies;[147] and from forcing profit sharing with employees.[148]

Other intergovernmental and nongovernmental organizations have suggested, however, that the range of tax incentives instituted by developing countries on the basis of the advocacy of the Bretton Woods institutions has led to a 'race to the bottom'.[149] The IMF,[150] as well as the NGOs Tax Justice and ActionAid International,[151] have claimed that such incentives do not attract foreign direct investment, and that the tax privileges granted transnational corporations 'have far exceeded reasonable limits'.[152] This became acutely apparent during the 2002–8 commodities boom and its aftermath, when commodities prices soared. The revenues of the world's largest mining companies increased fivefold, and net profits more than tenfold.[153] Even the World Bank acknowledged in 2010 that '[m]ining fiscal regimes developed in the past (often under Bank guidance) were not adequate to capture much of the large increase in rents generated by these price increases'.[154]

---

[141] *Strategy for African Mining* (n 26) 30.
[142] *Strategy for LAC Mining* (n 27) 24.
[143] *Strategy for African Mining* (n 26) 33.
[144] *Strategy for LAC Mining* (n 27) 23.
[145] *Strategy for African Mining* (n 26) 27, 28.
[146] Ibid 33.
[147] Ibid 34.
[148] *Strategy for LAC Mining* (n 27) 24–5.
[149] UNCTAD (n 10) 180.
[150] IMF, *Fiscal Regimes for Extractive Industries: Design and Implementation* (2012).
[151] Tax Justice – Africa and ActionAid International, *Tax Competition in East Africa: A Race to the Bottom?* (2012). See also the sources cited in fn 40 in this source.
[152] UNCTAD (n 10) 182.
[153] Ibid.
[154] World Bank, 'The World Bank's evolutionary approach to mining sector reform', Extractive Industries for Development Series No. 19 (2010) 9.

More recently, a collaborative project on tax incentives conducted by the OECD and the Intergovernmental Forum for Mining and Metals concluded that '[t]here is little evidence that tax incentives are effective at attracting mining investment in developing countries'.[155] The three findings advanced from studies that have studied the effect of tax incentives more generally have found that: tax incentives have no 'compensation effect' if the investment climate is weak overall; if nontax factors are unfavourable, developing countries are unlikely to attract foreign direct investment; and while incentives may have a small positive effect on foreign direct investment, they have no positive effect on fixed assets,[156] which would signal the conversion of natural into fixed capital. These findings seriously challenge calls for tax incentives in the mining industry to reduce perceived 'investor risk'.

2.2.2.1 Corporate income tax

Mining companies' profits are usually subject to standard corporate income tax over and above the payment of mineral royalties.[157] The policy issues arising from this kind of tax include the overall rate of corporate tax, affording the mining industry special treatment or exemptions, the extent to which mining companies can benefit from broad exemptions tailored for other sectors, the extent and rate at which losses may be set off against the corporate income tax payable and the interaction between the corporate income tax and other taxes payable within the mining jurisdiction and beyond.

A reduction in corporate income tax rates – attributed to the competition among governments to attract and retain 'mobile investors' – has been a trend in all regions.[158] In OECD countries corporate income tax rates declined from an average 45 per cent in the 1980s to 25 per cent in 2012, and for developing countries from an average of 38 per cent in the early 1990s to 27 per cent in 2012.[159] In some countries, lowering the corporate income tax rate has not reduced the revenues from this fiscal stream as a result of a broadened tax base and increased profits, but in others the reduction in public revenues has been amplified by tax holidays, direct tax breaks and reduced statutory rates for particular sectors.[160] The latter trend is acutely observable in the mining industry. Kumar *et al*, for instance, highlight the case of Guatemala in which the Marlin

155 Alexandra Readhead, *Tax Incentives in Mining: Minimizing Risks to Revenue* (IGF and OECD 2018) 11.

156 Ibid.

157 Boadway and Keen (n 2) 42.

158 UNCTAD (n 10) 168.

159 Ibid.

160 Ibid.

gold mine was granted *maqila* status in 2003.[161] The mining company that owned the mine thus avoided paying income tax, VAT or corporate income tax, at the same time as the Mining Law of 1997 lowered the mineral royalty rate from 6 to 1 per cent.[162]

Corporate income tax is also reduced through generous loss carry forward positions, which are not uniquely applicable to the resources sector. These provisions allow a company to carry losses incurred in a given year forward to following years, thereby reducing taxable income and tax payable. A typical example in this regard would be losses incurred for exploration and development. If losses are substantial, or if they accumulate over a number of years, the company will only start paying tax several years after it starts earning profits. Many jurisdictions have extended loss carry forward provisions for extractive companies, to hasten payback of initial outlays.[163] Loss carry forward provisions are offset by the ringfencing of operations, however, which restricts the extent to which losses can be offset against profits by carrying the loss from one project over to another.[164]

Accelerated depreciation allowances also allow mining companies to reduce tax payable.[165] There is even the theoretical possibility of a depletion allowance, which would allow the value of depletion of a mineral reserve to be set off against taxable income. Boadway and Keen note that such an allowance would only be appropriate in a system in which mining companies have paid for the right to extract, otherwise the allowance would amount to a kind of negative royalty.[166]

The distortionary effect of other taxes – a mineral royalty, for instance, or even the carbon tax – depends in part on their treatment under the general corporate income tax regime. Allowing mineral royalties to be set off against taxable income under the corporate tax regime reduces the overall level of corporate taxation. Boadway and Keen argue that this would be 'structurally irrelevant' if the royalties were simply set at a lower rate.[167] However, where royalties accrue to the provincial level of government and corporate taxation

---

[161] Kumar (n 39) 10. In Latin America *maquila* is a term typically reserved for companies manufacturing for export who use low skilled labour and are often located in export processing zones. See also Lyuba Zarsky and Leonardo Stanley, 'Can extractive industries promote sustainable development? A net benefits framework and a case study of the Marlin mine in Guatemala' (2013) 22(1) *Journal of Environment and Development* 131.

[162] Kumar (n 39) 10.

[163] Hogan and Goldsworthy (n 50) 124.

[164] Boadway and Keen (n 2) 43.

[165] Hogan and Goldsworthy (n 50) 124.

[166] Boadway and Keen (n 2) 43.

[167] Ibid 44.

accrues to the central or federal level of government, such an incentive for balancing the corporate and royalty taxes would not exist.[168]

2.2.2.2 Value-Added Tax (VAT) and import and export taxes

States may charge import duties on the large capital goods which mining companies require to undertake exploration and extraction.[169] This provides assurance on revenue flows right from the start of a project, but most States put exemptions in place for large resource projects to facilitate mining development. Writing in 2006, for example, Otto *et al* noted that most of the 35 countries included in the study on mineral royalties had eliminated or greatly reduced import duties.[170]

VAT is also rarely significant for mining taxation. In most countries the export of mining ores/products does not attract VAT as it is a tax on domestic consumption and most mining production is exported. Many mineral-rich jurisdictions have therefore zero rated or exempted minerals from VAT and export duties.[171] Because mining companies would have paid VAT on the inputs to the mining processes, they also commonly receive a VAT refund. However, in many developing countries the domestic tax authorities have found it difficult to pay these taxes in a timely manner, resulting in an implicit export tax.[172]

The investment-promoting State therefore functions according to a well-worn script: upholding the principles of neutrality, flexibility and stability to play the game of competing for limited private investment. Notwithstanding research to the contrary, States have been encouraged to incentivize mining through tax measures, including keeping in step with lowered corporate tax income rates and offering other forms of tax incentive.

2.3 Environmental and Social Externalities: The State as Behaviour Incentivizer

Under the Polanyian double movement, the State could protect society through mineral taxation in two ways: either by applying revenues gained from productive tax bases to social and environmental causes, or by designing fiscal measures that incentivized more socially and environmentally responsible

---

168 For a discussion on how the Australian MRRT intersected with corporate income tax and State mineral royalty regimes see Murray (n 70) 119ff.

169 Ibid.

170 Otto (n 28) 37.

171 Boadway and Keen (n 2) 44.

172 Ibid.

behaviour in the first place. The latter brings the State's role as behaviour incentivizer to the fore.

For the most part, the environmental and social costs of mining are treated as externalities that do not feature in the design of mineral fiscal frameworks. To control for mining impacts, governments tend to rely on command and control regulation and not economic instruments.[173] Special taxes or tax arrangements may nevertheless be imposed to correct externalities.[174] This section focuses on special taxes or arrangements pertaining to decommissioning and closure, green taxes and the carbon tax.

2.3.1 Tax treatment of decommissioning costs

The decommissioning and closure of mines are recognized elements of the mining production cycle. As discussed in Chapter 7, the mining industry has recognized mine closure as a core business activity. The dominant model for mine closure accords the State a watchdog role to ensure that integrated closure planning and concurrent rehabilitation are properly implemented over the life of the mine, and that funds are set aside as a form of assurance for decommissioning and closure activities. In this way, States try to protect themselves from becoming the 'mender of last resort'.[175] In addition to rules determining the setting aside of financial assurance for mine decommissioning and closure, States need to consider the tax treatment of such funds. The manner in which decommissioning costs are treated has the potential to impact upon the success of the longterm process of mine closure, and the funds available to secure the socioecological sustainability of postmined land.

A number of mineral-rich jurisdictions treat decommissioning costs as a tax deduction. In essence this means that the State subsidizes decommissioning, either in the form of lower tax revenues or in tax refunds. In its *Handbook on Extractive Industries Taxation*, the UN notes that there are generally three models for treating decommissioning costs as a tax deduction for mineral, oil and gas projects: (1) providing a tax deduction when cash is expended on decommissioning (for example, in Chile, Peru and some states in Canada and Australia); (2) providing a tax deduction when decommissioning is accrued, that is, when the expense is charged to the profit and loss account (for example, in various jurisdictions of the USA); and (3) providing a tax deduction when decommissioning is prefunded, through payments into a decommissioning

173 John E Tilton, 'What's the optimal tax on mining?' *Resources for the Future* (9 July 2010), www.rff.org/blog/2010/what-s-optimal-tax-mining, accessed 26 February 2019.

174 Garnaut (n 55) 347.

175 See the discussions in sections 2.1 and 2.3, Chapter 7.

fund out of which the decommissioning liability can be settled (for example, in Ghana, South Africa and Zambia).[176]

These different models for tax deduction of decommissioning costs present different risks for the State and mining companies. In general, greater risks are associated with the first model, in which expenditure on decommissioning usually occurs at a time when the mine has stopped producing income. This generates a large tax loss, which is advantageous to the State to the extent that it has received tax receipts throughout the profit generating phase of the mine and allows deductibility only at the end. It is problematic, however, if tax refunds for decommissioning costs impact upon the availability of government revenues for other social and developmental programmes.[177] Tax refunds can arise if the State allows for loss carry back provisions and ringfencing of operations. Such rules either reduce the total amount of tax payable, or facilitate the payment of a tax refund by allowing companies to offset losses against the amount of tax paid in earlier periods.[178] For example, under new tax relief rules in the United Kingdom, oil companies operating in the North Sea can claim a significant portion of their decommissioning costs as a tax refund, and carry the loss back against taxable profits as far as 2002.[179] It is estimated that this could result in significant corporate tax refunds, with operators receiving as much as 50 per cent of the decommissioning costs.[180] The underlying rationale for such tax relief, at least in the context of oil projects in the United Kingdom's North Sea, is that it stimulates innovative decommissioning projects.[181] In Kenya, such loss carry back provisions have been implemented in the oil, gas and mining sectors where the amount of loss can be carried back as a deduction against income, to a maximum of three years from the year in which the loss arose and the operation ceased.[182] However, in anticipation that

---

176 United Nations (n 42) 200. The UN Report on Taxation in the Extractive Industries was preceded by H Choudhury *et al*, 'Guidance note on the tax treatment of decommissioning for the extractive industries' (October 2016), Draft prepared for the UN Sub-Committee on Extractive Industries Taxation Issues for Developing Countries.

177 Choudhury (n 176) 15.

178 United Nations (n 42) 201.

179 Alistair Dunbar 'Decommissioning – a tax perspective', http://pwc.blogs.com/energy_spotlight/2015/04/decommissioning-a-tax-perspective.html, accessed 26 February 2019.

180 Ibid.

181 Ibid.

182 EY Global Tax Alert Library, 'Kenya revises taxation applicable to the Oil and Gas & Mining Sectors', 23 February 2015, www.ey.com/Publication/vwLUAssets/Kenya_revises_taxation_applicable_to_the_Oil_and_Gas_and_Mining_sectors/$FILE/2015G_CM5238_Kenya%20revises%20taxation%20applicable%20to%20the%20Oil%20and%20Gas%20and%20Mining%20sectors.pdf, accessed 26 February 2019.

the government may change the rules of deductibility, or if the loss cannot be carried back for long enough, mining proponents may be incentivized to decommission prematurely.[183]

The other models offer some advantages over the risks of the first model by allowing for the deduction of decommissioning costs to be better phased over the life of the mine. Other risks nevertheless arise. For example, the second (accrual) model requires robust controls and monitoring processes to ensure that mining companies are not making excessive provision for decommissioning.[184] And the third model (payment into a decommissioning fund) may require additional complex rules regarding the use of the financial provision, protection of the fund from insolvency, treatment of deficits and surpluses and repayment of the funds to mining companies.

The broader sustainability question that the tax deductibility of decommissioning costs raises, however, is largely unaddressed in the literature, which is that the host jurisdiction and its taxpayers effectively subsidize decommissioning and mine closure. Whether this policy and approach results in improved innovation in decommissioning and closure projects is an empirical question worthy of further investigation.

2.3.2 Green taxes

The overall level of taxation would increase if States used fiscal instruments to deal with the negative environmental and social externalities arising from mining. Commenting on a meeting of the Intergovernmental Forum on Mining, Minerals and Metals and Sustainable Development that took place in 2018, Macey notes for example that discussions on the fiscal regime for mining do not integrate environmental concerns at all. Instead, the substantial environmental challenges of the mining sector are dealt with on a separate track of the agenda. 'This separation is typical', he writes, 'and conceals the unexplored potential for the fiscal regime to be used as a tool for environmental protection in the mining sector'.[185]

The mining sector's economic and social impacts are significant and range from longlasting and possibly irreversible damage to landscapes, biodiversity and water resources, to the intensive use of water and energy, to the importa-

---

183 Choudhury (n 176) 23.

184 United Nations (n 42) 202.

185 Steve Macey, 'Designing a green fiscal regime for the mining sector', UNEP Green Fiscal Policy Network, http://greenfiscalpolicy.org/policy-insights/mining/green-fiscal-regime-for-mining/ accessed 26 February 2019. See also UNEP Green Economy, 'Fiscal reforms in the extractives sector for green finance', www.greenfiscalpolicy.org/wp-content/uploads/2016/11/Fiscal-reforms-in-the-extractives-sector-for-green-finance_EN_Web.pdf, accessed 26 February 2019.

tion of machinery and products that use fossil fuels and rely upon fossil fuel dependent international transportation, to the largescale generation of waste.

Rather than treating such impacts as a matter of regulation or corporate social responsibility, the call is for the fiscal regime to tax environmentally damaging inputs or outputs directly.[186] For example, governments could tax fuel usage, greenhouse gas emissions, excessive water usage, units of waste generated, units of biodiversity loss, and so on. There are already precedents for taxes on fuel usage, and on greenhouse gas emissions (see the discussion on the carbon tax in section 2.3.3 below). Macey notes that the corporate tax regime could be used to incentivize the introduction of innovative technologies for dealing with environmental and social impacts by allowing for accelerated depreciation. To reduce the total tax liability on mining companies, other taxes (for example, payroll tax) could also be reduced.[187]

Environmental taxes in the extractives industry have only been imposed or mooted in a handful of jurisdictions. In Iran, following a contentious policy development process, under the Parliamentary-approved sixth five year development plan, mining companies whose operations harm 'regional agriculture and residents' may be required to pay up to 1 per cent of their total sales revenues to the treasury, in order to rectify the damage and revitalize the environment.[188] Provincial councils made up of 15 members, comprising voting and nonvoting members, must decide whether operations at a mine are environmentally harmful or not. The voting members include the heads of provincial departments responsible for environment; forests, rangeland and watershed management; and the provincial agricultural jihad organization respectively.[189] In 2014, Mexico also introduced an annual extraordinary fee aimed at financing the environmental erosion impact of the gold, silver and platinum mining industries as part of a broader taxation reform package. The tax is applied at a rate of 0.5 per cent of the gross income arising from the sales of these commodities, but is deductible for tax purposes bringing the effective rate to 0.35 per cent.[190] In South Africa, the imposition of an environmental tax on the mining sector was mooted following State expenditure

---

[186] Macey (n 185).

[187] Ibid.

[188] Amir Havasi, 'Iran mining sector censures new environmental tax', *Financial Tribune* (31 May 2017), available at https://financialtribune.com/articles/economy-business-and-markets/65647/iran-mining-sector-censures-new-environmental-tax, accessed 26 February 2019.

[189] Ibid.

[190] David Cuellar and Caroline Paris, 'Mexico: New mining and environmental royalties' (28 March 2014) available at www.internationaltaxreview.com/Article/3325223/Mexico-New-mining-and-environmental-royalties.html, accessed 26 February 2019.

to deal with acid mine drainage (AMD) from abandoned mines (amounting to expenditures of R3.6 billion per annum in 2016).[191] In its policy report on the mining industry, the Davis Committee (a structure set up to review more general taxation reform) acknowledged the seriousness of the AMD issue and urged the Treasury to collaborate with the governmental departments responsible for mineral resources, environmental affairs and water and sanitation, respectively, to develop a joint governmental strategy and framework to deal comprehensively with the problem.[192]

Placing environmental protection alongside the policy objectives of revenue generation and investor promotion for the design of mineral fiscal regimes would mark a 'major change' to the advice and practice currently dispensed on the part of international organizations to mineral-rich jurisdictions.[193]

2.3.3 Mining and carbon taxes

While environmental taxes in the mining sector are rare, the extent of the mining industry's greenhouse gas emissions (GHGs) has exposed the industry to States' attempts to establish an international carbon price through carbon taxes or carbon emissions trading systems (ETS).[194]

Mining is a significant contributor to anthropogenic forcing of climate change although finding disaggregated statistics covering the global mining sector as a whole is challenging.[195] In a report on the GHG emissions of the world's top 500 companies issued by the Carbon Disclosure Project, mining and metals form part of the materials sector, a category that includes compa-

---

[191] Megan van Wyngaardt, 'Environmental tax could make appearance in budget speech', *Mining Weekly* (27 January 2016), www.miningweekly.com/article/environmental-tax-could-make-appearance-in-budget-speech-2016-01-27, accessed 26 February 2019.

[192] Davis Tax Committee, *First Interim Report on Mining for the Minister of Finance* (December 2014) 101.

[193] Ibid.

[194] There are significant differences between a carbon tax and an ETS. For example, a carbon tax provides more price certainty, since the level is set by the government, while an ETS will deliver clearer emissions reductions, as this is set by controlling the volume of allowances through the cap. A carbon tax is also administratively easier to administer and can build on existing tax administration institutions. However, both carbon taxes and ETS sales raise government revenues – the latter frequently through auction sales of the allowances. Based on 2014 data, a larger proportion of government revenues is raised through carbon taxes – USD 10 billion of the more than USD 15 billion raised in 2014 (see World Bank Group: Climate Change, *State and Trends of Carbon Pricing (2015)* (World Bank Group and Ecofys 2016) 27, 30.

[195] See R Irarrázabel, 'Mining and climate change: Towards a strategy for the industry' (2006) 24(3) *Journal of Energy and Natural Resources Law* 403, 410.

nies providing and manufacturing chemicals and construction materials.[196] In 2013 the materials sector was the third highest emitting sector of Fortune 500 companies, responsible for 26.2 per cent of total G500 emissions; that is, 953 $MtCO_2e$ of scope 1 and 2 emissions.[197] Moreover, while the GHG emissions of other sectors declined, those of the materials sector increased by 13 per cent over scope 1 and 2 emissions in 2012.[198]

While the largest mining companies typically publish their total annual GHG emissions in sustainability reports, comparing this information is difficult because they have different commodities in their portfolios.[199] Although the value chain of mining, processing and production is broadly the same across the industry, the specifics of the chain and hence the emissions profile of particular mineral commodities (and even between commodities produced in different regions) will differ along a number of variables, including grade of ore, amount of ore, extraction technology, processing requirements and accessibility of the mining site.[200] In the case of scope 2 emissions, the emissions intensity of any particular product will also depend largely on the fuel used for the production of electricity in that nationality or region.

The extent of these emissions renders the mining industry vulnerable to the imposition of carbon taxes (or carbon pricing imposed through an ETS) on the part of both national and subnational governments. In a 2016 World Bank review on trends in carbon pricing, the authors found that 39 national and 23 subnational jurisdictions had imposed a price on carbon through taxes or ETS as of 31 August 2015, a 90 per cent increase from the number of instruments

[196] CDP (formerly the Carbon Disclosure Project), *What Is Driving Climate Change Action in the World's Largest Companies? Global 500 Climate Change Report 2013* (CDP 2013) 34.

[197] The definition of scope 1 and scope 2 emissions derives from the Greenhouse Gas Protocol, the most widely used accounting framework for greenhouse gas inventories developed by the World Resources Institute and the World Business Council for Sustainable Development. The *Corporate and Accounting Standard* (rev. 2013) forms part of this Protocol and distinguishes between GHG emissions of three different scopes: Scope 1 emissions occur from sources actually owned or operated by a company, for example, boilers, furnaces, vehicles and other heavy duty equipment owned and operated by a mine; scope 2 operations are GHG emissions from the generation of purchased electricity, for example, the emissions that occur from operating a smelter with purchased electricity; and scope 3 emissions arise from the activities of a company, but from sources not owned or controlled by that company.

[198] CDP (n 196) 34.

[199] Irarrázabel (n 195) 412.

[200] ICMM, *The Cost of Carbon Pricing: Competitiveness Implications for the Mining and Metals Industry* (ICMM 2013) 30.

in 2012.[201] Of these, 38 carbon pricing instruments had already been implemented or were scheduled for implementation.[202] Mineral-rich jurisdictions that have implemented or are considering implementing a carbon tax or ETS include Poland (from 1990), British Columbia (from 2008), Mexico (from 2014), South Africa (from 2016) and Chile (from 2017).[203] Australia's federal experiment with a carbon tax – much criticized by the mining industry in that jurisdiction – lasted from 2012 to 2014.

A number of mining companies are taking measures to address climate change, largely through attempts at mitigation.[204] Internationally, the ICMM has put out a *Climate Change Position Statement* (May 2006), a *Policy on Climate Change* (November 2009),[205] Principles for Climate Change Policy Design (June 2011), a letter to the United Nations Framework Convention secretariat on the eve of the conclusion of the Paris Agreement and a global study on the industry cost of carbon pricing,[206] among other climate change-specific reviews.[207] These statements policy outputs emphasize the need for a clear, gradual, predictable and measured transition to a price on carbon. They also advocate for applying climate change policy revenues primarily to developing climate-friendly technologies, and assisting exposed sectors (such as the mining industry) to adjust to the costs of a carbon-limited future. This policy matrix also highlights the danger of carbon leakage – the phenomenon by which companies relocate investment and production to regions having a more lenient regulatory regime – arising from fragmented approaches to carbon pricing in national and subnational jurisdictions.

The ICMM's policy statements on climate change taxes emphasize the variability of carbon pricing mechanisms, the detriment such variability poses for competitiveness and the consequent danger of carbon leakage. Their

---

[201] World Bank Group and Ecofys (n 194). This figure nevertheless still only represented 12 per cent of global GHG emissions.

[202] Ibid.

[203] Ibid 23.

[204] JD Ford *et al*, 'Canary in a coal mine: Perceptions of climate change risks and response options among Canadian mine operations' (2011) 109 *Climatic Change* 399–415; TD Pearce *et al*, 'Climate change and mining in Canada' (2011) 16(3) *Mitigation and Adaptation Strategies for Global Change* 347.

[205] ICMM, 'ICMM principles for climate change policy design position', www.icmm.com/en-gb/members/member-commitments/position-statements/icmm-principles-for-climate-change-policy-design-position-statement, accessed 26 February 2019.

[206] Smith (n 14) 320.

[207] See also ICMM, *Adapting to Changing Climate: Implications for the Mining and Metals Industry* (March 2013); and ICMM, *Options in Recycling Revenues Generated through Carbon Pricing: How 16 Governments Invest Their Carbon Revenues* (ICMM 2013).

review on the cost of carbon pricing notes that carbon pricing mechanisms differ according to whether emissions from the mining and metals industry are incorporated into the regime, whether there are compensatory measures to cushion the effects of carbon pricing on emissions intensive and trade-exposed industries (EITE) and the uses to which revenues derived from carbon pricing are applied. Recommended compensatory measures include the free allocation of emission allowances to EITE-exposed industries, tax rebates and direct financial aid to such industries and border tax adjustments. The carbon pricing review, however, noted that while all systems that define EITE industries include at least some forms of metal processing and production, only a handful classify mining activities as EITE.

The mining industry's rigorous advocacy on the carbon tax is notable. Needless to say, if the full range of recommended measures were implemented it would be questionable whether the State's imposition of carbon taxes would incentivize behaviour towards lower GHG emissions.

2.4 Tax Avoidance and Tax Evasion: The Outsmarted State

Under the dominant model, States are not only expected to design fiscal regimes that capture mineral resource rents, promote private investment and (possibly) avert environmental and social externalities. They are also required to respond to the various ways in which tax obligations can be sidestepped through tax avoidance and evasion. 'Taxpayers adapt' and accordingly 'an overriding principle of intelligent tax design must be to account for behavioural reactions to the set of tax instruments under consideration'.[208] Such 'behavioural reactions' include treaty shopping, trade mispricing and transfer mispricing.

The narrative of the outsmarted State in the field of tax avoidance and tax evasion is broader than the extractives industries, with roots in the literature on both IFFs and BEPS. IFFs have been defined as 'money illegally earned, transferred or used'.[209] Two dimensions of this definition bear emphasis. First, the emphasis on illegality throughout the flow of funds (place of earning, transfer and use) is deliberate, to underline that a legal act in one jurisdiction does not nullify the intent and purpose of the outflow, which is to hide money, either to evade or avoid taxes or to launder funds obtained from criminal activities.[210] Second, emphasis placed on illicit rather than illegal financial flows is consid-

---

[208] Smith (n 14) 10.

[209] High-Level Panel on Illicit Financial Flows, *Illicit Financial Flow: Report of the High-Level Panel on Illicit Financial Flows from Africa* (AU/ECA 2014) 15.

[210] Ibid 23.

ered a fairer description of activities that, 'while not strictly illegal in all cases, go against established norms and principles'.[211] The OECD's definition of base erosion and profit shifting is narrower, referring to 'tax avoidance strategies that exploit gaps and mismatches in tax rules to artificially shift profits to low, or no tax jurisdictions'.[212]

IFFs arise from a broad range of unrecorded, illegal and criminal activities across different economic sectors. Civil society reports on massive IFFs out of developing countries started to emerge in the early 2000s.[213] For example, in 2005 Baker estimated that USD 540 billion flowed out of developing countries each year as a result of tax evasion, international tax fraud, drug trafficking and corruption.[214] This fed into the more systematic work conducted by Kar *et al* in collaboration with Global Financial Integrity.[215] A 2012 report on the *magnitude* of IFFS from developing countries for the period 2001–10 put the figure at between USD 585.9 billion and USD 918.6 billion per annum.[216] A 2013 report on IFFs out of Africa concluded that cumulative IFFs from Africa for the period 1980–2009 amounted to USD 1.2 to 1.3 trillion, with most of these outflows coming from sub-Saharan Africa.[217] The AU/ECA report of the High Level Panel on IFFs from Africa, adopted by the Assembly of the African Union in 2015, found that Africa was losing USD 50 to 60 billion per annum due to IFFs, approximately double the amount of official development

---

211 Ibid.

212 OECD, 'Base erosion and profit shifting', www.oecd.org/ctp/beps/, accessed 26 February 2019.

213 The reports included Transparency International, *Global Corruption Report 2004* (Transparency International 2004); RW Baker, *Capitalism's Achilles Heel: Dirty Money and How to Renew the Free-Market System* (Wiley and Sons 2005); Tax Justice Network, *Closing the Floodgates: Collecting Tax to Pay for Development* (TJN 2007); and S Kapoor, *Haemorrhaging Money: A Christian Aid Briefing on the Problem of Illicit Capital Flight* (Christian Aid 2007).

214 Baker (n 213).

215 See the sources cited in n 40 above.

216 Kar and Freitas (n 41) 9. This figure relates to IFFs originating from all economic activities, and not only activities in the extractives sector.

217 African Development Bank and Global Financial Integrity (n 40) 3. The methodologies used by the tax and environmental justice movements to estimate the quantum of IFFs have not gone unchallenged. In a recent contribution, for example, Nitsch has claimed that the annual trillion dollar estimated of IFFs from developing countries lacks evidence and corroboration. See Volker Nitsch, 'Trade mispricing and illicit flows' in Peter Reuter (ed.), *Draining Development? Controlling Flows of Illicit Funds from Developing Countries* (World Bank 2012) 309; Volker Nitsch, 'Working Paper: Trillion dollar estimate: Illicit financial flows from developing countries' Darmstadt Discussion Papers in Economics, No. 227. GFI, Kar and Freitas responded to Nitsch's 2012 critique in their 2012 reports (see n 41 above).

aid.[218] IFFs are considered to be rife in extractives, a sector which includes mining, oil and gas projects. In 2013 the African Development Bank and GFI concluded that the *main* source of IFFs in resource rich African countries was the natural resource sector.[219] The High Level Panel on IFFs from Africa also noted a high correlation between reliance on extractive industries and IFFs.[220]

The OECD has recognized base erosion and profit shifting in the mining sector as a particular concern for developing countries.[221] To strengthen tax administration, the OECD Centre for Tax Policy and Administration has been collaborating with the Intergovernmental Forum on Mining, Minerals and Sustainable Development (IGF) to produce various forms of guidance on BEPS practices in the mining sector.[222] Over time, the programme of collaboration between the two organizations is intended to address the full range of tax revenue risks arising in the mining industry, namely international tax treaties, undervaluation of mineral exports, abusive transfer pricing, excessive interest deductions, tax incentives, tax stabilization, offshore indirect transfers of mining assets, metals streaming, abusive hedging arrangements and inadequate ringfencing. The following sections highlight risks arising from treaty shopping and trade and transfer mispricing only.

2.4.1 Treaty shopping

Jurisdictions rich in natural resources lose tax revenues when extractive companies abuse tax treaties and bilateral investment treaties. This involves setting up holding or financing companies in countries that function as 'tax conduits' or 'tax havens'. In 2010, for example, Heritage Oil sold its exploration licences in the Albertine Rift in Uganda to Tullow Oil for the princely sum of USD 1.45 billion.[223] The Uganda Revenue Authority charged Heritage Oil USD 434 million in capital gains taxes on the basis that the assets sold were all located in Uganda, and that the sale had been completed with the consent of the Ugandan

---

218 High-Level Panel on Illicit Financial Flows, *Illicit Financial Flow: Report of the High-Level Panel on Illicit Financial Flows from Africa* (AU/ECA, 2014) 13, 79.

219 African Development Bank and Global Financial Integrity (n 40) 4.

220 High-Level Panel on Illicit Financial Flows (n 218) 16, 58.

221 For an overview of the OECD's work in this regard see www.oecd.org/ctp/tax-global/work-on-extractive-industries.htm, accessed 26 February 2019.

222 Dan Devlin, *Limiting the Impact of Excessive Interest Deductions on Mining Revenue* (IGF and OECD 2018); Alexandra Readhead, *Monitoring the Value of Mineral Exports: Policy Options for Governments* (IGF and OECD 2018).

223 Angelo Izama and Hashim Wassa Mulangwa, 'Understanding the tax dispute: Heritage, Tullow and the Govenrment of Uganda', Advocates Coalition for Development and Environment, Infosheet No. 16 (2011), www.acode-u.org/Files/Publications/infosheet_16.pdf, accessed 26 February 2019.

government.[224] Heritage disputed the tax, arguing that the sale was not taxable as it had taken place in the Channel Islands off the coast of France, and the company was domiciled in Mauritius.[225] Uganda had a double taxation agreement with Mauritius, and since Mauritius did not impose any capital gains tax Heritage could reduce its tax bill to zero.[226] Legal proceedings between the government of Uganda and Heritage Oil, and between Heritage Oil and Tullow Oil regarding the disputed tax were subsequently lodged in London, in which the Tullow Oil prevailed in 2013,[227] and the Uganda Revenue Authority in 2015.[228] Release of the Panama Papers in 2016, however, revealed how Heritage had changed the domicile of the company from the Bahamas to Mauritius on the advice of tax accountants a few days before the conclusion of the sale. An email penned by one of Heritage's accountants stated that the move to Mauritius would be a 'second line of defence' in efforts to 'eliminate the potential tax charge imposed by the Ugandan authorities'.[229]

The tax avoidance strategy evident in the example cited above is commonly associated with tax havens – or 'offshore financial centres' (OFCs) as they are euphemistically known – such as Bermuda, the British Virgin Islands, the Cayman Islands and others. A staggering 50 per cent of the world's crossborder assets and liabilities are estimated to pass through OFCs.[230] These places functions as critical nodes in complex international flows of capital that divert revenues away from mineral-rich jurisdictions. The use of OFCs to minimize tax payments has prompted policy concerns that have led to initiatives such as the OECD's BEPS programme. Accordingly, identifying OFCs has become a politically contentious issue.

In recent research, Garcia-Bernardo and others used a novel data-driven research method based on global ownership relations to identify OFCs. Their

---

[224] Ibid.

[225] Ibid 2.

[226] Staff Reporter, 'Panama Papers: how Jersey-based oil firm avoided taxes in Uganda', *BBC News*, 8 April 2016, www.bbc.com/news/world-africa-35985463, accessed 26 February 2019.

[227] Emily Gosden, 'Tullow Oil wins $313 millioni from Heritage in Ugandan tax dispute', *The Telegraph*, 14 June 2013, www.telegraph.co.uk/finance/newsbysector/energy/oilandgas/10121062/Tullow-Oil-wins-313m-from-Heritage-in-Ugandan-tax-dispute.html, accessed 26 February 2019.

[228] Ismail Musa Ladu, 'Govenrment wins Heritage Oil case', *Daily Monitor*, 26 February 2015 www.monitor.co.ug/News/National/Government--wins--Heritage-----Oil--case/688334-2635614-ip6po4/index.html, accessed 26 February 2019.

[229] Ibid.

[230] Javier Garcia-Bernardo *et al*, 'Uncovering Offshore Financial Centers: Conduits and sinks in the global corporate ownership network' (2017) *Scientfic Reports* 7, www.nature.com/articles/s41598-017-06322-9, accessed 26 February 2019.

research also highlighted an important distinction between 'sink' and 'conduit' OFCs – the former being jurisdictions where money is 'stored' to facilitate objectives such as tax minimization, the latter being 'attractive intermediate destinations in the routing of international investments that enable the transfer of capital without taxation'.[231] The researchers identified 24 'sink' OFCs.[232] However, they also found that a small group of five countries – the Netherlands, the United Kingdom, Ireland, Singapore and Switzerland – are responsible for channelling the vast majority of corporate offshore investment.[233] These countries facilitate the transfer of value from and to sink OFCs. As the authors point out, their research challenges the notion that tax havens are exotic, small island destinations that defy regulations. Instead, all conduit and many sink OFCs are highly developed countries.[234]

Civil society has, for example, scrutinized the role of the Netherlands in the transfer of mineral value. The Netherlands is well known for being a jurisdiction with a 'beneficial tax system' that enables multinational companies to 'design, set-up and maintain tax efficient corporate and holding structures'.[235] Research conducted in 2016 by Profundo and partners found that 34 per cent (43) of the 128 mining companies exploiting mineral resources in five developing countries were directly or indirectly owned by 38 Dutch financing and holding companies,[236] belonging to 11 international mining groups.[237] Based on a comprehensive literature review, case studies and interviews with 14 experts, the authors identified 28 risk indicators that could point to tax avoidance, such as a subsidiary located in a known tax haven, intragroup loans and interest payments, redirected dividend payments and a relatively limited number of employees.[238]

---

[231] Ibid 1.

[232] See Table S3 in the electronic supplementary information to the article. The research identified the British Virgin Islands, Taiwan, Jersey, Bermuda and the Cayman Islands as the top five sink OFCs. The list of 24 sink OFCs included Mauritius, Hong Kong, Monaco, Qatar, Norway, the United States, Canada and France.

[233] Garcia-Bernardo (n 230) 6.

[234] Ibid.

[235] See International Tax Review, 'Netherlands: The advantages of a Dutch holding company' (30 July 2012), www.internationaltaxreview.com/Article/3068219/Netherlands-The-advantages-of-a-Dutch-holding-company.html, accessed 26 February 2019. The range of tax benefits include a 100 per cent exemption of dividends and capital gains for holding companies, coupled with a network of 90 double tax treaties and around 100 bilateral investment treaties 'that offer direct access to international arbitration as opposed to being obliged to exhaust proceedings with a local court first'.

[236] The developing countries were the Democratic Republic of the Congo, Ghana, Indonesia, Mongolia and Zambia.

[237] Van Gelder (n 39) 2.

[238] Ibid 16–24.

The existence of 'sink' and 'conduit' OFCs is coextensive with the highly complex corporate structures of parents and subsidiaries which multinational companies have set up to organize ownership and operations across the globe. Complex parent–subsidiary relationships are further complicated by multiple stock exchange listings. For example, BHP – the largest mining company by market capitalization in the world – is a dual listed company, with BHP Group Limited listed on the Australian Securities Exchange, and BHP Group plc having a primary listing on the London Stock Exchange. The two companies nevertheless conduct business as one operation, with identical boards and a single management structure.[239] Undated documents submitted to the United States Securities Commission showed that these two companies had almost 400 subsidiaries between them. Unincorporated joint venture agreements, where multiple corporate entities undertake a mining venture by way of contractual agreements among themselves, add a further layer of complexity to taxation administration.[240]

The narrative of the outsmarted State in the field of tax avoidance and tax evasion tacitly assumes that the 'problem' is lack of capacity on the part of developing countries and their tax administrations. This attitude is constituted by actors in developed and developing countries alike. It is evident, for example, in the opening lines of the UN's recent *Handbook on Extractive Industries Taxation*, a document developed in response to the need often expressed by developing countries 'for clearer guidance' on the policy and administrative aspects of applying taxes to multinational enterprises in the extractive industries.[241] The 'helpful guidance' in this 'complex area' – as contained in the *Handbook* and the recently commissioned OECD/IGF collaboration on BEPS in the mining sector – is full of technical detail and is no doubt well intentioned. Developing countries, for example, are advised to pay attention to the scope of their tax treaties, and to ensure that special mining taxes are excluded from blanket provisions that limit the taxing rights of the source State.[242] But the narrative shifts attention away from the larger systemic problems associated with the transfer of mineral wealth, namely the behaviour of corporations and the governments of conduit and sink OFCs, and the international institutional framework for taxing crossborder investment flows, which currently comprises a patchwork of domestic legislation and bilateral treaties that limit the taxing right of source (host) States and allow for minimal international guidance or oversight.

---

[239] Wikipedia, 'BHP', https://en.wikipedia.org/wiki/BHP, accessed 26 February 2019.

[240] United Nations (n 42) 36.

[241] Ibid 1.

[242] Ibid 42.

2.4.2 Trade mispricing and transfer mispricing

The narrative of the outsmarted State is also evident in the framing and policy prescriptions associated with trade mispricing and transfer mispricing in the mining industry.

Trade mispricing involves misrepresenting the price or quantity of imports or exports to hide or accumulate money in other jurisdictions, simultaneously facilitating a transfer of revenue out of the host country.[243] Kumar, for example, notes that while trade mispricing is barely discussed in taxation reform forums in Latin America, the underpricing of mineral exports is consistently problematic in Peru, Brazil, Mexico, Chile and Colombia.[244] OECD/IGF guidance to developing countries notes that undervaluation arises as a problem when tax revenue depends on both the quantity and price of mineral exports, that is, when *ad valorem* royalties are applied. Checking the price of mineral exports is more complicated than checking quantity as a result of different stages of mineral beneficiation, deductions for transport and insurance, related party sales and lack of publicly quoted prices for some mineral commodities.[245] The belief is nevertheless widespread that companies intentionally or accidentally undervalue their mineral exports, contributing to an erosion of trust and impairment of companies' 'social license to operate'.[246]

Policy guidance for the outsmarted State in the arena of trade mispricing also rests on an assumption of lack of capacity. As the OECD/IFG guidance explains, 'the skills, expertise and facilities to monitor mineral value are lacking'.[247] Assistance accordingly focuses on policy options for 'improving government oversight of mineral product export valuation', such as direct measurement, monitoring companies' own valuation processes and a hybrid approach.[248] The well intentioned nature of this guidance, once again, distracts attention from other problems and policy options, such as measures States can take to seize underdeclared revenues and punish corporations and their directors. That States may not be lacking in capacity to such a great extent is evident from recent developments in Tanzania, where the government issued a subsidiary of a large Canadian company with a tax bill of USD 40 billion in July 2017 for alleged underdeclared export revenues from the Bulyanhulu and

243 High-Level Panel on Illicit Financial Flows (n 218) 10–11; Kumar (n 39) 2.
244 Kumar (n 39) 2.
245 Readhead (n 222) 2.
246 Ibid.
247 Ibid.
248 Ibid.

Buzgwazi mines over the period 2000–17, together with USD 150 billion in interest and penalties.[249]

Transfer pricing refers to the price of transactions occurring between related companies, particularly those in the same company group, and affects the level of taxable profits of the different branches and subsidiaries of the firm. Abusive transfer pricing occurs where the prices for internal goods and services are manipulated in a manner that does not respect the 'arm's length principle' (the price of the good or service between unrelated companies) and the intent is to reduce taxable profits or shift profits from one jurisdiction to another.[250] Transfer pricing can include trade mispricing but covers a broader range of practices, such as loan payments between related companies and the interest payable on such, payments for managerial services or charges for intellectual property such as royalties or patents. In April 2017, for example, the Federal Court of Australia unanimously dismissed an appeal brought by Chevron against a ruling of the Australian Tax Office that Chevron had used an intracompany loan to shift its profits offshore and avoid paying tax on its Australian income.[251] Chevron had borrowed USD 2.5 billion in the United States of America at an interest rate of less than 2 per cent and on-lent the loan to its Australian subsidiary at 9 per cent. The Federal Court found that this interest rate was too high and not in line with the arm's length principle.[252] Chevron initially indicated it would appeal this ruling, but subsequently reached a USD 1 billion-plus settlement with the Tax Office over its treatment of intercompany loans.[253]

The narrative of the outsmarted State in the field of mineral taxation thus assumes both an incapable and capable State. The tax administration systems in developing mineral-rich jurisdictions are represented as lacking in skills, expertise and facilities. And yet, with enough straightforward and 'helpful' guidance it is hoped that States will be able to outsmart the nimble corporations that shift costs and profits around the world. This guidance comes at the

---

[249] Thomas Biesheuvel, 'This miner's $190 billion tax bill would take centuries to pay' (24 July 2017), www.bloomberg.com/news/articles/2017-07-24/acacia-gets-190-billion-tax-bill-it-would-take-centuries-to-pay, accessed 26 February 2019.

[250] High-Level Panel on Illicit Financial Flows (n 218) 10–11.

[251] Stephen Long, 'US oil giant Chevron faces $300 million tax bill after ATO court victory', www.abc.net.au/news/2017-04-21/chevron-faces-massive-tax-bill-after-ato-court-victory/8460874, accessed 26 February 2019.

[252] Michael West, 'Chevron: A game-changer for multinational tax avoiders', *The Conversation*, 24 April 2017, http://theconversation.com/chevron-a-game-changer-for-multinational-tax-avoiders-76587?utm_source=linkedin&utm_medium=linkedinbutton, accessed 26 February 2019.

[253] Matt Chambers, 'Chevron drops High Court tax appeal, with win "to yield $10 billion in revenue"', *Australian Business Review*, 18 August 2017.

expense of harsher, more direct State action against corporate tax abuse, and at the expense of more concerted international action against the behaviour of conduit and sink OFCs.

2.5 Fiscal Decentralization and Natural Resource Revenue Sharing: The State as Wealth Distributor

A more recent addition to the dominant model of mineral taxation focuses on the State's role as wealth distributor through fiscal decentralization and/or natural resource revenue sharing. This role corresponds with the issue of how mineral and mining taxes should be generated, allocated and used by and among different spheres of government within a mineral-rich jurisdiction.

'Fiscal decentralization' and 'revenue sharing' are related but not synonymous terms.[254] Fiscal decentralization refers to how the State empowers its various parts and levels to transform private into public capital for the use and benefit of society.[255] Revenue sharing, on the other hand, is a consideration in the budgeting process, whereby revenue collected by one branch of government is distributed to other governmental entities.[256] Brosio identifies four systems for sharing natural resource revenues between different levels of government: A system of separate (own) taxes, which entitles national and subnational levels of government to levy separate natural resource taxes on the firms or projects in their jurisdiction; tax base sharing, where two or more levels of government use the same tax instrument to generate revenues, such as a surcharge on mineral royalties; revenue sharing, where the central government determines tax rates and revenue shares and allocates such to producing and nonproducing regions; and intragovernmental transfers in kind, involving infrastructure provision by companies exploiting the resources.[257]

From a Polanyian lens, fiscal decentralization and revenue sharing arrangements strengthen the double movement, roping an increasing number of governments into dependence on mineral resource revenues – whether or not the minerals actually lie in the region of the subnational government concerned. At the same time, such revenues could be used to address the socioecological impacts of mining, especially in the localities where commodities are mined. Many mineral-rich jurisdictions already have systems in place for various forms of intergovernmental transfers of revenue, and creating special

---

[254] James M Otto, 'Fiscal decentralization and mining taxation', Occasional Paper: World Bank Group Mining Department (March 2001) 1.

[255] Ibid 1–2.

[256] Ibid 1.

[257] Giorgio Brosio, 'The assignment of revenue from natural resources' in Ehtisham Ahmad and Giorgio Brosio, *Handbook of Fiscal Federalism* (Edward Elgar 2006) 440.

regimes to allocate nonrenewable natural resource revenues to subnational governments is an increasing trend.[258] The motivations for establishing these systems vary from country to country but include the idea of compensating local communities for environmental degradation and other negative effects of extraction.[259]

In Canada, fiscal decentralization of mineral revenues is being instituted as part of a broader process of devolving control and administration of land and resources to territorial and indigenous governments. Prior to the conclusion of negotiations on devolution in some provinces and territories, Canada received resource revenues pursuant to federal legislation and regulations, alongside royalty shares set out in indigenous land claim agreements.[260] Devolution and resource revenue sharing agreements were first finalized in the Yukon with the passage of the Yukon Oil and Gas Accord in 1998; arrangements for forests, mines and minerals followed in 2003.[261] These devolution and revenue sharing agreements transfer the administration and control of public lands and associated natural resources to the Yukon government, empowering it to also collect all associated royalties, rents and fees.[262] In 2014, devolution and resource revenue sharing arrangements were also finalized in Canada's Northwest Territories.[263] New mining regulations now provide for an *ad valorem* royalty to be paid to the Government of the Northwest Territories.[264] Critics argue, however, that the devolution discussions have failed to consider how devolved powers and authorities might address social, cultural and envi-

---

[258] According to a 2016 survey conducted by the Natural Resource Governance Institute and the UNDP, in the following countries the national government collects oil, gas and mineral revenues and then transfers these funds back to their area of origin or adjacent areas: Angola, Bolivia, Brazil, Cameroon, some regions in Canada, Chad, China, Colombia, the Democratic Republic of the Congo, Ecuador, Ethiopia, Ghana, Guinea, India, Indonesia, Iraq, Kyrgyzstan, Madagascar, Malaysia, Mexico, Mongolia, Niger, Nigeria, Papua New Guinea, Peru, the Philippines, South Sudan, Uganda and some regions of the United States of America. See Andrew Bauer *et al*, *Natural Resource Revenue Sharing* (NGRI and UNDP 2016) 5, 8.

[259] Ibid. Other motivations include addressing local claims about resource ownership and distributing resource revenues to help defuse violent resource-related conflicts.

[260] Stephanie Irlbacher-Fox and Stephen J Mills, 'Devolution and resource revenue sharing in the Canadian North: Achieving fairness across generations', Discussion Paper, Walter and Duncan Gordon Foundation, 11.

[261] Ibid 5.

[262] Ibid.

[263] Government of Canada: Indigenous and Northern Affairs Canada, 'Mining Regulations'.

[264] Regulation 69, Northwest Territories Lands Act, Mining Regulations (R-015-2014).

ronmental sustainability.[265] The changes initiated through devolution could have ushered in innovative arrangements for protecting the interests of future generations. Indigenous governments have generally adhered to the principle of intergenerational equity in managing the financial endowments associated with land claims agreements. This in turn derives from the principle of respect, which suffuses all relations – reaching back to the ancestors and forward to the welfare of future generations in addition to encompassing community, lands and resources.[266] The Canadian government required, however, that new mining regulations should substantively mirror the corresponding federal regulations, driving strong federal and industry interest in maintaining continuity for the sake of economic stability. The 'mirroring' requirement watered down the opportunity for change to promote sustainability that the devolution negotiations potentially presented.[267]

Academic literature on the State's role as wealth equalizer advances conflicting principles, at least insofar as shifting wealth between mineral producing and nonproducing regions is concerned. On the one hand, inhabitants of producing regions expect to receive a share of the wealth generated in their territories.[268] According to the derivation principle adopted in some petroleum producing States, resources should stay where they are produced.[269] Failure to respect this principle has led to interregional conflicts and even demands for secession.[270] The principles of intra and intergenerational equity may also require that mineral revenues remain in producing regions, given the disproportionate and extensive localized social and environmental impacts these regions typically bear.[271] As Irlbacher-Fox and Mills state: 'We know that the needs of future generations will include servicing the social, environmental, cultural and economic costs inflicted by previous generations, and inflicted by our generation.'[272] On the other hand, nonproducing regions have relied upon the argument of equitable federalism.[273]

Unlike some of the other areas of mineral taxation, the sustainable mineral development consensus has not pushed a clear policy agenda on resource revenue sharing. The MMSD observed that there is no simple rule of thumb

---

265 Irlbacher-Fox and Mills (n 260) 9.

266 Ibid 14.

267 Ibid 10.

268 Cut Dian Agustina *et al*, 'Political economy of natural resource revenue sharing in Indonesia' (March 2012) Asia Research Centre Working Paper 55, 6.

269 Brosio (n 257) 446.

270 Ibid.

271 See Kumar (n 39) 5.

272 Irlbacher-Fox and Mills (n 260) 14.

273 Ibid; A Ikein and C Briggs-Anigboh, *Oil and Fiscal Federalism in Nigeria* (Ashgate 1998).

regarding the allocation of mineral revenues among different tiers of government, and that it was a political decision few countries had resolved satisfactorily.[274] The ICMM-sponsored review of mineral fiscal regimes was agnostic on the benefits of fiscal decentralization, pointing out that the theoretical and practical experiences were inconclusive.[275] Mining dissenters have pointed out that mineral royalties can be ringfenced for development in the localities most heavily impacted by mining activities. But even here the policy advice has been anodyne. The Natural Resource Charter, for example, states that 'in some cases' governments may consider distributing more revenues to communities near extraction sites, and that where groups disproportionately bear extraction costs such as environmental damage or social disruption, the government should 'actively seek to prevent or compensate for this'.[276] However, it also espouses the contrary view that in light of the national ownership of mineral resources, communities near to extraction sites have no inherent claims to greater shares of resources than other communities in the country.[277]

To date there has been only sporadic research on the design and implementation of systems of resource revenue sharing.[278] It is accepted, however, that resource revenue sharing schemes can generate perverse incentives, as much as they may also raise standards of living and reduce poverty in resource-rich regions, address the demands of local groups' special claims on resources, and compensate mine-affected communities for environmental damage.[279] Perverse incentives include local governments' extreme dependence on such revenue streams, the tendency for the volatility of natural resource revenues to exacerbate boom and bust cycles of development, and the potential to accentuate regional disparities, and even contribute to violent conflict in some regions.[280] There is also a lack of strong empirical evidence to suggest that resource revenue sharing schemes advance economic growth and development.[281] For example, in Peru, around 60 per cent of the revenue collected from the mining sector is distributed to municipal and regional governments on a derivation-based system.[282] Transferred mining revenues are earmarked for

[274] *Breaking New Ground* (n 7) 182.
[275] Choudhury (n 176) 63.
[276] Natural Resource Governance Institute (n 35) 26–7.
[277] Ibid 27.
[278] Bauer (n 258) 5.
[279] Ibid 9.
[280] Ibid 8–9.
[281] Ibid 9.
[282] The taxes distributed to subnational governments include the *canon minero* (50 per cent of the corporate income tax collected from mining firms, mineral royalties and the annual subsurface fee. See María Lasa Aresti, 'Mineral revenue sharing in Peru' (April 2016) Natural Resource Governance Institute: Revenue Sharing Case Study, 5.

particular uses – such as spending all resource transfers on investments for the benefit of the community and funding universities to undertake technical and scientific investigations.[283] However, findings of the limited studies into the use and impact of earmarked mining revenues thus far show an underutilization of transferred revenues and an increasing incidence of conflict as a result of revenue transfers.[284]

One of the policy prescriptions for mineral resource revenue sharing is that any system of this nature must clarify its objectives, for example, whether the resource sharing is intended to compensate for extractive activities, avoid disputes or ensure equitable development between regions.[285] However, none of the case studies reviewed in a recent NRGI/UNDP report on revenue sharing expressly positions environmental rehabilitation as a scheme objective. Although there are systems where the idea of compensating for environmental harm is a driver,[286] compensating for environmental harm is not the same as ensuring resources are reinvested into the productive capacity of ecological systems. For example, in China, the government has levied mineral compensation fees since 1997. Together with other royalties, compensation fees need to be spent in their region of origin, but these are largely spent on further State geological exploration, thus driving an extractivist/neoextractivist paradigm.[287] In the Philippines, the 1987 Constitution expressly states that 'local governments shall be entitled to an equitable share in the proceeds . . . of national wealth within their respective areas',[288] and the Local Government Code stipulates that subnational governments must utilize national wealth revenues to finance local development and livelihood projects, in consultation with local development councils and elected representatives. In practice, revenues received from hydropower, geothermal and other energy projects are earmarked for lowering electricity costs,[289] rather than rehabilitating the environment.

In conclusion, although fiscal decentralization and resource revenue sharing systems are theoretically attractive as a potential mechanism for either compensating local communities for environmental degradation or ensuring that funds are reinvested in the productive capacity of ecological systems, there is

---

283 Ibid 7.

284 Ibid.

285 Bauer (n 258) 10–11.

286 Ibid 24. The NRGI/UNDP report cite the examples of the USD 1 dollar Eucador levies on production of oil in the Amazon region.

287 Ibid 83.

288 Constitution of the Philippines (1987), Article 10.7.

289 Bauer (n 258) 101.

limited empirical evidence to demonstrate that such schemes are being successfully used in this manner.

2.6 Tax Transparency: The Accountable State

An increasing number of global governance institutions have endorsed 'transparency' as a governance ideal and a practice.[290] The reasons for transparency are frequently consequentialist in nature, such as improvements in reputation, positioning or operational efficiencies, or simply as a means to adhere to 'best practice'.[291] In the extractives sector, tax transparency initiatives such as Publish What You Pay (PWYP) and the EITI gained ground in the late 1990s and early 2000s to promote the broader ideal of 'free political debate' about how mineral wealth is managed.[292] The tax transparency narratives that have emerged around these programmes rest upon multiple and at times contradictory State roles.

PWYP and the EITI evolved in tandem at the same time that the formal mining industry began reckoning with its sustainable development performance. In response to the burgeoning literature on the resource curse,[293] organizations such as Global Witness, Human Rights Watch and Oxfam America started agitating for transparency in the flow of funds from extractive companies to governments. In 2002, these NGOs and three other London-based organizations launched PWYP to pressure extractive companies to publish their payments to governments.[294] Linked to this campaigning, in February 2001, British Petroleum had already published details of a signature bonus paid to the Angolan government for an offshore licence. This sparked a cold and vitriolic reaction from the Angolan government, with threats of a backlash.[295] Fearing how a global standard focused only on corporate disclosures would affect their 'social licence to operate', oil companies argued for a voluntary initiative to which governments could subscribe. The government of the United Kingdom supported this idea and took the idea of the EITI forward.[296]

---

[290] Megan Donaldson and Benedict Kingsbury, 'The adoption of transparency policies in global governance institutions: Justifications, effects and implications' (2013) 9 *Annual Review of Social Science* 119, 120.

[291] Ibid 131.

[292] *Breaking New Ground* (n 7) 194.

[293] The resource curse is discussed more fully in in section 2 of Chapter 3.

[294] Today, there are more than 700 civil society coalition partners in the PWYP campaign, working in seven continents: Publish What You Pay, 'Who we are', www.pwyp.org/about/, accessed 26 February 2019.

[295] Extractive Industries Transparency Initiative, 'History of the EITI' https://eiti.org/history#eiti-history-timeline, accessed 26 February 2019.

[296] Ibid.

The belief at the core of the EITI was that secrecy between governments and corporations fuelled the resource curse.[297]

Today, there are 51 EITI member countries, at various stages of implementation of the standard. Notably, major mineral-rich jurisdictions such as the USA, Canada, Australia, Russia, India, Chile, Brazil and South Africa have not signed up to the standard. PWYP has evolved as a civil society coalition that lobbies corporates to adopt transparency best practice, while the EITI is a global standard to which countries may voluntarily subscribe to demonstrate their commitment to transparency and hence 'free political debate' on mineral resource wealth. The two initiatives are closely articulated: for example, PWYP coordinates the civil society constituency on the international EITI board, and at a national level PWYP members support EITI implementation.[298] Of the two initiatives, the EITI is more significant for purposes of excavating the State's roles.

The EITI standard evolved over time, beginning with a formulation of the 12 EITI principles in 2003.[299] These principles resonate with key tenets of the sustainable mineral development consensus and responsible mining. The first principle, for example, affirms the belief that the 'prudent use of natural resource wealth should be an important engine for economic growth that contributes to sustainable development and poverty reduction'.[300] This principle also acknowledges that improper management of natural resource wealth can lead to negative social and economic consequences. Revenue streams are affirmed as a core benefit of extractive activity, although with the warning that such streams 'can be highly price dependent'.[301] The theme of free political debate emerges strongly: the key to the 'proper' management of natural resource wealth lies in public understanding of government revenues and expenditures and informed, public debate on appropriate and realistic options for sustainable development. For this to occur, governments and companies in the extractive industries must be more transparent, principally through disclosing tax payments on the part of extractive companies to governments. This, the principles espouse, will not only encourage high standards of transparency

---

[297] Nathan Andrews, 'A Swiss-Army knife? A critical assessment of the Extractive Industries Transparency Initiative (EITI) in Ghana' (2016) 121(1) *Business and Society Review* 59, 63.

[298] Publish What You Pay, 'EITI', www.publishwhatyoupay.org/our-work/eiti/, accessed 26 December 2018.

[299] Extractive Industries Transparency Initiative (n 295).

[300] Extractive Industries Transparency Initiative, 'The EITI Principles', https://eiti.org/document/eiti-principles, accessed 26 February 2019. See also Extractive Industries Transparency Initiative, *The EITI Standard 2016* (Rev. 24.5.2017) (2017) 10.

[301] Ibid, principle 3.

and accountability in public life, government operations and business, but also create an enhanced environment for domestic and foreign direct investment.

The EITI principles, and the Standard of which they form part, rest on a complex set of assumptions regarding the State. On the one hand, the principles affirm that how the natural resource wealth of a country is 'managed' for the benefit of citizens and national development is 'in the domain of sovereign governments'.[302] But given the global system of mining production described in Chapter 1 – a system whereby developing countries have been locked into a system of raw material supply export over many centuries – this principle is false, because the choices that some mineral-rich jurisdictions are able to exercise over their natural resource wealth are in fact highly circumscribed. The State's sovereign role is nevertheless affirmed by the operation of the EITI, as it is only States that can voluntarily subscribe to the EITI certification process. In the operation of the EITI Standard, however, the State is positioned as one roleplayer among equals. This much is clear from the EITI principle 12, which states that 'all stakeholders have important and relevant contributions to make – including governments and their agencies, extractive industry companies, service companies, multilateral organisations, financial organisations, investors and non-governmental organisations'. The design features of the EITI carry through this conviction, as they require establishment of a multistakeholder government–industry–civil society group to oversee the programme's implementation at a national level.

The value and effectiveness of the EITI has been criticized and commentators have highlighted numerous problems in design and implementation.[303] These include, for example, the fact that corporate participation remains voluntary, delays in time between submission of the information and publication of the EITI report and lack of alignment between Corporate Social Responsibility (CSR) initiatives and reporting of EITI payments.[304] Further, and similarly to other transparency initiatives, PWYP and the EITI may be constituting the rhetorical priority of transparency while belying the enduring importance of secrecy in governments and corporations – both in daily practice and as an idea.[305] And from the perspective of the double movement, tax transparency initiatives do little to strengthen scrutiny of the State's protective role – for, as McHenry *et al* have pointed out, the EITI is limited as it does not mandate

---

[302] Ibid, principle 2.

[303] Andrews (n 297), G Hilson and R Maconachie, 'Good governance and the extractive industries in sub-Saharan Africa' (2008) 30 *Mineral Processing and Extractive Metallurgy Review* 52.

[304] Andrews (n 297) 68.

[305] Ibid 120.

environmental payments, or the inclusion of legislative mine rehabilitation and closure information.[306]

Over time, the EITI has shifted from a standard focused on revenue collection, to a broader set of open data concerns relating to beneficial ownership, contract transparency and the transparency of commodity trading.[307] Emphasis is now also being placed on country-by-country reporting. Following the launch of the EITI, the US Dodd–Frank Wall Street Reform and Consumer Act, EU Accounting Directives, the UK's Reports on Payments to Governments Regulations 2014, Norway's Country-by-Country Reporting Law and Canada's Extractive Sector Transparency Measures Act have been formulated to promote fairer and more prudent stewardship of the revenues generated by oil, gas and mineral extraction. All these initiatives give effect to bifurcated assumptions regarding the State: on the one hand, the administratively efficient and accountable institutions of the global North, intent on scrutinizing their listed corporations' payments to governments on a country-by-country or even project-by-project basis; on the other, the outsmarted and undercapacitated State institutions in developing regions, unable to conduct this oversight on their own.

3. CONCLUSION

The resource rent capturing State, the private investment promoting State, the behavior incentivizing State, the outsmarted State, the wealth redistributing State and the transparent and accountable State – these are the roles constituting the dominant model for State taxation of minerals and mining. Taken together, these roles illustrate the paradox at the heart of the double movement: The State depends on mineral resource revenue streams for its existence and must use those revenues to advance and protect society. At the same time, it is expected to design fiscal frameworks in a manner that facilitates a global market for mineral commodities and mineral extraction.

While mining does generate significant tax revenues in many mineral-rich jurisdictions, those revenues are not protecting society against social, environmental or economic harms, nor generating significant developmental gains, notwithstanding initiatives such as the EITI. Instead, the bias of the double movement in the field of mineral and mining taxation is skewed towards promoting and supporting the market. This bias arises from numerous elements of policy advocacy and practice: the convoluted debates around the nature of the

---

306 MP McHenry *et al*, 'Puzzled: Navigating extractive policy information jigsaws for best practice and transparency' (2015) 2 *Extractive Industries and Society* 401, 403.

307 Extractive Industries Transparency Initiative (n 295).

'pure' economic rents arising from mining; the push for mineral royalties to be narrowly circumscribed to profit-based royalties or economic rent taxes; the entrenched construction of investor risk and the associated mantra of neutrality, stability and flexibility; the promotion of 'longtermism' alongside a range of tax incentives for the mining industry; State subsidization of commissioning and closure; the lack of any provision for a green fiscal regime; the strong industry pushback on the carbon tax, replete with requests for carbon tax revenues to be used to assist 'exposed' industries; the fragmented institutional framework for taxing crossborder investment; and extensive tax avoidance and evasion through the elaborate corporate architecture of multinational companies and the facilitating behaviour of State conduit and sink OFCs.

The contours of these policy areas, and the debates that have taken place therein, allow little space for considering how fiscal measures can strengthen the State's protective role. In particular, the reality of socioecological harm is rarely considered – either as a factor that shapes the principled basis for the design of a mineral fiscal regime, or in terms of specific fiscal instruments. The plethora of guidance documents surveyed in this chapter – from advice on treaty shopping, to tax incentives, to fiscal decentralization – do little to reverse this state of affairs.

6. The State, mining and environmental assessment

1. INTRODUCTION

This chapter extends the analysis of Polanyi's double movement in the system of global mining production to the area of the State, mining and environmental assessment. In line with Polanyi's theorizing, this book argues that the State is the site of paradox: it must both protect and defend disembedded markets in mineral exploration and exploitation, and secure their political and social legitimacy by addressing mining's worst environmental, social and economic effects. Chapter 4 demonstrated the critical role that property institutions have played in establishing disembedded markets for the production of mineral commodities. In this area the State strongly promotes the first arm of the double movement through a variety of roles centred on ownership of mineral resources and concessioning of extraction rights. Chapter 5, on mining and taxation, introduced some ambiguity: States must strengthen the second arm of the double movement by capturing a fair share of mineral resource rents for 'development' or (less prominently) to address the negative impacts of mining. But they are also expected to design fiscal frameworks that promote (or at least do not deter) private investment.

In this chapter, and the following on mine closure, the State's protective role under the double movement appears to loom large. Mining's far reaching, and oftentimes irreversible, impacts on the environment, society and economy have most obviously been mediated through various forms of prior assessment which have their roots in environmental impact assessment (EIA). In 2002 the MMSD project observed that EIA was arguably the most widely used tool of environmental management in the minerals sector,[1] and was already at that time being expanded to include social impact assessment and cost–benefit analysis.[2] The prevalence of EIA as the 'pre-project standard for outlining

---

[1] International Institute for Environment and Development and World Business Council for Sustainable Development, *Breaking New Ground: Mining, Minerals and Sustainable Development* (Earthscan 2002) 248 (henceforth *Breaking New Ground*).

[2] Ibid.

potential environmental and social risks related to large-scale mining' continues to the present day.[3]

EIA has been defined as 'the process of identifying, predicting, evaluating and mitigating the biophysical, social and other relevant effects of proposed development proposals, prior to major decisions being taken and commitments made'.[4] Over 40 years the broad EIA procedure, as it emerged from the National Environmental Policy Act (NEPA), 1969 in the USA, has been joined by a growing family of assessment tools which Sadler has labelled forms of 'environmental assessment' (EA).[5] Social Impact Assessment (SIA), Strategic Environmental Assessment (SEA) and Health Impact Assessment (HIA) have all emerged as strong and distinct areas of theory and practice,[6] usually in response to some level of dissatisfaction with EIA as practiced.[7] Consultative and participative methodologies have evolved as an integral element of these EA processes, giving effect to the core sustainable development value of public participation. Implicitly critiquing broader democratic processes, Baker and McClelland observe that often impact assessment processes present the only opportunity for local and indigenous communities to influence mine and infrastructure development directly.[8]

From this, the modality of the State's protective role becomes apparent. Through the various forms of EA, the State institutionalizes various forms of foresight that draw upon principles of prevention and precaution and rest upon scientific expertise. Knowledge is gained as a result. The State must then use that knowledge for at least two ends: for boundary setting purposes, to decide whether and how mining should proceed in its jurisdiction, and – linked to this – to institutionalize and police the 'management' of environmental impacts on the part of mining proponents. A third element of the protective role is to entrench democratic decisionmaking, or at least give the appearance of doing so.

---

[3] Heather Bedi, 'Environmental mis-assessment, development and mining in Orissa, India' (2013) 44(1) *Development and Change* 101.

[4] International Association of Impact Assessment, *What Is Impact Assessment?* (Fargo 2009).

[5] B Sadler, *Environmental Assessment in a Changing World: Evaluating Practice to Improve Performance* International Study on the Effectiveness of Environmental Assessment (Canadian Environmental Assessment Agency 1996).

[6] Alan Bond and Jenny Pope, 'Editorial: The state of the art of impact assessment in 2012' (2012) 30(1) *Impact Assessment and Project Appraisal* 1.

[7] Richard K Morgan, 'Environmental impact assessment: The state of the art' (2012) 30(1) *Impact Assessment and Project Appraisal* 1, 7.

[8] Douglas C Baker and James N McLelland, 'Evaluting the effectiveness of British Columbia's environmental assessment process for first nations' participation in mining development' (2003) 23 *Environmental Impact Assessment Review* 581, 582.

Like the area of taxation, the State's role is therefore ambiguous. On the one hand, rigorous design and implementation of EA processes could genuinely protect society from the worst of mining's excesses. On the other, EA could simply be an elaborate form of market facilitation, bolstering proponents' 'social licence to operate' but not protecting particular societies from the very troubling longterm systemic impacts of extractivism and neoextractivism. This critique has been voiced by mining dissenters, who argue that the protections of EA (deliberation, evaluation and recordkeeping) are only paper-based, and that in reality these spaces often prioritize procedure over content and circumscribe which risks are flagged for management interventions in a manner that does not change, or even worsens, the familiar power imbalances of neoliberalism.[9] Like taxation, therefore, the framing of EA in the mining sector is particularly powerful in 'locking' the double movement into place.

This chapter explicates the dominant model for the State's framing of mining and EA. This model is constituted by three main State roles centred on (1) the institutionalization of precaution; (2) the setting of boundaries; and (3) the promotion of democratic environmental decisionmaking. In the case of boundary setting, the chapter considers whether States can use EA to delineate 'no go' areas for mining and to manage cumulative impacts.

2. THE STATE, MINING AND ENVIRONMENTAL ASSESSMENT: EXPLICATING THE DOMINANT MODEL

Narratives on mining and environmental assessment first arose from national processes of legislated EIA, and practitioner and academic reflections on their application to mining. In 1980, for example, Palmay and Gwilym observed that '[t]hroughout the world, the preparation of Environmental Impact Statements is rapidly becoming an integral part of any mining development'.[10] Atkinson and Morrison report on how environmental assessments were being undertaken in Australia even prior to the implementation of the NEPA in the USA.[11] Although having no legislative base for EIA procedures, the New South Wales government introduced assessment procedures in the late 1960s and the

[9] Fabiana Li, 'Documenting accountability: Environmental impact assessment in a Peruvian mining project' (2009) 32(2) *Political and Legal Anthropology Review* 218.

[10] F Palmay and RD Gwilym, 'Preparing and presenting environmental impact statements in support of mining operations with particular reference to uranium mining' (1980) 2(3) *Minerals and the Environment* 114.

[11] Warren Atkinson and Kerry Morrison, 'Dealing with social and biological environmental impact assessment' in *Mining and Environment: A Professional Approach (Symposia Series)* (Australasian Institute of Mining and Metallurgy 1987), 57.

Australian Commonwealth Government worked under procedures agreed by Cabinet up until 1974. Prior to 1970, there are no papers on EIA held by 'One Mine', a repository containing more than 124,000 mining and minerals-related documents – including many authored by industry practitioners – but from this date onwards, research on the topic picks up steadily.

EIA has become synonymous with the sustainable development movement and most countries have some form of legislated EIA procedure. Prior environmental assessment is a key tenet of sustainable development, as enshrined in Principle 17 of the Rio Declaration, which states: 'Environmental impact assessment, as a national instrument, shall be undertaken for proposed activities that are likely to have a significant adverse impact on the environment and are subject to a decision of a competent national authority.'

In mineral-rich jurisdictions, EIA may be legislated in mining-specific laws, or more commonly in laws relating to environmental management or land use planning. By the early 2000s, a number of countries had already drafted specific environmental regulations for the mining industry.[12]

The normative framing of mining and EA, however, extends beyond national EIA processes and is the product of guidance emanating from a wide variety of social actors. The significance of mining's adverse impact on the environment has prompted the United Nations, international organizations such as the International Organization for Standardization (ISO), international financing institutions (IFIs), international and national mining associations and environmental justice organizations to articulate their expectations of the State and the mining industry in this area.

At the level of the UN, a narrative on mining and environmental management emerged in the early 1990s and was developed over the next ten years. In 1991, the United Nations Department of Technical Cooperation for Development organized an International Roundtable on mining and the environment, which culminated in the formulation of 15 Fundamental Principles for the Mining Sector (the Berlin Guidelines).[13] The Berlin Guidelines were subsequently revised after a second roundtable in 1999.[14] The revised Guidelines recognized the importance of both environmental and socioeconomic impact assessments.[15] In 2002 the UN published *Berlin II*, which incorporates guidelines on

[12] United Nations, *Berlin II: Guidelines for Mining and Sustainable Development* (United Nations 2002) 9.

[13] UN Department of Technical Cooperation for Development and Deutsche Stiftung für Internationale Entwicklung, *Mining and Environment: The Berlin Guidelines* (Mining Journal Books 1992) (henceforth *Berlin Guidelines*).

[14] UNEP, 'Mining and Sustainable Development II: Challenges and Perspectives' 23 *Industry and Environment* (UNEP 2000) 9.

[15] Ibid.

community consultation and development and the various dimensions of environmental management, including environmental and socioeconomic impact assessment. Voluntary standards developed by international organizations and associations are also influential in framing the conduct of EA in the mining sector. The premier internationally-agreed standard for an environmental management system is the ISO's Standard 14001:20015 and, like its 2004 counterpart, the standard requires implementing companies to comply with the environmental legislation of the country in which operations take place.[16] This would obviously include any laws mandating EA.

Over the years, IFIs have developed environmental performance standards for the projects they finance, which incorporate guidance on various forms of EA. These performance standards apply when the mining industry seeks debt and equity funding or insurance from such institutions for the activities of exploration,[17] mine development,[18] construction,[19] production,[20] and mine closure.[21] Project finance for mines has become increasingly difficult to procure

---

[16] International Organization for Standardization, 'ISO 140001:2015' www.iso.org/standard/60857.html accessed 26 February 2019.

[17] Different financial institutions feature in the financing of the different stages of the mining cycle, as these stages present different levels of risk. Exploration is high risk and was traditionally financed by the public equity markets; however, post-2010 these sources of capital contracted. Alternative sources of equity, including private capital providers, were being explored by the mid-2010s. See Sam Jordan Jones (ed.), *Global Mining Finance Guide* (Aspermont 2013) 9, 10–12.

[18] Equity remains the preferred form of funding during the development phase of the mine life cycle when detailed feasibility studies need to be undertaken to secure permits and licences. Access to equity finance, although easier than the exploration stage, is still challenging and the cost of capital is usually higher than most projects are able to bear (Jones (n 17) 18). As a result, mine developers are exploring debt financing, including from development finance institutions and multilateral development banks, to take the project forward. Obtaining funding from such institutions may require compliance with strict social and environmental standards. Commercial banking institutions may also consider project finance at this stage (ibid).

[19] A variety of debt and equity instruments provided by an increasingly diverse set of service providers finance the critical construction phase of a mine (Jones (n 17) 43). Such instruments include streaming, offtake agreements and private royalty agreements. During the construction phase national export credit agencies may also provide forms of finance, for example for equipment.

[20] During the production phase of the mine the need for financing is reduced, as the mine will be generating cash flows that can service prior debt. Cash flows can provide security and assure lenders, facilitating the taking on of additional debt to expand and upgrade operations, diversify assets or restructure the company's balance sheet (Jones (n 17) 55). Most debt during this stage is sourced from the public bond markets, and in recent years equity has played less and less of an important role (ibid 56).

[21] Mine closure, considered in the following chapter, is typically funded through various forms of financial assurance, including setting aside financial provision, rather

and companies must now draw upon an innovative combination of sources to secure finance.[22]

World Bank and IMF environmental standards have had an enduring impact, notwithstanding that only a small percentage of mining projects are funded by these institutions.[23] The final report of the MMSD noted, for example, that the broad appropriation of EIA in the mining sector was due in part to the World Bank, which had been instrumental in spreading its use.[24] Following the publication of Environmental Guidelines in 1988,[25] the World Bank introduced its first Operational Directive on Environmental Assessment in 1989,[26] and it again highlighted the importance of EA in its Pollution Prevention and Abatement Handbook of 1998.[27] Operational Policy 4.01 on Environmental Assessment came into effect in January 1999, with the current revision dating from April 2013.[28] An operational policy on Indigenous Peoples was subsequently developed in 2005.[29] These Operational Policies addressed deficiencies in the World Bank Group's Safeguard Policies in the extractives industries, highlighted in the Extractives Industries Review of the early 2000s. But other than these operational policies, issues of environmental governance were only tangentially addressed in the World Bank's 1992 and 1996 Strategies for mining in Africa and Latin America and the Caribbean respectively.[30]

---

than through debt or equity provided by financial institutions. However, forms of financial assurance may include bank guarantees or insurance provided by such institutions.

[22] Norton Rose Fullbright, 'Finding finance in the mining and minerals sector – A guide for mine developers' (May 2010).

[23] Jones (n 17).

[24] *Breaking New Ground* (n 1) 248.

[25] Environment Department, World Bank Group, *Environmental Guidelines* (September 1988).

[26] World Bank, 'Operational Directive 4.00: Annex A: Environmental Assessment'.

[27] World Bank Group (in collaboration with UNEP and UNIDO), *Pollution Prevention and Abatement Handbook 1998: Towards Cleaner Production* (April 1999). The *Handbook* sets out industry sector guidelines for base metal and iron ore mining, coal mining and production and onshore oil and gas development.

[28] World Bank, *Operational Manual: OP 4.01 – Environmental Assessment* (January 1999, rev. April 2013).

[29] World Bank, *Operational Manual: OP 4.10 – Indigenous Peoples* (January 1999, rev. April 2013).

[30] Mining Unit, Industry and Energy Division, *Strategy for African Mining* World Bank Technical Paper No. 181 (World Bank 1992) (henceforth *Strategy for African Mining*); Industry and Mining Division, *A Mining Strategy for Latin America and the Caribbean* World Bank Technical Paper No. 345 (World Bank 1996) (henceforth *Strategy for LAC Mining*).

The International Finance Corporation has also actively developed performance standards for EA in the extractives industries with the current 'Environmental, Health and Safety Guidelines for Mining', dating from 2007.[31] The IFC's more general Performance Standards on Environmental Sustainability date from 2012.[32]

Commercial banks are increasingly reluctant to lend money to the mining sector owing to its high inherent risks,[33] and are more likely to provide short term bridging finance.[34] Nevertheless, to the extent that commercial banks do finance mining, they may require the mine developer or operator to comply with the Equator Principles (EPs), a risk management framework developed by financial institutions in 2003 'to encourage responsible and sound environmental and social policies in project finance'.[35] As of early 2019, 94 Equator Principles Financial Institutions in 37 countries had adopted the EPs, covering more than 70 per cent of global project finance.[36] Principles 2 and 5 of the EPs deal with Environmental and Social Assessment and Stakeholder Engagement respectively.[37]

National export credit agencies are the 'quiet giants' of mining finance, although their activities are generally not subject to public scrutiny and they are generally unaccountable for the environmental and social consequences of their financing.[38] Export credit agencies play a particularly important role during the construction phase of the mine, where they may facilitate the financ-

---

[31] International Finance Corporation, *Environmental, Health and Safety Guidelines for Mining* (December 2007) www.ifc.org/wps/wcm/connect/1f4dc280488 55af4879cd76a6515bb18/Final%2B-%2BMining.pdf?MOD=AJPERES&id= 1323153264157, accessed 26 February 2019.

[32] International Finance Corporation *Performance Standards on Environmental Sustainability* www.ifc.org/wps/wcm/connect/Topics_Ext_Content/IFC_External _Corporate_Site/Sustainability-At-IFC/Policies-Standards/Performance-Standards, accessed 26 February 2019.

[33] *Breaking New Ground* (n 1) 136; John Muchira, 'Rwanda mulling credit guarantee fund to encourage lending to mining sector', *Engineering News*, 11 March 2016 www.engineeringnews.co.za/article/rwanda-mulling-credit-guarantee-fund-to-en courage-lending-to-mining-sector-2016-03-11, accessed 26 February 2019.

[34] Norton Rose Fullbright (n 22).

[35] Olaf Weber and Emmanuel Acheta, 'The Equator Principles: Ten teenage years of implementation and and a search for an outcome' (January 2014) CIGI Papers No. 24, 5.

[36] Equator Principles Association, 'Equator Principles' (2011) www.equator -principles.com, accessed 26 February 2019.

[37] Equator Principles Association, *The Equator Principles* (June 2013) https:// equator-principles.com/wp-content/uploads/2017/03/equator_principles_III.pdf, accessed 26 February 2019.

[38] *Breaking New Ground* (n 1) 135.

ing of much needed equipment. A 2007 OECD Council Recommendation, however, requires Member States to screen all applications for officially supported export credits to identify projects requiring a review due to their potential adverse environmental impacts, and, where necessary, to undertake an EIA.[39]

Since the mid-1990s, mining industry associations have also actively developed and promoted EA guidelines. The International Council on Mining and Metals (ICMM) has sponsored extensive research into the impacts of mining on water, climate change, biodiversity, mine closure and tailings management.[40] And Principle 6 of the ICMM Sustainable Development Principles requires member institutions to 'assess positive and negative, direct and indirect, and cumulative environmental impacts of new projects – from exploration to closure'.[41] The ICMM has also been active in developing impact assessment methodologies, both for occupational health and for the health and wellbeing of mining-impacted communities.[42] At a national level, the Minerals Council of Australia (MCA) developed a Leading Practice Guidance on cumulative environmental assessment.[43] In Canada, the Mining Association of Canada recently made detailed submissions to the Expert Panel tasked with reviewing Canada's federal environmental assessment process, and is thus an active discursive player in this field.[44]

---

[39] OECD Council, 'Recommendation on common approaches to the environment and officially supported export credits' www.oecd.org/newsroom/21684464.pdf, accessed 26 February 2019.

[40] ICMM, 'Environment' www.icmm.com/en-gb/environment, accessed 26 February 2019.

[41] ICMM, 'ICMM 10 Principles: Principle 6' www.icmm.com/en-gb/members/member-commitments/icmm-10-principles/icmm-principle-6, accessed 26 February 2019.

[42] ICMM, 'Health impact assessments' www.icmm.com/en-gb/health-and-safety/health/health-impact-assessments, accessed 26 February 2019; ICMM, 'Health Risk Assessment Guidance for Metals' www.icmm.com/herag, accessed 26 February 2019. The ICMM's *Good Practice Guidance on Health Impact Assessment* was published in 2010 (www.icmm.com/en-gb/publications/health-and-safety/good-practice-guidance-on-health-impact-assessment, accessed 26 February 2019), while a second edition of the sister publication, *Good Practice Guidance on Occupational Risk Assessment*, was published in 2009.

[43] See further the discussion on cumulative environmental impacts in section 2.3 below.

[44] Mining Association of Canada, 'MAC Submission to the Expert Panel Review of Environmental Assessment Processes' (8 November 2016) http://mining.ca/sites/default/files/documents/MAC-Submission-CEAA-Expert-Panel-Nov-2016.pdf, accessed 26 February 2019.

Civil society organizations and indigenous groups contribute to the discourse on environmental assessment and mining through development of standards,[45] commentary upon standards or law reforms,[46] and litigation challenging the application and interpretation of EA laws.[47] In some mineral-rich jurisdictions, where political and economic powers collude to ensure either that strict environmental assessment laws are not in place or that they are weakly enforced, civil society organizations may be the only actors able and willing 'to monitor mining-related environmental destruction, point fingers at the perpetrators, demand stricter environmental regulations, and take legal steps'.[48]

It is from this variety of sources that the double movement of the State in mining and EA has been constructed, as constituted by the ensuing overview of State roles.

2.1 Forms of Environmental Assessment: The State as Regulator of Precaution

The first of the State's roles under the dominant model for mining and EA is to institutionalize precaution through various forms of EA. Growth in

---

[45] The Natural Resource Governance Institute's *Natural Resource Charter* (2nd edn), for example, contains guidelines on environmental assessment in Precept 5.

[46] For example, see MiningWatch Canada, 'Environmental groups send letter to ministers re: Reforming Federal Environmental Assessment Law' https://miningwatch.ca/blog/2017/8/30/environmental-groups-send-letter-ministers-re-reforming-federal-environmental, accessed 26 February 2019; Fair Mining Collaborative, 'Environmental Assessment for Mining Activities' www.fairmining.ca/code/environmental-assessment-for-mining-activities-2/, accessed 26 February 2019.

[47] Seminal decided and pending cases include *Mining Watch Canada v. Canada (Fisheries and Oceans)*, 2010 SCC 2 (whether the environmental assessment track is determined by the project as proposed or by the discretion of the regulatory authority); *Fort Nelson First Nation v. British Columbia (Environmental Assessment Office)* 2016 BCCA 500; the extensive litigation against the environmental approvals granted for the Carmichael Coal Mine in Queensland, Australia (see http://envlaw.com.au/carmichael-coal-mine-case/, accessed 26 February 2019); *Diné Citizens against Ruining Our Environment v. United States Office of Surface Mining Reclamation and Environment* (see www.hurriyetdailynews.com/court-in-canakkale-halts-exploration-activities-of-four-gold-mining-companies-in-kaz-mountains-59495, accessed 8 November 2017); *Wild Earth Guardians v. U.S. Office of Surface Mining, Reclamation and Enforcement* (see http://climatecasechart.com/case/wildearth-guardians-v-u-s-office-of-surface-mining-reclamation-and-enforcement/, accessed 26 February 2019); *Montana Environmental Information Center v. U.S. Office of Surface Mining* Civ. No. 15-106-M-DWM (D.Mont 2017); *Kangwa v. Environmental Council of Zambia* (2008/HP/245) [2011] ZMCH 85 (31 December 2010).

[48] Christoph H Stefes and Katherine Weingartner, *Environmental Crime in Armenia* (European Union Action to Fight Environmental Crime 2015) 4.

the use of EA occurred in parallel with the liberalization, privatization and globalization trends affecting the mining industry in the latter quarter of the twentieth century. New opportunities for the private sector opened up with the demise of State-owned mining companies and the dismantling of regulatory frameworks that had previously disallowed or discouraged private investment. This occurred just as environmental controls in some of the more developed and established mining jurisdictions were becoming more stringent.[49] At the same time, environmental activism also underwent a global expansion, with a proliferation of NGOs devoted to organizing and representing mine-affected communities and the growth of the Indigenous Peoples' movement.[50] The swathe of mining law reforms during the latter portion of the twentieth century reconstituted the primary role of the State in most mineral jurisdictions as the regulator of private activity, which has included regulation of the environmental and socioeconomic assessment of mining operations.[51]

In addition to EIA, the State has been expected to institutionalize SIA, SEA and HIA. As the ensuing discussion shows, these forms of EA have been expressly contextualized for application in the mining industry.

2.1.1 Environmental impact assessment (EIA)

With the enactment of the NEPA in 1969, the US government formally established EIA as a proactive planning tool for environmental management.[52] Following the example of the USA and early adopters such as Australia, Canada, Ireland, Sweden and New Zealand, over the last quarter of the twentieth century virtually all the countries of the world incorporated some form of impact assessment process into planning or environmental decisionmaking legislation.[53] Even without a framework treaty or the exhortation of a UN resolution, the consensus among member countries of the UN to use EIA

---

[49] John P Williams, 'Legal reform in mining: Past, present and future' in Elizabeth Bastida, Thomas Wälde and Janeth Warden-Fernández, *International and Comparative Mineral Law and Policy: Trends and Prospects* (Kluwer 2005) 37, 49.

[50] Robert A Bassett and Ricardo I Becker, 'Myth or reality – Has environmental regulation destroyed the US mining industry' in E Bastida, T Wälde and J Warden-Fernández, *International Comparative Mineral Law and Policy: Trends and Prospects* (Kluwer 2005) 49.

[51] Williams (n 49) 52.

[52] John Glasson, Riki Therivel and Andrew Chadwick, *Introduction to Environmental Impact Assessment* 4th edn (Routledge 2012) 31.

[53] Morgan (n 7) 5, Glasson (n 52) 31; Nicholas A Robinson, 'International trends in environmental impact assessment' (1992) 19 *B.C. Environmental Affairs Law Review* 591, 594 and 597 ff.

within a range of policy contexts is almost universal.[54] As is evident from the overview above, multilateral and development organizations including the World Bank and the IFC have adopted lending-linked EIA operational or performance standards, and the approach and methodology is recognized in a number of multilateral environmental agreements, including the Convention on Transboundary Impact Assessment and the United Nations Framework Convention on Climate Change.[55]

There is broad-based consensus that EIA should be applied to operations throughout the mineral value chain. For example, the first principle of the 1992 Berlin Guidelines called upon governments to include early and comprehensive EIAs for mining as an integral element of environmental management systems.[56] The revised 1999 Guidelines underlined the need for socioeconomic impact assessments, and for socioeconomic impacts and gender issues to be taken into account during the earliest phase of project development.[57] The 2002 *Guidelines for Mining and Sustainable Development* present EIA as the process 'by which environmental factors are integrated into project planning and decisionmaking in a way that is consistent with sustainable development',[58] and as a means to 'protect' the environment from exploration all the way through to decommissioning.[59] Best practice EIA, these *Guidelines* stress, involves 'the delivery of high quality information from the company to the community, the government and other decision-makers', not only for purposes of determining environmental conditions for the project, but for deciding whether the project should proceed at all.[60]

In addition to controversy over the State's boundary setting and democracy-facilitating role (elaborated in sections 2.2, 2.3 and 2.4 below), conflict over the State's approach to and execution of its protective role has emerged over the screening of projects for EIA, and the correct approach to EIA-related decisionmaking.

2.1.1.1 Screening projects for EIA

The International Association for Impact Assessment (IAIA) defines screening as the process to determine whether or not a proposal should be subject to

---

[54] Morgan refers to an ECOLEX search conducted in 2011 in which he found that 191 of 193 UN member States had national legislation or had signed some form of international instrument referring to the use of EIA (see n 7) 6.

[55] Ibid.

[56] UNEP (n 14) 15.

[57] Ibid.

[58] United Nations (n 12) 36.

[59] Ibid.

[60] Ibid.

EIA, and if so, at what level of detail.[61] Screening – or 'qualification', as it is also known – is one of the most crucial elements of an EIA system,[62] as it determines what types of projects require scrutiny, and thereby the institutional capacity, resources and time needed to undertake the task. A State's approach to screening is very important from a sustainability perspective, as it positions the entire EIA system as more or less centred on the longterm sustainability of local, regional or national ecosystems. Rajaram and Das state, for instance, that '[t]he Screening guidelines for EIA reflect the first level of commitment the nation displays towards tightening its environmental protection system'.[63]

Determining which projects should be subject to an EIA is complicated in any jurisdiction, but even more so in developing countries. Here, the burden that an EIA places on small enterprises, or even the delays associated with the construction of large projects deemed necessary for socioeconomic development, ground arguments for restricting the ambit of EIA – so that developing States can grow faster and be in a position to eliminate poverty.[64] Developed States may in turn be swayed to roll back the scope of EIA by so-called green tape reduction arguments. For example, as a result of the 'de-ecologization'[65] of the Russian Law on Environmental Protection over the past decade, the law only applies to a restricted number of projects (for example, if these are located in conservation areas or on the continental shelf). Although the 1992 Subsoil Law requires some consideration of environmental issues, the overwhelming majority of all mining projects are no longer covered by the provisions of the Environmental Protection Law. In Australia over the past decade, Queensland initiated a policy reform process on greentape reduction;[66] additionally, the federal government also undertook an inquiry into streamlining environmental regulation and creating 'one-stop shops' for the review of

---

[61] IAIA, *Principles of Environmental Impact Assessment Best Practice* (IAIA 1999) para 2.3.

[62] Slàvka Galas and Andrzej Galas, 'The qualification process of mining projects in environmental impact assessment: Criteria and thresholds' (2016) 49 *Resources Policy* 204, 205.

[63] T Rajaram and Ashutosh Das, 'Screening for EIA in India: Enhancing effectiveness through ecological carrying capacity approach' (2011) 92 *Journal of Environmental Management* 140.

[64] Ibid.

[65] Joshua P Newell and Laura A Henry, 'The state of environmental protection in the Russian Federation: A review of the post-Soviet era' (2017) *Eurasian Geography and Economics* 1, 7.

[66] Department of Environment and Resource Development, Queensland Government, *Greentape Reduction – Reforming Licensing under the Environmental Protection Act, 1994* (2011) www.ehp.qld.gov.au/management/pdf/greentape-reduction-discussion-paper.pdf, accessed 26 February 2019.

environmental assessments that would have shifted decisionmaking power to state governments.[67] Encouraged by the Trump Administration's regressive moves regarding environmental regulation of the US coal mining industry, the organized mining and petroleum industry in Australia is still calling strongly for a reduction of environmental regulation.[68]

There are various approaches to screening. Projects may be filtered on the basis of thresholds or on the basis of case-by-case assessment, or may utilize a mixture of both approaches.[69] In either case the approach could be more 'ecologically' or 'developmentally' centred, with the former placing emphasis upon ecosystem carrying capacity and the latter focusing on the thresholds that would be most conducive to stimulating mining investment.

To implement an approach based on ecological carrying capacity, States would need to maintain detailed databases of ecological processes and functions, the natural ecosystem's capacity to assimilate pollution and maintain productivity, the current trend of resource use and its sustainability and linkages between ecological components and the local populace.[70] Rajaram and Das suggest that the scope of ecological carrying capacity differs for four major impacts associated with extractive projects – the extraction of water, the discharge of liquid effluents, the disposal of solid and hazardous wastes and air emissions. They propose that the pollution of water resources should be determined with reference to the carrying capacity of local ecosystems, the acceptable level of solid and hazardous wastes should be determined based on regional ecosystems (as solid waste can be transferred from one ecosystem to another, although at great cost) and air emissions should be determined on the basis of the national ecosystem's carrying capacity.[71]

However, few States, if any, base EIA screening upon ecological carrying capacity, although some have funded work along this vein. With monies from a fine that had been levied against a mining company for mining in a wetland, the South African Water Research Commission funded work on reframing

---

[67] Parliament of Australia: House of Representatives Committees, 'House standing committee on the environment: Inquiry into streamlining environmental regulation' www.aph.gov.au/parliamentary_business/committees/house_of_representatives_committees?url=environment/greentape/index.htm, accessed 26 February 2019. For an opinion on the policy implications of the proposed reform in a mining context see Jeff Smith, '"Green tape cuts": Industry wins, locals and the environment lose' *The Conversation* 13 May 2014 https://theconversation.com/green-tape-cuts-industry-wins-locals-and-the-environment-lose-26443, accessed 26 February 2019.

[68] See Simon Breheny, 'Greentape's 80-fold explosion costing $176 billion a year', *The Australian* 29 April 2017.

[69] Rajaram and Das (n 63) 141.

[70] Ibid 145.

[71] Ibid.

mining licensing processes in terms of the concepts of ecological infrastructure, ecosystem services, complex socioecological systems, integrated water resource management and adaptive management.[72] This project found, for example, that there was a need to place certain wetlands, biodiversity and ecological infrastructure beyond the realm of contestation, that is, as off limits to mining.[73] The project also recommended that public authorities should have the power to determine ecological thresholds for uses within particular regions, which should bind the authority responsible for issuing mining concessions or licences.[74]

In mineral-rich jurisdictions the approach to EIA screening is ordinarily based on thresholds linked to the mining project itself. These could be based on a particular quantitative threshold for the project, such as the area covered by the production, the volume of the production or the amount of investment; or a particular qualitative characteristic of the project, such as the location of the mine in a protected area or the method of extraction; or a combination of both quantitative and qualitative features.[75] A particular State's approach may also evolve over time. For instance, India's first set of screening guidelines, issued in 1994, was based on excluding certain categories of projects based on investment thresholds.[76] However, it was found that this approach encouraged rampant 'salami slicing' by project proponents in order to circumvent the EIA process, and so the screening guidelines of 2006 opted for capacity-based exclusions.[77]

There is little in the way of international guidance on screening mining projects for EIA. The *Berlin Guidelines* simply state that the level of EIA 'depends on the nature of the proposal, its complexity, the local environment, its expected effects and the degree of controversy that the project might create'.[78] The World Bank Group's Extractive Industries Review addressed problems associated with screening, and suggested that extractive industry projects should always be classified as Category A projects, that is, as likely to have significant adverse environmental impacts.[79] The EU's EIA Directive

---

[72] T Humby, V Munnik and GCR Palmer, *Deliverable 4: The Extent to which Current Mining Licensing Processes Align with Biodiversity Goals and Options to Address Contestation* (Water Research Commission 2015).

[73] Ibid 4.

[74] Ibid.

[75] Galas and Galas (n 62) 209.

[76] Rajaram and Das (n 63) 141.

[77] Ibid 142.

[78] *Berlin Guidelines* (n 13) 37.

[79] World Bank, *Striking a Better Balance Volume I: The World Bank Group and Extractive Industries* (December 2003) iv (henceforth *Striking a Better Balance*) 54.

provides something by way of guidance on a regional level,[80] and has been used as a basis of comparison for EIA screening in developing countries.[81] Even with this guidance, there are significant differences in terms of how EU States have codified screening requirements. In their review of qualification criteria for mining projects in the Visegrad countries (Poland, the Czech Republic, Slovakia and Hungary), for example, Galas and Galas found that the screening requirements for mining projects in these countries were at times more detailed than the specifications of the EU EIA Directive, and at times differed significantly from each other. For example, in the Czech Republic all new mining projects are subject to a mandatory EIA procedure, while in Hungary all mining projects are always screened first.[82] The authors found little support for the hypothesis that the mining industry's importance to the economy of a mineral-rich jurisdiction could result in the application of more liberal criteria and threshold values.[83]

Although exploration is the fundamental process initiating the mining industry, not all mineral-rich jurisdictions require that an EIA be conducted for exploration activities. Exploration activities produce waste, use natural resources, have effects on cumulative effects on water and soil and pose accident risks. In April 2016, for example, the European Commission referred Poland to the Court of Justice for the EU, based on the complaint that the environmental impacts of exploratory drilling (for shale gas) were not being adequately assessed.[84] In Polish law it was possible to conduct drilling up to 5000m without conducting an EIA.[85]

Where the EIA law establishes thresholds for mining projects, State authorities may encounter the problem of 'parcelling'. In India, for example, the Mines and Minerals (Development and Regulation) Act, 1957 empowered subnational governments to make rules for minor minerals (sand, gravel, clay, marble and other stones).[86] Under the Indian Environment Protection Act, 1986, EIAs for minor minerals were only required for mining leases in excess

---

80 Directive 85/337/EEC of 27 June 1985 on the assessment of the effects of certain public and private projects on the environment, codified by Directive 2011/92/EU of 13 December 2011, and as amended by Directive 2014/52/EU of 16 April 2014.

81 See Rajaram and Das (n 63).

82 Galas and Galas (n 62).

83 Ibid 210.

84 European Commission, 'Environmental Impact Assessment: Commission refers POLAND to the Court of Justice of the EU over inadequate assessment of exploratory mining drillings' http://europa.eu/rapid/press-release_IP-16-1454_en.htm, accessed 26 February 2019.

85 Ibid.

86 Kumar Sambhav Shrivastava, 'MoEF's must for mining minor minerals, too: Supreme Court' (7 March 2012) www.downtoearth.org.in/news/moef-s-clearance

of five hectares. Miners owning large tracts of land were circumventing this provision by breaking up the mining area into smaller parcels and obtaining separate leases from state governments for these smaller operations.[87] In *Deepak Kumar etc. v. State of Haryana & others*,[88] the Supreme Court of India ruled that mining of minor minerals would not be allowed to proceed without the approval of the central government and the implementation of a host of existing guidelines and recommendations on an environmental regulatory framework for minor minerals. The court found that the cumulative impact of the smaller operations over time would lead to longterm and irreversible damage to lakes, groundwater and riverbeds, and contribute to a situation of water scarcity.[89]

Mining proponents may parcel projects not only to avoid an EIA altogether, but also to position a project under a lower rather than a higher level of scrutiny. Desiring mining investment, some States even appear to collude in this strategy. In *Mining Watch Canada v. Canada (Fisheries and Oceans)*,[90] for example, an open pit copper/gold mining and milling operation in British Columbia triggered the requirements for a comprehensive study under the federal Canadian Environmental Assessment Act, 1992.[91] The Department of Fisheries and Oceans initially concluded that the project required a comprehensive study, but then subsequently advised that it had scoped the project to exclude the mining and mill. As such, the project could proceed by way of screening rather than a comprehensive study.[92] A Screening Report was released in April 2006, concluding that the project was not likely to cause significant adverse environmental effects, and in May 2006 the project was allowed to proceed. Mining Watch Canada subsequently took this decision on judicial review to the Federal Court, the Federal Court of Appeal and finally the Supreme Court of Canada.[93] At issue was whether the environmental assessment track is determined by the project as proposed by the proponent, or by the federal authority's discretionary authority to scope a decision. The

---

-must-for-mining-minor-minerals-too-supreme-court-37198, accessed 26 February 2019.

87 Ibid.

88 Supreme Court of India, Case No. 19628-19629 of 2009 (27 February 2012) https://indiankanoon.org/doc/60071241/, accessed 26 February 2019.

89 Ibid.

90 2010 SCC 2.

91 Miller Thomson Lawyers, 'The environmental assessment track – Discretion to scope is not discretion to track?' www.millerthomson.com/en/publications/communiques-and-updates/environotes/april-2010/the-environmental-assessment-track-2/, accessed 26 February 2019.

92 Ibid.

93 Ibid.

Supreme Court found for Mining Watch Canada, concluding that the environmental assessment track should be determined by the project as proposed by the proponent.[94] In the wake of this decision, the Federal Parliament amended the Environmental Assessment Act, 1992, as the Supreme Court's interpretation did not find favour.[95] Subsequently, however, the Conservative Harper government overhauled Canadian federal environmental assessment legislation entirely, passing a new Environmental Assessment Act, which came into effect on 6 July 2012. This selfsame Act is now the subject of a comprehensive legislative review process.[96]

States are required to institutionalize precaution. For project-level EIA, this requires identifying which projects should be subject to an EIA and which projects should be subject to more or less rigorous processes of scrutiny. As this brief overview shows, most States opt for an approach to EIA screening that is development-centred, rather than focused on ecological carrying capacity. Allowing exploration to proceed without an EIA and failing to address, or even supporting, practices of 'parcelling' are just some of the ways in which States are complicit in driving extractivism and neoextractivism.

2.1.1.2 Approach to EIA-related decisionmaking

The model of EIA promoted by institutions of neoliberal governance assumes a scientific, rational approach to decisionmaking. The underlying faith is that a holistic and linear approach, a systematic information gathering process, objectivity and the consideration of alternatives will generate scientific facts and facilitate logical decisionmaking.[97] This rationalist–technical view of EIA posits 'planners and other professionals acting as neutral processors of information, producing independent evaluations of the alternatives, to be provided to decision-makers'.[98] The model is State-led, as it requires the State to define the target, parameters and conditions for the neutrality of the information gathering process. It is still the dominant form of institutionalized EIA,[99] even

---

94 Ibid.

95 Sara Seck, Associate Professor, Dalhousie University, email communication with author, 20 December 2017.

96 Government of Canada, 'Environmental and regulatory reviews: Discussion Paper' (June 2017) www.canada.ca/en/services/environment/conservation/assessments/environmental-reviews/share-your-views/proposed-approach/discussion-paper.html, accessed 26 February 2019.

97 Glasson (n 12) § 1.5.2 'EIA in its theoretical context'. See also F Retief, 'The evolution of environmental assessment debates: Critical perspectives from South Africa' (2010) 12(4) *Journal of Environmental Assessment Policy and Management* 375.

98 Morgan (n 7) 8.

99 Ibid.

as legislated EA processes have incorporated theoretical insights stressing the need for political tradeoffs, incrementalism, and a participatory approach.[100]

The rationalist–technical model of EIA, however, has been subjected to scathing criticism from a variety of theoretical quarters. Influenced by Habermas, academics have urged project proponents and professional technocrats to opt for more collaborative and consensus-oriented models of EA.[101] Collaborative and consensus-oriented models place greater emphasis on stakeholder and community inclusion, communication as a means of negotiating consensus solutions and a facilitative role for the State.[102] Foucauldian-inspired critiques of environmental assessment methodology, on the other hand, draw attention to the power relations that hold sway among the different parties and the potential for power imbalances to bias the substantive outcome of EA processes.[103] To remedy the power asymmetry between mining companies and communities the State is expected not merely to facilitate engagement, consultation and dialogue, but to act as a guarantor and referee of procedures associated with environmental assessment.[104]

The prevailing dominance of the rationalist–technical model and the tensions among competing theoretical models for EA are well illustrated by research recently conducted on dialogue, conflict and regulatory processes in EIA studies in Peru and other Latin American States.[105] At a workshop convened for more than 70 participants involved in a range of dialogue initiatives for conflict in the mining sector, one of the key messages was that environmental impact studies in Peru and elsewhere are 'often treated as a merely technical affair' characterized by a lack of dialogue and tokenistic participation.[106] As a regulatory process, environmental impact studies (EIS) could not in fact manage all the tensions that emerged in relation to mining projects. Echoing

---

[100] Glasson (n 12) § 1.5.2 'EIA in its theoretical context'.

[101] Morgan (n 7) 8; H Wilkins, 'The need for subjectivity in EIA: Discourse as a tool for sustainable development' (2003) 23(4) *Environmental Impact Assessment Review* 401.

[102] Morgan (n 7) 8.

[103] Ibid.

[104] César Rodríguez-Garavito, 'Ethnicity.gov: Global governance, indigenous peoples, and the right to prior consultation in social minefields' (2010) 18(1) *Indiana Journal of Global Legal Studies* 1, 38; Mariel Aguilar-Stoen and Cecile Hirsch, 'Bottom-up responses to environmental and social impact assessments: A case study from Guatemala' (2017) *Environmental Impact Assessment Review* 225, 230.

[105] Diana Arbeláez-Ruiz, *Dialogue, Conflict and Regulatory Processes in Environmental Impact Studies for Mining Projects: Learning from the Peruvian Experience in the Latin American Context* (June 2015) IM4DC Action Research Project.

[106] Ibid 10.

Habermas, participants insisted that those responsible for undertaking an EIS were accordingly dutybound to implement participatory, dialogue-driven processes in a timely fashion that continued well beyond the conclusion of the EIS.[107] And recalling Foucault, social actors also needed to recognize the 'political and relational nature' of EIS processes, and take the initiative to build capacity for engagement.[108]

Related to the critique of the rationalist–technical approach is the charge that State-led EIAs stimulate a compliance-based or a 'regulatory' approach that stands in contrast to the more organic and rigorous processes necessary to support a mining company's social licence to operate, or a community's entitlement to environmental justice.[109] This has led, in some instances, to non-State action aimed at reinvigorating EIA processes.

Aguilar-Stoen and Hirsch, for example, report on a trend of resistance to the practice of EIAs in mining and energy projects in Guatemala.[110] They argue that EIAs for mining projects in Guatemala are contested, generate conflicts and constrain the resistance's conditions of possibility.[111] Using a Foucauldian frame that sees resistance as never external to power, they document cases in which Guatemalan resistance groups have used transnational networks to reach out to international experts who offer alternative (and ostensibly more rigorous) evaluations of EIA reports. This has enabled community-based resistance groups to access alternative sources of knowledge, ground the legitimacy of their claims and in some cases even reclaim their right to participate in decisionmaking processes. The La Puya resistance, for example, came about when communities were completely excluded from plans to build a gold mine extraction project about 20km from Guatemala City.[112] The exploitation licence and EIA for the project had been approved by State authorities without the communities' involvement. Increasingly concerned about water quality and water demand from the mine, along with other environmental impacts, the communities set up a peaceful roadblock to disrupt mining operations and also engaged two USA-based engineers to review the EIA. The latter confirmed that the EIA lacked details on water use and water treatment.[113]

---

[107] Ibid.

[108] Ibid.

[109] Some contributors nevertheless still highlight the gains made from formalizing EIA. See for example Douglas C Baker and James N McLelland, 'Evaluating the effectiveness of British Columbia's environmental assessment process for first nations' participation in mining development' (2003) 23 *Environmental Impact Assessment Review* 581.

[110] Aguilar-Stoen and Hirsch (n 104) 230.

[111] Ibid.

[112] Ibid 229.

[113] Ibid 230.

This independent assessment did not persuade the government to revoke the EIA or exploitation licence, but after several failed attempts to evict the roadblock the government installed a 'dialogue table' with representatives from the government, mining company and communities. This process also stagnated, however, and violent conflict escalated in the area, even as another independent assessor affirmed the gross inadequacy of the EIA. In July 2015, a Guatemalan appeals court ruled in favour of the La Puya movement, which ordered suspension of construction activities at the mine and ruled in favour of residents' right of consultation.[114] This victory was therefore achieved by communities reaching beyond the foil of legislated EIA.

Critiques of compliance or regulatory-based EA processes assume an ineffective or weak State. Alternatively, one can view EA processes as knowledge practices that recreate the State as both powerful and elusive. Li argues, for example, that while the practice of EIA is couched in the language of transparency, democratic participation and environmental management, accountability is skewed in favour of the mining companies who set the standards of performance upon which the government will enforce compliance.[115] This bias is driven by the fact that the risks identified in the EIA are those that the mining company deems technically feasible to address. Further, the collaborative relationships that emerge among State agents, mining companies, communities and NGOs through the EIA process strengthen the claims of that process to accountability and legitimacy – at the same time constituting the State's 'due diligence' environmental management role.[116] But these forms of collaboration also circumscribe the spaces of resistance to a proposed project, leading activists to question whether they should step outside the official process and resort to political strategies of refusal to be informed, and of nonparticipation.[117] Li's arguments in this regard support the claim that EA processes in particular have a 'lock in' effect on the double movement – that is, they provide a façade of legitimacy that keeps the hope of sustainable mining alive.

2.1.2 Social impact assessment (SIA)

Under the dominant model, the duty vesting in the State to institutionalize precaution in relation to social impacts is less well entrenched than in the case of environmental impacts. Initially, Social impact assessment (SIA) grew out of a landmark Canadian judicial process regarding an extractives project. In

---

[114] Ibid.

[115] Fabiana Li, 'Documenting accountability: Environmental impact assessment in a Peruvian mining project' (2009) 32(2) *Political and Legal Anthropology Review* 218, 219.

[116] Ibid 219–20.

[117] Ibid 220.

the mid 1970s the Canadian Parliament set up a judicial inquiry to investigate the social impacts of the proposed MacKenzie Valley gas pipeline. This State-initiated inquiry marked the first time that social impacts were formally considered in project decisionmaking. Justice Berger, who led the inquiry, recommended that the project be postponed for at least ten years to allow for the settlement of land claims and for supportive programmes and institutions to be put into place for the Native American population.[118]

In the mining industry, one of the earliest and best known SIA studies was conducted for the proposed mine at Coronation Hill in the Northern Territories of Australia – work that is also frequently cited to demonstrate that SIAs can dramatically impact project development.[119] Here, the Northern Land Council of Australia concluded that the effects of mining would be too adverse for the Jawoyn Aborigines, and Australia's federal Cabinet accordingly voted against permitting the mineral development.[120]

The sustainable mineral development consensus has tended to promote SIA as an integral part of the EIA process. The 2002 *Guidelines for Mining and Sustainable Development*, for example, contain separate sections on EIA and SIA, but note that SIAs can be done as part of the EIA or as a standalone study.[121] SIAs can provide invaluable information on the type, duration, spatial extent and distribution of impacts arising from the intersection between mining, the key social features of the host environment and interactions with mining-induced transformation of both physical and social environments. The World Bank Group's (WBG) Extractives Industries Review put forth more explicit policy guidance on integrated environmental and social impact assessments. The final project report recommended that WBG interventions in the extractives industries should require integrated environmental and social impact assessments for all activities including project expansion.[122] The Review said that environmental and social impact assessments should be 'holistic and multidimensional, identifying cumulative impacts of projects and socioeconomic linkages to environmental issues'.[123] Social impact assessments also needed to cover health impacts and impacts on vulnerable groups.[124] In

---

118 Susan A Joyce and Magnus MacFarlane, 'Social impact assessment in the mining industry: Current situation and future directions' (2001) Report commissioned by the MMSD project of the IIED, 5.

119 Ibid 9.

120 Ibid 9–10.

121 United Nations (n 12) 39.

122 Extractive Industries Review, *Striking a Better Balance: Volume I – The World Bank Group and Extractive Industries (Final Report of the Extractive Industries Review)* (December 2003) 54.

123 Ibid.

124 Ibid.

recent years, however, SIA has evolved from being a technique for predicting social impacts within an EIA into an amalgam of processes for analysing, monitoring and managing the social dimensions of project interventions.[125]

In most mineral-rich jurisdictions SIAs do not constitute a standalone legislative requirement, but are integrated into the carrying out of a more broad-ranging EIA. Both mining companies and communities have nevertheless sought ways to extend and deepen SIA processes. Lockie *et al*, for example, report on two SIAs conducted by a university research unit for the Coppabella coalmine in Queensland, Australia.[126] The studies, funded by the mine, were undertaken outside of Queensland's legislative EIA framework, which limited impact assessment to the startup of major new projects, and did not require consideration of exogenous factors that could interact with the proposed project to affect social and economic outcomes.[127] But because misassessed or misaligned project proposals could lead to project delays, reputational damage and other costs from unmitigated social impacts, it was becoming increasingly common, Lockie *et al* report, for mining companies to undertake a series of voluntary SIA or community consultation activities.[128]

The need for State-led action on SIAs – either as integrated with the EIA or as a standalone study – is therefore uncontentious. Remaining controversial, however, are questions relating to the stage at which SIAs are carried out, the balance between reliance upon expert opinion or the lived experiences and visions of mining-affected communities themselves, the focus on social indicators versus understanding the social processes leading to particular outcomes and the institutional safeguards necessary for postauthorization monitoring and management. To an arguably greater extent, therefore, State-led SIAs are vulnerable to being characterized as deficient.

2.1.3 Strategic environmental assessment (SEA)

SEA entered the lexicon of environmental management practice in the late 1980s, although the concept of evaluating the environmental impacts of plans, policies and programmes, and not merely projects, was already inherent in the USA's 1969 NEPA.[129] Similarly to EIA, the origin of SEA was grounded

---

125 Ana Maria Esteves, Daniel Franks and Frank Vanclay, 'Social impact assessment: The state of the art' (2012) 30(1) *Impact Assessment and Project Appraisal* 34.

126 S Lockie *et al*, 'Coal mining and the resource community cycle: A longitudinal assessment of the social impacts of the Coppabella coal mine' (2009) 29(5) *Environmental Impact Assessment Review* 330.

127 Ibid.

128 Ibid.

129 Monica Fundingsland Tetlow and Marie Hanusch, 'Strategic environmental assessment: The state of the art' (2012) 30(1) *Impact Assessment and Project Appraisal* 15.

in modernist, rational planning traditions, although subsequently SEA was strongly influenced by postmodernist and collaborative planning traditions that stressed the importance of understanding the institutional framework in which planning occurs.[130]

A rapidly evolving field of theory and practice, SEA grew out of and responded to some of the deficiencies of project-based forms of EA but has since developed to encompass a wide range of policy objectives.[131] Bina pinpoints a conceptual shift in the SEA community in the late 1990s, when the potential for SEA to actively shape and formulate strategic initiatives was recognized.[132] It is for this reason that SEA is frequently described as a family or continuum of approaches rather than a single approach.[133] Ahmed and Sánchez-Triana distinguish between impact-based SEA, which involves scaling up the predictive and mitigatory objectives of EA to the level of policies, plans and programmes, and institution-centred SEA, which is focused on mainstreaming the environment and sustainability across high levels of decisionmaking, with a focus on assessing the capacity of the institutional and policy framework to detect environmental risks and manage them in a timely and effective manner.[134] Arguments in favour of SEA can thus range from countering the limitations of project-level EIA by considering environmental impacts and alternatives much earlier in the decisionmaking process and addressing cumulative and regional impacts, to more indirect benefits such as providing space for dialogue, raising environmental awareness, improving the transparency of planning and decisionmaking processes and providing opportunities for individual and organizational learning.[135]

The range of application of SEA is thus varied and extends from impact-oriented assessment of a number of projects, to sectoral, issue or area-based studies, to SEA of legislation or lending policies.[136] For example, in the mid-2000s the WBG was urged to take up a stronger leadership position in applying SEA to country assistance strategies, adjustment and programme

---

130 Ibid 16.

131 Ibid.

132 O Bina, 'A critical review of the dominant lines of argumentation on the need for strategic environmental assessment' (2007) 27 *Environmental Impact Assessment Review* 585.

133 OECD, *Applying Strategic Environmental Assessment (SEA): Good Practice Guidance for Development Cooperation* (OECD Publishing 2006) 17.

134 Kulsum Ahmed and Ernesto Sánchez-Triana, 'SEA and policy formation' in K Ahmed and E Sánchez-Triana, *Strategic Environmental Assessment for Policies: An Instrument for Good Governance* (World Bank 2008) 1, 3.

135 Fundingsland Tetlow and Hanusch (n 129) 16.

136 Ibid 18.

lending, sectoral environmental assessment, and annual budgets.[137] Goodland observes, for example, that the Extractive Industry Review was essentially a SEA of the WBG's adjustment and programme lending for oil, gas and mining.[138] He also points out that even seemingly anodyne technical assistance can impose 'major damage' and should thus be subjected to the rigours of SEA.[139] He specifically mentions the WBG's technical support of mining code reform in more than 70 countries over a period of two decades and opines that '[m]ost new [mining] codes make mining so industry-friendly that civil and environmental legislation is gutted, and hard-won freedoms prohibited, such as collective bargaining'.[140]

On an international level, there is little to bind most mineral-rich jurisdictions to formalizing SEA. There are two international law frameworks for SEA, but these largely only apply to countries that are members of, or that have consultative status with, the European Union. In 2001 the European Commission adopted the European SEA Directive, which required Member States to bring laws, regulations and administrative measures necessary for implementation into force by 21 July 2004.[141] The Directive aims to integrate environmental considerations into the preparation of plans and programmes, that is, generally those subject to preparation or adoption by local, regional or national authority or required by legislative, regulatory or administrative provisions.[142] The second international law framework for SEA is the 2003 United Nations Economic Commission for Europe's (UNECE) Supplementary Protocol on Strategic Environmental Assessment to the Espoo Convention on Environmental Impact Assessment in a Transboundary Context.[143] Since 26 August 2014 the Espoo Convention has been open to accession by UN members that are not part of the UNECE. However, accession to the SEA Protocol is still largely restricted to UNECE members.[144] The Espoo SEA

[137] Robert Goodland, 'Strategic environmental assessment and the World Bank Group' (2005) 12 *International Journal of Sustainable Development & World Ecology* 1, 4ff.

[138] Ibid 5.

[139] Ibid 7.

[140] Ibid.

[141] 2001/42/EC. However, most EU countries had only transposed the Directive by 2009.

[142] Article 2(a), Directive on the assessment of the effects of certain plans and programmes on the environment.

[143] UNECE, 'Environmental Assessment' www.unece.org/env/eia/welcome.html, accessed 27 February 2019. The Supplementary Protocol entered into force on 11 July 2010.

[144] UNECE, 'Introduction to Espoo Convention' www.unece.org/env/eia/eia.html, accessed 27 February 2019.

Protocol obligates State Parties to conduct a SEA for industry plans and programs for mining (among others) that (1) set the framework for development consent projects listed in annex I and any other project listed in annex II, and (2) require an EIA under national legislation.[145] Annex I projects include 'major mining, on-site extraction and processing of metal ores and coal', while annex II projects list quarries, opencast mining and peat extraction and underground mining (to the extent not included under annex I), along with the extraction of minerals by marine or fluvial dredging.

Interestingly, under the Ramsar Convention on Wetlands of International Importance especially as Waterfowl Habitat (which has near universal membership of UN member States), the Conference of the Parties (COP) have adopted a number of resolutions emphasizing the application of SEA to the extractive industries.[146]

The extent to which States outside of the EU have formalized SEA varies and there is no exact overview of the number that have legalized SEA requirements.[147] Mineral-rich jurisdictions differ according to whether they have policy or law-based guidance on SEA. For example, the Australian Commonwealth government first introduced formal legal provisions on SEA in the Environment Protection and Biodiversity Conservation Act, 1999. Independent reviews of this Act in 2009 recommended strengthening the SEA provisions and incorporating them in a part dedicated to strategic and landscape approaches to environmental protection,[148] but these recommendations were not adopted. In Canada, the federal government adopted a policy-based approach to SEA in the mid-1980s, and a series of amendments eventually culminated in the *Cabinet Directive on the Environmental Assessment of Policy, Plan and Program Proposals*, which underwent an indepth review process between 2006 and 2008.[149] The recommendations of this process to adopt a law- and policy-based approach to SEA were not adopted, however, and the Directive is still the basis for SEA for federal policies, plans and

---

[145] Article 4.2 UNECE Protocol on Strategic Environmental Assessment to the Convention on Environmental Impact Assessment in a Transboundary Context (Kyiv 2003).

[146] See for instance 'Wetlands and extractive industries', Resolution X.26, adopted at the 10th Conference of the Parties in Changwon, Korea (2008).

[147] Fundingsland Tetlow and Hanusch (n 129) 17.

[148] Simon Marsden, 'A critique of Australian environmental law reform for strategic environmental assessment' (2013) 32(2) *University of Tasmania Law Review* 276.

[149] Robert B Gibson *et al*, 'Strengthening strategic environmental assessment in Canada: An evaluation of three basic options' 20 *Journal of Environmental Law and Practice* 175.

programmes.[150] In China, the Environmental Impact Assessment Law, 2003 provided an institutional basis for SEA, including the massive SEA for the Long-Term Industrial Development of Five Mega-Regions in China initiated by the Ministry of Environmental Protection.[151] In Indonesia, SEA must be undertaken for various spatial plans and where policies, plans and/or programmes have the potential to cause environmental impacts and/or risks.[152] Chile, similarly, recently introduced a mandatory SEA regulation.[153] In South Africa and Brazil, the environmental laws allow for SEA to be conducted, but in practice impact assessment is largely applied at the project level.[154]

In extractives, SEA has been used more systematically in oil and gas development, for both on and offshore developments and including conventional and unconventional sources.[155] Advocacy for the application of SEA to deep seabed mining has also been prominent.[156] In the mining sector proper it has been applied to the development of the sector overall,[157] and to assessing the cumulative effects of a number of projects, but these examples are the excep-

---

[150] Government of Canada, 'Strategic Environmental Assessment' www.canada.ca/en/environmental-assessment-agency/programs/strategic-environmental-assessment.html, accessed 27 February 2019.

[151] Ministry of Environmental Protection of China and Netherlands Commission for Environmental Assessment, *Strategic Environmental Assessment Effectiveness: Learning from Experience in China and the Netherlands* (2014) 4 http://api.commissiemer.nl/docs/mer/diversen/sea-effectiveness-china-nl2014.pdf, accessed 27 February 2019.

[152] Article 15(2) Environmental Protection and Management Act, 2009 (Indonesia).

[153] Chile's General Framework Law, 2010 introduces SEA as an environmental management instrument. Regulation of Strategic Environmental Assessment (4th Decree NO 32/2015) only applies to policies.

[154] PMPS Cavalcanti and EL La Rovere, 'Strategic environmental assessment of mining activities: A methodology for quantification of cumulative impacts on the air quality' (2011) (1995) 61(March) *Journal of the Air & Waste Management Association* 377. In South Africa, the National Environmental Management Act, 1998 (NEMA) provides for environmental assessment to be applied to 'activities', which includes 'policies, programmes, processes, plans and projects' (National Environmental Management Act, section 1).

[155] L Lamorgese, D Geneletti and MR Partidario, 'Reviewing strategic environmental assessment practice in the oil and gas sector' (2015) 17(2) *Journal of Environmental Assessment Policy and Management* 1.

[156] See for example the submission of the Deepsea Conservation Coalition and Greenpeace to the 21st session of the International Seabed Authority (13–24 July 2015) www.savethehighseas.org/publicdocs/DSCC-Briefing-21st-Session-International-Seabed-Authority-July-2015.pdf, accessed 27 February 2019.

[157] See for example the SEA conducted for the mining sector in Kenya: Habitat Planners *Strategic Environmental Assessment (SEA) for the Mining Sector in Kenya* (May 2017).

tion rather than the rule.[158] The most successful sector of SEA application, however, has been in spatial planning.[159] Thus spatial plans developed using the SEA methodology may also determine the extent to which mining can take place in a particular region.

2.1.4 Health impact assessment (HIA)

States have institutionalized health impact assessment (HIA) to an even lesser extent than EIA, SIA or even SEA. However, the duty to institutionalize precaution over the impacts of mining on community health easily aligns with the State's protective role under the double movement. States may choose to incorporate HIA into other forms of impact assessment, or define standalone procedures. A rich variety of sources already exists to assist them in this role.[160]

HIA is a new, evolving form of assessment that has its origins both in EIA and in the environmental concerns of public health professionals.[161] An early articulation of the principled basis and procedural aspects of HIA was set out in the Gothenburg Consensus Paper, which defined HIA as 'a combination of procedures, methods, and tools by which a policy, programme, or project may be judged as to its potential effects on the health of a population, and the distribution of those effects within the population'.[162] Since then, the International Association for Impact Assessment (IAIA) has updated this definition to note that the health effects of a policy, programme or project are at times unin-

---

[158] Terence Day, 'Strategic environmental assessment of marine sand and gravel extraction', Paper presented at the 26th Annual Underwater Mining Institute, held from 29 October to 1 November 1995 in Newfoundland, Canada; Jan de Leeuw *et al*, 'Strategic assessment of the magnitude and impacts of sand mining in Poyang Lake, China' (2010) 10 *Regional Environmental Change* 95.

[159] Fundingsland Tetlow and Hanusch (n 129) 18.

[160] For example, in 1992 the Asian Development Bank formulated guidelines for the HIA of development projects – see Ben Harris-Roxas *et al*, 'Health impact assessment: The state of the art' (2012) 30(1) *Impact Assessment and Project Appraisal* 43, 45. The IFC's Performance Standard 4 on Community Health, Safety and Security (2012) addreses HIA. See www.ifc.org/wps/wcm/connect/115482804a0255db96fbffd1a5d13d27/PS_English_2012_Full-Document.pdf?MOD=AJPERES, accessed 27 February 2019. For the IFC's Guideline Document on HIA see www.ifc.org/wps/wcm/connect/a0f1120048855a5a85dcd76a6515bb18/HealthImpact.pdf?MOD=AJPERES, accessed 27 February 2019; see also the IAIA 'Health Impact Assessment' www.iaia.org/wiki-details.php?ID=14, accessed 27 February 2019.

[161] Harris-Roxas (n 160) 43.

[162] WHO European Centre for Health Policy, *Health Impact Assessment: Main Concepts and Suggested Approach: Gothenburg Consensus Paper* (WHO Regional Office for Europe 1999).

tended, and to underscore that HIA also incorporates 'appropriate actions to manage those effects'.[163]

Prior to and after the Gothenburg Consensus, a number of development, professional and industry institutions and associations formulated voluntary guidelines on the conduct of HIA. For example, in 2010, the ICMM published its *Good Practice Guidance on Health Impact Assessment*, one of only two industry associations that have developed a context-specific guide.[164] The ICMM HIA *Good Practice Guidance* outlines the community health and wellbeing impacts of mining and metals projects. Thereafter it provides guidance on undertaking an inhouse rapid HIA, integrating health into EIAs and SIAs, commissioning and managing an HIA and managing and following up on community health and wellbeing impacts.[165] The *Good Practice Guidance* does not address the role of the State or government directly, but hints at some tensions. For example, it points out that one of the reasons for conducting an HIA is to facilitate negotiations with local government and local public services as to which aspects of community health and wellbeing are the responsibility of the project, and which aspects remain with the State.[166] In general, the *Good Practice Guidance* emphasizes the role of local governments as a 'partner' for developing projects that will enhance community health and wellbeing.[167]

Whether standalone or integrated into an EIA, SIA or SEA, the ICMM's *HIA Guidance* advises, an HIA should address three distinct but related areas of public health: the potential health risks of major infrastructure projects ('environmental health'); the wider 'determinants of health', which could be biophysical, social, economic or institutional in nature; and health equity, or the distribution of health effects.[168] The *HIA Guidance*, for example, identifies five major categories of mining-induced health effects,[169] and 16 wider deter-

---

[163] IAIA, *Health Impact Assessment International Best Practice Principles* Special Publication Series No. 5 (Fargo 2006).

[164] ICMM *Good Practice Guidance on Health Impact Assessment* (2010) 8–23 (henceforth *HIA Guidance*); the other industry association that has formulated HIA guidance is the International Petroleum Industry Environmental Conservation Association, which published its *Guide to Health Impact Assessments in the Oil and Gas Industry* in 2005.

[165] *HIA Guidance* (n 164).

[166] Ibid 6.

[167] Ibid 19.

[168] Harris-Roxas (n 160) 44.

[169] These being infectious diseases (for example malaria, tuberculosis); chronic diseases (heart disease, cancer, asthma and bronchitis); nutritional disorders; physical injury (arising both from accidents and community violence and heavy metal or chemical poisoning); and mental health (stress and anxiety, depression and suicide).

minants of health in mining areas.[170] The complex interactions a mining project triggers among health effects, determinants of health and distributional pathways can lead to positive or negative outcomes. For example, mining investment can lead to the construction of or new access to public health facilities, new employment opportunities, increased income, new transport infrastructure and skills development, among others, which can lower the incidence of some health effects, such as nutritional disorders. However, mining also causes negative health effects for all the major health determinants; for example, employment opportunities for some segments of the population may decline, reducing their chances of accessing good healthcare; hostel accommodation and community in-migration facilitates the spread of infectious diseases; mining may overuse or contaminate sources of water supply, and so on. The *HIA Guidance* also recognizes that mining can increase health inequality, as the negative effects of a project (loss of land and agricultural livelihoods, air and water pollution, increased food costs) tend to disproportionately affect those segments of the population that are already vulnerable, that is, women, children, the elderly and the disabled.[171]

Very few States have institutionalized precaution in the form of a HIA. Thailand stands out globally for having constitutionalized this requirement. The Thai Constitution states that '[a]ny project or activity which may seriously affect a community's environmental quality, its natural resources or its people's health, is prohibited, unless (a) these environmental and health impacts are studied and assessed'. In some developing regions of the world the political will to institutionalize HIA is nevertheless apparent. For example, in 2008, African ministers responsible for health and environment signed the Libreville *Declaration on Health and Environment in Africa*, which incorporates the commitment to institute 'the systematic assessment of health and environment risks, in particular through the development of procedures to assess the impacts on health'.[172]

The lack of a formal statutory framework for HIA does not preclude health impacts from being assessed as part of an EIA, SIA or SEA. In 2014 the

---

[170] Namely, employment and economy; housing and shelter; water supply and sanitation; transport and connectivity; learning and education; crime and safety; health, social care and public services; commercial goods and services; social capital and community cohesion; spirituality, faith and traditions; arts and cultural activities; leisure and recreation; lifestyle and daily routines; governance and public policy; energy and waste; land and spatial planning.

[171] *HIA Guidance* (n 164) 20.

[172] Article 9, *Libreville Declaration on Health and Environment in Africa*, 29 August 2008 www.ehrn.co.za/download/libreville_declaration.pdf, accessed 27 February 2019.

World Health Organization commissioned a study on the effectiveness of HIA when paired with these other processes, or when conducted as a standalone procedure.[173] The WHO Study found that while health as a topic is not foreign to EIA, SEA, SIA or Sustainability Impact Assessment, and while they all aspire towards a more comprehensive inclusion of human health, in practice coverage is still limited.[174] To improve the extent to which HIA can institutionalize precaution, the WHO advised, it is necessary to clearly conceptualize health (including its physical, social and mental dimensions) and to use this conception consistently; to have access to reliable health data and information; to draw upon the substantive and methodological insights of health experts from the earliest stages; and to raise awareness among the community of impact assessors and decisionmakers of the interconnections between policies, programmes and health.[175]

However, in extractives, the policy preference of the dominant model is to integrate HIA into EIA or SIA rather than to conduct standalone assessments. The ICMM *Good Practice Guidance*, for example, advocates for integrated environmental, social and health impact assessments, outlining the potential integration benefits (a more holistic and comprehensive overall assessment, integrated consultation with affected communities, fewer inconsistencies and conflicts in findings, and so on) and pitfalls (domination of the EIA or SIA at the expense of health, leading to a shallow assessment).[176] With a focus on mining in low and middle-income countries, Harris, Villiani and Spickett also argue strongly that connecting with EIA is an essential task for the health system, and that EIA regulations provide the best current mechanism for bringing health impacts to the fore in decisionmaking processes.[177]

2.2 The No Action, 'Zero Alternative' or 'No Go' Option: The State as Boundary Setter, Part I

In theory, the dominant model concedes that it is not enough for the State to institutionalize precaution in relation to mining's environmental, social and economic impacts by prescribing that studies be undertaken. The State must

---

[173] Rainer Fehr *et al*, *Health in Impact Assessment: Opportunities Not to Be Missed* (World Health Organization Regional Office for Europe 2014).

[174] Ibid 112.

[175] Ibid.

[176] *HIA Guidance* (n 164) 58.

[177] Patrick Harris, Francesca Viliani and Jeff Spickett, 'Assessing health impacts within environmental impact assessments: An opportunity for public health globally which must not remain missed' (2015) 12(1) *International Journal of Environmental Research for Public Health* 1044.

also use the information generated by an EIA to improve decisionmaking on how mining should be conducted within its jurisdiction. This may include deciding whether and how mining should proceed at all, and/or what conditions should apply to the various operational phases.

One of the most intractable issues associated with EIA in the extractives industry is whether the process can lead to refusal of the project based on the precautionary principle and longterm sustainability concerns. This touches upon, but does not exhaust, the issue of considering alternatives in EIA, and the 'zero alternative' of not proceeding with the project at all. According to Steinemann, developing a set of alternatives is the 'most important' part of an EIA process.[178] The rigorous identification and analysis of alternatives can improve decisionmaking in a manner that protects, restores and enhances the environment.[179] The IAIA insists that 'consideration of alternatives is central to sound decisionmaking; it increases public participation and improves transparency, thus ensuring better accountability of the decision – in short alternatives are important for better governance and sustainability'.[180]

There is a line of argument that because mines can only be located where ore reserves are found, the range of alternatives is limited to mining methods, the location of mining infrastructure, siting of waste disposal sites and the sourcing of power, water and raw materials. Weaver and Caldwell, for example, hold: 'The choice as to where a mine should be placed is predetermined by the location of mineral deposits. Alternatives in mining projects differ from other developments where alternative sites could be considered or, conversely, there could be a wide variety of development options for a specific site.'[181] However, this argument begs the question: Is mining developmentally appropriate for a locality or region in the first place?

The EA systems of mineral-rich jurisdictions differ according to whether the consideration of alternatives is mandatory or subject to the discretion of the authority, whether alternatives are limited to operational or production requirements and whether alternatives include the 'no action', 'zero alternative' or 'no go' option. In British Columbia, for example, there is no explicit legal requirement to carry out alternative analyses when conducting an EA. The scope, procedure and methods of a reviewable project are determined by the executive director of the Environmental Assessment Office and/or the min-

---

[178] Anne Steinemann, 'Improving alternatives for environmental impact assessment' (2001) 21 *Environmental Impact Assessment Review* 3, 4.

[179] Ibid.

[180] J de Jesus *et al*, 'Alternatives in project EIA' (IAIA 2015).

[181] Alex Weaver and Paula Caldwell, 'Environmental impact assessment for mining projects' in Judith Petts (ed.), *Handbook of Environmental Impact Assessment* (Blackwell 1999) 377, 393.

ister.[182] In other jurisdictions there may be no explicit requirement to consider the 'no action' alternative, as is reportedly the case in the Philippines.[183]

However, proceeding from the example in the USA NEPA (discussed below), many mineral-rich jurisdictions do require project proponents to consider alternatives when submitting their EA documentation. For example, the EIA procedure for mining projects in Finland, as set out in the Environmental Impact Assessment Act (468/1994) and the EIA Decree (713/2006), stipulates that EIA programmes must contain details of alternatives for implementing the project, one of which is usually the no action alternative.[184] Finnish Guidelines on EIA for mining projects distinguish between a '0 alternative' and a '0+ alternative' – the former being a description of how the area would develop in the absence of any mining project, the latter the situation where further developments are limited to further studies of local ore deposits, with no actual mine commissioned.[185] These guidelines also provide an illustrative list of the production factors a project proponent could examine for alternatives, ranging from mining different ore deposits in different orders, to different mining methods, to annual production levels, and so on.[186] Economic viability is expressly identified as the basis for all the various project alternatives and scheduling of activities.[187] South African EIA law requires the consideration of alternatives,[188] although the political authorities may grant a project proponent an exemption from the requirement to do so.[189] The South African EIA regulations define alternatives as

> different means of meeting the general purpose and requirements of the activity, which may include alternatives to the (a) property on which or location where the activity is proposed to be undertaken; (b) type of activity to be undertaken; (c) design or layout of the activity; (d) technology to be used in the activity; and (e) operational aspects of the activity, and includes the option of not implementing the activity.[190]

---

182 Environmental Assessment Act, 2002 (British Columbia), sections 11, 14.

183 Allan Ingelson, William Holden and Meriam Bravante, 'Philippine environmental impact assessment, mining and genuine development' (2009) 5(1) *Law, Environment and Development Journal* 1, 10.

184 EIA Decree (713/2006) (Finland) s 9.

185 Ministry of Employment and the Economy, *Guide: Environmental Impact Procedure for Mining Projects in Finland* (2015) 31.

186 Ibid 32.

187 Ibid 31.

188 National Environmental Management Act, 1998 (South Africa), section 24(4)(b).

189 Ibid, section 24M.

190 Environmental Impact Assessment Regulations, 2014 (South Africa), reg. 1.

Rather than purely economic criteria, however, the authorities must take a broadranging set of sustainable development principles into account in evaluating the application for an environmental authorization.[191]

The consideration of alternatives, including the alternative of no action, was an integral part of the EIA process under the NEPA from the start. Particular design features of this regulatory regime, however, have undermined the consideration of genuine alternatives.[192] Under the NEPA process, if a project proponent puts forward a major federal action, a lead agency must be assigned to undertake the EIA.[193] The lead agency must determine whether the proposed action will have potentially significant impacts on the quality of the human environment and, in the event of a positive finding, the agency must prepare an EIA. The NEPA then contains detailed provision on the consideration of alternatives. For example, the lead agency must rigorously explore and objectively evaluate 'all reasonable alternatives', discuss the reasons for the elimination of alternatives from the detailed study, devote 'substantial treatment' to every alternative considered in detail, include the alternative of no action, include alternatives that fall outside the jurisdiction of the lead agency and identify the agency's preferred alternative.[194] The problem with this system, however, is that the rigorous evaluation of alternatives applies only to those that are included once an initial process of screening has determined which alternatives are relevant to the project's objectives and goals, as determined by an agency-authored statement of 'purpose and need'.[195] The statement of purpose and need also inevitably frames the problem to be addressed, which can be defined so narrowly as to screen out all other alternatives other than the project proposed. Other factors that constrict consideration of possibly more sustainable alternatives include agency agendas and autonomy, where the lead agency may be reluctant to consider alternatives outside their purview, or have a bias towards infrastructural development.[196] Public participation in the agency EIA process starts too late to influence key decisions on alternatives, most critically in the formulation of the purpose and need statement that frames the problem to be addressed.[197]

These factors, among others, led Steinemann to argue that the consideration of alternatives under the NEPA system is dominated by consideration of alternative designs, not alternative approaches. An alternative approach is

---

[191] National Environmental Management Act, 1998 (South Africa), section 24O.
[192] Steinemann (n 178) 3.
[193] Ibid 5.
[194] Ibid 6.
[195] Ibid 7.
[196] Ibid 12.
[197] Ibid 9, 15.

a functionally different way to address the problem that the project attempts to solve and the project's objectives. An alternative design is a functionally similar way of addressing the same problem.[198] For example, expanding public transport would be an alternative approach to constructing a highway; presenting a different alignment of the highway would be an alternative design.[199] This example illustrates how critical it is to frame the problem in a manner that admits a broad enough range of alternatives based on longrun sustainability. IAIA guidelines directed to consultants that usually conduct EIAs endorse the consideration of both alternative approaches and alternative designs. They state that the alternatives process 'should consider different ways of achieving the same objective (for example, alternatives to building a hydro-electric scheme might be to import power or build wind farms)',[200] but also state that 'project EIAs require consideration of projects of a similar technical character or functionality that will meet the specified objective'.[201]

Over time, States have incorporated checks and balances to lessen the likelihood of bias on the part of either the agency or the project proponent. Checks and balances have included reforms focused on the allocation of the EA licensing function,[202] requiring that the project proponent appoint an independent

---

198 Ibid 6.

199 Ibid.

200 De Jesus (n 180) 2.

201 Ibid.

202 To address problems relating to conflicts of interest the Peruvian Congress passed *Proyecto de Ley* 1461/2012PE reforming the regulatory institutions in charge of assessing and approving projects likely to have a significant environmental impact. The law creates a new institution – the National Environmental Certification Service for Sustainable Investments (SENACE) – within the Ministry of Environment. For the functioning of the SENACE see D Arbelaez-Ruiz *et al*, *Institutional and Political Frameworks of Environmental Licensing Processes* (2013) IM4DC Action Research Project 45. In Queensland, amendments to the Environmental Protection Act transferred the environmental regulation of mining from the Department of Mining and Energy to the Environmental Protection Agency in 2000. After examining the amendments Peel concluded that the efficacy of the proposed changes would ultimately depend on the degree of resources and commitment the state government provided to the Environmental Protection Agency. See Jacqueline Peel, 'An Environmental Revolution in the Queensland Mining Industry or Just a Changing of the Guard? An Analysis of the New Regime for the Environmental Regulation of Mining under the Environmental Protection Act (Qld)' (2001) 20 *Australian Mining and Petroleum Law Journal* 137. In South Africa, the 'One Environmental System' was established in September 2014. The Minister responsible for the Environment determines the 'rules of the game' for the impacts of mining on the environment, but the Minister of Mineral Resources receives and considers applications for environmental authorization under the national environmental management law. See Tracy-Lynn Humby, 'One envi-

'environmental assessment practitioner' to conduct the assessment,[203] allowing for the appointment of independent review panels,[204] institutionalizing public participation and consultation at an earlier stage in the project cycle,[205] and, lately, calls for the better incorporation of indigenous knowledge systems into assessment processes.[206]

The inefficacy of these checks and balances to entrench a no action decision in situations where the economic benefits of a mining project seem to be clearly outweighed by the sociocultural and environmental losses that the project would initiate are well illustrated by the ongoing saga of the New Prosperity mine in British Columbia, Canada. Initially dubbed the Prosperity Mine, and proposed by a NYSE-listed company, the project included an open pit copper–gold mine, concentrator facility, supported infrastructure and tailings and waste rock facilities with a 20-year mine life.[207] The mineral deposit is estimated to be the seventh largest undeveloped gold–copper resource in the world, with government revenues of nearly USD 10 billion over the life of the

---

ronmental system: Aligning the laws on the environmental management of mining in South Africa' (2015) 33(2) *Journal of Energy and Natural Resources Law* 110.

[203] Environmental Impact Assessment Regulations, 2014 (South Africa), reg. 12.

[204] The federal Canadian Environmental Assessment Act (CEAA), 2012 (currently under review) allows for environmental assessments to be conducted by a state agency or by an independent review panel. If the Minister responsible for the Environment is of the view that an EA is 'in the public interest' he or she may refer the assessment to a review panel (CEAA, section 38).

[205] Steinemann (n 178) 18.

[206] The process to review the federal CEAA acknowledges that the current system does not afford Indigenous Peoples and the public sufficient opportunity to meaningfully participate. Indigenous groups in Canada are rigorously contesting the adequacy of the federal and provincial processes for EA in Canada, and are in some instances formalizing their own review panels. In 2015/2016 for example, the Stk'emlúpsemc te Secwepemc Nation, a governance body of the Secwepemc Nation, constituted an indigenous-led review panel to conduct a social, cultural and environmental impact assessment and community consultation process of Polish-owned KGHM's plans to open the low-grade copper–gold Ajax mine near their traditional territory in British Columbia (see SSN, 'Honoring the vision of our ancestors' https://miningwatch.ca/sites/default/files/ssn_project_review_process_4pages_0.pdf, accessed 27 February 2019). The indigenous-led panel concluded its deliberations in March 2017 and rejected the project on the basis that it would cause irreversible and unacceptable impacts to land, waters and people (see MiningWatch Canada, 'MiningWatch urges B.C. & Canada to honour indigenous-led environmental review panel's decision to reject KGHM's Ajax mine' https://miningwatch.ca/news/2017/3/7/miningwatch-urges-bc-canada-honour-indigenous-led-environmental-review-panel-s, accessed 27 February 2019).

[207] Canadian Environmental Assessment Agency, 'New Prosperity Gold-Copper Mine Project' www.ceaa-acee.gc.ca/050/details-eng.cfm?evaluation=63928, accessed 27 February 2019.

mine.[208] To make way for mine tailings, the company's initial proposal would have partially drained Teztan Biny (also known as Fish Lake), a site sacred to the Tsilhqot'in Nation in British Columbia, in one of the few areas in Canada with a court declaration of proven Aboriginal rights.[209] Although approved by the British Columbia government, the project was rejected by a federal review panel under the CEAA in 2010, with the panel finding that the project would result in several significant and unacceptable environmental effects.[210] The company submitted an updated proposal for the New Prosperity Mine in 2011, putting forward a project design that it maintained would preserve Teztan Biny. A new federal review panel was convened, which handed down its decision in October 2013 to once again refuse the mine.[211]

The manner in which the company and other participants framed alternatives against the need for and purpose of the project in the second federal review process for the project is illuminating. The company maintained that the project met the needs of a range of beneficiaries, spanning from sustaining the economic and social health of rural British Columbia communities, to boosting jobs, GDP and tax revenues in British Columbia and Canada, to entrenching Canada's position as a gold and copper producer, to meeting a predicted global shortage of copper concentrate and demand for gold.[212] Participants' views on the purpose of the project were polarized, with industry associations and aligned groups affirming the flow of tax revenues and employment and civil society groups questioning the financial viability and economic benefits of the mine, highlighting the manner in which the State would subsidize the project and claiming that the project would generate significant net cost to British Columbia and Canada as a whole.[213] Alternatives to the project were described as 'functionally different ways to meet a project's need and achieve a project's purpose'.[214] The company stated that the only functionally different way to

---

[208] Review Panel established by the Federal Minister of the Environment, *Report of the Federal Review Panel: New Prosperity Gold-Copper Mine Project, Taseko Mines Ltd, British Columbia* (31 October 2013) 25 (henceforth Review Panel).

[209] MiningWatch Canada, 'First Nations celebrate Federal rejection of New Prosperity mine proposal' https://miningwatch.ca/news/2014/2/27/first-nations-celebrate-federal-rejection-new-prosperity-mine-proposal (accessed 30 December 2017).

[210] MiningWatch Canada, 'Prosperity Mine – A precautionary tale: The importance of environmental assessments' https://miningwatch.ca/blog/2017/1/31/prosperity-mine-precautionary-tale-importance-environmental-assessments, accessed 27 February 2019.

[211] Review Panel (n 208).

[212] Ibid 25.

[213] Ibid 26.

[214] Ibid 27.

meet the purpose and need of the project was to develop alternative copper and gold mines in Canada, preferably in British Columbia. It also conceded, however that it had no economically viable alternative at the same advanced level of geological definition, engineering and environmental assessment, and that it was already maximizing copper production at an existing mine.[215] A divergent participant view emphasized different opportunities for economic development in the region. If the same kind of government subsidies and investments were put into building a more diverse and healthy economy, this participant said, the citizens of the region would create many more jobs than the mine could create in sustainable alternatives.[216]

The remaining deliberation on alternatives focused on alternative means of conducting the project.[217] The Federal Review Panel did not engage with the broadranging arguments relating to mining as a development alternative in its assessment and review on alternatives. Instead it concentrated on the reasonableness of the mining company's methodology to select a site that would impact upon Tetzan Biny for its mine waste disposal facility, alongside other infrastructure that needed to be built for the mine.[218]

The federal review process did not bring closure for the Tsilhqot'in Nation. The company challenged the second review panel's report in a federal court, claiming that the panel's findings that the project would have serious effects on the water quality of Tetzan Biny were flawed.[219] In July 2017 the provincial government approved the company's extensive drilling programme to advance the rejected New Prosperity Mine.[220] Far from having minor impacts, the drilling programme involved drilling 122 exploration holes, digging 357 test pits, constructing 48km of new access trails, modifying 28km of existing trails and establishing a 50-person labour camp.[221] The permit was issued at a time when wildfires were ravaging the Tsilhqot'in region and communities were working to relocate elders, children and others to safety while trying to protect their homes and future.[222] The company voluntarily suspended the

---

[215] Ibid.

[216] Ibid 28.

[217] Ibid 28–33.

[218] Ibid 36–8.

[219] MiningWatch Canada (n 210).

[220] MiningWatch Canada, 'Tsilhqot'in Nation seeks injunctions from BC court to stop (again) Taseko Mines' https://miningwatch.ca/news/2017/7/31/tsilhqot-nation-seek-injunctions-bc-supreme-court-stop-again-taseko-mines, accessed 27 February 2019.

[221] Derrick Penner, 'Taseko mines halts exploration work at New Prosperity' *Vancouver Sun* 15 August 2017 http://vancouversun.com/news/local-news/taseko-mines-halts-exploration-work-at-new-prosperity, accessed 27 February 2019.

[222] Ibid.

exploration programme after the Canadian Environmental Assessment Agency indicated it would petition the British Columbia Supreme Court to grant an injunction against the drilling programme.[223] And in December 2017, a federal court dismissed the company's challenge to the federal environmental review panel report.[224] The court found it reasonable for the review panel to reject claims that 'adaptive management' would be applied to serious environmental problems as they arose, and was critical about the company's failure to supply details on mitigation measures related to water quality.[225] The company may nevertheless still appeal this ruling.

The New Prosperity mining case is thus illustrative of the failure of the EIA process to accommodate deliberation and decision on development alternatives. Instead, in this case it has facilitated ongoing development uncertainty that places the cultural survival of the Tsilhqot'in at risk. Through multiple review processes and court challenges associated with the EIA process, Tsilhqot'in communities have been subjected to ongoing stress. The protracted legal battles around the EIA process are likely to wear communities down over time. The case is also illustrative of the fracturing of the State, with the provincial government keenly in favour of the project, and the federal government and judiciary offering resistance.

In 1996, an update prepared for the World Bank's Environmental Assessment Sourcebook incorporated the statement: 'It is still common to encounter proposed projects in which the decisions up to and including selection of site and technology have been made with little or no environmental consideration.'[226] The projects outlined above indicate that little appears to have changed. To avoid the 'disruptive and sometimes artificial process of examining alternatives once the site and technology have been chosen', the recommendation put forward by the World Bank at the time was to adopt a tiered approach to EA, relying upon the integrated use of strategic, sectoral and regional EA in addition to project-level EIA to finesse the development trajectory.[227] The use of SEA at an earlier stage of agency planning and budget development is also

---

[223] Ibid.

[224] MiningWatch Canada, 'Dead mine walking? Federal Court reconfirms Taseko Mine's "New Prosperity" mine a "no go"' https://miningwatch.ca/news/2017/12/7/dead-mine-walking-federal-court-reconfirms-taseko-s-new-prosperity-mine-no-go, accessed 27 February 2019.

[225] Ibid.

[226] A Davey, TE Walton and T Ziegler, 'Analysis of alternatives in environmental assessment', *Environmental Assessment Sourcebook Update* (December 1996) 2.

[227] Ibid.

a key recommendation emanating from Steinemann's analysis of alternatives under NEPA in the USA.[228]

2.3 Cumulative Impacts: The State as Boundary Setter, Part II

Apart from deciding whether mining can proceed in certain areas at all, States may also be faced with the question of *how much* mining to allow in particular localities and regions. This second form of boundary setting is accommodated by the process of Cumulative Impact Assessment (CIA), or Cumulative Effects Assessment (CEA) as it is known in some jurisdictions.[229]

The origin of CIA dates back to the early 1970s – the term 'cumulative effects' was first mentioned in guidelines published by the USA Council on Environmental Quality in 1973.[230] The Minerals Council of Australia (MCA) has defined CIA as an EIA approach 'that aims to consider the effects of multiple actions or impacts on the environment'.[231] This broadranging definition accommodates much variation in CIA, for example, the combined effects of a single mining project on multiple environmental values, the combined effects of a single proposed project on an existing baseline or current state of health of an ecosystem (that is, taking into account historical context), the cumulative effect of multiple projects on a single environmental value or asset and the cumulative effect of multiple projects on multiple/all environmental values or assets.[232]

According to Duinker and Greig, cumulative effects are the only real effects worth assessing in any EIA.[233] They argue that in its initial conception the whole point of EIA was environmental protection, with the process of EIA designed to sustain environmental values in the face of development proposals that may compromise them.[234] In this light, the central role of EIA is to sustain Valued Ecosystem Components (VECs), and if CEA is to do so properly, if must be implemented in a manner as if VECs were centre stage.[235] Instead of

---

228 Steinemann (n 178) 18.

229 Peter N Duinker and Lorne A Greig, 'The impotence of cumulative effects assessment in Canada: Ailments and ideas for redeployment' (2006) 37(2) *Environmental Management* 153.

230 Larry Canter and Bill Ross, 'State of practice of cumulative effects assessment and management: The good, the bad and the ugly' (2010) 28(4) *Impact Assessment and Project Appraisal* 261, 262.

231 Minerals Council of Australia, *Cumulative Environmental Impact Assessment: Industry Guide* (July 2015) 7.

232 Ibid 11.

233 Duinker and Greig (n 229) 157.

234 Ibid 154.

235 Ibid.

attention being focused on whether the impacts of a single project on ecosystem components are acceptable, the sustainability of VECs can be understood properly only by examining the full range of human-generated stresses.[236] The role of CIA is to ensure that the *total* effects of all stressors on VECs are kept within tolerable and acceptable levels.[237] The goal is to sustain VECs for the future; accordingly, if done well, CIA demands the specific creation of alternative development scenarios and the potential cumulative effects associated with each.[238]

The consideration of cumulative environmental impacts is an integral and frequently legislated component of many project-related and/or regional EAs, although there is much variation in State approach. In some jurisdictions the need to consider cumulative impacts is express. For example, the EU EIA Directive requires a developer to prepare and submit an EIA report that includes a description of the project's likely significant effects on the environment.[239] The EIA report must describe the accumulation of the project's effects with other existing and/or approved projects 'taking into account any existing environmental problems relating to areas of particular environmental importance likely to be affected, or the use of natural resources'.[240] In Canada, the assessment of cumulative impacts became mandatory under the Canadian Environmental Assessment Act, 1995.[241] The Canadian Environmental Assessment Act, 2012 scaled back on this requirement,[242] but the review process of this legislation initiated in 2017 identifies addressing cumulative impacts as an express policy reform focus.[243] At a provincial level, however (with the exception of Nunavut), there are no binding policies on cumulative effects assessment.[244] The South African EIA system requires assessment of

---

236 Ibid.

237 Ibid.

238 Ibid 158. See also Peter N Duinker and Lorne A Greig, 'Scenario analysis in environmental impact assessment: Improving explorations of the future' (2007) 27 *Environmental Impact Assessment Review* 206.

239 Article 5(1), Directive 2011/92/EU (as amended by Directive 2014/52/EU) (henceforth EU EIA Directive).

240 Annex IV, item 5(e), EU EIA Directive.

241 CEEA, 1995 s 16(1)(a).

242 CEAA, 2012, section 4(1)(a)(i) of the Canadian Environmental Assessment Act, 2012, for example, simply provides that the purposes of the Act include encouraging the study of the cumulative effects of physical activities in a region and the consideration of those study results in environmental assessments.

243 Government of Canada (n 96).

244 E Tovilla, 'Reviewing Canada's cumulative effects assessment guidelines for the metal mining sector' *Environmental Science and Engineering*, 24 October 2017 https://esemag.com/hazmat-remediation/reviewing-canadas-cea-guidelines-for-the-metal-mining-sector/, accessed 27 February 2019.

cumulative impacts for both basic assessment and the more complex scoping and environmental impact reporting process. The definition of cumulative impact in the 2014 EIA regulations requires proponents to consider the past, current and reasonably foreseeable future impact of an activity, considered together with the 'impact of activities associated with that activity'.[245] This definition is therefore considerably vaguer than the European Directive, and it is not clear whether such activities are ones associated only with the project or undertaken by other proponents. The focus also remains on the activity, rather than the ecosystem component or natural resource. Ghana's 1999 EIA Regulations, on the other hand, while not directly requiring a project proponent to consider cumulative impacts, require a description of 'alteration in ecological processes such as transfer of energy through food chains, decomposition and bio-accumulation which could affect any community, habitat or specie of flora or fauna' and the decline in existing or potential use of valued resources arising from concentration of pollutants, ecological changes, alteration in ecological processes and so forth.[246]

In other jurisdictions, however, there is no requirement to consider cumulative impacts. For example, Botswana's EIA framework simply requires a project developer to identify and evaluate the environmental impact of an activity with reference to a variety of anthropocentric values.[247] In Australia, federal and provincial legislation does not expressly mention cumulative impacts or distinguish between cumulative and other impacts. Nevertheless, in practice requirements to address cumulative impacts are usually addressed in the terms of reference developed by agencies overseeing the EA process.[248] In State jurisdictions, some Australian courts have upheld a requirement to consider cumulative impacts.[249]

Incorporating CIA into EIA systems is a fairly recent development. Commentators have noted that this area of assessment is comparatively

---

245 Environmental Impact Assessment Regulations 2014 (South Africa), reg. 1.

246 Environmental Assessment Regulations, 1999 (Ghana), reg. 14(1).

247 Environmental Assessment Act No. 10 of 2011 (Botswana), section 9(2).

248 Daniel M Franks, David Brereton and Chris J Moran, 'Managing the cumulative impacts of coal mining on regional communities and environments in Australia' (2010) 28(4) *Impact Assessment and Project Appraisal* 299, 305.

249 For example, *Gray v. Minister for Planning & Others* (2006) 152 LGERA 258 (holding that the EIS for the Anvil Coal Project should have investigated cumulative impacts); *Bulga Mibrodale Progress Association Inc. v. Minister for Planning and Infrastructure and Warkworth Mining Limited* (2013) 194 LGERA 347 (successful challenge to the extension of an open cut coal mine on the basis of cumulative impacts relating to noise and dust); and *Hancock Coal Pty Ltd v. Kelly & Others* [2014] QLC 12 (challenge to the Alpha Coal Project on a number of grounds, including cumulative impacts particularly related to groundwater).

underdeveloped,[250] and that execution of legislative mandates to undertake CIA is generally inadequate and weak.[251] Commenting on the execution of the CIA provided by EU regulations in Sweden, for example, Wärnbäck and Hilding-Rydevik observe that cumulative effects are rarely described or included in Swedish environmental assessment documents.[252] In Brazil, based on a study of 37 EIA applications in the states of Sao Paulo and Minas Gerais (which included mining, mineral processing and mining-related projects), researchers found that cumulative assessment featured in a particularly negative way: when cumulative effects were presented, they were merely treated as an attribute of already identified impacts, and were not subjected to any type of specific analysis or assessment.[253] In 2010 Franks *et al* observed that notwithstanding requirements and guidance regarding cumulative assessment in Australia, the treatment of this aspect in actual EA processes was mixed; for example, assessments acknowledged the potential for cumulative impacts on communities situated near multiple mines but offered no proposed management or mitigation measures to address the issues.[254]

A number of reasons have been put forward for the poor development and implementation of CIA. First, there is a lack of a common understanding of 'cumulative effects' and a lack of agreed approaches and methods for conducting a CIA.[255] In the absence of State guidance, precise operational definitions of cumulative effects and CIA remain elusive, significantly impacting how the analysis is conducted.[256] An empirical study on cumulative effects in Swedish EIA practice found that perceptions varied widely as to what cumulative assessments are and how they arise. Some participants in the study, for example, considered cumulative effects to be merely additive, whereas others noted the possibility of synergistic effects arising from multiple project-related

---

[250] Morgan (n 7) 9.

[251] Duinker and Greig (n 229) 158.

[252] A Wärnbäck and T Hilding-Rydevik, 'Cumulative effects in Swedish EIA practice – Difficulties and obstacles' (2009) 29(2) *Environmental Impact Assessment Review* 107.

[253] MR Raimundo e Almeida and M Montano, 'The effectiveness of environmental impact assessment: Systems in Sao Paulo and Minas Gerais states' (2017) 20(2) *Ambiente & Sociedade* 77, 87.

[254] Daniel Franks *et al*, *Cumulative Impacts: A Good Practice Guide for the Australian Coal Mining Industry* (Centre for Social Responsibility in Mining, Centre for Water in the Minerals Industry and Australian Coal Association Research Program 2010) 306.

[255] Morgan (n 7) 8; Jill Gunn and Bram F Noble, 'Conceptual and methodological challenges to integrating SEA and cumulative effects assessment' (2011) 31 *Environmental Impact Assessment Review* 154, 156.

[256] Gunn and Noble (n 255) 156.

impacts or the impacts of multiple projects in a region.[257] Only a few participants mentioned that past activities could contribute to cumulative effects or required looking at what could happen to a given area in the future.[258] The Good Practice Guidelines on Cumulative Effects Assessment developed for the Australian Coal Mining Industry define cumulative effects very broadly, as 'the successive, incremental and combined impacts of one, or more, activities on society, the economy and the environment. Cumulative impacts result from the aggregation and interaction of impacts on a receptor, and may be the product of past, present or future activities.'

Cumulative impacts can be both positive and negative and can vary in intensity as well as spatial and temporal extent. Cumulative impacts may interact such that they trigger or are associated with other impacts. They may aggregate linearly or exponentially or reach 'tipping points' after which major changes in environmental, social and economic systems may follow.[259]

Notable in this very broad definition of cumulative impacts is the shift away from VECs to a broader conception of the interlinked systemic cumulative impacts on environmental, social and economic systems.

Second, if the role of CIA is to ensure that the total effects of all stressors on VECs are kept within tolerable and acceptable levels, it is necessary to determine thresholds over ecologically meaningful spatial and temporal scales.[260] Notwithstanding the extensive work undertaken on planetary and social boundaries,[261] thresholds are difficult and sometimes impossible to determine and are usually beyond the capacity of a project-level EIA to address.[262]

Third, the responsibility for conducting a CIA rests at the door of project proponents,[263] who may legitimately ask why they should care about future developments and their impacts on valued components of ecological systems.[264] In 1999, Kennett highlighted the reactive and project-bound nature of CIA, and cited giving project proponents primary responsibility for driving cumulative assessment and the lack of a developed policy and planning context as elements of a largely ineffective 'conventional EA paradigm' for cumulative effects management.[265] He proposed a new paradigm for

---

257 Wärnbäck and Hilding-Rydevik (n 252) 110.

258 Ibid.

259 Franks (n 254) 10.

260 Duinker and Greig (n 229) 156.

261 See the discussion in Chapter 1.

262 Duinker and Greig (n 229) 156; Gunn and Noble (n 225) 155.

263 Morgan (n 7) 9.

264 Duinker and Greig (n 229) 156.

265 Steven A Kennett, 'Towards a new paradigm for cumulative effects management', CIRL Occasional Paper #8 (December 1999) v.

cumulative effects management resting on five pillars: vesting primary responsibility for cumulative effects management in the State, adopting a proactive, planning-based approach, establishing overall objectives and specific thresholds for both impacts for land and resource use, opting for a regional rather than a project-specific focus and developing an integrated legal and policy framework for EA and land use planning.[266] Franks *et al*, on the other hand, argue that management of cumulative impacts requires strategic and regional planning, information exchange, networking and forums, pooling of resources to start initiatives and programmes and multistakeholder and regional monitoring.[267]

Commenting on the Canadian framework mid-2000, Duinker and Greig said that while it would probably be best to scrap project-level CIA in favour of an aggressive, regionally oriented programme, this was admittedly politically infeasible due to the entrenched legislated nature of the former and the lack of institutions to drive the latter.[268] Moving forward, both technical improvements to project-level CIA and institutional improvements to regional CIA were indicated[269] – advice that would arguably be applicable to other mineral-rich jurisdictions as well. Technical improvements to project-level CIA would include assuming that all effects are cumulative, integrating CIA through the EA and instituting mechanisms to monitor these impacts throughout the mine's lifecycle, taking a VEC-centred approach to the analysis and obliging proponents to share data and plans for relevant future developments.[270] Good Practice Guidelines developed for CEA in the Australian coal mining industry stress that data access and sharing is one of the major challenges in undertaking CIA.[271] Mining companies' concerns regarding commercially sensitive information and intellectual property, alongside practical difficulties related to compatibility, archiving and accessing data, are impediments to the free flow of information that could establish communities of practice around different development scenarios.[272] These Good Practice Guidelines identify different models for data sharing and access, ranging from government-funded statutory assessments and lead studies, to government–industry–community partnerships, to industry collaborations, nongovernment/industry initiatives and the purchase of data.[273]

266 Ibid.
267 Franks (n 254) 307–10.
268 Duinker and Greig (n 229) 158.
269 Ibid.
270 Ibid 159.
271 Franks (n 254) 40.
272 Ibid.
273 Ibid 41.

The State thus has a role to play in generating and making available broader-based area studies of cumulative impacts to project proponents, or requiring proponents to share information among themselves. The Upper Hunter Cumulative Impact Study and Action Strategy, conducted by the New South Wales Government in the mid-1990s, serves as an example of how a State-led data gathering process can intersect with cumulative assessment at project-level EIA. The study was focused on the cumulative impacts of coal mining in the Upper Hunter Valley Region, a mature and high density mining region.[274] The study incorporated four local government areas and entailed both a qualitative review of potential cumulative relationships among a variety of land uses and the environment, using a set of environmental indicators (thus incorporating a VEC-centred approach), and an analysis of the more significant cumulative impacts using quantitative techniques.[275] Although the study found there were no major cumulative impacts that warranted additional regulatory interventions or restrictions on development at that time, it recommended that the outcomes of the study be used in future EIS and planning studies. Action strategies thus applicable to the coal mining industry in the region thus included the need to address cumulative impacts in EIS preparation, and the need for the State to develop a landscape master plan to coordinate between existing and future mines.[276]

The institutional improvements needed to entrench regionally focused CIA are less clear, although there are a number of recent examples of regional CIAs involving or applying to the mining industry across the actions of assessment, monitoring and management. One of the obstacles to regionally focused action is uncertainty regarding the unit requiring regional assessment (and subsequent monitoring and management).[277] In the case of project-level EIA the unit of assessment – the project – is clear. Regional CIA assessment on the other hand, may be focused on land use plans (thus triggering land use planning legislation), integrated resource plans (thus triggering legislation governing the use of natural resources, inclusive of energy or water), or simply development pressures within a particular region. Surveying the mining-related CIA initiatives that have taken place in Australia, concerns relating to developmental pressures within particular regions appear to be the primary motivating force for conducting CIAs.[278] Pressure from communities,

---

[274] Franks (n 254) 21.

[275] Ibid.

[276] Ibid.

[277] Duinker and Greig (n 229) 159.

[278] Tom Kaveney, *Cumulative Environmental Impact Assessment Industry Guide: Adaptive Strategies* (July 2015) 43. Examples include the Fitzroy Basin Water Quality Program (CIA undertaken in Queensland in 2008 following concerns about mine water

indigenous organizations and environmental justice organizations highlighting developmental pressures could therefore prompt environmental authorities or mining companies to undertake CIAs, even when this falls beyond the purview of statutory obligations.

Over and above the assessment of cumulative impacts, States have a role to play in instigating or participating in institutions set up to monitor and manage cumulative impacts. Drawing on notions of collaborative adaptive management, there are a variety of such institutions emerging in the world, including in mining-related contexts. Examples include the Moranbah Cumulative Impacts Monitoring Group, a collaborative group set up on the basis of a collective agreement to monitor and improve upon the management of cumulative environmental and socioeconomic impacts arising from multiple mining, petroleum and agricultural projects affecting the town of Moranbah in Australia's Bowen Basin.[279] In Canada, Nunavut and the Northwest Territories have a clear policy on and institutional framework for monitoring and managing cumulative effects.[280] The Northwest Territories Cumulative Impacts Monitoring Program, for instance, coordinates, conducts and funds studies that track the collection, reporting and storage of information relating to environmental conditions in the Northwest Territories. Set in place as a result of the requirements of settled Northwest Territory land claims and the MacKenzie Valley Resource Management Act, which stipulate cumulative impact monitoring, the vision of this programme is '[t]o watch and understand the land so that it can be used respectfully forever'.[281] This surely captures a vision of CIA that can inspire and guide mineral resource-rich States the world over.

---

releases and the impacts on water quality in the Fitzroy Basin; CIA of the impact of multiple projects on the salinity of the Hunter River, which led to the Hunter Salinity Trading Scheme; and independent CIA of mining-related impacts on the town of Camberwell, Australia, particularly dust and noise emissions).

[279] See Moranbah Cumulative Impact Group, 'What is the Moranbah Cumulative Impact Group?' http://mcig.org.au, accessed 27 February 2019; and Carol Bond, Jo-Anne Everingham and Daniel M Franks, 'Managing the cumulative impacts of mining through collaboration' (February 2013), paper prepared for the Centre for Social Responsibility in Mining, University of Queensland.

[280] Edgar Tovilla, 'Reviewing Canada's cumulative effects assessment guidelines for the metal mining sector' *Hazmat & Remediation* 24 October 2017 https://esemag.com/hazmat-remediation/reviewing-canadas-cea-guidelines-for-the-metal-mining-sector/, accessed 27 February 2019; NWT CIMP, *Cumulative Impact Monitoring Program: Action Plan 2016–2020* (September 2015).

[281] NWT CIMP (n 280) 1.

2.4 Participation and Consultation: The State as Promoter of Democratic Environmental Decisionmaking

The State's role to promote democratic environmental decisionmaking through participation and consultation is a key pillar of the dominant model for mining and EA. This role could bolster the State's protective function under the double movement, giving people themselves a voice against the impingements of the market upon society. However, as the ensuing discussion shows, States and mining companies have generally eschewed the more far reaching forms of participation in EA that could democratize and decentralize mine-related decisionmaking in favour of more anodyne forms of participation associated with 'community engagement' or 'meaningful engagement'.

'Environmental issues are best handled with the participation of all concerned citizens' – so begins Principle 10 of the 1992 Rio Declaration.[282] Together with access to information and access to justice, participation has been heralded as one of the key aspects of neoliberally inspired notions of environmental governance.[283] But public participation also has a longer history as part of EA. The system in which the NEPA system was conceived already provided for an array of participation rights – detailed notice and comment procedures under the Administrative Procedures Act, substantial statutory and judgemade participation rights and the US Freedom of Information Act, which provided public interest groups with a lever to extract information from the government.[284]

The institutionalization of participation rights in EA affects the relative power of groups in the decisionmaking process because it crystallizes their expected benefits of action. Where interest groups are able to participate in policy and decisionmaking processes as a matter of right, they have greater incentives to do so, as the costs of participating are lowered.[285] Stronger and more pervasive participation rights lead to potentially decentralized policymaking and decisionmaking. Green brings this into sharp relief by contrasting the ability of the public to participate in environmental governance in Canada and the United States during the 1970s and 1980s. Until the mid-1980s the Canadian system entrenched fewer participation rights and fewer points of access, with the result that environmental governance was characterized as relatively closed and informal, 'providing industry with considerable power to

---

[282] *Rio Declaration on Environment and Development* (1992) www.unesco.org/education/pdf/RIO_E.PDF, accessed 27 February 2019.

[283] UNEP, 'UNEP implementing Principle 10 of the Rio Declaration'.

[284] Andrew J Green, 'Public participation, federalism, and environmental law' (1999) 6 *Buffalo Environmental Law Journal* 169, 177.

[285] Ibid 174.

influence policy while leaving the public without any serious manner in which to access policy-makers'.[286]

From the 1990s onwards increasing prominence was afforded to public participation in EIA theory and practice, spurred on by new thinking on deliberative democracy, collaborative rationality and environmental justice.[287] Formulations of EA 'best practice' routinely assert that EA processes are intended to be open and participatory, allowing various experts and members of the public to be consulted and to voice their concerns.[288] The overwhelming view from the literature is that public participation is highly desirable and a key area of focus for scholars and practitioners to suggest ways in which it can be made more effective.[289]

The assumed benefits of public participation are also evident in discourses of mining dissent. Commenting on the inadequacies of public participation at the Rito Seco mine in the USA, for example, Smith states: 'It is widely thought that a useful tool in the fight for environmental justice is increasing the public involvement of previously disadvantaged communities in the political processes surrounding the management of the environments they live in.'[290] Public participation is associated with multiple benefits that are assumed to be obvious and substantial, such as sharing information, filling information gaps, providing space for the contestability of projects, strengthening the democratic process, empowering communities, promoting social learning and avoiding litigation.[291]

Given the wide range of benefits attributed to participation and consultation, it is unsurprising that there are differences in terms of how States institutionalize public participation for mining-related EA.[292] The public participation mandate for EA typically derives from the national mining or EA or management law, which must be viewed within the larger statutory and constitutional

---

[286] Ibid 172.

[287] Morgan (n 7) 9.

[288] Jeffrey Thomson, 'The duty to consult and environmental assessments: A study of mining cases from across Canada' (2015) Thesis presented to the University of Waterloo (Ontario) in fulfilment of the requirements for the degree of Master of Environmental Studies, 27–8.

[289] Ciaran O'Faircheallaigh, 'Public participation and environmental impact assessment: Purposes, implications and lessons for public policy making' (2010) 30 *Environmental Impact Assessment Review* 19.

[290] Everett Smith, 'The Rito Seco mine and inadequacies in public participation' (November 2016), https://sites.coloradocollege.edu/ejsw/tag/public-participation/ accessed 27 February 2019.

[291] Ibid.

[292] George (Rock) Pring, 'The law of participation in mining and resources development' (December 2001) Report commissioned by the MMSD of the IIED.

framework for participation rights in a particular mineral-rich jurisdiction. States usually require that mining proponents prepare and submit reports on environmental baseline data, impacts and management programmes, but differ according to whether public participation in the EA process is mandatory, or at the discretion of the competent authority.[293] While some States also establish project or stakeholder engagement groups to conduct or oversee the assessment,[294] in most States it is conducted by apparently 'independent' consultants. States also differ quite dramatically in the extent to which EA documents are freely available to the public,[295] provided upon request or application or closed to public scrutiny. Public participation is conducted during the preparation of the reports and/or immediately after they have been submitted to the authority. Many countries also allow for public participation during the scoping phase of the EA process.[296] In some mineral-rich jurisdictions a public hearing is mandatory, while in others it is only required if the project is contentious.[297]

In both developing and developed mineral-rich jurisdictions, however, the State's legal framework for public participation has been criticized as ineffective. In the Philippines, for example, Ingelson *et al* highlight the following shortcomings in the EIA system: the discretionary nature of public hearings; the narrow definition of who may participate to exclude parties that are not directly affected; failure to disseminate the results of the impact assessment, as the findings of environmental impact studies are still treated as confidential;

---

[293] In British Columbia, for example, the Executive Director determines the scope, procedure and methods of the environmental assessment, including the persons and organizations (including but not limited to the public), first nations, government agencies, and (if warranted) the neighbouring jurisdictions a proponent must consult (Environmental Assessment Act, 2002, section 11(f)). This discretion extends to the means by which persons and organizations are to be provided with notice of the assessment, access to information during the assessment and opportunities to be consulted.

[294] In Western Australia, for example, the EPA established a Stakeholder Reference Group (SRG) comprising representation of governmental, industry and civil society groups in the areas of conservation, health and water; planning; the resources industry; and other industry. The SRG provides feedback to the EPA on issues of process, policy and performance, including the EA process (see www.epa.wa.gov.au/stakeholder-engagement, accessed 27 February 2019).

[295] In Western Australia, for example, the Environmental Protection Authority (EPA) publishes all documents for public comment on its consultation hub. See Environmental Protection Authority, Government of Western Australia, 'EPA consultation and public comment' https://consultation.epa.wa.gov.au, accessed 27 February 2019.

[296] Zambian Environmental Protection and Pollution Control (Environmental Impact Assessment) Regulations, 1997 (Statutory Instrument No. 28 of 1997), reg. 8(2).

[297] Environmental Protection and Pollution Control (Environmental Impact Assessment) Regulations, 1997 (Zambia), regs 18–19.

and failure to disseminate the results of impact studies in the language of affected parties.[298] Baker and McLelland developed a detailed framework to evaluate the effectiveness of First Nations' participation in British Columbia's environmental assessment process (prior to its 2002 reform).[299] Examining First Nation participation in three mining developments (Mt Milligan, Kemess and Huckleberry), they found that all three cases failed to achieve procedural, substantive and transactive efficacy.[300] A later review of environmental assessment in British Columbia found that the credibility of the process was questioned by the majority of citizen participants.[301] The major concerns highlighted by this 2010 review were summarized as '[c]onsultation is not simply telling people what you intend to do and then listening to their comments' and questions over the 'perceived sincerity' of the dialogue.[302] These concerns emerged from a host of State action and nonaction, such as a lack of State response to correspondence from the public, reluctance to extend review and comment procedures in technically complex projects with voluminous documents, refusal to allow concerned citizen group representatives to attend working group meetings, refusal to hold public meetings in the main population centres affected by developments, failure to ensure that relevant documentation is made publicly available and a lack of participant funding resources to level the playing field.[303]

O'Faircheallaigh challenges the idea that the central issue is how to make public participation more effective, and highlights the problem of pursuing multiple objectives.[304] Different objectives involve different concepts, activities and consequences (contrast providing access to information with promoting social learning, for example); public participation is usually invoked in the highly charged political environment of authorizing contentious projects, which places limits on the range of potential benefits such processes can achieve; some objectives are complex and admit a wide variety of implementation approaches (for example, allowing community aspirations to be taken

---

[298] Allan Ingelson, William Holden and Meriam Bravante, 'Philippine environmental impact assessment, mining and genuine development' (2009) 5(1) *Law, Environment and Development Journal* 1.

[299] Douglas C Baker and James N McLelland, 'Evaluating the effectiveness of British Columbia's environmental assessment process for First Nations' participation in mining development' (2003) 23 *Environmental Impact Assessment Review* 581.

[300] Ibid 598.

[301] Mark Haddock, *Environmental Assessment in British Columbia* (Environmental Law Centre, University of Victoria 2010) 38.

[302] Ibid 36.

[303] Ibid 37–8.

[304] O'Faircheallaigh (n 289) 19–20.

into account); and objectives may interact in a manner that is reinforcing or undermining.[305]

To enable more careful thinking about the benefits of public participation, O'Faircheallaigh divides the purposes of public participation into three broad areas that are neither discrete nor precisely delineated: 'Benefits that are associated with public participation as an aid to decisionmaking, which yet remains separate from the participating public (for example, public participation in EIA as a means to provide the public with information, fill information gaps, allow for the contestability or projects, and promote social learning)';[306] 'as a mechanism for constituting the public as a joint decision-maker or collaborator (for example, where the goal of EIA processes is respecting democratic principles, improving democratic practice and capacity, and representing EIA as a pluralistic arena in which the conflicts between representatives of different interests groups are resolved)';[307] and 'as a means for reconstituting decision-making structures (for example, public participation in EIA as a means to empower marginalized groups and shift the locus of decision-making)'.[308]

These broad areas are distinguished on the basis of the level of State control over decisionmaking, with different implications for the State and corporate actors. In the first broad area, public participation is an input to decisionmaking centrally controlled by the State or corporate actors; in the second, the public begins to exert an element of control over decisionmaking but existing decisionmaking structures are assumed to be acceptable and remain unchanged, with the mantra being 'meaningful engagement' rather than public participation as an 'input'; in the third, the goal is to achieve a more equitable distribution of power and to change decisionmaking structures.[309]

This spectrum of public participation benefits is present in narratives on mining-related EA. The picture is rendered more complex, however, by the mining industry's association of public participation with 'community engagement' and 'community development'. In its *Community Development Toolkit*, for example, the ICMM defines 'community development' as '[t]he process of increasing the strength and effectiveness of communities, improving people's quality of life, and enabling people to participate in decisionmaking and to achieve greater long-term control over their lives'.[310] Ensuring consultation and participation is one of a select number of good practice principles for ensuring 'sustainable community development'. A blend of O'Faircheallaigh's

---

305 Ibid 20.
306 Ibid 20–21.
307 Ibid 21–2.
308 Ibid 22–3.
309 Ibid.
310 ICMM, *Community Development Toolkit* (2012) 203.

broad areas of public participation is evident in the ICMM's counsel that communities should be 'actively involved in all stages of project conception, design and implementation, including closure and post-closure'.[311] In addition to ensuring diversity of representation, mining companies must ensure that communities are enabled to 'participate fully' in decisions pertaining to the flow of benefits from the mine. This will be achieved, the ICMM states, through 'concerted stakeholder engagement activities that demystify the mining and metals process, empowering community members to understand the motivations as well as project plans of the companies so that they can make informed choices'.[312] The 'business case' for community development, according to the ICMM, includes an enhanced reputation of mining with the financial community, government and other stakeholders; improved access to ore bodies in challenging environments; easing of the approvals processes for project development, expansion and closure; and the reduction of closure costs and liabilities, among other reasons.[313]

An Australian *Guide to Leading Practice Sustainable Development in Mining* also underlines the point that 'community engagement' is central to risk management in the industry, inclusive of the highest risk that future mining in a particular area will be completely jeopardized. This *Guide* states, for instance, '[f]rom a future operations aspect, it is essential that the company focuses on the community engagement side'.[314] Community engagement is an integral part of community development, the *Guide* explains, although engagement can be undertaken for other purposes, such as addressing community concerns about environmental impacts.[315] The types of activity that give effect to community engagement and development cover the full range of public participation benefits, ranging 'from information provision through to empowerment'.[316]

Such corporate conceptions of public participation benefits almost completely dominate the recent State-led *Due-Diligence Guidance for Meaningful Stakeholder Engagement in the Extractive Sector*.[317] This document was developed under the auspices of the OECD's Declaration on International Investment and Multinational Enterprises by the OECD Secretariat, with

---

311 Ibid 17.

312 Ibid.

313 Ibid 17–18.

314 Australian Centre for Sustainable Mining Practices, *A Guide to Leading Practice Sustainable Development in Mining* (2011) 33.

315 Ibid.

316 Ibid.

317 OECD, *OECD Due Diligence Guidance for Meaningful Stakeholder Engagement in the Extractive Sector* (OECD 2017).

input from an Advisory Panel cochaired by the governments of Canada and Norway and including representation of major extractive industry associations, international NGOs and the Centre for Social Responsibility in Mining.[318] The *Due-Diligence Guidance* provides pointers on risk-based due diligence for meaningful stakeholder engagement in the extractive sector. 'Meaningful stakeholder engagement' refers to 'ongoing engagement with stakeholders that is two-way, conducted in good faith and responsive'.[319] However, the reasons for undertaking meaningful stakeholder engagement in this *Guidance* do not accommodate the powershifting dimension of public participation.

Costanza agrees that mining companies are predominantly interested in participation as a means to obtaining a social licence, rather than as a means to empower participants and truly democratize decisionmaking.[320] However, this may also be a goal of the State, particularly in developing countries where State actors are closely networked with the owners of private capital.[321]

In their study of socioeconomic impact assessment and community participation in the Bowen Basin in Australia, Lockie *et al* report on mining companies' tendency to separate community engagement/participation from public participation conducted as part of EAs.[322] Writing prior to the finalization of the Australian *Guide to Leading Practice Sustainable Development in Mining*, they observed that 'community engagement' did not connote a well defined methodological or legislative framework.[323] Its provenance lay in a 'pragmatic agenda' on the part of the Australian government and industry groups to use consultation processes as a means to factor in community concerns and priorities throughout the mining cycle.[324] Based on a review of impact assessment and community engagement processes in Australia's coal-rich Bowen Basin, they found that while mining companies were undertaking consultation for impact assessment beyond the strict ambit of legislative requirements, 'community participation' was relatively independent of the impact assessment process.[325] While they regarded the emphasis placed on community engagement throughout the lifecycle of the mine as a positive development, they also emphasized that the framing of public participation as community engagement,

---

[318] Ibid 5.

[319] Ibid 18.

[320] Jennifer Noel Costanza, 'Mining conflict and the politics of obtaining a social licence: Insight from Guatemala' (2016) 79 *World Development* 97, 98.

[321] Ibid.

[322] Stewart Lockie *et al*, 'Democratisation versus engagement? Social and economic impact assessment and community participation in the coal mining industry of the Bowen Basin, Australia' (2008) 26(3) *Impact Assessment and Project Appraisal* 177.

[323] Ibid 179.

[324] Ibid.

[325] Ibid 186.

as opposed to democratization, represented an opportunity lost.[326] A State–industry aligned emphasis upon community engagement and community development can thus be seen as resistance to moving to O'Faircheallaigh's second broad area of public participation, where such processes are intended to strengthen democracy.

A distinction between public participation and consultation with Aboriginal and indigenous groups has further complicated the locus of control in EIA decisionmaking. Consultation with and accommodation of Aboriginal and Indigenous People has followed a different trajectory, influenced by the International Labour Organization's Convention No. 169 Concerning Indigenous and Tribal People in Developing Countries, 1989,[327] and the adoption of the principle of free, prior and informed consent.[328] In some mineral jurisdictions the approach to consultation has also been heavily influenced by constitutional development and decisions of the courts, as has been the case in Canada. The potential for a differential locus of control in decisionmaking applies just as strongly in the sphere of consultation as it does to public participation, and even in Canada, where there has been rich development of the concept of consultation with Aboriginal and indigenous groups, it is not evident that consultation has moved beyond the second area of benefits, that is, 'meaningful engagement'.

A stronger indictment against the State is that it is complicit with resource extraction companies in constituting public participation as 'the new tyranny'.[329] There is an extensive literature on how citizen's voices can be weakened when participatory spaces are captured by local elites.[330] Elites dominate discussions in these spaces and influence the State's decisions because they are equipped with better information and education in a context where both the State and community groups may be weakly organized and few accountability mechanisms are in place.[331] World Bank sponsored research has found that elite capture is most likely when citizen participation is promoted by the policy actions of the State and implemented through its bureaucracies.[332] Costanza confirmed this to be the case in her documentation of Guatemalan firm

---

[326] Ibid.

[327] International Labour Organization, 'C169 Indigenous and Tribal Peoples Convention, 1989 (No. 169) 1 www.ilo.org/dyn/normlex/en/f?p=NORMLEXPUB:12100:0::NO::P12100_ILO_CODE:C169, accessed 27 February 2019.

[328] See section 3.4.2 of Chapter 3 for a discussion of the adoption of the principle of free, prior and informed consent (FPIC) in relation to Indigenous Peoples.

[329] Costanza (n 320) 100.

[330] Ibid 99.

[331] Ibid 100.

[332] G Mansuri and V Rao, *Localizing Development: Does Participation Work?* (World Bank 2013) 32.

Cemento Progreso's quest to acquire a social licence to operate in a municipality in Guatemala through participatory democracy.[333]

What can be done to improve participation and consultation in EA processes such that they have a transformative rather than a reinforcing effect on the paradigm of extractivism? There is no shortage of suggestions in the literature. O'Faircheallaigh notes that it is unhelpful to place different forms or levels of public participation into rigidly bounded categories. Rather, the three broad areas of public participation outlined above interact in the politically charged dynamic that inevitably characterizes large resource projects.[334] For example, increased access to information regarding mining projects is likely to raise public awareness of the project and fuel demands for more substantive participation. Although the EIA literature, and the literature on public participation more generally, supports the view that ultimate control over decisionmaking should remain vested with public officials, the central conundrum in public participation processes is that unless the public feels that participation will result in real influence over decisionmaking, they will be reluctant to participate. This reluctance may transcend a particular project or policy area and manifest 'in a general cynicism that makes it very difficult to involve citizens when officials wish to do so and ultimately threatens the legitimacy of government'.[335] Public actors may then find ways to undermine or circumvent existing structures and processes, including independently establishing contact with international technical experts and constituting their own environmental and health tribunals.[336] When crafting public participation regimes, therefore, State officials are not faced with a 'menu' of participation options, but rather with a need to accommodate an ongoing negotiation regarding the terms on which the public will participate.[337] This does not negate the need to be clear about the different forms of public participation and transparent about the motives for constructing participatory spaces.[338]

3. CONCLUSION

This chapter has shown how various forms of EA have developed over the past few decades to mediate mining's impacts on the environment, society and economy. EIA, SIA, SEA, HIA and CIA hold out the promise of expert

---

[333] Costanza (n 320) 109.

[334] O'Faircheallaigh (n 289) 24.

[335] Ibid 25.

[336] See Aguilar-Stoen and Hirsch for an overview of these developments in Guatemala.

[337] O'Faircheallaigh (n 289) 25.

[338] Costanza (n 320) 110.

and rational identification, predication, evaluation and mitigation of impacts. Mining-affected communities and the broader citizenry are supposed to participate in these processes alongside various organs of the State, bolstering democratic decisionmaking and lowering the potential for social conflict. These processes of EA align with the second arm of the double movement and the rapidity of their uptake speaks to a concern to protect society from mining's worst impacts. The State's roles centre upon institutionalizing forms of EA in the first place, using the information generated by these processes to set boundaries relating to where and when mining should take place, and promoting democratic decisionmaking.

The real protection afforded by these processes, however, is frequently only paper thin. A rationalist–technicist approach to EA prevails over more collaborative and consensus-based models that recognize the significance of power relations. In general, States have restricted their gaze to project-level EIA and shied away from identifying and enforcing clear thresholds that could apply spatially (no go areas) or temporally (cumulative impacts). The entire model for EA therefore aligns closely with the growth assumptions of extractivism and neoextractivism and shows little regard for socioecological limits. The State remains centrally positioned as ultimate decisionmaker. Participation and consultation are not robust and it is unclear whether they even function as an aid to decisionmaking, let alone instituting interested and affected parties as joint or even key decisionmakers. In the main, EA processes are front-ended in nature, and their protective ambit wanes as the mineral cycle unfolds from exploration, through development and operation, to closure. It is at this point, as the following chapter explains, that the State must reckon with whether EA has functioned to support longterm development and sustainability.

7. The State and mine closure

1. INTRODUCTION

This is the last of four chapters outlining the State's role in various areas of mining policy, governance and law, selected in order to illustrate Polanyi's conception of the double movement.[1] Thus far, the State's roles in mining property institutions, taxation, and environmental assessment have been examined. This chapter journeys to the end of the mining trajectory and the activities of closure, relinquishment and postclosure monitoring and management.[2]

Mine closure lacks the prestige associated with exploration or the development and operation of a mine: 'The excitement and fanfare that surrounds the opening of a new mine is never present when it finally closes.'[3] If there are negative impacts associated with the growth of mining in an area (the 'doom side of the boom'), mine downscaling and closure is the 'doom side of the doom'.[4] Closure has nevertheless been described as 'the most tangible indicator of sustainable development for the mining industry'.[5] Indeed, closure is arguably the point at which extractivism or neoextractivism is fully and finally laid bare, and the State's roles – as landlord, concessionary, receiver of revenues and environmental custodian – are exposed as a triumph or a sham. There is no shortage of case studies documenting the pernicious aftershocks of mining. Many States also document the numbers of 'orphaned and abandoned'

---

1 See further section 6.1 of Chapter 1.

2 In general, this chapter uses the concept of 'mine closure' to include the activities of decommissioning a mine, relinquishment and postclosure, unless the context indicates otherwise.

3 D Laurence, 'Optimisation of the mine closure process' (2006) 14(3–4) *Journal of Cleaner Production* 285.

4 Lochner Marais *et al*, 'Mine closure, the resource curse, and the Marikana flu: Response to mine downscaling in Matlosana and Matjhabeng' www.erln.co.za/images/jevents/5624bd447aa5e4.90993032.pdf, accessed 28 February 2019.

5 MC Moller, R Flugge and S Anstee, 'Closure – The most tangible indicator of sustainable development for the mining industry: Rio Tinto's approach' (2007) Proceedings of the Second International Seminar on Mine Closure held from 16–19 October 2007 in Santiago, Chile, 199.

mine sites.[6] The price of failure is heavy: as national landlord of mineral resources the State assumes custodianship of such sites and must step in as 'mender of last resort' to address the worst socioecological impacts.

Closure is also the point at which the market disappears. In Polanyi's theoretical framing, it is the point at which land – or the shattered and wasted residues thereof – becomes reembedded within society. To date there is no marketable or tradable basket of rights in closure liabilities, akin, for example, to trade in air emissions. The dominant financial model for dealing with residual and latent closure liabilities is through so-called financial provision or assurance. The corporate form, convenient for raising the capital necessary to undertake mining exploration and exploitation, fails at the gate of mine closure, even as it facilitates a 'pass the parcel' approach to liabilities.

And yet, the idea of restoring mine sites to some level of socioecological functionality has been alive since the late nineteenth century, instantiating the double movement. Over the course of a century, mine closure has emerged as an interdisciplinary field and a dominant governance model for mine closure has become apparent through 'best practice guidance' closely aligned with the sustainable mineral development consensus. As this guidance has crystallized over the past few decades, the State's attempt to protect *itself* from the longterm, and even perpetual, environmental liabilities associated with worked-out mine sites has become apparent. This protection, a limited form of the double movement, has taken the form of enforced closure planning and requirements for various forms of upfront financial guarantees ('financial assurance'). In some regions, the effectiveness of mine closure standards has been tested in commodity downturns, but overall it is far from clear that closure governance protects States from the longterm future liabilities of mined sites. That closure rules are protecting people and planet is even less clear.

This chapter presents the dominant model for mine closure, which revolves around three State roles: a watchdog role during the long period of developing and operating the mine, a relinquishing role at the point of mine closure and a 'mender of last resort' role for abandoned and orphaned mines. As part of its watchdog role the State formalizes integrated closure planning, determines financial assurance requirements, and frames the conditions for mining rights transfers. Relinquishment entails approving compliance with closure requirements, which may also shift responsibility for mining-related liabilities from the private to the public sphere. As 'mender of last resort', the State may undertake a variety of functions, from monitoring compliance with rules relating to the management of postclosure landscapes, to actually undertaking mining rehabilitation work with public funds.

---

6 See the discussion in section 2.3 below.

2. THE STATE'S ROLE IN MINE CLOSURE: PRESENTING THE DOMINANT MODEL

The idea of mine closure has developed differently by region and industry sector and has been driven by both social conflict and broader environmental concerns.[7] In the USA, for example, damage caused to farmland by hydraulic gold mining in California's Sacramento Valley in the 1870s and 1880s prompted farmers to take legal action against the miners.[8] In the 1960s broader environmental concerns were added to natural resource conflicts as a driver of modern ideas of mine closure and increased calls for legislative intervention. From the 1970s onwards, and continuing to the present, many jurisdictions incorporated mine closure provisions into their mining laws to respond to these environmental concerns. But it was not until the 1990s or 2000s that many mining jurisdictions passed laws dealing expressly with closure issues.

Mine closure expanded rapidly as an interdisciplinary field during the latter half of the twentieth century. More than 170 articles on mine reclamation and more than 200 articles on acid mine drainage (AMD) had already been published by 1960, but the field expanded most rapidly from the 1990s onwards. By 2015 there were more than 4000 papers on mine closure and a few dedicated conference series.[9]

Bibliometric analysis of the extensive mine closure literature reveals a shift away from reclamation as a master concept, to a preference for 'mine closure' and 'remediation'. Hockley and Hockley proffer two reasons for this shift: there is now a more indepth appreciation and consideration of the myriad physical, chemical and socioeconomic factors that feature in the stabilization of a site and its ultimate closure; and increasing emphasis on chemical contamination has led to mine sites being thought of as problems necessitating 'remediation'.[10] Lately, there have been calls to shift the emphasis again – to the 'regeneration' of mining sites – based on the claim that successful mine closures around the world are based on economic occupation of the site. Instead of focusing on stabilizing physical and chemical conditions and reestablishing ecosystems, regulators and companies are now being urged to adopt

---

[7] D Hockley and L Hockley, 'Some histories of mine closure, the idea' in A Fourie *et al* (eds), *Proceedings of the Mine Closure Conference, 2015* (Australian Centre for Geomechanics 2015) 1.

[8] Ibid 2.

[9] Ibid 1, 14. For example, since 2006 the Australian Centre for Geomechanics has convened an annual Mine Closure Conference: see www.mineclosurehub.com accessed 28 February 2019.

[10] Hockley and Hockley (n 7) 5.

an adaptive approach to the end of the mining trajectory that accommodates opportunities for creative human enterprise.[11]

State responsibilities under the dominant model for mine closure merge with those of other roleplayers. The mining industry is expected to play a key role in mine closure, at least insofar as mine closure planning is concerned. The International Council of Mining and Metals (ICMM) has insisted that 'planning for closure needs to be a *core business practice* of mining companies'.[12] Communities are also expected to pull their weight. *Breaking New Ground*, the final report of the Mining, Minerals and Sustainable Development Project (MMSD), for example, exhorted 'communities' to own the process of sustaining ongoing economic activities and 'to understand and manage residual environmental concerns'.[13] Anglo-American's 'Mine Closure Toolbox' notes that sustaining postclosure landscapes is a 'complex challenge' and that 'sustainability beyond mine closure will not happen if not taken up seriously and vigorously by mining companies in partnership with government, NGOs and communities'.[14] Ultimately, it seems, everyone must pull together.

States are nevertheless expected to regulate mine closure through the rule of law and effective State institutions.[15] District and local authorities also come

---

[11] B Harvey, 'The eye of the beholder – Utility and beauty in mine closure' in A Fourie and M Tibbett (eds), *Proceedings of the Mine Closure Conference 2016* (Australian Centre for Geomechanics 2016).

[12] International Council of Mining and Metals, 'Mine closure' www.icmm.com/en-gb/environment/mine-closure, accessed 28 February 2019 (my emphasis). See also ICMM, *Planning for Integrated Mine Closure Toolkit* (2008) 4 (henceforth *Integrated Mine Closure Toolkit*).

[13] International Institute for Environment and Development and World Business Council for Sustainable Development, *Breaking New Ground: Mining, Minerals and Sustainable Development* (Earthscan 2002), 220 (henceforth *Breaking New Ground*).

[14] Anglo American, *Mine Closure Toolbox* version 2 (2013) www.angloamerican.com/~/media/Files/A/Anglo-American-PLC-V2/documents/approach-and-policies/environment/toolbox-main-brochure-lr.PDF, accessed 28 February 2019.

[15] The policy advice on this topic is constituted by diverse sources. The World Bank, *Strategy for African Mining* (1992) World Bank Technical Paper No. 181 (henceforth *Strategy for African Mining*) at 50 acknowledged the problem of 'mine reclamation' and outlined some suggestions for meeting reclamation costs through charges on the company, or sharing the costs between companies and the government. The 1996 *Mining Strategy for Latin America and the Caribbean* (1996) World Bank Technical Paper No. 345 xiii (henceforth *Strategy for LAC Mining*), used the concept of mine closure and noted the need for early consideration of closure issues (at xiv), and the importance of consultation (at 105). In line with the 'toolkit' and 'toolbox' approaches developed by the ICMM and others, the World Bank published its *Towards Sustainable Decommissioning and Closure of Oil Fields and Mines: A Toolkit to Assist Government Agencies* version 3.0 (March 2010) (henceforth *World Bank Mine Closure Toolkit*).

into focus, and they are expected to play a key role in maintaining physical and social infrastructure in postclosure areas.[16]

Some developed jurisdictions began elaborating mine closure regimes during the 1970s,[17] but many only left the starting blocks during the early 1990s,[18] or even in the 2000s.[19] The relative immaturity of mine closure regimes is reflected in the World Bank's 1996 *Strategy for LAC Mining*, which held:

> Host country governments have an interest in assuring that exhausted mines will be closed in an environmentally sound manner; that the mine infrastructure will become part of the national or regional infrastructure, or else decommissioned as appropriate; and that mining communities will be able to sustain themselves or relocate. The mining regulations of the LAC countries reviewed for this study do not appear to contemplate a role for the mining ministries in assuring that a proper coordinating mechanism for this planning and transition process exists and functions effectively; nor how closure costs are to be borne or shared between the private and public sectors. Additional reflection and work should be devoted to this issue.[20]

There is no global standard on mine closure and reclamation management – a state of affairs that recently prompted the International Organization

---

The MSSD commissioned a working paper on 'Mining for the Future' which includes appendices on mine closure and abandoned mines (see D van Zyl *et al*, 'Mining for the future: Main report' (April 2002) Working Paper No. 68, Mining, Minerals and Sustainable Development Project). *Breaking New Ground* addresses mine closure at a number of points with the main discussion occurring in Chapter 9, under the banner of 'Local Communities and Mines'.

The ICMM commissioned a study on public policy measures relating to mine closure in 2015 (the author was part of the research team), but this report was never made public. The ICMM has not issued a position statement on mine closure, but has developed 'toolkit' resources for integrated closure planning and financial assurance, respectively.

[16] *Breaking New Ground* (n 13) 220–21.

[17] The western states in the USA were among the first to enact reclamation/rehabilitation legislation to improve control over their extensive mining industries. California's Surface Mining and Reclamation Act was enacted in 1975. In the USA, the federal Surface Mining Control and Reclamation Act was enacted in 1977, but it only regulates the environmental effects of coal mining.

[18] Arizona (Mined Land Reclamation Act, 1994), for example, only finalized mine closure-specific legislation in the 1990s. In South Africa, environmental rehabilitation of the environment was only elevated to the level of a policy objective of the primary mining legislation in 1991 with the enactment of the Minerals Act.

[19] Chile, the global leader in liberalized property rights for minerals and mining, only enacted closure-specific legislation after 2010 (Law No. 20,551 Regulating Closure of Mines and Mining Installations, in force from 11 November 2012; and Decree 21 approving Regulation, 22 November 2012).

[20] *Strategy for LAC Mining* (n 15) 22.

for Standardization (ISO) to convene a subcommittee for this task.[21] Industry-driven initiatives on mine closure best practice,[22] particularly from Canada[23] and Australia,[24] are also only partially reflected in the mining laws of the world.

Notwithstanding the immaturity and partiality of mine closure guidelines and policy and legal frameworks, consensus on the variety of State closure roles is discernible. The following section outlines the first of these, namely the State's watchdog role over integrated mine closure planning, financial assurance and the transfer of extraction authorizations.

2.1 Integrated Mine Closure Planning, Financial Assurance and Transfers: The Watchdog State

2.1.1 Integrated mine closure planning

The dominant model for mine closure rests on the assumption that the State will entrench, oversee and enforce legal requirements to develop a closure plan

---

21 Corinne Unger, 'Mirror-committee for development of ISO standards on "mine closure and reclamation standards" initial meeting for Australia' *AusIMM Bulletin* (July 2017).

22 Anglo American (n 14).

23 Canada has more than 10,000 orphaned and abandoned mines. In 1999 and 2000 a number of stakeholders requested the Mines Ministers of Canada to convene a multistakeholder workshop to discuss a number of issues pertaining to orphaned and abandoned mines. A National Advisory Committee representative of federal/provincial/territorial governments, the mining industry, environmental nongovernmental organizations and Aboriginal people and their communities has been mandated since 2002 to conduct research on the topic of orphaned and abandoned mines in Canada and elsewhere. For an overview of the NOAMI initiative see www.abandoned-mines.org/en, accessed 28 February 2019. For a succinct account of best practice from this initiative see WR Cowan, WO Mackasey and JG Robertson, *The Policy Framework in Canada for Mine Closure and Management of Long-Term Liabilities: A Guidance Document* (2010) National Orphaned/Abandoned Mines Initiative.

24 See Australian and New Zealand Minerals and Energy Council (ANZMEC) and Minerals Council of Australia (MCA) *Strategic Framework for Mine Closure* (2000). During the early 2000s, the Australian government developed a number of guideline documents on mine closure under the Leading Practice Sustainable Development Programme for the Mining Industry (see www.archive.industry.gov.au/resource/Programs/LPSD/Pages/default.aspx, accessed 28 February 2019). Australian state governments and/or state mining industry associations have also developed policies and guidelines documents on mine closure. See, for example, the *Guidelines for Preparing Mine Closure Plans* (2015) jointly developed by the Department of Mines and Petroleum and Environmental Protection Authority, Government of Western Australia www.dmp.wa.gov.au/Documents/Environment/ENV-MEB-121.pdf, accessed 28 February 2019; or the Queensland Mining Council's *Guidelines for Mine Closure Planning in Queensland* (2001).

as a 'living document' throughout the mining cycle. This reinforces the State's protective role under the double movement, affording it a long lead time to oversee management of the worst longterm impacts of mining in a locality. Policy recommendations from Canada's National Orphaned and Abandoned Mines Initiative (NOAMI) provide an implicit, sample statement of this State role:

> Closure plans must be required to ensure that mine sites will be returned to a safe, physically and chemically stable state … Because a mine site evolves with time, initial closure plans may be conceptual subject to amendment or revision on a periodic basis. In this regard closure plan development and implementation must be assured with a competent inspection and enforcement program.[25]

This stance on closure plans is mirrored in the mining industry's policy guidance on 'integrated mine closure'. As advocated by the ICMM, integrated mine closure has at least three forms of integration. Operational integration requires that closure planning should be integrated into the systems and decisionmaking processes that support a mining operation, and not be undertaken as a separate process tagged onto a project as it nears the end of its cycle.[26] Temporal integration requires mining companies to commence with closure from the earliest stages of a mining project, and then extend the overall phases of the mine cycle to cover exploration, prefeasibility, feasibility, construction, operation, decommissioning, closure and postclosure.[27] In line with the NOAMI policy statement above, the ICMM's guidance on operational and

---

[25] Cowan (n 23) 47. The World Bank's *Mine Closure Toolkit* (n 15) similarly includes as an essential element of a mine closure policy and regulatory regime the development, approval and periodic updating of appropriately scoped decommissioning and closure plans as a condition of exploration and resource exploitation permits (see T1-11).

[26] ICMM, *Integrated Mine Closure Toolkit* (n 12) 8.

[27] Ibid 10. Closure planning from mining inception is in line with research confirming that early decisions in the process of developing a mine can critically influence postmining outcomes. Although project proponents are usually only required to submit formal closure plans to regulatory authorities at the feasibility stage of a mine, actions impacting on the cost and effectiveness of closure already take place during the exploration and prefeasibility stages. For example, while reconnaissance exploration is largely nonintrusive, advanced stages of exploration usually involve a more concentrated drilling programme, leading to land disturbance and associated impacts. For example, already at this stage, there are a number of common procedures that should be taken to minimize these impacts, such as locating fuel storage and refuelling facilities away from watercourses and constructing appropriate retaining walls (bunding); stockpiling topsoil from cleared areas for rehabilitation use at a later stage; restricting the use of heavy road transport and construction equipment to established access tracks (to minimize soil compaction); and locating drillholes in a manner that avoids unneces-

temporal integration centres on progressively more detailed closure plans, commencing with a 'conceptual closure plan' at the exploratory stage that transitions to a detailed closure plan through annual processes of review.[28] As the project nears its end, mining companies are supposed to develop decommissioning and postclosure plans to ensure that closure goals have been met.[29] Stakeholder integration, finally, requires mining companies to incorporate the expectations of communities and 'other stakeholders' in closure planning processes. Other stakeholders include local government, nongovernmental organizations and regulators.[30] An integrated approach 'requires the active participation of local communities in planning and implementation of actions, so that lasting benefits can be recognized'.[31] Stakeholder integration also has an extended temporal component. Communities and other stakeholders serve as a sounding board for the ongoing testing of assumptions and recommendations 'to match evolving social, economic, environmental conditions and expectations'.[32] According to the ICMM, ongoing stakeholder consultation on closure risks and postclosure goals is thus critical, facilitated by transparency and ease of communication.[33]

A number of States require mining proponents to submit mine closure plans at the time of submission of an application for an exploration or exploitation authorization, or as part of the environmental impact assessment requirements associated with such authorization. For example, in Western Australia an application for a mining lease must include a mining proposal, which is defined as inclusive of a 'mine closure plan',[34] and in Indonesia mining title holders must submit a reclamation and postmining plan at the time of submitting an application for a licence.[35] In British Columbia, no work may start in, on or about a mine without a permit issued by the chief inspector of mines.[36] At the time of submitting a permit application, a mining proponent must also file 'a program for the conservation of cultural heritage resources and for the

---

sary tree felling. See CH Leiner, KP Hammerschmid and IF Bell, 'Environmental management plans to reduce mine closure costs' (1995) *PACRIM Congress 1995* 333.

[28] ICMM (n 12) 23ff.

[29] Ibid 43.

[30] Ibid; Commonwealth of Australia, *Leading Practice Sustainable Development Program for the Mining Industry* (2015) 99.

[31] ICMM, 'Integrated mine closure' www.icmm.com/en-gb/environment/mine-closure/planning-for-integrated-mining-closure, accessed 28 February 2019.

[32] Ibid.

[33] Ibid; see also ANZMEC and Minerals Council of Australia (n 24) 1–4 on 'stakeholder involvement' in mine planning.

[34] Mining Act, 1978 (Western Australia), section 70O.

[35] Mineral and Coal Mining Law, 2009 (Indonesia), Article 99.

[36] Mines Act 1996 (British Columbia, Canada), section 10(1).

protection and reclamation of the land, watercourses and cultural heritage resources affected by the mine'.[37] The owner, manager or agent of the mine must submit operational reclamation plans for the ensuing five years, a conceptual final reclamation plan for the closure or abandonment of all aspects of the mining operation and an annual report of reclamation and environmental monitoring.[38]

In Queensland and South Africa, planning for closure is an integral part of the environmental assessment process. South Africa's 2014 environmental impact assessment regulations require submission of a closure plan for both mining exploration and exploitation projects, which must include details of financial provision for rehabilitation, closure and postclosure of mining operations.[39] In Queensland, mining proponents must submit applications for progressive and final rehabilitation approvals under the environmental protection legislation, which requires compliance with statutorily defined environmental values for 'ecologically sustainable development'.[40]

In their review of mine closure institutional frameworks in Australia and Africa, Murdoch *et al* found that all of the jurisdictions examined had specific regulations on mine closure and/or environmental assessment 'with the broad intention that it occurs early in the development planning and assessment cycle with appropriate refinements and updates occurring during mining operations especially as the closure period draws near'.[41]

While not exhaustive, this brief review of State practice on closure planning demonstrates how some States have at least formally heeded the 'best practice' of integrated closure planning. The legal obligation to consider closure upfront speaks of rigour, foresight and precaution that bolsters the State's protective role. But legislated closure planning ultimately serves as a thin and fragile veneer to address the profound and far reaching changes mining that inflicts on the environment, society and economy. A generic, statutorily prescribed mine closure planning process also downplays the fact that there is no 'one size fits all' template for managing the intractable environmental, social and economic problems that arise when mines near the end of their cycle.[42]

---

[37] Ibid.

[38] Health, Safety and Reclamation Code for Mines in British Columbia, 2008, Article 10.1.4 (5), (6), (7).

[39] Environmental Impact Assessment Regulations, 2014 (South Africa), regs 19(5), (6).

[40] Environmental Protection Act, 1994 (Queensland, Australia), section 125.

[41] A Morrison-Saunders *et al*, 'Integrating mine closure planning with environmental impact assessment: Challenges and opportunities drawn from African and Australian practice' (2016) 34(2) *Impact Assessment and Project Appraisal* 117.

[42] J Stacey *et al*, 'The socio-economic aspects of mine closure and sustainable development: Literature overview and lessons for the socio-economic aspects

What institutional controls need to be in place for closure planning to transition mined landscapes into sustainable postclosure States? Much will depend on the actual content of the plan, as well as inclusivity, progressive rehabilitation and enforcement, as discussed below.

2.1.1.1 Mine closure plan content

States differ widely in their approach to prescribing the substance of mine closure plans, a matter that is closely interwoven with the level of control States choose to exercise over the formulation of closure objectives, standards and/or the specification of the postmining land use.

Some States have expressly endorsed a 'risk-based approach' to mine closure planning. The mining industry has supported this approach, but there are differing emphases among the various industry guidelines. In Australia and New Zealand the *Strategic Framework for Mine Closure* (2000) urges a risk-based approach as a basic principle of closure planning to ensure the physical and chemical stability of mined sites.[43] A risk-based approach, involving 'technical review and analysis of risk and cost benefit in both engineering and environmental terms', will reduce both cost and uncertainty, it is argued.[44] Later on, a sense of the *type* of risks deemed most significant can be gleaned from the recommended 'Typical contents of a closure plan'.[45] While cautioning that mine closure plans must always take into account the 'unique environmental, economic and social properties of the operation', the ANZMEC and MCA suggest that public health and safety and the 'environmental effects' of mining operations are the most salient risks. These risks highlight the physical and chemical stability of disturbed sites. This also reduces the need for longterm monitoring and maintenance on the part of mining companies.[46] The need for mine closure planning to ensure a 'safe, physically and chemically stable state' is also emphasized in the Canadian NOAMI guidelines.[47]

It bears emphasizing that ensuring the physical and chemical stability of mined sites into perpetuity is in itself an enormous undertaking. Contrary to the common assumption that mining is a temporary land use, mining intersects with land in a manner that disrupts geotechnical stability, flows of surface and underground water and the dispersal of airborne contaminants over long periods of time. One of the major risks for perpetual maintenance and care is

---

of closure – Part 1' (2010) 110 *Journal of the South African Institute of Mining and Metallurgy* 379, 380.

[43] ANZMEC and Minerals Council of Australia (n 24) viii.

[44] Ibid 5.

[45] Ibid 7.

[46] Ibid.

[47] Cowan (n 23).

the potential for AMD. AMD occurs when 'sulphidic rock and soil materials oxidize with the assistance of moisture and bacterial action to generate sulphuric acid solutions, which in turn may dissolve and transport metals'.[48] The acidity of the solution, the sulfates and the mobilized heavy metals can wreak havoc on the environment, human and animal health. AMD management is the feature of postclosure management most likely to be deemed as 'perpetual' in nature. Some jurisdictions consider AMD to be so destructive that they have banned (or are considering banning) the mining of acid-generating potential.[49]

Ensuring the longterm physical and chemical stability of the solid wastes produced by mining is also critical. This applies, in particular, to tailings storage facilities (TSFs). The MMSD cautions:

> Where they [TSFs] are not physically stable, erosion or catastrophic failure may result in severe or long-term impacts. Where they are not chemically stable, they can serve as a more or less permanent source of pollutants to natural water systems. These impacts can have lasting environmental and socio-economic consequences and be extremely difficult and costly to address through remedial measures.[50]

As this quotation indicates, apart from managing erosion and the longterm contamination of natural water systems, TSF failures can result in the catastrophic uncontrolled release of millions of cubic metres of waste material into the environment, potentially resulting in loss of life, damage to property and irreversible environmental degradation. Research indicates that the lower number of TSF failures and incidents since 2000 is countered by an 'emerging and pronounced' trend since the 1960s of 'serious' and 'very serious' failures.[51]

Even the relatively straightforward action of erecting signs and fences around a mined-out site in the interest of public safety can be a challenging venture over the long term, especially if the area is subsequently mined by artisanal and smallscale miners and the signage or fencing is constantly removed.

A 'risk-based' approach to closure planning is not necessarily confined to the physical and chemical stability of mine sites, however. The ICMM *Mine Closure Toolkit* extends risk to a broader range of risk types, albeit that these are narrowly formulated, reflecting a mining company perspective. Six risk types are identified (in no particular order): health and safety, natural environment, social, reputational, legal and financial.[52] Including social risk

---

48 Ibid 12.

49 Ibid, where the authors refer to Wisconsin Act 171, 1997: Mining Moratorium Law.

50 *Breaking New Ground* (n 13) 234.

51 Lindsay Newland Bowker and David M Chambers, 'The risk, public liability and economics of Tailings Facility Storage Failures' (2015).

52 ICMM, *Integrated Mine Closure Toolkit* (n 12) 25.

significantly extends the range of considerations meriting attention in closure planning processes.[53] 'Typical' social closure risks include unemployment, unemployability, poverty, vandalism of infrastructure and facilities, obstruction and impairment of the community's use of natural resources, sickness and disease, unrest and conflict, uncontrolled artisanal and smallscale mining and the infiltration of criminal elements.[54] Mine closure can lead to a profound deterioration of the social fabric with serious human rights implications.[55]

Even where States have not expressly endorsed a risk-based approach to mine closure planning, the formulation of closure objectives in law affirms a risk hierarchy, either expressly or implicitly. Many mineral-rich jurisdictions now require a core set of risks to be addressed comprising public health and safety, decommissioning of mine infrastructure and physical and chemical stability of the mine site.

Public health and safety concerns manifest in legal obligations to erect fences and signage, remove hazardous materials and seal shafts. Finnish law, for example, requires as 'aftercare measures' for mineral exploration that the holder 'immediately restore the exploration area to the condition required by public safety, remove temporary constructions, and equipment, [and] attend to rehabilitation and tidying of the area'.[56] In Arizona, the law requires reclamation plans for mining to specify postmining land uses and proposed reclamation measures. The latter must include information on restriction of public access to pits, adits and shafts, in addition to information on addressing erosion control and stability, revegetation, conservation and the care of revegetated areas, and ways in which specific wildlife or fish habitats will be rehabilitated.[57]

In some States, the closure objective appears to be limited to public safety requirements – an old model of 'fence and walk away'. In Ghana, the mining law does not include an express provision on rehabilitation, and criteria for obtaining a 'certificate of surrender' simply indicate that the minister must be satisfied that the site is 'in a condition that is safe and accords with good mining practice'.[58]

In line with the objective of ensuring public safety, the dominant State approach to decommissioning mine infrastructure is developed countries is one

---

[53] Ibid 68–9.

[54] See Stacey (n 42).

[55] For a recent human rights-based analysis of risks associated with the declining gold mining industry in South Africa see International Human Rights Clinic, Harvard Law School, *The Cost of Gold: Environmental, Health, and Human Rights Consequences of Gold Mining in South Africa's West and Central Rand* (2016).

[56] Mining Act, 2011 (Finland), section 15(1).

[57] Mined Land Reclamation Act, 1994 (Arizona), section 27-974.

[58] Minerals and Mining Act, 2006 (Ghana), section 67(4)(c).

of removal: removing or demolishing buildings, taking down or demolishing processing facilities, draining pipelines, taking electrical installations out of service, and so on. The New South Wales *Mining Operations Plan Guidelines*, for example, include the statement that '[a]ll non-heritage infrastructure will be removed to ensure the site is safe and free of hazardous materials'.[59] In developing countries, however, mine infrastructure, including roads, may be repurposed for postmining land uses and alternative livelihoods. In Peru, if the community or local, regional or national governments are interested in the alternative and economically viable use of an installation or infrastructure related to a mining unit for the public interest, they may jointly request the operator to exclude such from closure commitments. The further use of such mining infrastructure must not pose risks to human health or the environment. Environmental responsibilities attached to the use and potential closure of such installations lie with the beneficiaries, removing further responsibility from the mining title holder.[60]

More progressive jurisdictions require some level of ecosystem function restoration.[61] The mining law of Indonesia, for example, defines 'reclamation' as 'an activity carried out during the whole phases of mining business to arrange, restore and improve the quality of the environment and ecosystem to enable them to function again according to their appropriation'.[62] Philippine law is even more elaborate in this regard. The law requires every mining contractor to undertake an 'environmental protection and enhancement program'.[63] The environmental protection programme must be incorporated into the work programme that a contractor submits as part of an application for a mining agreement or permit. The law goes on to provide that work programmes 'shall include not only plans relative to mining operations but also to rehabilitation, regeneration, re-vegetation and reforestation of mineralized areas, slope stabilization of mined-out and tailings covered areas, aquaculture, watershed development and water conservation; and socioeconomic development'.[64] Guidelines on mine closure planning in New South Wales, Australia require a commitment to the principles of ecologically sustainable development, with effective rehabilitation as a key component of mine operations. Rehabilitation should, at a minimum, achieve postmining land uses that are

---

59 NSW Trade and Investment, 'ESG3: Mining Operations Plan (MOP) Guidelines' (September 2013), 32.

60 Centre for Sustainability in Mining and Industry, *Draft Review of Current Public Policy Measures relating to Mine Closure* (April 2015) 47.

61 Mined Land Reclamation Act, 1994 (Arizona), section 27-974.

62 Mineral and Coal Mining Law, 2009 (Indonesia), Article 1.26.

63 Mining Act, 1995 (Philippines), section 69.

64 Ibid.

stable, nonpolluting and sustainable. Ecosystem establishment is identified as one of the discrete phases of rehabilitation and ecosystem resilience is included under criteria for completion.[65] When it was enacted, the revised New Mexico Mining Act contained some of the most extensive, specific and substantive performance and reclamation requirements in the western USA.[66] The Act specifically addresses wildlife protection, hydrological balance, stream diversions, surface stability and erosion control and revegetation.[67]

References to addressing social closure risks are rare in the laws of mineral-rich jurisdictions. The need for mining companies to address the socioeconomic aspects of closure are usually cited in very high-level, nonspecific terms. For example, the 'Guidelines for Preparing Mine Closure Plans' in Western Australia simply state that the authorities 'encourage regular engagement between a mining company and the local community(s) throughout all stages of a mine development in order to manage the potential socio-economic and environmental impacts of mine closure'.[68] In Peru, the 'Guide for the Preparation of Mine Closure Plans' advises the conceptual mine closure plan to include information on the socioeconomic problems foreseen, which must be assessed in the various scenarios for mine closure.[69]

South Africa is somewhat of an outlier in requiring mining companies to expressly address social closure risks in a mandatory 'social and labour plan' for the grant of a mining right.[70] These provisions must be seen in the light of South Africa's chronic and serious structural problem of unemployment. Social and labour plans articulate with the objective of the country's mining law to promote broad-based economic empowerment through the socioeconomic development of communities immediately hosting, affected by or supplying labour to mining operations.[71] One of the elements of a social and labour plan is to detail processes relating to retrenchment and downscaling, thus addressing one of the key constituencies of interest in mine closure –

---

65 NSW Trade and Investment (n 59) 39.

66 JR Kuipers, *Hardrock Reclamation Bonding Practices in the Western United States* (National Wildlife Federation 2000) 416.

67 New Mexico Department of Game and Fish, 'Habitat Guidelines for Mine Operations and Reclamation (2004) www.wildlife.state.nm.us/download/conservation/habitat-handbook/project-guidelines/Mining-Guidelines.pdf, accessed 28 February 2019.

68 Department of Mines and Petroleum and Environmental Protection Authority, Government of Western Australia (n 24) 28.

69 Centre for Sustainability in Mining and Industry (n 60) 43.

70 Mineral and Petroleum Resources Development Act Regulations, 2004 (South Africa), reg. 43.

71 Mineral and Petroleum Resources Development Act, 2002 (South Africa), section 1.

employees. In the social and labour plan, mining rights applicants must detail 'mechanisms to save jobs losses and a decline in employment',[72] alongside providing 'alternative solutions and procedures for creating job security where job losses cannot be avoided'.[73] The mine is also required to establish a 'Future Forum' to oversee downscaling and retrenchment.[74] Extending the scope of concern, regulations also require that mining companies 'ameliorate the social and economic impact on individuals, regions and economies where closure of the mine is certain'.[75] The efficacy of these provisions, however, is questionable.[76] Apart from South Africa, the closure risks suffered by mining employees (redundancy and retrenchment) would generally fall under relevant labour laws. These laws are unlikely to address the specific working conditions of mineworkers.

Recent South Africa litigation on the occupational diseases of silicosis and tuberculosis starkly illustrates how mining companies have been forced to bear liability for risks traditionally carried by workers and the State. Following a groundbreaking constitutional judgment that allowed for sick workers to claim compensation from mining companies under the common law,[77] representatives of tens of thousands of mineworkers instituted a class action against more than 30 companies engaged in the gold mining industry. The court certified the class action in a resounding success for the mineworkers,[78] paving the way for an historic and unprecedented settlement between some of the gold mining companies and workers.[79] Illustrating how longterm liability can extend beyond the closure of the mine, and of the mine site, these developments support the business case for social closure risks to be addressed more explicitly in mine closure planning.

---

[72] Mineral and Petroleum Resources Development Act Regulations, 2004 (South Africa), reg. 46(d)(ii).

[73] Ibid reg. 46(d)(iii).

[74] Ibid reg. 46(d)(i).

[75] Ibid reg. 46(d)(iv).

[76] The Centre for Applied Legal Studies, University of the Witwatersrand has undertaken extensive work on the design and implementation of social and labour plans. See their research at www.wits.ac.za/cals/our-programmes/environmental-justice/social-and-labour-plans/, accessed 28 February 2019.

[77] *Mankayi v. Anglogold Ashanti* 2011 (3) SA 237 (CC).

[78] *Nkala & others v. Harmony Gold Mining Company Limited & others* 2016 (5) SA 240 (GJ).

[79] Richard Spoor Inc and Others, 'Media Release: Settlement of the silicosis and TB class action', www.mining.com/wp-content/uploads/2018/05/Occupational-Lung-Disease-media-release-SETTLEMENT-OF-THE-SILICOSIS-AND-TB-CLASS-ACTION03052018.pdf, accessed 28 February 2019. The agreement establishes the 'Tshiamiso Trust' (a Setswana word meaning 'to make good' or 'to correct') to disburse compensation exceeding R5 billion to mineworkers.

Finally, mine closure planning jockeys for position among a variety of planning instruments emanating from the discipline of town planning as well as the newer discipline of environmental spatial planning. National, regional and local level spatial planning instruments associated with these disciplines potentially conflict with each other as well as with any evolving mine closure plan. The dominant model for mine closure planning has little to say about the integration of mine closure planning with broader processes of spatial planning. As a recent review of mine closure policy and law notes, '[t]here are only tenuous linkages in a handful of jurisdictions (the DRC, South Africa, New South Wales) aligning mining planning and permitting with spatial development plans and frameworks developed by different spheres of government, which may lead to significant disconnects post-closure'.[80]

While formal mine closure plans are touted as a means to ensure sustainable and integrated closure, the foregoing review has illustrated the extent of variability in policy guidance and law on the actual content. At the very first hurdle of planning, States are at very different levels in terms of formally acknowledging the full range of closure risks necessary to secure sustainable, postclosure mining landscapes.

2.1.1.2 Progressive rehabilitation

The task of planning is only one element of an integrated mine closure and rehabilitation regulatory framework. Progressively more detailed planning throughout the life of the mine should be accompanied by action in the form of progressive rehabilitation. As developed in the best practice guidance of the sustainable mineral development consensus, progressive rehabilitation gives effect to the preventative principle of international environmental law.[81] The essence of this principle is that rather than responding to environmental catastrophes, it is cheaper, easier and less environmentally damaging to prevent harm from manifesting in the first place.[82]

Progressive rehabilitation 'involves the staged restoration of disturbed areas during the exploration, construction or development and resource extraction phases of [a mining] project, instead of large-scale works at the end of [the] project'.[83] Typical activities include backfilling, establishing a vegetative

---

[80] Centre for Sustainability in Mining and Industry (n 60) 23.

[81] Leslie-Anne Duvic-Paoli, *The Prevention Principle in International Environmental Law* (Cambridge University Press 2018).

[82] Encyclopaedia Britannica, 'Principles of Environmental Law' www.britannica.com/topic/environmental-law/Principles-of-environmental-law, accessed 28 February 2019.

[83] Business Queensland, 'Progressive rehabilitation and certification for an environmental authority' www.business.qld.gov.au/running-business/environment/licences-permits/rehabilitation/certification, accessed 28 February 2019.

cover and testing rehabilitation and waste management techniques.[84] At times, progressive rehabilitation simply involves thoughtful action that may be more costly in the short term but that reduces costs over the long term. As the Australian Government's 'Leading Practice' Guide on Mine Closure explains:

> [W]hen waste rock is being hauled out of an open pit and placed into a landform, it could be transported to an adjacent landform that needs a rock mulch cover over the final landform to reduce erosion. Rather than double-handling the material, the incremental initial cost in transporting it the extra distance is more than compensated for by the resulting cost-effective and timely progressive rehabilitation.[85]

The business case for progressive rehabilitation is therefore not difficult to make. The 'enormous cost' incurred when mining operations are not closed correctly has been well documented.[86] From the perspective of the mining company, tangible benefits include reducing overall final decommissioning and closure costs, allowing space for the trial of rehabilitation measures using an adaptive management approach, avoiding the risk of failure and reducing the required level of financial assurance.[87] Intangible benefits include the goodwill (continuing 'social licence to operate') gained from demonstrating to external stakeholders that rehabilitation is being conducted in a socially responsible manner. Under the dominant model for mine closure, therefore, there is support for progressive rehabilitation.[88]

While many jurisdictions expect mining companies to undertake progressive rehabilitation, it is rare to find an express legal duty in this regard, and rarer still for this duty to be supported by administrative or criminal penalties for noncompliance. Queensland is a jurisdiction where legally enforceable requirements for progressive rehabilitation have been considered as part of a broader review on the adequacy of financial assurance. In Queensland the legal requirement to undertake rehabilitation has taken the form of conditions attached to an environmental approval granted under the Environmental Protection Act, 1994. In 2016 the Queensland Treasury Corporation was commissioned to review the financial assurance system for the resources sector.[89] Worryingly, this review found an increasing gap between disturbed land and

---

[84] State of Queensland, *Better Mine Rehabilitation for Queensland: Discussion Paper* (2017) 14 (henceforth *Better Mine Rehabilitation*).

[85] Commonwealth of Australia, *Mine Closure*, Leading Practice Sustainable Development Program for the Mining Industry (September 2016) 22.

[86] Ibid 21.

[87] Ibid 21–2.

[88] Ibid 5, 22; Government of Western Australia (n 24) 14; *Better Mine Rehabilitation* (n 84) 14.

[89] *Better Mine Rehabilitation* (n 84) 10.

land under rehabilitation: in 2006 the area of disturbed land was only three times greater than areas under rehabilitation; by 2016 areas under rehabilitation had shrunk to only 9 per cent of areas disturbed, and areas of certified rehabilitation represented less than 0.25 per cent of the area of disturbed land.[90] Concerned by the risks this growing discrepancy posed, the review recommended an alternative financial assurance system and a raft of complementary measures to reduce the State's exposure to the financial and environmental costs of unrehabilitated land.[91] 'Enforceable requirements for progressive rehabilitation' was among six elements of a proposed integrated mined land management framework.[92] Under the system of environmental approvals, the enforceability of progressive rehabilitation had been hampered by a lack of information and by failure to specify timeframes.[93] The discussion paper for the overhaul of the Queensland mine closure regulatory project accordingly recommended including actions and time-based milestones for achieving rehabilitation milestones in the new proposed 'Progressive Rehabilitation and Closure Plan'.[94] Following a period of consultation, the Queensland government's finalized Mined Land Rehabilitation Policy states that 'progress and outcomes of progressive rehabilitation activities will be monitored and reported on to demonstrate how successful they have been in achieving progress towards the approved post-mining land form, and to inform corrective action where required'.[95]

As the Queensland model demonstrates, the dominant model for institutionalizing progressive rehabilitation in law is to incorporate rehabilitation requirements as part of the conditions of an environmental authorization. Philippine law serves as an example of this approach. Here the mining regulations provide:

> During every stage of the mining operation, as well as after the termination stage thereof, all open pit work areas, underground workplaces, mine waste and tailings impoundment systems, quarry sites and other mining-disturbed landforms, including those disturbed during exploration, shall be progressively rehabilitated to a condition prescribed in the Environmental Compliance Certificate and/or Environmental Protection and Enhancement Program.[96]

---

[90] Ibid.
[91] Ibid.
[92] Ibid 16.
[93] Ibid 19.
[94] Ibid.
[95] Queensland Government, *Mined Land Rehabilitation Policy* (n.d.).
[96] Revised Implementing Rules and Regulations of Republic Act No. 7942 (Philippines), reg. 167(a).

The lack of any reference to timebound actions in this provision – the problem noted in the Queensland model – is notable.

Some States incentivize progressive rehabilitation through a certification process. For example, under the Queensland Environmental Protection Act, 1994, the holder of an environmental authority for a resource activity can request certification of progressive rehabilitation. If successful, the certification allows a holder to reduce their financial assurance payment.[97] As noted above, however, the 2016 Treasury Corporation review of financial assurance in this jurisdiction found that less than 0.25 per cent of disturbed land had been certified as progressively rehabilitated.[98]

Policy guidance and laws on formal closure planning might instil a sense of confidence that measures are progressively being put in place to secure sustainable postclosure landscapes. However, without an undertaking to secure progressive rehabilitation in line with the mine closure plan's contents, such plans are not optimally effective. Although the dominant model for mine closure supports the notion of progressive rehabilitation, policy guidance and law on this aspect is underdeveloped, and there is little in the way of legal measures to incentivize progressive mining proponents and to punish those who fail to keep their mines in order with a view to the postclosure outcome.

2.1.1.3 Inclusivity in mine closure planning

Inclusivity in mine closure planning is critical for longterm socioecological sustainability. Again, this is no easy task. As literature on mine closure acknowledges, the complex and high risk subject of mine closure 'requires engagement over years, delivers few quick wins, and requires cooperation and understanding between internally and externally heterogenous groups of people'.[99]

Inclusivity evokes the topic of public participation. Front-ended public participation in the form of environmental assessments has been comprehensively canvassed in Chapter 6. The discourses of the sustainable mineral development consensus and responsible mining advocate initial and ongoing stakeholder engagement as best practice, and there are a variety of guidelines that support this.[100] With few exceptions, the laws of mineral-rich States require mining proponents to conduct some form of public participation on environmental

---

[97] Queensland Government, 'Progressive rehabilitation and certification for an environmental authority' www.business.qld.gov.au/running-business/environment/licences-permits/rehabilitation/certification, accessed 28 February 2019.

[98] *Better Mine Rehabilitation* (n 84) 10.

[99] Stacey (n 42) 379.

[100] See for example, Department of Industry, Tourism and Resources (Australia) *Community Engagement and Development* (2009a).

issues when submitting an application for a mining authorization. The ongoing and backend nature of closure-related public participation is neglected, however. Although best practice guidelines and policies exist, the laws of mineral-rich jurisdictions do not generally facilitate the longterm engagement among internal and external stakeholders necessary to secure socioecological sustainability.

As an example of a best practice guideline, the *Strategic Framework for Mine Closure* developed by ANZMEC and the Minerals Council of Australia incorporates principles on stakeholder engagement around closure. These principles call attention to the importance of identifying stakeholders and interested parties, ensuring that consultation is an inclusive process that encompasses all parties and occurs throughout the life of the mine, developing a targeted communication strategy that reflects the needs of stakeholder groups and interested parties, allocating effective resources to the consultation process and working with communities to manage the potential impacts of mine closure, whenever practicable.[101] The Government of Western Australia's *Guidelines for Preparing Mine Closure Plans* appropriated these process-oriented principles.[102]

The ICMM's *Integrated Mine Closure Toolkit*'s guidance on stakeholder engagement adds a touch of realism to substantive consultation outcomes. The ICMM concedes that '[t]he process of engagement may not result in full consensus on closure outcomes'.[103] Nevertheless, engagement can be considered successful if it leads to 'fully informed' decisions.[104] The ICMM emphasizes the need for a 'balanced, realistic and achievable closure outcome that can be funded and supported by the relevant parties'.[105] Their closure guidelines also take the position that while environmental closure outcomes largely rely on the expertise of mining companies, social closure outcomes depend on government and communities playing a 'pivotal role'.[106] This concession highlights one of the central tensions in mine closure – the allocation of responsibility among industry, State and community on different social closure risks, and the extent of responsibility in each case.

These best practice policies and guidelines for engagement around mine closure distinguish between 'external' and 'internal' stakeholders. Western Australia's *Guidelines for Preparing Mine Closure Plans*, for example, iden-

---

[101] ANZMEC and Minerals Council of Australia (n 24) viii.

[102] See Government of Western Australia (n 24) at 27–8, where the *Guidelines* elaborate on each of these principles.

[103] ICMM *Integrated Mine Closure Toolkit* (n 12) 17.

[104] Ibid.

[105] Ibid 20.

[106] Ibid.

tify mine managers, mine planners, engineers and 'relevant staff involved in mine planning and technical/operational decision-making' as internal stakeholders.[107] 'External stakeholders' are identified as regulatory agencies and local authorities, postmining landowners or managers, indigenous/traditional landowners, local community members or groups, interested NGOs, adjacent landholders and downstream users of surface or groundwater resources. Postmining landowners or managers and relevant regulators are identified as 'key stakeholders'.[108] While comprehensive, this list also includes notable omissions – employees and stakeholders as a critical internal stakeholder group, for example. Reference to gender sensitivity in consultation is also notably absent.

However, there are very few examples of States incorporating these guidelines on stakeholder engagement in law, or really attempting to frame the difficult, ongoing process of engagement among heterogenous groups of stakeholders that is needed. Chilean law now requires a 'community dissemination plan' to accompany compulsory mine closure plans. The dissemination plan must inform communities as to closure actions, implementation dates and terms of execution, and specify the methods of dissemination.[109] However, these laws hardly give effect to the notion of ongoing engagement throughout the life of the mine, as the dissemination plan must only be compiled two years before starting the execution of measures for final closure, one year before in the case of partial closure, and thirty days before temporary closure.[110] Western Australia serves as a better example of State-enforced ongoing stakeholder engagement. Here, mine closure plans must include a stakeholder engagement register identifying the rehabilitation and consultation that has been conducted during the period of the plan,[111] along with a stakeholder engagement strategy identifying the stakeholder engagement to be undertaken prior to the submission of the next revision.[112]

Transparency is a necessary precondition for inclusivity in closure planning. In a closure context, this relates to the ease with which closure plans, reports and audits are publicly available. With some notable exceptions,[113] many

---

[107] Government of Western Australia (n 24) at 27.

[108] Ibid.

[109] Law 20, 551 (Chile), Article 13(k) read with Articles 18–21 of the accompanying Regulatory Decree.

[110] Ibid.

[111] In Western Australia mine closure plans must be reviewed and approved by the Department of Minerals and Petroleum every three years or such other period that is stipulated.

[112] Government of Western Australia (n 24) at 26.

[113] For example, South Africa and British Columbia.

mineral-rich jurisdictions in developed and developing countries contain such stipulations. Mine reclamation law in Arizona, for example, incorporates liberal provisions on disclosure of reclamation information.[114] However, the same level of transparency is not always extended to the financial assurance.[115]

Mine closure is a highly emotive topic characterized by relations of dependence and power imbalances. The idea of inclusivity is laudable, and is supported by 'best practice' policy guidance aligned with the sustainable mineral development consensus. However, the institutional controls necessary to secure inclusive decisionmaking among heterogenous internal and external stakeholders over the cycle of a mine are still poorly developed, even as some States have entrenched transparency around mine closure plans.

2.1.1.4 Enforcement

Legal requirements relating to planning, progressive rehabilitation and consultation are only as good as the State enforcement backing them up. State enforcement in this area could take the form of inspections, following up on industry self-reporting, suspension and cancellation of permits and even prosecution of offenders.

The inadequacy and inefficacy of State enforcement in this arena can be illustrated by the case of British Columbia, arguably a better resourced mineral-rich jurisdiction. Here the Auditor-General was engaged to determine whether the compliance activities of two primary provincial mining agencies – the Ministry of Energy and Mines (MEM) and the Ministry of Environment (MoE) – were protecting the province from significant environmental risks.[116] The audit was instigated prior to the disastrous TSF failure at Mount Polley.[117] The audit concluded that the compliance activities of both the MEM and the MoE were failing to protect the province.[118] The MEM's compliance and enforcement programme was found to be limited and as a result the ministry was deficient in carrying out most of its expected regulatory activities, including undertaking inspections, monitoring industry self-reporting and enforcing

---

[114] Mined Land Reclamation Act, 1994 (Arizona), section 27-930.

[115] See the discussion in section 2.1.2 below.

[116] Auditor-General of British Columbia, *An Audit of Compliance and Enforcement of the Mining Sector* (May 2016) 3.

[117] On 4 August 2014, the tailings facility at Mount Polley (an open-pit copper–gold mine in South Central British Columbia) breached its walls, flushing 25 million m^3 of tailings into nearby water resources. The tailings collapse was the largest in Canadian history, and among the largest in the world over the past 50 years: see Erica Shoenberger, 'Environmentally sustainable mining: The case of tailings storage facilities' (2016) 49 *Resources Policy* 119, 124ff.

[118] Auditor-General of British Columbia (n 116) 41, 79.

noncompliance.[119] On reclamation, in particular, the audit found that the MEM did not meet the minimum requirements of its reclamation inspection policy (conducting reclamation inspections at all major mines at least annually),[120] that only a little more than half of mining companies submitted their annual reclamation reports timeously or at all,[121] and that the agency did not have a policy for tracking and reviewing industry-reported data, nor enforcement tools to compel permit holders to submit reports.[122]

In a developing country context, enforcement is even more problematic. In their review of mine closure planning and environmental assessment in Australia and eight African countries, for example, Morrison-Saunders *et al* found that in Africa there were numerous problems with regulation and agency capacity to uphold mine closure laws.[123] These included general capacity development, coordination between different government ministries, limited budget allocations, lack of supervision at provincial and local levels, lack of guidelines and political interference.[124] Without effective enforcement, the integrity of the entire integrated mine closure planning framework falls flat.

2.1.2 Financial assurance

The second major element of the State's watchdog role pertains to setting up a legal frame for financial assurance. The dominant model for mine closure therefore stipulates the provision of some form of regulator-approved financial assurance,[125] to guarantee the availability of sufficient funds for decommissioning of facilities, rehabilitation and the management of postclosure liabilities. States are expected to provide guidance on the forms of acceptable financial assurance in a particular jurisdiction, quantification of the amount, allocation of responsibility and liability when the mining proponent is unable or unwilling to complete the closure process and the conditions under which the financial assurance can be returned to the project proponent.

Financial assurance is only one form of closure cost estimating. The first closure cost estimates were voluntary internal measures used by the mining industry to plan, budget for and manage actual closure activities.[126] According

---

[119] Ibid 41.
[120] Ibid 56.
[121] Ibid 57.
[122] Ibid.
[123] Morrison-Saunders (n 41) 10.
[124] Ibid 11.
[125] Also termed financial provision, reclamation security or reclamation bonding.
[126] JV Parshley, W Bauman and D Blaxland, 'An evolution of the methods for and purposes of mine closure cost estimating' in AB Fourie and M Tibbett (eds), *Mine Closure 2009* (Australian Centre for Geomechanics 2009) 187.

to contemporary guidelines, this internal 'life of mine' estimate has evolved to include existing and future disturbance according to the current mine plan, liabilities associated with any and all legal and nonlegal obligations, project management costs and postclosure monitoring and maintenance costs.[127]

The earliest legal requirements stipulating financial assurance as a form of *State-enforced* closure cost estimating date from the late 1940s.[128] Federal reclamation and financial assurance requirements for hard rock minerals and coal mining came into force in the USA during the late 1970s.[129] Under these rules closure cost estimating became more externally focused, a means to assure the State and the public that sufficient funds would be available for the mining company to meet its statutorily defined closure obligations.[130]

Over the next 30 years, mineral-rich jurisdictions the world over strengthened their laws and regulations or passed similar ones, requiring mining companies to estimate and maintain a form of financial security for responsible closure. For example, in the mid-1980s, the amount of mine reclamation security held by the government of British Columbia was virtually zero. By the year 2000 this had increased to just under CAD 200 million, rocketing to about CAD 1 billion by 2014.[131] In China the first mine reclamation bonding system was introduced in Zhejiang Province in 1998, after China passed its first national law on reclamation in 1986.[132] Globally, the effectiveness of financial assurance standards was not tested until the late 1990s, when a downturn in commodity prices forced a number of mining companies into insolvency.[133] These developments highlighted a number of deficiencies in the financial assurance systems of several jurisdictions, prompting 'an urgent and frank appraisal by government, industry and the public'.[134]

---

127 Commonwealth of Australia (n 30) 78.

128 Linlan Cheng and Jeffry G Skousen, 'Comparison of international mine reclamation bonding systems with recommendations for China' (2017) 4(2) *International Journal of Coal Science Technology* 67, 69. In the USA, Pennsylvania's Anthracite Strip Mining Law introduced a legal requirement for reclamation bonding in coal mining in 1947.

129 United States Forest Service (USFS) Hard Rock Minerals Regulations, 1974 (36 CFR 228); Surface Mining Control and Reclamation Act, 1977 (for coal mines); and US Bureau of Land Management (BLM) Hard Rock Minerals Management Rules, 1980 (43 CFR 3809).

130 Parshley (n 126) 187.

131 BC Ministry of Energy and Mines, *EY Report and Recommendations for BC's Mine Reclamation Financial Security Policy* (February 2017) 11.

132 Cheng and Skousen (n 128) 73–4.

133 Parshley (n 126) 188.

134 Ibid.

The most recent developments in closure cost estimating have been driven by tightened compliance with accounting standards, most notably the International Financial Reporting Standards (IFRS)[135] and the US Generally Accepted Accounting Practice standards. Following the exposure of illegal accounting practices in largescale corporate failures such as Enron, awareness of the potential consequences of financial misreporting forced a number of mining companies to reevaluate their systems for financial reporting of closure liabilities.[136]

In its 2005 review of financial assurance, the ICMM found that many States had strengthened their financial assurance requirements, and that the trend towards higher standards would continue.[137] Nevertheless, the relative novelty of strengthened systems for financial assurance means that many mines may have already been operating within regulatory frameworks that did not assure sufficiency of funds for mine closure, a red flag for States unless adequate transitional measures are put in place.

For the purposes of this work, the policy issues of greatest importance for socioecological sustainability are arguably the form and the quantum of the financial guarantee.[138] While the preferences of the mining industry in respect of these issues are discernible, State practice is quite varied.[139]

2.1.2.1 Form of financial assurance

Two key tensions lie at the heart of determining the form and quantum of financial assurance: the need to provide State and society with reasonable assurance that funds will be available for decommissioning, rehabilitation

---

[135] The IFRS are standards issued by the IFRS Foundation and the International Accounting Standards Board to provide a comparable global accounting language for company accounts. They have been adopted by a number of States, including the European Union and the important mining jurisdictions of Australia, Canada, Brazil and Ghana.

[136] Parshley (n 126) 188. The legally defined term used by the US and other IFRS-compliant countries for financial reporting on abandonment costs is the 'asset retirement obligation' (ARO) cost estimate. This figure 'is the fair value of abandonment liabilities associated with mining and mineral processing operations for financial reporting' (ibid 190). The reporting standards associated with this concept are set out in the Financial Accounting Standards Board Statement 143 (FAS 143) and the London-based International Accounting Standards Board Statement 37 (IAS 37).

[137] ICMM, *Financial Assurance for Mine Closure and Reclamation* (February 2005) 5–6. Countries expressly mentioned included Botswana, Canada (Yukon), Chile, Ghana, India, Peru, South Africa, Sweden and the United States (hereafter *ICMM Financial Assurance Survey*).

[138] Other policy issues include the tax treatment of financial assurance, and the conditions under which monies set aside can be returned to the project proponent (if at all).

[139] *ICMM Financial Assurance Survey* (n 137) 5.

and postclosure care, and the need to ensure that the instrument(s) selected will not unnecessarily burden the liquidity and creditworthiness of the mining proponent. The form of financial assurance is the kind of financial instrument used to provide the guarantee. Broadly, there are two models of financial assurance: (1) individualized checks or bonding requirements, incorporating refundable security payments for a set amount; (2) regular, nonrefundable contributions to a central or pooled fund. The policy advice of the sustainable mineral development consensus has been concentrated on the former, which is the more common approach.

In the case of individualized checks and bonding requirements, the literature distinguishes between 'softer' and 'harder' forms of financial assurance. Softer forms include balance sheet checks, various forms of accreditation, parent company guarantees or self-bonding. 'Harder' financial assurance takes the form of sureties or bonds (guarantees issued by third parties, such as a bank, insurance company, bonding company or other financial institution), a cash deposit made to a responsible government authority or trust funds.[140]

The issue of unduly burdening mining companies is more conspicuous in the case of individualized bonding, as there is no pooling of responsibility. Here harder forms of financial assurance create 'out of pocket' expenses for mining companies, but even softer forms of assurance may impact the credit rating and borrowing ability of the firm.[141] For example, a mining company will not be able to obtain a letter of credit unless it is a subsidiary of a parent company that provides a guarantee,[142] or where it places the full value of the letter of credit on deposit with the bank. Even if a company's credit rating is good enough to obtain the letter of credit in the first instance, the borrowing power of the company will be correspondingly reduced.[143] Harder forms of assurance nevertheless provide the State with greater confidence that closure and postclosure risks will not become a State liability.

Apart from emphasizing the burden of harder forms of financial assurance, the global mining industry has not pushed very strongly for a particular form of assurance. The emphasis has rather fallen on 'fit': ensuring that an instrument is matched to the reclamation needs of the site. The ICMM Guidance on Financial Assurance, for example, advises: 'Each specific type of instrument may be appropriate in a given situation or set of circumstances, depending on the financial strength of the mining company, the amount of the potential

140 Ibid 8.

141 Ibid 12.

142 A letter of credit is an agreement between a mining company and a bank, surety company or insurer in favour of a third party such as a State agency, allowing funds to be drawn down for mine closure.

143 *ICMM Financial Assurance Survey* (n 137) 49.

environmental liability, the timeframe over which the liability is to be extinguished, and so on.'[144]

This nonprescriptive approach to financial assurance is reflected in the wide choice of options some mineral-rich jurisdictions afford mining proponents. For example, in British Columbia, the Chief Inspector of Mines may accept guaranteed investment certificates, cash, irrevocable standby letters of credit and reclamation security bonds as forms of security.[145] Less often, States may refuse some forms of financial assurance. In China, with the exception of Shandong Province, all reclamation bonds must be in cash.[146] In British Columbia and in the state of Montana, self-bonding and corporate guarantees are not acceptable, particularly for sites with longterm liability and water quality concerns.[147]

In a number of developed and developing mineral-rich jurisdictions, the trust fund is the instrument of choice when financial security for longterm treatment obligations is required. A trust fund is an account managed by a third party (the trustee), into which a mining proponent pays funds for a beneficiary (a State or federal agency). An agreement between these three parties outlines the rules for the management of the trust, and the investment and distribution of funds. Conrad summarizes the advantages of trust funds as follows:

> By using this mechanism, the [state agency] and the [mining proponent] can overcome the limits placed on cash accounts and allow for more aggressive investment strategies over time. The accounts normally provide for appreciation of the funds, with contributions from the [mining proponent], and therefore can compensate for increased reclamation costs or mine expansions. They also provide an opportunity to more effectively provide for longer term reclamation obligations, like water treatment.[148]

In the USA coal and hardrock mining sectors, the 'trust fund concept' has been gaining nationwide acceptance.[149] There is increasing awareness that the most common form of financial assurance – surety bonds – are ill suited to ensuring the longterm treatment of pollution discharges as they were usually only issued

---

144 Ibid 12.

145 Government of British Columbia, 'Securities' www2.gov.bc.ca/gov/content/industry/mineral-exploration-mining/permitting/reclamation-closure/securities, accessed 28 February 2019.

146 Cheng and Skousen (n 128) 74.

147 Ibid 70, 72.

148 Gregory A Conrad (Executive Director, Interstate Mining Compact Commission), 'Mine reclamation bonding – From dilemma to crisis to reinvention: What's a state regulator to do?' (February 2014) 5.

149 Ibid.

where there is an expectation of release from liability.[150] The Bureau of Land Management (responsible for regulating hardrock mining on public lands) stipulates the use of a trust fund when hardrock mining operations lead to longterm treatment or other longterm postmining maintenance requirements.[151] In the case of surface coal mining, Pennsylvania, Ohio, Kentucky, West Virginia, Utah, Alaska and Tennessee have explored the use of trust funds for longterm obligations.[152] Philippine law requires contractors to create a mine rehabilitation fund, based on the contractor's approved work programme. This takes the form of a trust fund in a government depository bank and 'must be used for physical and social rehabilitation of areas and communities affected by mining activities'.[153] Failure to fulfil this obligation is visited by the sanction of immediate suspension or closure of the operations of the contractor concerned.[154]

Some forms of financial assurance offer the potential for non-State, third party oversight. For example, banks will only reissue letters of credit after an annual financial review of the company.[155] The role such institutions may play in upholding the efficacy of a system of financial assurance is an unexplored topic of research.

Recently some States have shifted towards central or pooled funds to replace or to function as an alternative to individualized bonding. In the USA, the Surface Mining Control and Reclamation Act allows for bond pools as an alternative bonding system,[156] and bond pools became popular in some states during the 1990s.[157] Typically, the bond pool is maintained by a combination of member contributions and severance tax determined on the basis of the extent of bonded acreage or amount of coal extracted. For example, in Ohio revisions to the coal mining law in 2007 allowed for a dual bonding system, whereby companies with less than five years' experience of mining coal in the state were required to post a full cost bond, whereas those that met the five year eligibility criteria could choose to participate in the bond pool.[158] A biennially fluctuating tax on coal extracted, civil penalties and money from liens and fines is the source of funds for the Ohio bond pool, in addition to a one-off

---

150 Ibid 6.

151 Ibid 5.

152 Ibid.

153 Mining Act, 1995 (Philippines), section 71.

154 Ibid.

155 *ICMM Financial Assurance Survey* (n 137) 48.

156 30 Code of Federal Regulations § 800.11(e).

157 Conrad (n 148) 11. By 2014 at least six states in the USA maintained bond pools as an alternative bonding system.

158 Ibid 12.

participation fee.[159] The idea of spreading the risk among a variety of operators and avoiding the need for full cost bonding is attractive. However, in some states the solvency of bond pools has been threatened by the need for the pool to cover costs of a single operator being held liable for the longterm treatment of unanticipated AMD.[160] The state of Pennsylvania, for example, terminated its bond pool for coal mining operations and has shifted to the use of trust funds for longterm reclamation costs.[161]

In Australia, Western Australia and Queensland have recently introduced reforms that encompass pooled financial assurance systems. In Western Australia, the government introduced unconditional performance bonds (UPBs) during the 1980s as the dominant form of security against State liability for abandoned mines.[162] However, according to the government, the UPB system did not service funds for the true costs of rehabilitating abandoned mines, the financial impact on the mining industry of increasing UPBs to the level of full-cost bonding would have been significant, and UPBs discouraged investment by tying up funds that could have been used for the progressive rehabilitation or the development of new projects.[163] After extensive consultation with government, industry, conservation and community stakeholders, the state passed laws to establish a Mining Rehabilitation Fund (MRF). The MRF is a compulsory, government-administered pooled fund sustained by an annual levy, determined according to the environmental disturbance existing on a tenement on the reporting date.[164] Participation in the MRF does not remove a mining proponent's legal obligation to implement their mine closure plan and undertake rehabilitation.[165] However, MRF funds may be deployed to rehabilitate abandoned mined sites where every effort has been made to trace the responsible parties and recover rehabilitation funds.[166] Interest on MRF funds may be used to rehabilitate sites constituting part of Western Australia's abandoned mine legacy – in the order of some 11,400 sites, for which the

---

159 Ibid.

160 Ibid 11.

161 Ibid 4.

162 Chamber of Minerals and Energy of Western Australia, 'Rehabilitation of mining and resources projects as it relates to Commonwealth responsibilities: Submission to Environment and Communications References Committee' (April 2017) 5; Mining Act, 1978 (Western Australia), section 126.

163 Department of Mines, Industry Regulation and Safety, Government of Western Australia, *Mining Rehabilitation Fund – Guidance* (rev. 2017) 2.

164 Ibid.

165 Mine Rehabilitation Fund Act, 2012 (Western Australia), section 9A.

166 Department of Mines, Industry Regulation and Safety (n 163) 2.

rehabilitation costs were estimated at between AUD 4–6 billion in 2014.[167] The transition phase to the MRF allowed the government to release mining proponents from the UPBs if they made levy payments and were assessed as being of good standing, and the majority of UPBs were released between 2013 and 2016.[168] The State is nevertheless empowered to require a UPB, including where the Department of Mines and Petroleum considers there is a higher risk of a rehabilitation liability reverting to the State.[169] The MRF system was reportedly well received by the mining industry of Western Australia, and there has been a very high rate of compliance with the requirement to report land disturbance (almost 99 per cent).[170] Critics have argued, however, that the annual levy payable to the MRF may be insufficient to encourage exhaustive rehabilitation, and that the implementation of the scheme was poorly timed, when commodity prices were in a downward trend.[171]

Following a comprehensive process of review, Queensland is also introducing reforms to the state's financial assurance system. Financial assurance is currently provided for under the Queensland Environmental Protection Act, 1994, and takes the form of cash or a bank guarantee provided by an Australian-registered bank or other institution approved by the Australian Prudential Regulation Authority.[172] Following consultation, a tailored, risk-based framework will be implemented that entails differentiating between the resource extraction companies based on their risk of insolvency. For example, companies possessing a particular financial strength and level of rehabilitation liability will be allowed to participate in a pooled rehabilitation fund, whereas companies that pose a relatively high risk of default will be required to provide third party surety for the full estimated rehabilitation amount.[173] Other elements of the reform package include an expanded range of surety providers, and improved management of sites in care and maintenance.[174]

---

167 D Klopper and JA Wessels, 'Investigation of Western Australia's rehabilitation fund as a fiscal policy solution for South African abandoned mines' (2017) 117(11) *Journal of the South African Institute of Mining and Metallurgy* www.scielo.org.za/scielo.php?script=sci_arttext&pid=S2225-62532017001100017, accessed 28 February 2019.

168 Chamber of Minerals and Energy of Western Australia (n 162) 5.

169 Ibid.

170 Klopper and Wessels (n 167). See also the notes on Western Australia's abandoned mine programme in section 2.3 below.

171 Ibid.

172 Queensland Government, *Financial Assurance Framework Reform: Discussion Paper* (2017) 1.

173 Ibid 9, 11.

174 Ibid 4.

The foregoing review has shown that while financial assurance is a relatively recent addition to the field of mining regulations, States are taking a variety of measures to protect themselves against liability for longterm treatment and maintenance costs associated with mine sites. Under the double movement, the State's protective role incorporates, at its core, the imperative to protect the State itself from liability. The policy advice of the sustainable mineral development consensus is open ended as to the form of financial assurance. That States are becoming wise to the forms of financial assurance that lower their own risks is reflected in the consensus positions now beginning to crystallize on the best forms of financial assurance for particular kinds of risk.

2.1.2.2 Quantum of financial assurance

The overview of integrated mine closure planning in section 2.1.1 above has shown how the sustainable mineral development consensus encourages States to adopt a risk-based approach to closure planning. And yet the type and range of closure risks recognized in statutory mine closure plan requirements differ widely among States, from requirements to plan for the physical and chemical stability of the site, to ecosystem restoration, to dealing with the social risks of closure. These differing mine planning outcomes, framed by differing visions of the postmining land use, have vastly different cost implications for the mining proponent and the State.

The discursive construct of a 'risk-based approach' has also cropped up in policy work on determining the amount or quantum of financial assurance. For example, in British Columbia, in response to the Auditor-General's damning findings that the MEM and MoE were failing to protect the province from significant environmental risks, the government commissioned auditing firm Ernst & Young (EY) to assist it in ensuring 'a sound, risk-based approach to BC's financial security program for mine site reclamation'.[175] The EY report goes on to describe a 'risk-based approach' in this context as an approach that seeks to provide *reasonable* and not absolute assurance that the taxpayer would not need to contribute to reclamation costs.[176] A key tenet of a risk-based approach, the report states, 'is that absolute assurance over future outcomes is impossible to obtain, and would be prohibitively costly to do so if it was'.[177] But what range of reclamation costs (and associated risks) does financial assurance cover? And whose interests does 'reasonable' assurance protect?

---

[175] BC Ministry of Energy and Mines, *EY Report & Recommendations for B.C's Mine Reclamation Financial Security Policy* (February 2017) 3.

[176] Ibid 11.

[177] Ibid.

A number of mineral-rich jurisdictions link the amount of financial assurance to implementation of the reclamation or environmental rehabilitation plan, plus a period of postclosure monitoring and maintenance. In the Democratic Republic of the Congo, the 2002 Mining Law required any person conducting exploration or mining 'to provide financial security for the rehabilitation of the environment to guarantee or cover the cost of environmental rehabilitation measures'.[178] In terms of regulations issued under this law, the Budget and Finance Plan for implementation of these measures incorporates a postclosure monitoring period of between one and five years.[179] In Arizona the mined land reclamation law provides that in determining the amount of financial assurance the state mine inspector must 'consider the costs of approved reclamation measures stated in the reclamation plan'.[180] The law goes on to provide that each financial assurance mechanism for an existing exploration or new or existing mining unit must be equal to the cost (in current dollars) of performing the approved reclamation measures stated in the reclamation plan, as well as providing continued care and monitoring of the areas stated in the reclamation plan for revegetation 'for no more than three growing seasons without additional supplemental irrigation or other man-induced inputs after performing the reclamation measures'.[181] The reference here to 'supplemental measures' points to the potential need for longterm postclosure monitoring and maintenance. Recent reforms to the financial provision law in South Africa require mining rights holders to post financial assurance for decommissioning and closure activities, as well as the 'remediation and management of latent or residual environmental impacts which may become known in future, including the pumping and treatment of polluted or extraneous water'.[182] The applicant must draw up plans detailing the activities and costs associated with decommissioning, closure and the management of latent or residual risks postclosure to determine the financial provision.[183]

The amount of financial assurance could thus be seen as coextensive with the cost of measures aimed at mitigating the risks set out in the mine closure plan – the statutory closure liability. The sufficiency of the financial assurance is thus directly linked to the rigour and scope of this plan.

---

178 Mining Code, 2002 (Democratic Republic of the Congo), Article 294.

179 Schedules to the Mining Regulations, 2003 (Democratic Republic of the Congo), Directive IX, Title VI: Detailed budget and finance plan for rehabilitation of the environment.

180 §27-992B Article 5, Chapter 5, Title 27 (Arizona Laws).

181 §27-992C Article 5, Chapter 5, Title 27 (Arizona Laws).

182 Regulations Pertaining to the Financial Provision for Prospecting, Exploration, Mining or Production Operations, 2015 (South Africa), reg. 5.

183 Ibid reg. 6.

In line with the idea of reasonable assurance, not all jurisdictions require the mining proponent to cover 100 per cent of this statutory closure liability. In a recent survey of mine reclamation security in selected jurisdictions in Canada, the USA and Australia, for example, few of the jurisdictions surveyed required mining operators to post 100 per cent of the closure liability in all instances, although there are exceptions. In Alaska, although the regulations refer to 'acceptable, reasonable and likely' estimates of reclamation security, the practice is to require operators to provide 100 per cent, including for longterm water treatment.[184] Policy in British Columbia only specifies a 100 per cent security requirement for sites requiring longterm water treatment, or sites owned by single mining companies.[185] In his 2005 survey of mine reclamation security for the ICMM, Miller found wide variation in the extent to which the financial assurance covered closure liabilities: from 70 per cent in Quebec, for example, to as little as 5–10 per cent of the closure liabilities in Ghana.[186]

Financial assurance may assist States in identifying unexpected postclosure impacts but may not necessarily provide the resources for dealing with such. Conrad, for example, notes the 'increasing occurrences of unanticipated impacts to water quality from acid mine drainage or the presence of chemical constituents of concern like selenium that have disrupted self-bonding and surety arrangements in some States of the USA'.[187] Depending on the content of the mine closure plan, the financial assurance may not be sufficient to deal with unanticipated impacts. Further, financial assurance stipulations do not usually require the mining operator to make provision for catastrophic events, such as unexpected tailings dams failures.[188]

The gap in coverage between statutory closure liability and the required financial assurance highlights the two major underlying risks associated with financial assurance: the risk of operator default, and the risk of tying up funds in financial assurance that could be put to other uses.

Financial assurance is not infrequently described as the amount that must be made available to the State to undertake a reclamation program *if the mining proponent fails to do so*. The essential risk against which financial assurance mitigates is therefore the risk of mine operator default.[189] In line with the principle that mine closure is a core business activity of mining companies,

---

[184] Stantec Consulting Limited, *Policy and Process Review for Mine Reclamation Security* (September 20, 2016) iv.

[185] Ibid.

[186] *ICMM Financial Assurance Survey* (n 137) 61–2.

[187] Conrad (n 148) 4.

[188] Stantec (n 184) v.

[189] Ibid 12.

the assumption is that the financial assurance would not be needed. Through the mining proponent's progressive rehabilitation, decommissioning and final rehabilitation, a mining site would be left *at least* physically and chemically stable, and not in need of longterm post-reclamation care. In practice, however, mining proponents do default on their obligations, particularly during commodity downturns. Commonly also, mining companies transfer mines and their associated assets and liabilities to increasingly marginal operators, until the last mine standing is left with no option but to apply for liquidation.[190]

The factors that drive operator default are not usually included in the legal criteria which State authorities must apply to determine the quantum of financial provision, although this is starting to change in the laws of some jurisdictions. The review of mine reclamation security in British Columbia, for instance, identifies 'financial strength of the company' and 'compliance history' as 'risk assessment gates' that affect the calculation of reclamation security.[191] The reforms in Queensland are premised on differentiated financial assurance requirements based on the likelihood of the resource extraction company becoming insolvent. In Western Australia, which has implemented a pooled approach to financial assurance since 2012, the State will still require UPBs where the tenement holder or controlling business entity exhibits signs of corporate distress, or has failed to comply with key statutory provisions.[192]

For mining companies, unlike life of mine estimates or estimates reported under the IFRS or national accounting standards, the financial provision must be lodged in the prescribed and/or negotiated form with the regulator as part of a licensing requirement.[193] Rather than simply being an estimate, it imposes a financial obligation on mining companies, thereby carrying an opportunity cost – either for exploration work, further development of the mine, or progressive rehabilitation. The amounts tied up in financial assurance may be substantial.[194] As noted above, when Western Australia implemented a pooled approach to mine rehabilitation funding, the majority of some 5000 UPBs totalling more than AUS 1.2 billion were released.[195]

The State's quantification of financial assurance is thus critically driven by the *scope* of risks associated with closure, and the different weight and

---

190 This issue is discussed in section 2.1.3 below.

191 BC Ministry of Energy and Mines, *EY Report* (n 175) 12.

192 Government of Western Australia, Department of Mines and Petroleum, 'The administration of mining securities for mine sites regulated by the Department of Mines and Petroleum' www.dmp.wa.gov.au/Documents/Environment/ENV-MEB-017 .pdf, accessed 28 February 2019.

193 Ibid 79.

194 *ICMM Financial Assurance Survey* (n 137) 48.

195 Government of Western Australia (n 24).

importance attached to different risks. Advocacy for a 'risk-based approach' to determination of the quantum of financial assurance is facile unless these nuances are made clear.

Determining the financial assurance needed also involves placing a quantitative value on the risks involved. Before embarking on a new venture, mining proponents may draw upon a variety of valuation techniques to determine if a project is viable or not. Simplified valuation techniques such as net present value (NPV), discounted cash flows and internal rate of return remain the techniques of choice notwithstanding the existence of alternatives.[196] Evans *et al* point out that within the mining industry, an NPV analysis is usually the starting point to evaluate projects.[197] An NPV analysis is based on the present value of future costs and an appropriate discount rate.[198] The future, hypothetical costs of decommissioning, reclamation and postclosure case and maintenance must be estimated in real terms for each year of the project's operations, and then the discount factor (based on the true discount rate) is applied to determine the present value.[199] The cumulative value of the present value of costs is the quantum of the financial assurance that needs to be provided. By investing the present value of future costs in a longterm investment instrument that grows according to the discounted rate, the claim is that the funds will grow and be sufficient to cover the risks of operator default /incapacity for the activities of decommissioning, closure and postclosure care and maintenance.[200]

There is an extensive literature critiquing the adequacy of NPV as a method for valuing costs, particularly in the case of liabilities that can last for a very long time, or even into perpetuity, such as longterm treatment required to maintain adequate water quality.[201] An NPV analysis can artificially reduce the cost of activities associated with post-reclamation care.[202] This can beguile mines 'into selling a valuable commodity at prices that do not account for the actual costs of production'.[203] The longer the period for which obligations need to be calculated, the smaller the NPV and potentially the less meaningful the figure

---

196 R David Espinoza and Jeremy WF Morris, 'Towards sustainable mining (part II): Accounting for mine reclamation and post reclamation care liabilities' (2017) 52 *Resources Policy* 29, 30.

197 R Evans, CJ Moran and D Brereton, 'Beyond NPV – A review of valuation methodologies and their applicability to water in mining' Paper presented at the Water in Mining Conference, held from 14–16 November 2006 in Brisbane, Queensland, 97.

198 Cowan (n 23) 16.

199 Ibid 58.

200 Ibid.

201 Evans (n 197) 97–8.

202 Espinoza (n 196) 30.

203 Ibid.

becomes.[204] According to guidelines issued by the United States Bureau of Land Management, '[u]nfortunately, there are no economic standards or rules defining when the point is exceeded when additional present value calculations do not contribute in any meaningful way to the ultimate answer'.[205] However, a number of Canadian jurisdictions have adopted a 50-year timeframe in order to achieve a realistic value over the foreseeable future.[206]

The range of alternatives to the use of NPV include methods that fully capture the direct and indirect costs of activities and their alternatives; methodologies for attaching financial value to uncertain future events and contingencies, such as 'Monte Carlo' analysis or financial value at risk methodologies; 'real options' methodologies, which assign ownership to an option to do something in the future, attaching a financial value thereto; methods to incorporate the external economic impacts and externalities beyond the mining organization, such as a cost–benefit tool that can be used to assess the manner in which benefits and costs flow to a variety of agents and stakeholders;[207] and models that integrate financial and nonfinancial methodologies to arrive at a holistic assessment of value. Nevertheless, while there is clearly no shortage of valuation methodologies, 'there is no generally-accepted valuation framework that can be readily deployed to integrate different types of value'.[208]

States rarely specify the method of valuation that must be used to determine the amount of financial assurance, or they may expressly endorse an NPV approach. In Chile, for instance, the mine closure law specifies that the amount of the financial guarantee is determined on the basis of the periodical estimate of the NPV of the costs to implement all closure measures during the operational period and until the end of its life cycle, as well as the NPV of follow-up and monitoring measures during the postclosure stage.[209] But this is rare.

A number of mineral-rich jurisdictions have nevertheless attempted to standardize closure costs by developing codes, templates or spreadsheets itemizing closure, decommissioning and rehabilitation actions and providing standard unit costs for specific tasks.[210] One of the better known resources is the Standard Reclamation Cost Estimator, which the Nevada Division of Environmental Protection developed in collaboration with the Bureau of

---

[204] Cowan (n 23) 60.

[205] Ibid.

[206] Ibid 18.

[207] Parshley (n 126) 187; X Gu and Q Wang, 'Internalising ecological costs in evaluating and planning a mining project' Paper presented at the 35th APCOM Symposium held from 24–30 September 2011, in Wollongong, New South Wales, 547.

[208] Evans (n 197) 99.

[209] Law 20,551 (Chile), Article 50.

[210] Cowan (n 23) 16.

Mining Regulation and Reclamation, the Bureau of Land Management and the Nevada Mining Association.[211] This free, online tool grew out of the Nevada Standardized Unit Cost Project, a project aimed at providing consistency in estimating reclamation costs for mining operations in Nevada and also promoting administrative efficiency. There are two versions of the Cost Estimator: one is designed to meet the regulatory requirements of the State of Nevada; the other is designed as an international version.[212]

Notwithstanding the existence of statutory rules and more informal guidelines, the pressure to secure mining investment may induce States to depart from the letter of the law and secure a negotiated outcome for financial assurance.[213] The sociology of these dynamics is not well researched.

In many mineral-rich jurisdictions, the amount of mine reclamation security is shrouded in secrecy. The law may expressly allow for reclamation liability costing to be kept confidential,[214] or may simply not make any provision for public review of the amounts. This runs counter to the policy guidance of the sustainable mineral development consensus, which stresses the need for transparency. Canada's NOAMI Guidelines, for instance, underline that integrity and transparency in the determination of financial assurance is critical and recommend the use of qualified independent consultants to determine the quantum and form of financial assurance. They also recommend that funds should be readily identifiable in government accounts, demonstrating that appropriate investments are in place and facilitating scrutiny by all affected stakeholders.[215] Western Australia's *Guidelines for Mine Closure* emphasize that the financial provisioning process and methodology must be transparent and verifiable, but do not actually hold that the amounts determined must be open to the public. The USA serves as an example of better practice in this regard as the actual reclamation security amounts are open to public scrutiny in a number of jurisdictions.[216]

Lack of rigour and consistency in the setting and enforcement of standards relating to the amount of financial assurance can lead to a situation where there are insufficient funds to close a mine site and ensure adequate post-reclamation

---

211 Standardized Reclamation Cost Estimator https://nvbond.org/about/, accessed 28 February 2019.

212 Ibid.

213 *ICMM Financial Assurance Survey* (n 137) 34.

214 A number of Canadian laws allow for reclamation liability costing to be kept confidential. Examples include the Mining Act, 1990 (Ontario), section 145(10) and Mineral Resources Act (Nova Scotia), section 19(9), 175.

215 Cowan (n 23) 17.

216 This is the case in Nevada (§519A.185 Nevada Administrative Code) and Alaska (§46.03.110(b) Alaska Statutes).

care. As Espinoza and Morris point out, 'this means that society will sooner or later bear the unfunded PRC [post-reclamation care] costs'.[217] The only questions then remaining are which generation (the timing effect) and which region (the location effect) will bear such costs. If the mineral resources have largely been extracted to supply local needs, then the timing effect saddles future generations with the cost. However, where resources are extracted locally for global consumption, the artificial reduction of costs transfers wealth to the future generations of another region.[218] This becomes particularly problematic where global consumers leave socioecological liabilities to the future generations of developing or emerging economies with insufficient resources to take care of these problems.[219]

2.1.3 Corporate adaptation, corporate failure and the transfer of exploitation authorizations

The third major element of the State's watchdog role over mine closure relates to oversight over corporate adaptation, corporate failure and the transfer of exploitation authorizations. In recent times the metaphor of 'pass the parcel'[220] has been applied to mine closure liabilities, to capture the phenomenon of mining assets falling into the hands of increasingly marginal operators as the mine nears exhaustion of its reserves. In a recent media report on the effect of the global commodities downturn on mining in Queensland, for example, a senior analyst is reported as saying: 'we are moving to a situation where we will see a large number of mines closing and a number of the companies that have developed them wanting to play pass the parcel.'[221] The article reports, among other cases, a multinational mining company's sale of a thermal coal mine in Queensland to a much smaller company, with just 24 shareholders, who had raised only AUD 750,000. The multinational company's financial assurance for the site, held by the Queensland Department of Environment and Heritage Protection, stood at AUD 121 million, although experts estimated that the true rehabilitation costs were nearly double that amount.[222]

---

[217] Espinoza and Morris (n 196) 30.

[218] Ibid.

[219] Ibid.

[220] Pass the parcel is a children's party game that involves passing around a gift wrapped in many layers. Each layer is unwrapped until the last layer of wrapping is removed to reveal a prize – or a booby trap.

[221] Mike Seccombe, 'Who foots the bill for open-cut mine rehabilitation?' *The Saturday Paper* Edition 94, February 2016 www.thesaturdaypaper.com.au/news/politics/2016/02/06/who-foots-the-bill-open-cut-mine-rehabilitation/14546772002857, accessed 28 February 2019.

[222] Ibid.

In a developing country context, a media report on the Blyvooruitzicht gold mine in South Africa notes that 'large mining companies have a habit of selling to juniors, or scavengers, that can survive by mining lower grade ore but lack resources for environmental clean-up'.[223] In this case, the Blyvooruitzicht Gold Mining Company (BGMC) was listed in the late 1930s to exploit one of the richest gold mines on South Africa's West Rand. In the late 1990s a listed company acquired the majority shareholding in this company. Some ten years later the company found itself in financial difficulty and, under administration (or 'business rescue' as it is known in South Africa), the majority shareholding passed to a smaller company.[224] The BGMC subsequently filed for liquidation and was overrun with artisanal and smallscale miners, even as the liquidator tried to secure other investors.[225] A number of human rights groups highlighted the human rights violations at this mine, with one describing the conditions at the mine village as a 'humanitarian catastrophe' as 60 per cent of the 300 households in the area did not have enough to eat or the ability to support their children.[226] In 2015, industry estimates of the rehabilitation tag at Blyvooruitzicht ranged from ZAR 108 to 130 million, which experts criticized as too low. In the 1990s, the financial rehabilitation for this mine was set at ZAR 10,000.[227]

Relevant to a discussion of a 'pass the parcel' approach to mine closure liabilities, the *Breaking New Ground* report noted that a group of smaller intermediate and junior miners were problematic for the industry's reputation. Being 'undercapitalized, short of management expertise and under intense pressure to succeed' they had limited capacity to deal with failures or other unexpected events and were accordingly at high risk for creating negative environmental and social conditions at their operations.[228] A disproportionate number of the 'bad actors' in the mining industry had come from this sector, the report con-

---

[223] Staff Reporter, 'Mining companies skirting the law', *Cape Argus* 12 October 2015, www.iol.co.za/capeargus/mining-companies-skirting-the-law-1928734 accessed 28 February 2019.

[224] T Humby, 'Facilitating dereliction? How the South African legal regulatory framework enables mining companies to circumvent closure duties', Paper presented at the Mine Closure Conference 2014, held in Johannesburg, South Africa.

[225] Kevin Crowley, 'Ransacked Blyvooruitzicht gold mine gets a reboot after clashing partners quit' www.businesslive.co.za/bd/companies/mining/2017-04-11-ransacked-blyvooruitzicht-gold-mine-gets-a-reboot-after-clashing-partners-quit/, accessed 28 February 2019.

[226] Paul Burkhardt, 'Abandoned Blyvooruitzicht mine caused catastrophe – rights group' www.fin24.com/Companies/Mining/abandoned-blyvooruitzicht-mine-caused-catastrophe-rights-group-20170127, accessed 28 February 2019.

[227] Staff Reporter (n 223).

[228] *Breaking New Ground* (n 13) 63.

tinued, and one of the 'major challenges' facing the industry was ensuring how the performance of this small group of companies could be raised, or how their licence could be removed.[229] *Breaking New Ground* did not link this group of actors to irresponsible closure practices, but the cases cited above show that there is a subgroup of such miners that invest in mines towards the end of their cycle. Although there is little research on the business model for end of life mining, this niche is occupied by a particular type of junior miner that focuses on what may be termed scavenger mining, frequently involving the reprocessing of mine tailings, and the sale of scrap metal and other mine assets.[230]

But contrary to the representation of 'bad actors', miners investing in operations that are nearing the end of their 'life' form part of what *Breaking New Ground* described as a 'highly interdependent' industry.[231] The pass the parcel approach to closure liabilities shows that the entire chain of mining producers is complicit in irresponsible closure practices, notwithstanding the direction of industry (and taxpayer) ire at intermediate and smaller junior miners. Failure to acknowledge this is key to the maintenance of an unsustainable extractivist/neoextractivist paradigm.

The dominant model for mine closure rests on the assumption of a stable operator over time that undertakes integrated mine closure planning and maintains financial assurance. In practice, however, company laws allow mining firms to adapt and exit looming closure liabilities in a variety of ways. This may first occur simply through the sale of a mine asset, or through a change in major shareholding if the company is listed. Following commodity downturns, major miners seek to bolster their balance sheets by selling their assets or stakes in assets to other actors.[232]

Second, operators may place the mine into care and maintenance, 'an alternative to closure that companies use while hoping for improved prices',[233] or that some see as a strategy 'to avoid having to meet rehabilitation obligations'.[234] The Australian government's *Leading Practice Manual on Mine Closure* defines care and maintenance as 'a temporary cessation of operations when infrastructure, plant and equipment remain intact and are maintained in anticipation of production recommencing'.[235] This aspect of mine production,

---

229 Ibid.

230 Crowley (n 225).

231 *Breaking New Ground* (n 13) 60.

232 Reuters Staff Reporter, 'Major mining assets change hands in 2016' www.iol.co.za/business-report/international/major-mining-assets-change-hands-in-2016-7186136, accessed 28 February 2019.

233 Seccombe (n 221).

234 Ibid.

235 Commonwealth of Australia (n 30) 110.

however, remains poorly regulated in many mineral-rich jurisdictions (if at all), despite concern regarding social impacts and continuing compliance with the environmental obligations attached to the mine.

There are examples where the mining industry has pushed back on State attempts to regulate care and maintenance. For example, in South Africa, the Department of Environmental Affairs promulgated a regulation on care and maintenance following the introduction of the One Environmental System.[236] The regulation introduced a regulatory approval for 'care and maintenance' (the term not being defined), requiring mining rights holders to submit an application to the Minister of Mineral Resources detailing the merits of putting the mine under care and maintenance, along with a care and maintenance plan.[237] Approval of the care and maintenance application would not release the rights holder from any of their rehabilitation obligations, including the duty to maintain the financial assurance.[238] The Department of Mineral Resources and the mining industry opposed this regulation, however, on the basis that it exceeded the Department of Environmental Affairs' statutory mandate to regulate the mining industry. Soon after the new regulations entered into effect the environmental department initiated another intensive review process, which will likely see the care and maintenance regulation withdrawn.[239]

Finally, companies investing in a mine towards the end of its life may find themselves in corporate distress. The company laws of mineral-rich jurisdictions accommodate corporate distress by allowing struggling companies to be placed under administration with a view to facilitating their revival, or with a view to their dissolution and eventual winding up (bankruptcy or liquidation). These processes are of concern from a sustainability perspective to the extent that they do not facilitate the consideration of compliance with rehabilitation obligations, maintaining the financial assurance and ensuring that a new operator has the capacity to continue in the same vein as the previous rights holder. If a company is wound up and ceases to exist as a juristic person, there is no party to hold criminally or civilly liable unless the State pursues action against individual directors, investors or other parties in line with the notion of an 'environmental chain of responsibility'.

---

[236] The One Environmental System is a system of streamlined licensing and enforcement between the executive agencies responsible for mineral resources and mining respectively, introduced in 2014.

[237] Regulations pertaining to the Financial Provision for Prospecting, Exploration, Mining or Production Operations, 2015 (South Africa), reg. 16.

[238] Ibid reg. 16(5).

[239] Webber Wentzel, 'Tabling of amended NEMA financial provision regulations, imminent' www.polity.org.za/article/tabling-of-amended-nema-financial-provision-regulations-imminent-2017-09-28, accessed 28 February 2019.

The mining laws of mineral-rich jurisdictions articulate imperfectly with processes of administrative supervision and bankruptcy/liquidation and it is difficult to discern a dominant model. A key issue is whether the initiation of these company law processes also triggers the need to institute proceedings for closure approval under the mining law. A number of States, for example, require mining proponents to apply for closure approval (or 'relinquishment', as it is termed in some jurisdictions) upon the cessation or abandonment of mining activities. For example, in Arizona, the reclamation law requires that reclamation must be completed within two years of completing the mining unit or the cessation of mining activities.[240] Similarly, in South Africa, one of the conditions prompting the need for a mining proponent to apply for a closure certificate is the 'cessation' of the prospecting or mining operation. As mining activities may continue under the guise of new operators under processes of administrative supervision, however, it is not clear that they have in fact ceased.[241]

The mining laws of some jurisdictions contain provisions that specify how the State's concerns relating to closure should be accommodated in liquidation processes. Chilean mining law specifies that in the case of bankruptcy of the mining company, the State regulatory authority will participate in the Creditors' Assembly.[242] The value of the duly approved mine closure plan will also be considered as a 'first class' credit in such proceedings.[243] Furthermore, in the case of mergers or any operation implying the total or partial change of ownership or corporate status of the mining company, the same will continue to be subject to the obligations established under Law 20,551. In case of sale or assignment of the mine assets, the closure and guarantee obligations will be acquired by the new owner. All these changes must be reported to the mining agency.[244] South African law is far more opaque on these issues, although following a longstanding debacle over State liability to treat AMD, the national environmental law was amended to provide that the national insolvency law does not apply to any form of financial provision.[245] In *Orphan Well Association v. Grant Thornton Limited*,[246] in a ruling that will have major

---

240 §27-926 Article 2, Chapter 5, Title 27 (Arizona Laws).

241 Mineral and Petroleum Resources Development Act, 2002 (South Africa), section 43(3)(c).

242 Law 20,551 (Chile), Article 35.

243 Ibid.

244 Ibid.

245 National Environmental Management Act, 1998 (South Africa), section 24P(6).

246 2019 SCC 5. See Supreme Court of Canada, 'Case in brief: Orphan Well Association v Grant Thornton Ltd' www.scc-csc.ca/case-dossier/cb/2019/37627-eng.aspx, accessed 28 February 2019.

implications for the mining industry, the Supreme Court of Canada ruled that an oil and gas company that had gone into bankruptcy under the federal law had to fulfil environmental obligations to reclaim the land before any other creditors were paid. The case has been touted as a major victory for the polluter pays principle in this jurisdiction.[247]

Mining laws also commonly provide for State approval in the event that a mining right is transferred from one mining proponent to another. There is thus potential for regulatory oversight to mitigate the pass the parcel approach to mine closure obligations. However, such laws usually only require generic oversight of a new holder's capacity to undertake the rehabilitation plan. For example, in Botswana the minister must approve any transfer, assignment or encumbrance of a mining licence or interest therein. The same particulars required for the licence application in the first instance apply.[248] Thus the minister must be satisfied that the applicant has or has secured access 'to adequate financial resources, technical competence and experience to carry on effective mining operations'.[249] The law specifies no clear duty – on the part of the applicant or the State – to consider and justify continuity in the implementation of the closure plan.

Very few States stipulate public participation or transparency requirements when mining authorizations are transferred. Finland is something of an outlier. Here the assignment of a permit also requires approval by the mining authority.[250] The application itself is not subject to public participation, but once approved the assignee must report the matter in writing without delay to property owners within the exploration or mining area, publicize the decision in at least one newspaper in general circulation within the operation's impact area and ensure that municipalities having jurisdiction over the areas affected by the assignment also publish the decision without delay.[251] Ordinarily, however, a lack of transparency in the transfer of mining authorizations prevails.

Some States are considering an additional phalanx of enforcement measures to deal with the transfer of liabilities. In Queensland, the Department of Environment and Heritage Protection recently formulated an Environmental Protection (Chain of Responsibility) Amendment Bill to confront 'increasing difficulties in ensuring that sites operated by companies in financial diffi-

---

247 Sharon J Riley, 'What the Redwater ruling means for Alberta's thousands of inactive oil and gas wells', *The Narwhal*, 31 January 2019 https://thenarwhal.ca/what-the-redwater-ruling-means-for-albertas-thousands-of-inactive-oil-and-gas-wells/ , accessed 28 February 2019.

248 Mines and Minerals Act, 1999 (Botswana), section 50.

249 Ibid (Botswana), section 39(1)(d) read with section 50(3).

250 Mining Act, 2011 (Finland), section 73.

251 Mining Act, 2011 (Finland), section 74.

culty continue to comply with their environmental obligations'.[252] Such sites included the Texas Silver Mine, Collingwood Tin Mine and Mount Chalmers Gold Mine.[253] The inability of companies and their related parties to bear the cost of managing and rehabilitating sites in the context of a major mining downturn was a 'looming major problem'.[254] Without entrenching additional enforcement powers in the Environment Protection Act, 1994, the State risked incurring operational and financial responsibility for sites in financial difficulty. The proposed range of enforcement powers included allowing the State to issue environmental protection orders against a party having some relevant relationship to the company in financial difficulty (for example, a parent company or executive officers), enabling the Department to amend environmental authorities upon transference to specify the provision of financial assurance as a condition precedent for the transfer, and requiring the recipient of a protection order to pay the costs of taking the actions specified therein in the event of noncompliance.[255] Together with a range of procedural forms aimed at more effective enforcement, these measures could address some of the problems associated with pass the parcel closure in that jurisdiction.

2.1.4 Conclusion

The State's protective role in mine closure manifests in rules on integrated closure planning, provision of financial assurance and approval of mining rights transfers. Even as closure is a core business activity of the mining proponent, rules on mine closure present the State as precautionary and preventive – guarding against the possibility of miner default on closure obligations. In this, the State acts firstly to protect itself against future liabilities. This dynamic is most prominent in rules on financial assurance, which have become stricter over time in a number of jurisdictions. For various reasons, however, the State's watchdog role is ineffective. Such reasons include failing to accommodate the full range of closure risks; lack of attention to, or enforcement of, progressive rehabilitation; difficulties in entrenching longterm consultation and cooperation on closure between heterogenous internal and external stakeholder groups; failure to enforce closure obligations; allowing softer forms of financial assurance that have rendered some States vulnerable to longterm closure liabilities; failing to specify the valuation method for the quantum of financial assurance; and blocking access to financial information on mine closure. Finally, while many States allow for some form of oversight

---

[252] Environmental Protection (Chain of Responsibility) Amendment Bill, 2016 (Queensland) 1.

[253] Ibid.

[254] Ibid.

[255] Ibid 1–2.

over mining rights transfers, laws on the sale of major assets, business rescue and liquidation/bankruptcy in the same jurisdictions undermine the State's efforts to hold the 'polluter' liable to 'pay'.

2.2 Closure Authorization: The Releasing State

The dominant model for mine closure incorporates the process of returning mineral title to the State, with a view to limiting the mining proponent's future administrative, criminal and civil liability associated with a site. A number of terms describe these processes:[256] closure,[257] relinquishment,[258] surrender,[259] abandonment.[260] There are generally three reasons put forward for the need to have some form of relinquishment process: (1) through various processes of corporate adaptation or failure, the project proponent is going to disappear anyway; (2) mineral rights, leases or permits are issued for a specific duration of time and will at some point expire; and (3) a mining proponent may not wish to carry a wasted mining asset on their books into perpetuity.[261]

Viewed through the lens of the double movement, the concepts of 'closure', 'relinquishment' and so on are more closely aligned with the organizing principle of mineral promotion than with protection. Providing mining companies with a potential 'way out' of potential future liabilities is not dissimilar to the idea of 'limited liability' so key to company law. Through the process of relinquishment, risk for the longterm liabilities associated with a mined-out site shifts to the public sector. Clarity on a certain end to the potentially perpetual liabilities of mining promotes a climate of investment certainty.

States differ in how clearly they delineate the relinquishment process and whether they also regulate the cessation of operations associated with an operator putting a mine into care and maintenance. In some States, authorities

---

[256] These terms do not necessarily apply to the same legal phenomenon. For example, in South Africa the process of extinguishing liabilities associated with a mining right is referred to as 'closure', whereas 'abandonment' refers to an illegal relinquishment of title and evasion of responsibility for liability.

[257] Used for example in Chile and South Africa.

[258] A term used in the mining laws of Sweden and the Democratic Republic of the Congo respectively.

[259] See for example Mining Act, 2010 (Tanzania), section 62.

[260] Mines and Minerals Development Act (Zambia), section 70 of provides for a certificate of abandonment. This relates primarily to abandoning of land incorporated in a mining right, but is also linked to a closure certificate issued by the Director of Mines Safety. A certificate of abandonment does not affect liabilities previously acquired. The Tanzanian Mining Act, 2010 also provides for a certificate of abandonment (see section 64).

[261] Cowan (n 23) 25.

must be notified when production ceases. In others, the law either specifies the conditions triggering the need to apply for a certificate of closure, surrender or abandonment, or places a duty on the mining proponent to notify the State of the intention to close, surrender or abandon the mine or the land on which it is located within a set period of time.

South African law, for example, sets out a very clearcut closure certification process linked to preemptive conditions. The holder of a mining authorization *must* apply to the authorities for a closure certificate on the lapse, abandonment or cancellation of the right in question, when prospecting or mining operations cease, on relinquishment of any portion of the land in respect to which the prospecting or mining authorization relates or upon completion of the prescribed closure plan.[262] This approach thus merges the regulation of care and maintenance with more permanent cessation of mining operations. It does not advance regulatory certainty, as it is unclear what constitutes a cessation of operations; for example, can a cessation of operations can be assumed when a mining proponent applies for a winding up order? As a result, mining proponents may simply not apply for a closure certificate, allowing the mine to slip into a state of abandonment.

Ghana adopts a different approach, requiring a mining proponent to notify the authority of a cessation of operations. Where the holder of a mining lease intends suspending production at a mine, he or she must provide the minister with three months' advance notification, setting out the reasons for the suspension. In cases of operational suspension beyond the holder's control (such as market conditions), the minister must be notified within 14 days. The minister may approve the suspension, or order the holder of the mining lease to resume full production at the mine by a specified date. If approved, a suspension of production may not exceed 12 months without an approved extension.[263] The minister may determine conditions associated with the approved suspension, including conditions advised by the presidentially appointed Minerals Commission.[264] This regulatory process for suspending production, however, does not articulate with the regulatory process for obtaining a certificate of surrender under Ghanaian mining law.[265]

British Columbia regulates the cessation of production differently, but in a manner that also differentiates care and maintenance from closure. Here, the Health, Safety and Reclamation Code for Mines requires the owner, agent or manager of a mine to provide a mining inspector with seven days' notice

---

[262] Mineral and Petroleum Resources Development Act, 2002 (South Africa), section 43.

[263] Minerals and Mining Act, 2006 (Ghana), section 51.

[264] Ibid s 51(5).

[265] Ibid s 67.

of their intention to stop work in, on or about a mine.[266] No State approval is required, but if a mine ceases operation the owner, agent or manager must continue to carry out the conditions of the permit and carry out a programme of site monitoring and maintenance.[267] If cessation of work lasts for longer than a year, the owner, manager or agent must apply for a permit amendment, identify hazards at the site and make this information available to local emergency agencies, and make updated plans available at the site in a conspicuous location.[268] These provisions, accordingly, determine care and maintenance standards, but with less regulatory intervention by the State. When a mine is closed for an 'indefinite period, or otherwise left unattended for any length of time', an owner, manager or agent is also dutybound to ensure that mine workings and fixtures remain secure.[269] In order to close a mine, the owner, agent or manager must file various plans and drawings with the inspector within a period of 90 days.[270]

In 1994, Canada's Whitehorse Mining Initiative proposed that the terms of relinquishment centre upon compliance with the obligations set out in the closure or reclamation plan, verification that the longterm obligations associated with post-closure monitoring and maintenance can be met and provision of adequate funding for such obligations. The adoption of risk-based financial assurance vehicles could be required in addition to the financial assurance already laid out for the site.[271] In mineral-rich jurisdictions there are nevertheless wide differences in terms of the conditions needed for a mining operator to obtain a certificate of closure. In some jurisdictions the standard is outlined in a generic, broadranging fashion. Ghana's mining law, for example, states that the minister may not issue a certificate of surrender unless he or she is satisfied that the applicant will surrender the land 'in a condition which is safe and accords with good mining practice'.[272] Other States are more specific in terms of requiring the removal of buildings and infrastructure and securing hazardous sites.[273] In more developed jurisdictions, reclamation standards are

---

[266] Health, Safety and Reclamation Code for Mines, 2008 (British Columbia), section 10.6.1.

[267] Ibid s 10.6.2(a).

[268] Ibid s 10.6.2(b).

[269] Ibid s 10.6.5.

[270] Ibid s 10.6.3.

[271] Cowan (n 23) 25.

[272] Minerals and Mining Act, 2006 (Ghana), section 67(4)(c).

[273] See, for example, Mineral Act, 1992 (Namibia) section 54(3), which sets out duties relating to abandonment, including the demolition of works, removal of debris and remedying 'to the reasonable satisfaction of the Minister' any damage caused by the mining operations to the surface of and the environment on the land in question.

articulated in much greater detail.[274] In a number of mineral-rich jurisdictions the law requires mining proponents to file plans and maps of the mining area. Such plans and maps may serve different purposes – for example, public safety,[275] or facilitating the grant of further mining concessions in the area.[276]

From an industry perspective, relinquishment processes are a means to terminate future liability, particularly around longterm water management. However, with few exceptions, the release of liability does not affect liabilities already incurred. Tanzania's mining law, for instance, stipulates that a certificate of abandonment 'does not affect any liability incurred before the date on which the abandonment has effect in respect of the land' or affect the institution of legal proceedings commenced or continued against the applicant for such liability.[277] In other jurisdictions, a release from liability may accompany a specification of postclosure obligations. In Finland, a mine closure process culminates in an official decision to terminate mining.[278] However, after termination of mining activity the mining operator is still required to monitor the mining area and undertake necessary corrective measures to guard against significant detrimental impacts on public safety.[279] Even if relinquishment and a release of future liability are granted in terms of the mining law, permits issued by environmental and other natural resource authorities remain in place, with their attendant obligations and liabilities.[280]

Since financial assurance under the dominant model is simply a guarantee against operator default, certified relinquishment processes also often entail return or release of the financial guarantee. British Columbia's Health, Safety and Reclamation Code for Mines entitles the depositor of security to a partial or full refund if the chief inspector is satisfied that some or all of the conditions of the permit have been complied with.[281] Other jurisdictions allow for

---

274 See for example the Health, Safety and Reclamation Code for Mines, 2008 (British Columbia).

275 See for example section 45 of Mongolia's Minerals Law, 2006, which requires that a mining licence holder must notify the mining authority a year in advance of a planned temporary or complete mine closure. Among other steps, the holder must 'prepare a detailed map of an appropriate scale showing the dangerous or potentially dangerous areas created by mining operations marked with the necessary warnings and markings and submit the map to the [mining authority] and the local governor).

276 See Mines and Minerals Act, 1999 (Botswana) section 78(1) for an example.

277 Mining Act, 2010 (Tanzania), section 64(5). For a positively framed provision see Health, Safety and Reclamation Code for Mines, 2008 (British Columbia), section 10.7.31.

278 Mining Act, 2011 (Finland), sections 147, 148.

279 Ibid s 150.

280 Cowan (n 23) 29.

281 Health, Safety and Reclamation Code for Mines, 2008 (British Columbia), section 10.6.14.

a phased return of the guarantee. Indonesia's regulations on 'Reclamation and Post-Mining in Mineral and Coal Mining Business Activity', for example, require the holders of various mining authorizations to submit exploration, production and postmining guarantees.[282] Having executed phased reclamation, the holders may apply to the Minister for a disbursement of the reclamation guarantee at the associated phase.

Notwithstanding these elaborate provisions on relinquishment, in practice there are relatively few examples of successful closure.[283] State enforcement of mine closure rules may be minimal to nonexistent, or mining proponents may not see the benefit of applying for formal closure. Frequently, mines close prematurely and not according to any plan.[284] More or less elaborate provisions on closure and 'toolkit' solutions gloss over what is frequently an exceedingly difficult and expensive process.

Is the notion of the releasing State viable? Is the elaborate regulatory frame constituting mine closure achievable? Perhaps not, or perhaps only with great difficulty. The protracted nature of negotiating a closure plan, estimating financial assurance and arriving at agreed closure outcomes is well illustrated by the case of the Chino mine in New Mexico, USA.[285] Here, standards have had to be lowered to meet legal closure requirements despite the touted success of the reclamation and closure programme.

The Chino copper mine began operating in 1910, but regulatory oversight of closure was only consolidated during the mid-1990s. In 1977, regulations issued by the New Mexico Water Quality Control Commission established the need for groundwater protection permits to safeguard groundwater quality in the State. Closure requirements were specified in such permits from the 1980s onwards, while the need to post financial assurance to cover the risk of oper-

---

282 See Chapter V, Reclamation and Post-Mining in Mineral and Coal Mining Business Activity, 2014 (Indonesia).

283 HWB Lacey and KE Bennett, 'Updating the Leading Practice Sustainable Development (LPSD) Mine Closure Guide Australia 2015', Presented at Goldfields Environmental Management Group Workshop 2016, held 18–20 May 2016 in Kalgoorlie, Western Australia; JV Parshley and CS MacCullum, 'Attractive nuisances and wicked solutions' in AB Fourie and M Tibbett (eds), *Mine Closure 2016* (Australian Centre for Geomechanics 2016) 223, 226. Parshley and MacCullum point out that there have also been some 'remarkable successes' particularly in the East German coal mining regions.

284 Laurence (n 2) 285, 286.

285 M Phillip and K Myers, 'Regulatory perspective – Development of closure plan with adequate financial assurance for the protection of ground water quality at the Chino copper mine', Presented at the 6th ICARD Conference held 12–18 July in Cairns, Queensland, 671.

ator default became a requirement in the mid 1990s.[286] In 1994, regulations issued under the New Mexico Mining Act, 1993 established a deadline for mining proponents to obtain approval for mine closeout plans.[287] The regulations required establishment of a self-sustaining ecosystem as a postmining land use. For existing operations, the New Mexico Environmental Department needed to approve that all applicable environmental requirements would be met with 'perpetual care'.[288] The initial deadline for submitting a closeout plan was set as 31 December 1995;[289] however, this deadline was extended several times for the Chino mine.[290]

The extent of environmental degradation at the Chino mine was significant. The modern mine at Chino was among the first lowgrade, open pit copper mines globally.[291] In the early 2000s, mining and smelting operations wound down as the copper price fell.[292] At that point, open pit, stockpiles and waste rock piles (AMD generating potential) covered approximately 1942 ha, and tailings impoundments covered a further 1416 ha.[293] The New Mexico Environmental Department and the mining company estimated that approximately 240L/s of AMD would not meet State standards and would require treatment. The extensive level of groundwater contamination at the site was evidenced by 2001 monitoring results: 117 out of 160 wells failed New Mexico groundwater quality standards, and all 25 sites tested for compliance with concentration standards failed.[294] 'Vast quantities' of contaminated groundwater would remain postclosure.[295]

In the early 2000s, after many years of correspondence, meetings and a public hearing, the mining company and regulatory agencies agreed on a draft closure permit setting forth the conditions relating to the postclosure treatment of groundwater.[296] Despite civil society objections, a closure permit was issued on 24 February 2003.[297] The stipulated permit included a condition

---

[286] Ibid 672.

[287] Ibid.

[288] New Mexico Statutes, Chapter 69. Mines, §69-36-11(B)(4). For the corresponding provision for new operations see §69-36-12.B.4.

[289] Ibid §69-36-11(B).

[290] Phillip and Myers (n 285) 672.

[291] Freeport McMoRan, 'North America: Chino' www.fcx.com/operations/north-america#chino_link, accessed 28 February 2019.

[292] Phillip and Myers (n 285) 672.

[293] Ibid.

[294] Ibid 673.

[295] Ibid.

[296] Ibid.

[297] *Gila Resources Information Project & New Mexico Environment Department v. New Mexico Water Quality Control Commission and Chino Mines Company*, IN RE:

that 'water treatment would be conducted in perpetuity', but in effect limited to 100 years of monitoring, operation and management.[298] A closure cost of USD 394 million was estimated for all closure work proposed (water treatment and reclamation), discounted to USD 191 million as the NPV for the financial assurance.[299] A total of USD 1 million of that amount was to be put into a trust in the event that the State needed to operate Chino's water management system.[300]

Chino's 'accelerated reclamation programme', which incorporated the contributions of the Gila Resources Information Project (Gila), was subsequently implemented with some success. In 2014, Gila reported that the 2000 acres of land reclaimed at Chino had kept hundreds of workers employed over the preceding decade in regrading, covering and reseeding mine waste units.[301]

In addition to undertaking water treatment and reclamation, the mining company also reached a settlement with the Office of the New Mexico Natural Resources Trustee and the US Fish and Wildlife Service for natural resources damages.[302] Acting under the Comprehensive Environmental Response, Compensation and Liability Act, 1980 and the Federal Water Pollution Control Act, the State filed complaints against Freeport for groundwater resources damages and injury to wildlife and wildlife habitat. The damages were finalized in two consent decrees dating from 2011 and 2012 respectively. For groundwater resources damages Freeport paid approximately USD 13 million to the State in damages inclusive of damage assessment costs, while the settlement for wildlife and wildlife habitat was set at USD 5.5 million.[303]

In recent years, however, the success and rigour of the Chino reclamation and closure case study has been tempered by the so-called Copper Rule amendment to New Mexico's Water Quality Act. In 2009 the Water Quality Act was amended, requiring the New Mexico Water Quality Control Commission to adopt regulations setting out water pollution control measures particular to the

---

the Appeal Petition on Chino Mines Company's Proposed Ground Water Supplemental Discharge Permit for Closure-DP-1340 (decided 15 June 2005) https://caselaw.findlaw.com/nm-court-of-appeals/1393359.html, accessed 28 February 2019, para. 8.

298 Phillip and Myers (n 285) 673.

299 Ibid 674.

300 Ibid.

301 Gila Resources Information Project, 'Mining update: Major reclamation complete at Tyrone and Chino mines' http://gilaresources.info/wp/blog/2014/12/17/mining-update-major-reclamation-complete-at-tyrone-and-chino-mines/, accessed 28 February 2019.

302 New Mexico Office of Natural Resources Trustee, 'Chino, Cobre and Tyrone mines' https://onrt.env.nm.gov/chino-cobre-and-tyrone-mines/, accessed 28 February 2019.

303 Ibid.

copper industry.[304] In line with the amendments, the New Mexico Environment Department (NMED) set about developing the regulations consultatively. This included establishing a Copper Rule Advisory Committee incorporating representatives of environmental groups, the State and mine owners and operators. A former NMED Ground Water Quality Bureau Chief, William Olson, was engaged as a contractor to assist this committee.[305] Olson provided NMED with a draft of the copper regulations, but the Department then requested him to incorporate modifications suggested by the mining company. Olson was of the view that the modifications violated the State's Water Quality Act, but eventually complied.[306] The modifications, ultimately adopted, are based on a 'point of compliance concept', which essentially exempts copper miners from complying with groundwater quality standards as long as the pollution is contained. Environmental advocacy groups have argued that this allows copper miners (and potentially other industries) to pollute vast tracts of groundwater, a critically scarce and strategic resource in New Mexico.[307]

After a further round of public participation, the Commission adopted NMED's proposed new copper regulations in September 2013. Environmental advocacy groups and the New Mexico Attorney-General subsequently took the regulations on review, arguing that they violated the Water Quality Act. In 2015 their objections were overruled by the New Mexico Court of Appeals,[308] a stance also taken by the New Mexico Supreme Court in 2018.[309] Justifying its decision in 2015 that the copper regulations did not violate the Water Quality Act, the Court of Appeals said that in promulgating the Regulations the Commission was acting pursuant to a legislative mandate that required them to balance water pollution prevention or abatement with 'the social and economic value of the sources of water contaminants' and 'the technical practicability and economic reasonableness of reducing or eliminating them'. Part of this balancing act involved formulating regulations 'with which the mining industry could reasonably and practicably comply'. It was not within the Commission's purview to enact regulations that totally prevented mining

---

304 New Mexico Water Quality Act, §74-6-4(K).

305 *Gila Resources Information Project v. Freeport McMoran Chino Mines Company & others* (decided 8 April 2015) https://caselaw.findlaw.com/nm-court-of-appeals/1697338.html accessed 28 February 2019, para. 5.

306 Ibid.

307 Amigos Bravos, Gila Resources Information Project & New Mexico Environmental Law Center, 'Copper Rule Q & A'.

308 *Gila Resources Information Project v. Freeport McMoran Chino Mines Company & others* (n 305).

309 ABQ Journal News Staff, 'NM High Court affirms "copper rule" for mining' www.abqjournal.com/1143337/nm-high-court-affirms-copper-rule-for-mining.html, accessed 28 February 2019.

operations from polluting groundwater.[310] The NM Supreme Court noted that the Copper Rule contained an 'abundance' of protections affording 'significant' groundwater protection at copper mine facilities.[311] Environmental advocacy groups expressed their disappointment in the courts' view, however, arguing that the judiciary had essentially sanctioned the idea of groundwater sacrifice zones.[312]

In conclusion, the Chino case study arguably represents both the best and the limits of what is achievable under the current dominant model for mine closure. Even when significant strides have been made to hold a mining company to account, to articulate perpetuity requirements for water treatment, to recover natural resource damages and to accurately estimate financial assurance, the State has needed to step down on idealized notions of ecosystem restoration and tailor laws suited to 'technical practicability' and 'economic reasonableness'. This case thus points to the limits of the current discourse on mine closure and mine sustainability more broadly, and the need to squarely face irremediable degradation. This will entail acknowledging the failure of the State's protective role.

2.3 Postclosure Landscapes and Abandoned Mines: The State as Mender of Last Resort

In the shadow of this failure, as mines near the end of their cycles, the State's role as mender of last resort looms large. The mender of last resort concept captures the notion of the State stepping in to address the multiple hazards posed by 'orphaned', 'derelict' or 'abandoned' mines. Open or imperfectly closed mine openings, subsidence, unstable tailings dams, AMD, windblown dust, and unsafe gasses are among the hazards associated with abandoned sites.[313] Worldwide, there are numerous accounts of the environmental justice and human rights risks associated with such sites.[314] Artisanal and smallscale

---

310 *Gila Resources Information Project v. Freeport McMoran Chino Mines Company & others* (n 305) para. 37.

311 ABQ Journal News Staff (n 309).

312 Sierra Club: Rio Grande Chapter 'NM Supreme Court upholds water-sacrifice zones' www.riograndesierraclub.org/copper-rule-upheld/, accessed 28 February 2019.

313 Scott Fields, 'The Earth's open wounds: Abandoned and orphaned mines' (2003) 111(3) *Environmental Health Perspectives* 54, 55. In 2002, the MMSD project grouped these hazards into physical, environmental, socioeconomic and financial risks (see IIED & World Business Council for Sustainable Development 'Mining for the Future: Appendix C – Abandoned Mines Working Paper' Report No. 28, MMSD Project (April 2002)).

314 Jason Lee, 'China's sinking coal mining towns and villages – in pictures' *The Guardian* 9 September 2016 https://www.theguardian.com/global-development

mining (ASM) may also flourish in the shadow of largescale mining, and, when conducted informally or even illegally, can exacerbate such risks.[315]

Globally, the number of orphaned and abandoned mines is unknown and estimates vary widely. In part this is a problem of inconsistent terminology.[316] It is possible for example, to distinguish 'inactive mines' (nonoperational and unpermitted, for which it is still possible to trace an identifiable owner or operator) from 'abandoned' mines proper (no identifiable owners or operators).[317] But in general, mining laws do not recognize or provide distinct regulatory solutions for these two different scenarios.[318] Setting aside this nuance, there are reportedly 500,000 abandoned mines in the USA alone.[319] The US Bureau of Land Management, responsible for managing abandoned hardrock mining lands in the Western United States, maintains an inventory of 52,381 sites.[320] Australia reportedly has more than 50,000 recorded abandoned mines,[321] Canada has more than 10,000,[322] and a 2009 Auditor-General Report puts the

---

-professionals-network/gallery/2016/sep/09/chinas-sinking-coal-mine-towns-and-villages-in-pictures, accessed 28 February 2019; Fergus Jensen, 'Indonesia faces environmental time bomb after coal bust', *Reuters* 29 June 2016; Ewen Hosie, 'Australia needs to "address legacy" of abandoned mines, says environmental study', *Australian Mining* 28 November 2017, both accessed 20 June 2019; Sheyla Palomino, 'Evaluating risks from abandoned mines in the Puno region of Peru' *AusIMM Bulletin* (February 2015) www.ausimmbulletin.com/feature/evaluating-risks-from-abandoned-mines-in-the-puno-region-of-peru/, accessed 28 February 2019; Paul Burkardt, 'Abandoned Blyvooruitaicht mine caused "catastrophe" – rights group', *Fin 24* 27 January 2017 www.fin24.com/Companies/Mining/abandoned-blyvooruitzicht-mine-caused-catastrophe-rights-group-20170127, accessed 28 February 2019.

315 Parshley and MacCullum (n 283) 230.

316 IIED & World Business Council (n 313) C8; Fields (n 313) 156.

317 IIED & World Business Council (n 313) C5, referencing a definition put forward by the US Bureau of Land Management.

318 South African mining law empowers the State to intervene with urgent remedial measures to prevent ecological degradation, pollution or environmental damage in situations where the holder can and cannot be traced. See sections 45 and 46 of the Mineral and Petroleum Resources Development Act 48 of 2002.

319 Compare IIED & World Business Council (n 313) C8 and Fields (n 313) 156, citing a number put forward by the Mineral Policy Center.

320 US Bureau of Land Management, 'Abandoned mine lands' www.blm.gov/programs/public-safety-and-fire/abandoned-mine-lands, accessed 28 February 2019.

321 C Unger *et al*, 'Mapping and prioritizing rehabilitation of abandoned mines in Australia' Paper presented at the Life-of-Mine Conference held 10–12 July 2012 in Brisbane, Queensland.

322 Charlene M Hogan and Gilles A Tremblay, 'Abandoned mines in Canada', Paper presented at the 7th International Conference on Acid Rock Drainage held 26–30 March 2006 in St Louis, MO.

figure in South Africa at 5,906.[323] Figures listed for other countries include Japan (5,500) and Sweden (more than 1,000).[324] In other countries comprehensive surveys of abandoned mines have not even been attempted.[325] Apart from indicating the scale of the problem, however, such figures are essentially meaningless in a context where there are not enough financial resources to deal with the mines already found, even in the best resourced mineral jurisdictions.[326]

The sustainable mineral development consensus presents abandoned mines as a legacy issue – a result of mining that occurred decades, centuries or even millennia ago.[327] To a certain extent this is true, as many States only started to develop mine closure laws towards the latter half of the twentieth century. However, the pass the parcel approach to closure liabilities outlined above suggests that mine abandonment is a *systemic* feature of an unsustainable extractivist/neoextractivist paradigm. *Breaking New Ground*, for instance, held that it would be meaningless to estimate how many former mining sites exist around the world and how many of these carry environmental risks, and therefore impossible to estimate how much it would cost to rehabilitate them.[328] On the issue of responsibility, the report was ambivalent, suggesting that it would be in the industry's interest to rehabilitate the worst sites, but that this would only occur if all companies were forced to comply.[329] 'At the other end of the spectrum', the report conceded, 'the only prospect for cleaning up an historic mine site is with public funds'.[330]

Notwithstanding its position on how to estimate abandoned mines, the sustainable mineral development consensus encourages the State to develop inventories of abandoned mines. 'The first global priority must be for the public authorities to identify and register abandoned mines and assess the risk they pose.'[331] Not even developed countries had made much progress in this regard by the early 2000s,[332] but since that time some have made significant strides. The Western Australia Department of Mines, Industry Regulation and

323 Auditor-General, South Africa, *Report of the Auditor-General to Parliament on a performance audit of the rehabilitation of abandoned mines at the Department of Minerals and Energy* (October 2009).

324 Fields (n 313) 156.

325 Ibid.

326 Ibid.

327 *Breaking New Ground* (n 13) 246.

328 Ibid.

329 Ibid.

330 Ibid.

331 Ibid 247.

332 See the country surveys of abandoned mine inventories in IIED & World Business Council (n 313) C4–C10.

Safety, for example, maintains a publicly available database of abandoned mines searchable according to features (41 different parameters) and location (5 different parameters).[333] It is possible to identify all abandoned mines having a particular water condition, or by stage of revegetation. The database also records the commodity and the originator. This tool allows the State to cognize the scope and scale of abandoned mines in its jurisdiction and allows for better planning and allocation of public resources.

Unlike the extensive legal provisions on mineral property rights, taxation and even environmental assessment, rules on abandoned mines are not a given in the laws of mineral-rich jurisdictions. Where abandonment is mentioned, the law may empower the State to access a closed or abandoned mine in order to avoid danger to persons, property or to abate environmental degradation. In British Columbia,[334] for instance, abandoned mines are those for which all permit obligations have been satisfied and title has reverted to the government.[335] If an inspector is of the opinion that work may be necessary to remedy a danger to persons or property, or to abate pollution to the land or watercourses, he or she may enter on or below the surface of the mine and cause the necessary works to be effected.[336] The funds for this work must come out of the public purse.[337] However, the amount expended, plus interest at a prescribed rate, is a debt owed to the government and forms a lien and charge on the mineral right or mine.[338] The outstanding payment may also be registered as a charge in the land title office, obstructing title and other dealings with the mine until the debt is paid.[339] The provisions allow the State to address the pass the parcel approach to closure, although the whole regulatory edifice hinges upon an inspector deciding that works are necessary.

The mining law of New South Wales contains an unusual certification process for derelict sites. The law allows the minister to declare as a derelict mine site any land that has been used for or affected by mining or prospecting operations, and which has, in the opinion of the minister, been abandoned.[340] Land may be declared as a derelict mine site irrespective of whether it is possible to identify the landholder or the holder of a prospecting of mining

---

[333] Government of Western Australia: Department of Mines, Industry Regulation and Safety *MineDex* http://minedexext.dmp.wa.gov.au/minedex/external/common/appMain.jsp, accessed 28 February 2019.

[334] See also Mineral Resources Act, 1989 (Queensland) s 344ff.

[335] Mines Act 1996 (British Columbia), section 1.

[336] Ibid s 17(1).

[337] Ibid s 17(2).

[338] Ibid s 17(3).

[339] Ibid s 17(4).

[340] Mining Act, 1992 (New South Wales), section 242A.

authorization.[341] With land declared as a derelict mine site, the mining authorities may initiate steps to have the land fully or partially rehabilitated, and may enter into contracts and agreements for that purpose.[342] The financial resources for this work are appropriated from a special purpose Derelict Mine Sites Fund.[343] Parliamentary appropriations, money received from the sale of mining plant for a derelict site, the financial assurance and monies received from investment of fund monies replenish this Fund.[344] This institution serves as an example of the call for mining stakeholders 'to develop new sufficiently robust and sustainable funding mechanisms at the national and international level to tackle problems that will be a burden on future generations'.[345] Other than the financial assurance, however, States have not responded to this challenge, particularly in the developing world.

The legislative and financial resources needed to address abandoned mine sites need not be mining specific. The USA's leading practice 'Superfund' legislation, the Comprehensive Environmental Response, Compensation and Liability Act, 1980, was initially set up on the basis of a tax on the petroleum and chemical industries to fund cleanups of abandoned or uncontrolled hazardous waste sites.[346] Inclusion on the Superfund 'National Priority List' (NPL) is currently still the best option to obtain funds and support for remediating hazardous abandoned mine sites. However, many abandoned mines will simply not be candidates for the NPL list.[347] Developing countries could draw inspiration from the Superfund model, but may not be able to generate a sufficiently large trust fund from resource taxes, or have the administrative resources to manage the use and allocation of the funds. This occurs in a context where the tax base is already stretched and there are many competing demands for public funds.

Other than sourcing funds from the prior mining proponent, or polluting industries more generally, an alternative funding option is to turn to the holder or possessor of land. Here, Finnish law contains an interesting provision. Where it is necessary for public safety reasons, the possessor of a mining

---

[341] Ibid s 242A(4).

[342] Ibid s 242B(1).

[343] Ibid s 242C.

[344] Ibid s 242C(3).

[345] *Breaking New Ground* (n 13) 247.

[346] United States Environmental Protection Agency 'Superfund: CERCLA overview' www.epa.gov/superfund/superfund-cercla-overview, accessed 28 February 2019.

[347] Megan Glatzel and Bea Gordon, 'The West's sleeping giant: Abandoned mines and the role of the Good Samaritan' http://waterinthewest.stanford.edu/news-events/news-insights/wests-sleeping-giant-abandoned-mines-and-role-good-samaritan, accessed 28 February 2019.

area is responsible for monitoring and corrective measures. This will only apply however, where the mining operator no longer exists, is 'unavailable' or 'cannot be made to comply with the obligation'.[348] Further, the possessor can only be held responsible if the possessor knew or should have known the condition of the area when acquiring it, and responsibility for monitoring and implementing the required corrective measures 'is not apparently unreasonable'.[349]

In summary, to a greater extent than even the laws on mine closure itself, the institutional provisions on abandoned and orphaned mines are underdeveloped in many mineral-rich jurisdictions. Lines of responsibility are vaguely or imperfectly drawn, allowing abandoned mine sites to persist in a state of ecological, and frequently also social, disarray. The presence of hundreds of thousands of such sites around the world, which accrue not only from historical legacies, is a serious and persistent challenge to claims of mining 'development' and 'sustainability'.

3. CONCLUSION

This chapter has journeyed to the end of the mine cycle, the 'doom side of the doom'. It has presented an explanatory framework for a dominant model of State involvement in mine closure that has traversed the role of watchdog, relinquishing authority and mender of last resort. As the last of the substantive chapters in this work, it fits within a broader explanatory model – the double movement – that explains the global hold of an unsustainable extractivist/neoextractivist paradigm in coal and hardrock mining. It highlights the weaknesses, and the ultimate inefficacy of the State's overtures to protect society against the longterm socioecological harms arising from a disembedded market in mineral and mining rights.

The chapter has presented the main features of a dominant model for State involvement in mine closure: instituting a formal, legal requirement for upfront integrated mine closure planning; stipulating the form and quantum of financial assurance to guard against operator default on rehabilitation requirements; encouraging inclusivity in mine closure planning and progressive rehabilitation; and defining institutional controls for processes of closure or relinquishment. These features of State involvement must not obscure the fact that the dominant model rests upon the mining industry's acknowledgement of responsibility for closure.

---

348 Mining Act, 2011 (Finland), section 150.
349 Ibid.

At the same time, the chapter has identified a number of key contradictions, weaknesses, gaps and opacities that render the formal regulatory framework for mine closure ineffectual in many countries. While many jurisdictions require mining proponents to develop mine closure plans according to a risk-based approach, perceptions of relevant risks vary widely from country to country. Very few States recognize, let alone accommodate, the significant social risks upon closure that intersect in complex and systemic ways with ecological risks. Very few States frame progressive rehabilitation as a legal duty, or specify measures to incentivize or punish mining proponents for good performance or noncompliance. The institutional measures to ensure inclusivity in mine closure planning over the cycle of the mine are generally poorly developed in comparison to front-ended public participation. Consensus on the most appropriate forms of financial assurance is still emerging, and many States still allow for a wide variety of forms of financial assurance that are not suited to addressing operator default on postclosure monitoring and maintenance obligations, especially where risks extend into perpetuity. States do not necessarily require 100 per cent of the statutory closure liability, frameworks for determining the quantum of financial assurance do not always directly address the risk of operator default and the method of valuation that must be used to determine the amount of financial assurance is rarely specified. While a number of jurisdictions require mine closure plans to be submitted to public scrutiny, in some financial assurance estimates are still expressly kept away from the public eye. There is a lack of enforcement, even in the best resourced mineral-rich jurisdictions. By failing to regulate care and maintenance and properly oversee processes that facilitate corporate adaptation in the face of various threats, States tacitly endorse a pass the parcel approach to mine closure liabilities. By failing to clearly specify the process and implications of relinquishment, States affirm their unwanted role as mender of last resort, to the detriment of present and future generations and the environment.

The chapter has nevertheless highlighted a number of examples of 'better' and 'best' practice, ranging from social and labour plans in South Africa, to the comprehensive financial assurance review in Queensland, to New Mexico's Standard Reclamation Cost Estimator, to Western Australia's publicly available, searchable database of abandoned mines, among others.

Mine closure is a new, interdisciplinary field that has driven very recent legislative amendments worldwide. The immaturity of the regulatory field – compared, for example, to mineral property rights – undoubtedly makes mine closure a legacy issue. But it is only a legacy issue in part. As suggested in this chapter, the particular construction of legal controls over the process of responsibly closing a mine may well facilitate systemic dereliction, to which thousands of modern abandoned mines attest.

8. Conclusion: towards postextractivism

1. INTRODUCTION

The thesis of this book has been that a global system of unsustainable mineral extraction persists because of the dynamic relationship between contending social forces advancing and resisting mining. This dynamic ensures that mining is promoted while its worst immediate effects are curtailed, albeit with differing levels of rigour in different parts of the world. Working most acutely through the double movement of the State, the push for and push back against mining keeps the hope of a sustainable, developmental mining industry in its current form alive: there is an abiding sense that 'just maybe' mining could contribute much more.[1]

This book adds to the mental models that explain why an extractivist/neoextractivist paradigm is held in place with such force. The view, perhaps contentious, is that the reasons these paradigms remain entrenched owes as much to the power and resources of mining proponents and their State backers as it does to the focus of dissent. Moreover, the organizing principles of promotion and protection are deeply embedded in technical areas of policy, governance and law, each having their own potentially problematic core concepts, traditions, epistemic communities and vested interests. The first part of this final chapter summarizes the book's key insights on the double movement in mineral extraction. Building on the work in the preceding chapters, it explains why the double movement is only superficially balanced and does not guard against predatory relations and practices. It shows that overcoming extractivism/neoextractivism will necessitate a great undoing, at the level of technical frameworks that translate into legal rights and obligations; at the level of narratives that justify extraction with reference to other grand and globalized human quests ('development', 'sustainability'); and, at the root, at the level of understanding how the use of minerals relates to ideas and assumptions, such as a Cartesian knowledge system, restriction of ethical values to the human sphere, the duality of society and nature, and the onward march of 'progress'.

---

[1] Anthony Bebbington *et al*, 'Contention and ambiguity: Mining and the possibilities of development' (2008) 39(6) *Development and Change* 965, 969.

There is value in identifying what needs to be undone, for as Eduardo Galeano, the Uruguayan journalist who penned the iconic *Las Venas Abiertas de América* (*Open Veins of Latin America*), observed, 'the first condition for changing reality is to understand it'.[2] Any well thought out transition to a state of postextractivism, however, would also need to posit viable alternatives. This is an enormous project, joining the need for a 'great reimagining' to the project of a 'great undoing'. The second part of this chapter, accordingly, shifts focus to possible reimagined futures for mineral extraction and the governance systems that drive the production of mineral commodities. The emerging paradigm of 'postextractivism' mentioned in Chapter 1 offers a starting point for these thoughts. This section situates postextractivism within the broader framing of transition discourses and explores the normative and technical implications of adopting a postextractivist frame.

2. THE GREAT UNDOING: THE DOUBLE MOVEMENT AND UNSUSTAINABLE EXTRACTION

This book has assumed a global system of unsustainable mineral extraction. As outlined in Chapter 1, global material metabolism has grown exponentially over the past few centuries to a point where it now rivals global net primary production, amounting to billions of tons of extracted material every year. Nonrenewable materials are being used more than ever before, accounting for more than 70 per cent of total materials use in the global 'mineral economy'. But society's demand for nonrenewable mineral materials is highly unequal. While China emerged as the largest consumer of total main metals in 2003, fully industrialized countries have used a disproportionate quantity of metals and minerals over the course of the past two centuries to spur their industrialization and economic growth. Despite cyclical downturns, the primary mining industry is expected to grow over the coming decades, meeting the needs of a global sustainability transition and the fourth industrial revolution.

Society's demand for mineral commodities is met by both formal, largescale, capital-intensive mining and the artisanal and smallscale mining sector, which is growing. The formal mining industry exhibits the features of an integrated production system aligned with the mining cycle, with firms of different sizes occupying different niches. A trend of consolidation in the mining industry has been apparent over the past 50 years and, globally, a limited number of

---

[2] Eduardo Galeano, *Open Veins of Latin America: Five Centures of the Pillage of a Continent* transl. Cedric Belfrage, 25th anniversary edn (Latin American Bureau 1973/1997).

companies control an increasing share of the formal mining industry. Over the past 150 years, both the public and private sectors have invested extensively in the production of mineral commodities along the mining cycle. Although private ownership of the factors of mining production tends to dominate, this has fluctuated. Currently, countries pursuing a neoextractivist agenda are increasing their involvement in mining production. Public monies have also been expended on mining education, geological data, logistical infrastructure and the social and environmental externalities of mining. A geographic shift in mining investment following on the heels of extensive neoliberal reforms in developing countries has taken place, but mature mining destinations have continued to attract investment, and the level of investment in developing countries is not evenly spread. Over the long term and relative to other industries, the mining industry's performance is disappointing. However, the industry is volatile and exhibits boom and bust cycles that drive investment and speculation. Commodity pricing is viewed as one of the primary causes of the boom and bust nature of the industry, but critics point out that the industry's low average profitability is also linked to decisions around investment in production capacity and costcutting measures. The concept of peak minerals has been mooted, although peaks in production are more likely to be associated with social and environmental constraints.

Mining has far reaching, and oftentimes irreversible, impacts on the environment, society and economy of localities, regions, the nation State and even the globe. The distribution of environmental and social impacts is unequal, with the brunt of negative externalities being borne by the poor, Indigenous People, women, the elderly and children in developing regions. Accounting frameworks to measure these impacts exist but have not been mainstreamed, although extensive work is being undertaken on planetary and social boundaries. Diverse schools of thought – from neoliberals to Marxists – have rejected ecological limits to extractives-fuelled economic growth, minimized the impacts of the extractive industries or argued that losses can be compensated for economically.

Against this context, this book has argued that the 'double movement' keeps the hope of a sustainable, developmental mining industry alive. The double movement, a concept put forward by Karl Polanyi in his 1944 work *The Great Transformation*, stands for the conflicting principles of promoting mining but protecting society from its worst impacts. It organizes societal positions but manifests most acutely through the State. The double movement is part of Polanyi's broader explanatory framework for the emergence and persistence of the market economy and 'market society'. The market society troubled Polanyi, as he believed the fictitious commoditization of land, money and labour causes tremendous damage to society.

This book has presented evidence for the double movement in mineral production at the level of discourses/narratives and technical frameworks. The following sections summarize the key insights from the analysis in the preceding chapters of the book.

2.1 The Double Movement in Mining-Related Discourses

Chapters 2 and 3 provided a detailed treatment of the emergence and key claims of nine mining discourses: four arranged as 'pro-mining discourses' (sustainable mineral development consensus, responsible mining, neoextractivism and critical and strategic minerals), and five arranged on the side of 'discourses of mining dissent' (resource curse thesis, Indigenous Peoples' rights, environmental justice, mining and human rights and feminist critiques of mining). These discourses originate and are sustained by a variety of interest groups – from international financial institutions, mining companies, global and national mining associations and international and regional intergovernmental associations, to mining-affected communities, Indigenous Peoples' movements, international and national NGOs, community organizations and academics.

The range of these discourses, the varied imagery they present of the State and their different conceptions of the State's key role support a conception of the State as a 'polyvalent, poly-contextual phenomenon which changes shape and appearance with the political forces acting towards it and the circumstances in which they do so'.[3] The State is of course never simply a construct in the discourse of political actors – it has a material base and linkages to distinct forms of power. But the discursive construction of the State is significant because discourses shape perceptions of persons, social relations, action and interaction and our grasp of the material world. In this way they channel our thoughts and action in a manner that opens up certain opportunities and excludes others.

The arrangement of mining narratives into pro and dissenting camps illustrates the double movement, with the former emphasizing mining promotion and the latter foregrounding protection of various elements of society against mining's environmental and social impacts. This is not a hard and fast distinction, however, and elements of both organizing principles are sometimes evident. Recall the World Bank's Extractive Industry Review recommending that the Group's Natural Habitat Policy should adopt clear 'no go' zones for oil, gas and mining projects; the Mining, Mineral and Sustainable

---

3 Bob Jessop, 'Bringing the State back in (yet again): Reviews, revisions, rejections and redirections' (2001) 11(2) *International Review of Sociology* 149, 161.

Development Project's (MMSD) principled position on qualifying economic considerations by a concern for maximizing human wellbeing, ensuring the efficient use of all resources and internalizing environmental and social costs; the support for mining among some Indigenous Peoples; or the 'women in mining movement'.

Even within a predominating orientation (pro or dissenting), there are vast differences in the imagery and claims made of the State. Representations of States range from corrupt, weak, unstable, incompetent, colluding and abdicating, to competent, assertive, strategic and rule-governed. A bifurcation between developed/developing, stable/unstable and resource-consuming/resource-rich is an enduring theme. The relationship between developing, unstable, resource-rich States and 'development' is contentious, with proponents of different discourses assuming different positions on the causes of 'underdevelopment' and the role of extractives in the cure. The value of economic growth and a centralized State tends to be assumed.

Mining-related discourses nevertheless tend to be rooted in theories of development that rest on an ideology of progress. 'Development', with its connotations of growth and maturity, is an old concept that is deeply embedded in the human psyche. But the contentious cultural construction of development as perpetual economic growth, and the positioning of extractive industries within this construction, is more recent. A heterodox body of theory acknowledges the possibility of placing limits on the systematic disembowelling of the Earth's finite mineral resources – from the sustainable mineral development consensus itself, to Indigenous Peoples' movements, environmental justice and human rights movements and ecofeminism. The need for limits on untrammelled market and State promotion of the mining industry aligns with Polanyi's theory of the double movement, and has been institutionalized in complex technical policies and rules on environmental assessment and mine closure, among others. But the conception of limits in the varying pro and dissenting mining discourses outlined in Chapters 2 and 3 is too noisy, a cacophony of contending proposals that impedes political action. And even among dissenters, the developmental allure of the extractive industry is often overpowering.

The discourses constructed in this book are transnational in nature. And yet, what is quite remarkable is the comparative lack of effort on the part of the international community of States to come to grips with the longterm development and sustainability issues of mining. As far back as 1972, recommendations appended to the Stockholm Declaration called upon the UN Secretary-General to provide an appropriate vehicle for the exchange of information on the environmental conditions of mine sites, action taken in respect of the environment and the positive and negative repercussions of this sector. When the mining sector appeared to be getting out of kilter in the late 1990s, and the industry perceived that its 'social licence to operate' was under threat, it was the industry that led reform through the MMSD project. Industry, rather than the community of States, took the lead.

2.2 The Double Movement in Technical Frameworks

This book has argued that the double movement operates at the level of overarching narratives and technical areas of governance, each having their own particular history (sometimes ancient), key sources and dominant patterning of State roles. A detailed exposition of these State roles in the areas of property institutions, taxation, environmental and mine closure filled the pages of Chapters 4 through 7. A summary of these dominant patterns, and key related limitations, is provided in Figure 8.1 below.

Property institutions play a critical role in strengthening the State's capacity to promote mining. More than any other area, property rules commoditize minerals and create a global market for mineral exploration and exploitation. This in turn feeds a global, market-based mechanism of mineral supply for major energy, industrial minerals and precious metals. The rules around property, minerals and mining tend to be similar, irrespective of whether an extractivist or neoextractivist paradigm prevails. Taxation is different, exhibiting some key differences between private and State-led extractivist economies, with the latter leaning towards fiscal regimes that are viewed as decidedly less 'investor friendly'. Viewed from the double movement, the area of taxation is ambiguous. On the one hand, taxes are the means by which mineral-rich jurisdictions can secure a clear benefit from mineral extraction for 'development'. On the other hand, tax revenues bind the State to mining in a manner that can be unstainable. The contribution mining companies can make to the national fiscus is the Faustian bargain that ties the State to a disembedded global market in mineral production. Environmental assessment and mine closure are more squarely positioned around the State's protective role, with the former being older and more entrenched. The technical elaboration of different forms of environmental assessment conveys the impression of serious and rigorous engagement with the socioecological limits of mining. Mine closure conveys the impression that mines are opened with closure in mind and that integrated closure planning, financial assurance and 'relinquishment' will ensure that significant social and environmental costs do not land at the door of the State, and the people and environments of mineral-rich jurisdictions. The extent of orphaned and abandoned mines the world over paints a different picture. But where limits have been imposed, they are poorly conceptualized or policed. The limits that are in place – while sufficient to keep the hope of a sustainable, developmental mining industry alive – are insufficient to counter the real, longterm detrimental effects of mining, which proceeds with extensive State

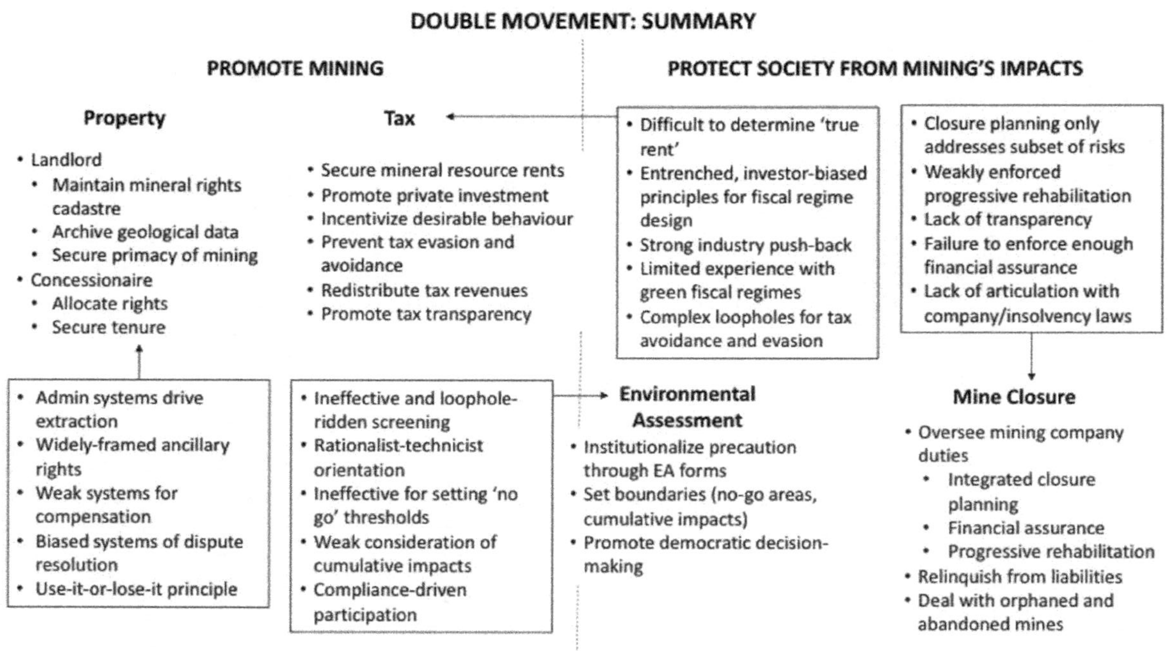

Figure 8.1 *Summary of the double movement and dominant patterning of State roles in the areas of property, taxation, environmental assessment and mine closure*

support and bias as a result of the older, more entrenched institutions of property and taxation.

The constellation of State roles around the axes of the double movement has a further, more insidious effect. As policy dialogues, guidelines, 'toolboxes' and 'toolkits' abound in each of these areas, they entrench a discursive architecture that appears to be more and more difficult to dislodge, crowding out alternatives. It is to such alternatives that this chapter now turns.

3. THE GREAT REIMAGINING: TRANSITION DISCOURSES AND POSTEXTRACTIVISM

A reimagined future for mineral extraction and the governance systems that drive the production of mineral commodities can only be contemplated outside familiar developmental logics. As the preceding section has argued, although there are glimpses of radical alternatives, contemporary forms of mining dissent are not at one on disputing development as growth or challenging the duality between nature and society. It is nevertheless an anticipatory sign of our times, Escobar urges, that over the past decade there has been a 'forceful emergence of transition discourses in multiple sites of academic and activist life'.[4] Transition discourses emanating from both the global South and the global North contemplate 'radical cultural and institutional transformation – a transition to an altogether different world'.[5] A dialogue among these broader framing narratives is essential for an 'effective politics of transformation'[6] that establishes a new normative and technical framework for postextractivism.

3.1 Transition Discourses

The range of transition discourses is wide. Transition discourses include degrowth;[7] postdevelopment;[8] a variety of 'sustainability transition'[9] and 'just

---

[4] Arturo Escobar, 'Degrowth, postdevelopment and transitions: A preliminary conversation' (2015) 10 *Sustainability Science* 451, 452.

[5] Ibid 453.

[6] Ibid 451.

[7] Giorgos Kallis, 'In defence of degrowth' (2011) 70(5) *Ecological Economics* 873; Joan Martínez-Alier *et al*, 'Sustainable de-growth: Mapping the context, criticisms, and future prospects of an emergent paradigm' (2010) 69 *Ecological Economics* 1741.

[8] Wolfgang Sachs (ed.), *The Development Dictionary* (Zed 1992); Majid Rahnema and Victoria Bawtree (eds), *The Post-Development Reader* (Zed 1997).

[9] FW Geels, *Technological Transitions: A Co-Evolutionary and Socio-Technical Analysis* (Edward Elgar 2005); J Meadowcroft, 'Engaging with the *Politics* of sustainability transitions' (2011) 1 *Environmental Innovation and Societal Transitions* 70.

transition'[10] initiatives; religious contributions such as Pope Francis' encyclical letter, *Laudato Si*;[11] *Buen Vivir* (the Good Life, collective wellbeing; *sumak kawsay* in Quechua; *Suma Quamana* in Aymara);[12] and the Rights of Nature.[13] Aspects of these discourses resonate with environmental justice, ecofeminism, deep ecology and decolonization theoretical framings.[14] In transition discourses emanating from the global North the 'age to come' tends to be defined as postgrowth, postmaterialist, posteconomic, postcapitalist and posthuman. In the global South, the same age is defined as 'postdevelopment', non/postliberal, biocentric and postextractivist.[15] Some scholars single out particular transition discourses for a 'dialogue' between orientations of the global North and South. Escobar, for example, encourages a conversation between degrowth and postdevelopment frameworks;[16] Acosta maintains that efforts to move towards postextractivism in the global South should be aligned with degrowth or at least stationary growth in the global North;[17] and Brand *et al* light upon degrowth and postextractivism for their frame of 'inclusive development'.[18] This section does not aim to rigorously map transition discourses, single out particular discourses, or set forth a comprehensive synthesis. It rather draws upon elements of various transition discourses in an eclectic fashion to sketch a framing narrative for postextractivism. These elements include the rela-

---

[10] Mark Swilling and Eve Annecke, *Just Transitions: Explorations of Sustainability in an Unfair World* (UCT Press 2012); Mark Swilling, Josephine Musango and Jeremy Wakeford, 'Developmental States and sustainability transitions: Prospects of a just transition in South Africa' (2016) 18(5) *Journal of Environmental Policy and Planning* 650.

[11] Encyclical letter *Laudato Si'* of the Holy Father Francis on Care for Our Common Home, http://w2.vatican.va/content/dam/francesco/pdf/encyclicals/documents/papa-francesco_20150524_enciclica-laudato-si_en.pdf, accessed 1 March 2019 (henceforth *Laudato Si'*).

[12] Raúl Prada Alcoreza, 'Buen vivir as a model for state and economy' in M Lang and D Mokrani, *Beyond Development: Alternative Visions from Latin America*, Permanent Working Group on Alternatives to Development (Rosa Luxemburg Foundation transl. 2013) 145.

[13] Global Alliance for the Rights of Nature, 'Rights of Nature', http://therightsofnature.org, accessed 1 March 2019.

[14] Val Plumwood, 'Decolonising relationships with Nature' (2002) 2 *PAN* 7.

[15] Escobar (n 4) 452–3.

[16] Ibid.

[17] Alberto Acosta, 'Extractivism and neo-extractivism: Two sides of the same cures' in M Lang and D Mokrani, *Beyond Development: Alternative Visions from Latin America*, Permanent Working Group on Alternatives to Development (Rosa Luxemburg Foundation transl. 2013) 61, 80.

[18] Ulrich Brand, Tobias Boos and Alina Brad, 'Degrowth and post-extractivism: Two debates with suggestions for the inclusive development framework' (2017) 24 *Current Opinion in Environmental Sustainability* 36.

tionship between the human and nonhuman spheres; human relationships, at different levels; economic growth and development; and the role of the State.

3.1.1 Relationship between the human and nonhuman spheres

The first element of a transition discourse-inspired framing narrative challenges the assumption of a duality between society and nature and restriction of ethical values to the human sphere. A common feature of transition discourses is that they assume that the environmental, social and economic polycrisis in which we are mired is inseparable from the model of social and economic life that has become dominant over the past few centuries[19] – a model of industrialism, globalized capitalism, rationalism, economism, patriarchy, racism, anthropocentrism and technocentrism.

The most innovative of these discourses recognize that this malady has a spiritual deficiency at its core and posit a return to sacred values. The concept of the 'ideal life' in the debate on *Buen Vivir* and corresponding indigenous terms, for example, rests on the idea that '[m]en and women, together with nature, are part of the Mother Earth and there is communion and dialogue between them mediated by rituals in which Nature is understood as a sacred being'.[20] Pope Francis' 'urgent challenge' to protect the Earth as 'our common home' rests on the belief that the Earth is God's creation, an endowment which we have used and abused irresponsibly, but of which we too are part.[21] To develop an ecology capable of remedying the damage we have inflicted, religion and the language particular to it cannot be left out.[22] The plurality of religious/spiritual expression should be respected here, including beliefs relating to the deceased (ancestors) and the not yet born, and their relationship to land and the environment. In a recent report on mining-affected communities, for example, the South African Human Rights Commission recognized that grave relocations were among the most sensitive and contentious issues between communities and mining companies. Ancestral graves had 'significant cultural and spiritual importance and their exhumation and re-interment should not be reduced to the physical process of relocation'.[23] The need for a more spiritual consciousness that recognizes the intrinsic worth of the nonhuman world is also central to ecofeminism and deep ecology.[24]

---

[19] Ecsobar (n 4) 452.

[20] Alcoreza (n 12) 145.

[21] *Laudato Si'* (n 11) para. 1.

[22] Ibid para. 63.

[23] South African Human Rights Commission, *National Hearing on the Underlying Socio-Economic Challenges of Mining-Affected Communities* (2018) 22.

[24] Ariel Salleh, 'The Ecofeminism/Deep ecology debate: A reply to patriarchal reason' (1992) 14 *Environmental Ethics* 195, 198.

A return to these forms of spirituality grounds arguments for the interconnection of the material, intellectual and spiritual realms; harmonious existence with nature; and the primacy of ecological values. This has certain practical consequences. As Alcoreza explains from the perspective of *Buen Vivir*, 'if Nature is sacred, then people should take from her only what is necessary to live'.[25] If we are able to feel intimately united with all that exists, Pope Francis says, then our attitude will not be one of 'masters, consumers, ruthless exploiters, unable to set limits on [our] immediate needs'.[26] We will refuse to turn reality 'into an object simply to be used and controlled'.[27]

The practical consequences flowing from these spiritual insights relate both to how we conceptualize nature and to the limits we impose on our own behaviour. The current dominant model of social and economic life is criticized because it supports an instrumental approach to nature based on abstraction and appropriation in the service of present needs. Abstraction and appropriation of nature are achieved – above all – by institutions of property and the rules and norms that influence how property is allocated among different social groups. As explained in this book, Polanyi recognized that assigning property rights in things that are not inherently suitable for market exchange – 'fictitious commodities' – lies at the heart of social and economic crisis. And within the degrowth movement, there is a general scepticism towards institutional reforms that attempt to substitute money relations for social relations.[28] In a world of globalized production and reproduction, property and associated rules of allocation render the chain of material transformations in goods and services invisible. A transition to an altogether different world seems unlikely without a fundamental change in basic institutions of property and allocation, as degrowth proponents have recognized.[29]

The question of limits ties in with, but is nevertheless distinct from, the issue of allocation. The idea of limits is not new and is even recognized in the mainstream discourses, as this book has demonstrated. For example, the discourse on planetary and social boundaries, as discussed in Chapter 1, shows the sophistication of this debate. And yet for all the scientific rigour of planetary/social boundaries debates, and earlier, fuzzier debates on the 'integration' of economic, social and environmental considerations under sustainable development, these narratives have less to say on *why* humans should limit their behaviour, or *what* the immediate focus of concern should be. Transition discourses fill some of these gaps. The *Buen Vivir* cosmovision, for example,

---

25 Alcoreza (n 12) 145.
26 *Laudato Si'* (n 11) para. 11.
27 Ibid.
28 Kallis (n 7) 5.
29 Ibid 3.

does not focus on the abstracted limits that are causing humanity to outstrip the carrying capacity of the Holocene period, but on the more grounded notion of ensuring that there is a 'harmonious relationship between living beings that ensures diversity, life and the equality of redistribution'.[30] Proponents of degrowth point out that we still live in a world of 'unchecked consumerism, excessive materials use, and fossil fuel addiction'.[31] The dominant economic paradigm, they say, 'rewards *more* instead of *better* consumption and *private* versus *public* investment in *man-made* rather than *natural* capital'.[32] A 'harmonious relationship between living beings' that remains within ecological limits would entail 'having to do with less high-speed transport infrastructures, space missions for tourists, new airports, or factories producing unnecessary gadgets, faster cars or better televisions'. Being able to imagine and follow through on limits requires decisionmakers to envision the ultimate purpose of material chains of production, a task current models of governance based on abstracted notions of property and rules of allocation mitigate against.

3.1.2 Human relationships

Recognizing the interconnection and interdependence of the material, intellectual and spiritual realms can also change the way we relate to each other. Transition discourses such as *Buen Vivir* hold that production and reproduction are possible only in the presence of links of mutual interdependence. The 'ideal life' is posited as one of reciprocal relationships and solidarity.[33] The current dominant model is not based on these values. Indeed, as Pope Francis has forcefully argued, the *majority* of the world's population – billions of people – can be classed as excluded. Rather being treated with equal dignity and respect, the problems of the 'excluded' are brought up in international economic and political discussions as if they were an 'afterthought', and they frequently remain 'at the bottom of the pile'.[34] (This tendency is ever more present in light of the migrant refugee crisis that has gripped parts of Europe and North America since 2010.) We have to realize, the Pope urges, 'that a true ecological approach *always* becomes a social approach; it must integrate questions of justice in debates on the environment, so as to hear *both the cry of the earth and the cry of the poor*'.[35]

The focus on mutuality and solidarity extends to the relationships – current and historical – between mineral-producing and mineral-consuming nations.

---

30 Alcoreza (n 12) 147.
31 Martínez-Alier (n 7) 1741.
32 Ibid.
33 Alcoreza (n 12) 145.
34 *Laudato Si'* (n 11) para. 49.
35 Ibid, emphasis in original.

Recognition of an asymmetrical power balance between the industrialized countries at the core and resource-rich countries on the periphery is as old as dependency theory. And yet the asymmetry persists, despite insights that should ground repugnance at the current state of affairs: that market-based systems of commodity pricing are inequitable; that tax avoidance, tax evasion and illicit financial flows have deprived host nations of mineral revenues; that failure to account and pay for environmental and social externalities has racked up a massive ecological debt owed to mineral-rich jurisdictions; that the debts incurred by many developing, mineral-rich jurisdictions in the 1980s that further locked them into mineral-exporting development models were odious;[36] and that the monetary policies of developed nations caused these debts to balloon artificially.[37] Alongside radical changes in the fundamental institutions of property, mainstream understandings of debt and credit and their application in the sphere of international relations need to be revised.[38] Furthermore, contemporary international relations in the extractive industries cannot be viewed outside of long colonial histories that entrenched asymmetries in wealth and access to technology. The nascent field of postcoloniality and decolonization in international law serves as a promising starting point for re-vision.[39]

3.1.3 Economic growth and development

'Development' as extractive-led economic growth is integral to all forms of extractivism: predatory extractivism, extractivism tempered by the sustainable mineral development consensus and the neoextractivist policies of developing countries. By the mid-twentieth century, Gudynas reminds us, the concept of development had become almost indistinguishable from that of economic growth.[40] Development still presents as a 'powerful myth', full of glowing, praiseworthy and apparently 'necessary' ideals: progress, modern life, technology, industrialization – 'ideas of advancing forward, and the uninterrupted

---

[36] See Naomi Klein, *The Shock Doctrine* (Picador 2008) 195–8 for the spending of military junta in South America during the late 1970s–80s.

[37] In the early 1980s Federal Reserve chairman Paul Volcker dramatically increased interest rates in the United States. Although this prompted a wave of bankruptcies in the United States, the greatest pain was felt by the developing world, because higher interest rates meant higher interest payments on foreign debts.

[38] Kallis (n 7) 3.

[39] See for example Antony Anghie, 'The evolution of international law: Colonial and post-colonial realities' (2006) 27(5) *Third World Quarterly* 739.

[40] Eduardo Gudynas, 'Debates on development and its alternatives in Latin America: A brief heterodox guide' in M Lang and D Mokrani, *Beyond Development: Alternative Visions from Latin America*, Permanent Working Group on Alternatives to Development (Rosa Luxemburg Foundation transl. 2013) 15, 16.

growth towards a civilization in the image and likeness of the countries of the North'.[41]

Eschewing the fetish of development as economic growth is integral to many transition discourses. The postdevelopment literature has trenchantly critiqued this association.[42] In 1992, the world's most eminent critics of development assembled a collection of essays in *The Development Dictionary: A Guide to Knowledge as Power*. The book exposed the 'historical obsolescence and intellectual sterility' of the development idea. Bidding farewell to development was 'urgently needed, in order to liberate people's minds in both North and South [to enable] bold responses to the environmental and ethical challenges . . . confronting humanity'.[43] Critics in this work, and a later volume on the postdevelopment era, dared to contemplate the 'end of development' and to parse open discursive space on alternatives to development, useful ideas which they argued could be gleaned from the practices of grassroots movements.[44]

The reasons for rejecting continuous development as economic growth are varied. Sustainable degrowth advocates, for example, maintain that additional economic growth simply cannot be delinked from increased materials consumption. If sustainable degrowth is defined from an ecological–economic perspective as 'a socially sustainable and equitable reduction (and eventually stabilization) of society's throughput',[45] then it will inevitably entail a smaller and qualitatively different economy.[46] In parallel to the emphasis on wellbeing in the *Buen Vivir* frame, advocates of degrowth envision multiple paths to 'happiness' such as the adoption of a 'voluntary simplicity' which would require reduced work hours, better selection of technical innovations and relocalizing economic activities.[47]

Others point to the 'productivity paradox' at the heart of the growth economy and its inevitable collision with a limited biophysical world. Fioramonti, for example, explains that to be 'competitive', companies must reduce production costs in terms of time and labour. However, if the same levels of production can be achieved with fewer workers (or their robotic counterparts), more stuff

---

[41] Alcoreza (n 12) 147.

[42] As an area of debate, postdevelopment emerged from critiques of the idea of development in the late 1980s, concurrently with the embedding of sustainable development in popular conscience.

[43] Zed Books, 'The Development Dictionary', www.zedbooks.net/shop/book/the-development-dictionary/, accessed 1 March 2019.

[44] Escobar (n 4) 455.

[45] 'Throughput' being understood in this context to mean the materials and energy a society extracts, processes, transports and distributes, and the consumption it returns back to the environment as 'waste' (Kallis (n 7) 2).

[46] Kallis (n 7) 2.

[47] Martínez-Alier (n 7) 1743; see also the writings of Serge Latouche.

must be produced and consumed to maintain the same levels of employment.[48] This argument resonates with the observation in Chapter 1 that mines have to operate at full or near full capacity at larger and larger scales in order to achieve cost targets.[49]

Still others highlight that the structural conditions necessary for fostering broadscale 'development' from economic growth are simply not present in developing countries, given an established system of globalized capital. After years of authoritarian rule, for example, Bolivia underwent a neoliberal revolution in the mid-1980s to address rampant inflation. The reforms were passed under the veneer of democracy, but in practice entailed significant repressive measures.[50] The poor bore the brunt of the reforms in the form of unemployment, increased prices, a reduction in the minimum wage and increased inequality. A broadranging increase in wealth and wellbeing did not materialize. The development as economic growth model in Bolivia was unviable and unequal, as Alcoreza explains, because only a few members of the Bolivian business class enjoyed links to international markets (and thus the benefits of globalization), and they were not committed to becoming a genuine modern bourgeoisie.[51] The 'road towards modernity', he continues, 'was basically oligarchic'.[52] This pattern has repeated itself all over the world – from Chile and Bolivia, to Poland, Russia, South Africa and numerous other sites.

Pope Francis associates a preoccupation with economic growth with faith in technological solutions, a stance he dubs the 'techno-economic paradigm'.[53] There are 'power structures' vested in this paradigm, he warns, that may overwhelm not only our politics but also freedom and justice.[54] Rather than a change in humanity, resource scarcity, pollution and waste are presented as technical problems requiring technological solutions.[55] But the alliance between the economy and technology is incapable of apprehending the 'mysterious network of relations between things', solves one problem but creates a myriad of others, and 'ends up sidelining anything unrelated to its immediate interests'.[56]

---

48 Lorenzo Fioramonti, 'The future of mineral mining' in Salimah Valiani, *The Future of Mining in South Africa: Sunset or Sunrise?* (Mistra 2018) 358.

49 See Chapter 1, section 4.4.

50 For an account of the neoliberal revolution in Bolivia, see Klein (n 36) 176–93.

51 Alcoreza (n 12) 148.

52 Ibid.

53 *Laudato Si'* (n 11) para. 53.

54 Ibid.

55 Ibid para. 20.

56 Ibid paras 20, 53.

Rejection of development as economic growth may include rejection of gross domestic product (GDP) as a hegemonic indicator of progress. Developed in the USA in the late 1930s to help governments tackle the Great Depression and the United States' involvement in the Second World War, GDP is a creature of politics that has many flaws. Chief among these are its failure to measure the *full* capital input into the production process, such as the depletion of natural capital and the contribution of services rendered within the household, and the informal and voluntary economy.[57] While alternatives such as adjusted net savings exist,[58] this measure has not been widely adopted in the national accounts of mineral-rich jurisdictions. And it too is based on an assumption of economic growth.

A number of alternatives to extractive-led, export-oriented economic models have been proposed. Herman Daly's concept of the 'steady state economy' was prescient in this regard.[59] In the early 1970s, he proposed that 'development' should be defined as 'development, without growth beyond environmental carrying capacity, where development means qualitative improvement and growth means quantitative increase'.[60] Daly believed in the accounting of natural capital, but insisted that natural capital should not be counted as income, and that labour and income should be taxed less while resource throughput is taxed more. He also recommended to the World Bank and governments that investments should be made to increase the supply of natural capital in the long run, and that governments should move away 'from the ideology of global economic integration by free trade, free capital mobility and export-led growth'.[61] Instead, policymakers should move towards a more 'nationalist orientation' that seeks first to develop domestic production for local markets, resorting to international trade only when this is clearly much more efficient.[62]

Referencing the Bolivian Constitution, for example, Alcoreza outlines the features of the 'social and communal economy', which is geared towards *Buen Vivir*. Rather than an overblown private or State-led economy, the social and communal economy strives for a balanced integration of the community,

---

[57] On the politics of GDP and its chief flaws see Lorenzo Fioramonti, *Gross Domestic Problem – The Politics Behind the World's Most Powerful Number* (Zed 2013).

[58] See Chapter 1, section 5.

[59] Herman Daly, *Towards a Steady State Economy* (Freeman 1973).

[60] Cited in Patrick Bond, 'Economic narratives for resisting extractive industries in Africa' (2018) 33 *Research in Political Economy* 6.

[61] Ibid.

[62] Ibid.

State, private and cooperative sectors.[63] This is a plural economy that does not exclude the possibility of State intervention to promote and industrialize strategic sectors such as mining. However, rather than mining for export earnings, the State must adopt a 'strategy of disconnection' by focusing on strengthening national and regional markets, opting to meet the basic needs of the population (including food sovereignty) and ensuring the survival of human beings, community and nature.[64]

Fioramonti advances the 'wellbeing economy' as a model that also recognizes the different ways of creating value in society. In models driven on growth-based industrialization, maximization (of efficiency, production) is the objective – producing more with less. But this results in an economy that fuels inequality, weakens the social fabric and consumes more resources than it generates. An economy of this nature must be seen as 'underdeveloped and underperforming'.[65] In a wellbeing economy, by contrast, the pillars of value creation are social relations and natural ecosystems.[66] As Fioramonti explains, optimization rather than maximization defines success:

> The well-being economy is a highly integrated system driven by locally-based and community-oriented businesses, which are more in tune with local needs, more labour intensive and better suited to customise the production of goods and services in order to avoid over-production, problems of scale and the resulting massive amount of pollution and waste.[67]

A comprehensive overview of the economic models assumed or proposed by transition discourses is beyond the scope of this section, or even this book. Suffice to underline, however, that economic models that can serve as alternatives to the fetish of development as growth have been, and are being, proposed.

3.1.4 Role of the State

In a transition to a different world, what role remains for the State? In the current dominant model of social and economic life, the State is a 'fundamental factor of societal domination':[68] it claims exclusive competence over solving certain problems and enjoys exclusive competencies (the power to tax,

---

[63] Alcoreza (n 12) 151.

[64] Ibid 149.

[65] Fioramonti (n 48) 362.

[66] Lorenzo Fioramonti, *Well-Being Economy: Success in a World Without Growth* (Macmillan 2017).

[67] Fioramonti (n 48) 361.

[68] Ulrich Brand, 'The role of the State and of public policies in transformation processes' in M Lang and D Mokrani, *Beyond Development: Alternative Visions from*

to make the law and to the legitimate use of armed force, for example). Current State structures are built on centuries of colonialism and exhibit the centric and reductionist modes of conceiving both nature and colonized peoples as Other.[69] And yet the main function of the State in a system of globalized capitalism is to consolidate the dominant social relations built on colonial histories, and to ensure their continuity.[70] One of the ways in which the State ensures such continuity is through the work of the double movement, as this book has argued. The State is a 'battlefield', as Brand recognizes, through which different social and political forces compete in an effort to promote their own interests, values and identities.[71] The battle is asymmetrical however, as the State tends to foster the interests of the dominant classes.

Transition discourses present competing conceptions of the State's role. Degrowth and postdevelopment perspectives converge on the position that on their own, neither State policy nor market forces will effect the necessary transitions.[72] Markets often wreak havoc, not gradual adaptation, and tend to discriminate in favour of the 'haves' rather than the 'have nots'.[73] Public policies can orchestrate social and political change, but these usually effect transitions (to new legal frameworks or political institutions), rather than the more profound social transformation required to address a global environmental, social and economic polycrisis.[74] However, while State intervention may not be regarded as sufficient to secure a state of degrowth or postdevelopment, it tends to be regarded as necessary. Speaking from a sustainability transition perspective, Meadowcroft believes that 'state intervention and governance reform are essential'.[75] In her view, changes to law and significant expenditure of social revenue are essential for driving sustainability transitions: the market will drive the uptake of a particular new technology (a smartphone, for instance), but it will not secure a CO_2 emission-free energy system on a timescale sufficient to avoid dangerous anthropogenic interference with the climate system.[76] Alcoreza also comes down in favour of a more interventionist State,

---

Latin America, Permanent Working Group on Alternatives to Development (Rosa Luxemburg Foundation transl. 2013) 105, 108.

69 For an overview of the logical structure of colonial relationship see Plumwood (n 14) 10–15.

70 Brand (n 68) 107.

71 Ibid.

72 Escobar (n 4) 457.

73 Kallis (n 7) 3.

74 Brand (n 68) 105–6.

75 Meadowcroft (n 9) 71.

76 Ibid.

but argues that it should play a more active part in the 'productive apparatus',[77] and not merely through law and social spending.

In line with the focus on a plural economy that recognizes localized community and cooperative economies, transition discourses have emphasized the decentralization of State authority. But rather than the simple devolution of State power, a plural State that advances a 'wellbeing' or 'social and community' economy will incorporate multiple spheres of authority with the flexibility to scale competencies up or down depending on the governance need at hand. Drawing inspiration from the plurinational Constitution of Bolivia, for instance, Alcoreza argues that there should be multiple structures – some more modern and bureaucratic, based on distrust and audits, and others more consensus- or community-based, based on trust and community relationships.[78] Society will reclaim its capacity to solve its own problems if the State establishes and supports the provision of goods and services at a community and local level. Whatever levels of government cannot manage at this level can be delegated upwards, to regional or national governments.[79] Through a two way process, central government will transfer competencies to departments, municipalities and autonomous indigenous territories, and community organizations will transfer competencies from the bottom up to regional authorities.[80] The hope is that these new forms of organization would break the old power and privilege associated with the centric State, and establish the conditions for meeting collective needs in harmony with nature.

3.2 Postextractivism

The foregoing narrative grounds and frames the calls for a transition to postextractivism. A transition discourse itself, postextractivism was originally proposed by the Centro Latinoamericano de Ecología Social in Montevideo in the mid-2000s, and has become an important topic of debate in intellectual activist circles in South America.[81] Recently, it has also gained traction in Africa.[82] The following sections outline the features of a postextractivist paradigm, alongside areas that still need further development.

---

[77] Alcoreza (n 12) 154.
[78] Ibid 149.
[79] Ibid.
[80] Ibid 150.
[81] Escobar (n 4) 455.
[82] See Womin (IANRA), *Background Note and Explanation of Key Concepts*, Women, Gender and Extractivism in Africa: A Collection of Papers (n.d.) 6; Samantha Hargreaves, 'Extractivism, its deadly impacts and struggles towards a post-extractivist future' in Mark Swilling, Josephine Kaviti Musango and Jeremy Wakeford

3.2.1 Relationship between the human and nonhuman spheres

Postextractivism does not call for a moratorium on mineral extraction.[83] But it requires reorientating extraction so that Rights to Nature are placed centre stage.[84] Because the Rights to Nature approach contests the idea of nature as property, a postextractivist orientation opposes practices that exploit, appropriate and commercialize nature. Although aligned with the cosmovision of *Buen Vivir*, the literature on postextractivism does not strongly feature calls for a spiritual orientation to minerals as such. But in exploring the possibility of a more integrated material, intellectual and spiritual approach, at least two avenues of research and practice merit further investigation.

First, there are already existing accounts of the place of the earth, the subsoil and minerals in the spiritual traditions of a variety of indigenous and nonindigenous groups. In the worldview of the Aymara people of Bolivia, for example, minerals feature as part of a system of reciprocity, duality and complementarity, grounded in male–female pairing. The Aymara worldview distinguishes various dimensions of life, each of which is overseen by a supernatural male or female protector. The realm of subsoils and minerals is governed by the masculine divinity *Tío*.[85] In the cosmologies of the Native Americans of North America, both nonorganic and organic entities constitute the living world, a 'fantastic and beautiful creation engendering extremely powerful feelings of gratitude and indebtedness, obliging us to behave as if we were related to each other'.[86] African ontologies are also based on the fundamental principle of the unity of being. The energy of cosmic origin permeates and lives within everything, including animals, plants and minerals alongside human beings, objects and events.[87]

These spiritual insights are by no means confined to so-called Indigenous Peoples. In Cornwall, Celtic-inspired spirituality centred on 'earth mysteries' has maintained that sacred sites are consistently built on areas exhibiting

---

(eds), *Greening the South African Economy: Scoping the Issues, Challenges and Opportunities* (UCT Press 2016) 145.

[83] Hargreaves (n 82) 153.

[84] Eduardo Gudynas, 'The new extractivism of the 21st century: Ten urgent theses about extractivism in relation to current South American progressivism' (2010) *Americas Program Report* 8.

[85] Vicenta Mamani-Bernabé, 'Spirituality and the *Pachamama* in the Andean Aymara worldview' in Ricardo Rozzi *et al* (eds), *Earth Stewardship: Linking Ecology and Ethics in Theory and Practice* (Springer 2015) 65, 71.

[86] Jack D Forbes, 'Indigenous Americans: Spirituality and Ecos' (2001) 130(4) *Daedalus* 283, 284.

[87] Mambo Ama Mazama, 'Afrocentricity and African spirituality' (2002) 33(2) *Journal of Black Studies* 218, 219.

a high magnetic or electrical force that can be accessed through ritual.[88] Within the Euro-Western Christian tradition, ecotheology has critiqued the 'intensely anthropocentric' Christian worldview, that consistently seeks to divorce humanity from, and lift it above the Earth.[89] Ecotheologians are now trying to revive and arouse a connection between spirit and nature, including through envisioning humanity as embedded in nature, as 'living matter' and even 'walking talking minerals' or the 'self-conscious element of the Earth's crust'.[90] These varied religious and spiritual accounts consistently emphasize the unity of all being and offer a language to enrich the impoverished minerals lexicon in extractivist discourses.

At the very least, the emphasis on unity and connectedness that flows from these spiritual accounts can fuel consciousness of the pervasiveness of minerals in our lives, and the sacrifices and contributions that are part and parcel of transforming subsoil resources into useful commodities. A postextractivist framing should incorporate modes of governance and monitoring that allow decisionmakers to cognize the entire mineral value chain. A commodity-specific approach will be important here. Rather than simply authorizing mineral extraction on the basis of the level of investment, or the financial and technical capacity of the mining proponent, consideration also needs to be given to the likely end use of the mineral commodity and the opportunity cost of extracting the resource. The Brundtland Report's warning on the opportunity cost of extracting minerals and metals for arms, for example, is apposite here.

A second avenue of research, paradoxically, should focus on the materiality of minerals and the 'magical' properties that are ascribed to mineral commodities in extractivist accounts. The relatively new field of resource geography studies how the properties and attributes of material things affect everyday life.[91] These include attributes that material objects do not have, or seem to manifest, such as attributing power to minerals to serve as the 'engine' of economic growth. The tendency to attribute qualities to a material object that are displaced, inordinate or inappropriate qualifies as resource

---

[88] Amy Hale, 'Whose Celtic Cornwall? The ethnic Cornish meet Celtic spirituality' in David C Harvey *et al* (eds), *Celtic Geographies: Old Cultures, New Times* (Routledge 2002) 157, 160.

[89] Eaton, 'Postscript: A spirituality of the Earth' in Graham Buxton and Norman Habel, *The Nature of Things: Rediscovering the Spiritual in God's Creation* (Pickwick 2016) 230, 231.

[90] Ibid 234.

[91] David Kneas, 'Necessary illusions: Fetishism and the becoming of subsoil resources' (2017) 4 *The Extractive Industries and Society* 846.

fetishism.[92] Fetishism is not benign, for it allows certain social relations and material processes to come into being, 'as if' the magical properties ascribed to resources were present. In his analysis of resource fetishism in Ecuador, for example, Kneas found that fetishized illusions of 'purified minerals' and a 'magical becoming' of Ecuador as a mining country paved the way for mineral exploration and the formation of a State-owned mining company, along with militarizing the copper-rich Intag region to quell local opposition.[93]

Postextractivism recognizes the need for limits and calls for reducing emissions and radically reducing pressure on ecosystems.[94] The existing work on planetary and social boundaries, discussed in Chapter 1, is pertinent here. In order to keep species and ecosystems alive, Gudynas argues, extensive protected areas will need be to be designated, as part of a connected and effectively managed network.[95] The potential for conflict between protected areas and mining activities is great. A recent survey, for example, found that approximately 7 per cent of mines for four key metals directly overlapped with the global protected area system, and a further 27 per cent lay within 10 kilometres of a protected area boundary.[96] As discussed in Chapter 4, States secure the primacy of mining over other surface uses of the land in various ways. In the case of protected areas this includes defining the area restrictively, failing to restrict mining as a land use within protected areas, and failing to protect buffer zones. Adoption of a postextractivist frame would entail opting for a far more rigorous system of protection, not only for representative areas of biodiversity but also for the purpose of protecting strategic water and food-producing zones.

This book has demonstrated the centrality of mineral property rights in perpetuating a global system of unsustainable mineral extraction. This applies to property rights inhering in minerals, and the property rights associated with extraction. Like other transition discourses, postextractivism is sceptical towards commodifying nature and substituting money relations for social relations, which often flow from the recognition of property rights. Postextractivism must question the primacy of property rights, and critique the

---

92 Ibid.

93 Ibid 850.

94 Gudynas (n 84) 9.

95 Eduardo Gudynas, 'Transitions to post-extractivism: Directions, options, areas of action' in M Lang and D Mokrani, *Beyond Development: Alternative Visions from Latin America*, Permanent Working Group on Alternatives to Development (Rosa Luxemburg Foundation, transl. 2013) 165, 177.

96 América P Durán, Jason Rauch and Kevin J Gaston, 'Global spatial coincidence between protected areas and metal mining activities' (2013) 160 *Biological Conservation* 272.

assumptions bound up with 'property'. Chief among these assumptions is the idea of 'ownership'.

Ownership is not an ideologically neutral concept. It is a social construct with particular historical, and even regional, assumptions. It carries different meanings in common and civil law systems, for instance.[97] Civil law concepts of ownership are based on the concept of *dominium*, the ultimate right in Roman texts to use and dispose of a thing in the most absolute way.[98] Rather than a right to exercise particular powers over things, *dominium* theories of ownership emphasize its residuary character, and its characterization by traits such as elasticity, exclusivity, independence and unlimited duration.[99] In Anglo American legal systems, ownership is more closely likened to a bundle of rights, which accommodates the idea that reasonableness must be used to place limits on the owner's powers in the interest of his or her neighbours.[100] The collation of rights comprising ownership include as 'standard incidents of ownership' the right to dispose of the property (*ius disponendi*), the right to use the property (*ius utendi*), the right to draw the fruits of the property (*ius fruendi*), and the right to neglect, or to fail to develop, the property (*ius abutendi*).[101] Even with these differences, ownership bears the connotation of the most complete set of entitlements towards the owned object.

In Western societies, ownership has also been imbued with assumptions relating to productivity and public enterprise. Gendered Western understandings of land ownership envision land as virgin territory, awaiting comingling with the fertility of human labour to be rendered productive for human purposes. This attitude was especially marked in the frontier and settler territories that constituted the New World, and in the frontier regions where much of the world's mining now takes place.[102] Speaking of the frontier mentality in Australia, Peterson and Sanders observe 'that a very general ideology throughout Australian history has rested on the imperative to make the land productive'.[103] Pragmatically, the legal construct of ownership also centralizes

---

97 Hanri Mostert, *Mineral Law: Principles and Policies in Perspective* (Juta 2012) 9.

98 Lanré Aladeitan, 'Ownership and control of oil, gas and mineral resources in Nigeria: Between legality and legitimacy' (2012) 38 *Thurgood Marshall Law Review* 159, 160.

99 Mostert (n 97) 9.

100 Bryan Clark, 'Migratory things on land: Property rights and a law of capture' (2002) 6(3) *Electronic Journal of Comparative Law* 1, 2–3.

101 Mostert (n 97) 9.

102 Joseph L Sax, 'Ownership, property, and sustainability' (2011) 31 *Utah Environmental Law Review* 1, 5.

103 N Peterson and W Sanders, 'Citizenship and indigenous responses to mining in the Gulf country' in Nicolas Peterson and Will Sanders, *Citizenship and Indigenous Australians* (Cambridge University Press 1998) 154, 155.

and focuses authority. From the perspective of investors, instituting the State as the centralized authority over unsevered minerals reduces transaction costs, contributing to a regulatory environment conducive to foreign, private investment. Instituting the State as centralized landlord and concessioning authority facilitates extractivism, because it removes the impediment of dealing with thousands of individual owners of unsevered minerals.

The nature of minerals as public property is, however, undertheorized. Unsevered minerals come in a myriad of forms and are extracted through a variety of technologies. Extraction inevitably and dramatically alters the environment, puncturing the landscape, changing the flow of surface and underground water and generating largescale waste rock dumps and tailings dams. Postextractivism must consider how the property concept aligns with these features of mining's aftermath. The reticence to characterize mining rights, and their essential character as a bundle of statutorily-defined entitlements given to an ephemeral corporate entity, support the misperception that mining is a temporary land use. The ideological function of the fuzzy legal characterization of extraction rights obfuscates liability for the longterm residual and latent impacts of mining, which revert to the State as residuary 'owner' under the rubric of orphaned and abandoned mines.

3.2.2 Human relationships

Postextractivism calls for extraction to contribute to 'eradicating poverty'.[104] This is hardly a novel request in itself, as the overview of the sustainable mineral development consensus and neoextractivist approaches in Chapter 2 attests. The novelty of a postextractivist approach lies in the means and not in the end, that is, in turning away from export-oriented growth models to 'indispensable' extraction that meets basic needs and expanded opportunities for recycling.[105]

A postextractivist approach values different stakeholder groups equally. Currently, some stakeholder groups (investors, mining executives, government officials) are valued disproportionately, while others are marginalized (women and their unpaid care, labourers, artisanal miners). The concern for particular stakeholders is not consistent throughout the mining cycle. For example, 'communities' are a matter of concern at the start of mining operations when a social licence to mine needs to be secured (hence the preoccupation with free, prior and informed consent and public participation in EIA). But this concern wanes rapidly, evidenced by the fact that mineral-rich jurisdictions rarely address social closure in their governance frameworks. Hargreaves urges

---

[104] Gudynas (n 84) 8.
[105] See section 3.2.3 below.

a postextractivist approach that foregrounds the interests of working class and peasant women. It is these women 'whose reproductive work in the fields and in the homes maintains a harmonious relationship with nature, regenerating and restoring natural resources and human relations', enabling the global economy to continue functioning.[106] The interests of labour, and the historical injustices of inadequate compensatory frameworks for occupational injuries and diseases along the entire mineral value chain, must also not be discounted, however. The unprecedented agreement between gold mining companies and labourers in South Africa on compensation for occupationally acquired silicosis and tuberculosis charts the way forward. A postextractivist approach would also recognize the points of articulation between artisanal, smallscale and formal mining, and innovative governance of ASM where this scale of mining is suited to the resource.

The technical means for securing the equal participation of stakeholder groups in the full mining cycle are not yet clear. The overview of public participation and consultation in environmental assessment procedures in Chapter 6 highlighted many deficiencies. Some progress may be made by according full respect to the principle of free, prior and informed consent. Even then, however, questions will hang over how 'consent' is procured. Changing the governance and reporting structures of resource extraction companies to accommodate representation of labour, affected communities and different levels of the State is a possible unexplored area of reform.

Gudynas maintains that postextractivism also requires closing 'unfair' material and resource flows and undergirding extraction with public policies on, for instance, the disproportionate accumulation of wealth.[107] Cognizing and addressing the asymmetry that still persists between resource-rich countries on the periphery and industrialized countries at the core should top the agenda of a postextractivist approach. This asymmetry will only be partly addressed by a 'strategy of disconnection', that is, by addressing the needs of domestic and regional markets going forward, as some have maintained.[108] It will also require a long historical view of unfair material and resource flows that takes social and environmental injustice and ecological debt seriously. It will necessitate international support for the range of measures currently being designed to address illicit financial flows, tax evasion and tax avoidance in the mining industry. A postextractivist approach would also not reject out of hand attempts to impose retrospective tax liability for disproportionate tax benefits secured in the past. And it would consistently bear in mind the strategies of domination

---

[106] Hargreaves (n 82) 155.
[107] Gudynas (n 84) 9.
[108] Alcoreza (n 12) 154.

which industrialized and newly industrialized countries have employed in their attempts to secure access to mineral resources, including conditional aid.

3.2.3 Economic growth and development

Postextractivism calls for a break with export-oriented and import substitution-driven policies, as both view nature as an exploitable resource.[109] The economic model imposed by the international market – extractives-based, export-driven economic growth – must be eschewed in favour of the plural economy, the 'steady state economy', the 'social and community economy', the 'wellbeing economy', and so forth. Mineral extraction should be vastly reduced.[110] Ideally, extraction should be aligned with a responsible programme of degrowth, and should satisfy local and regional needs.[111] The norm should be 'indispensable' extraction, to be decided by local and regional interests.[112] There should be a preference for low intensity and smaller scale projects with minimal social and environmental impacts.[113] There should be full accounting of positive and negative externalities.[114] In breaking their dependence on commodities and foreign direct investment, resource-rich countries should also promote forms of industrialization that are labour intensive, to provide employment for the youth bulge in their population pyramids.[115]

Apart from sustainable agriculture, tourism and the knowledge sector, proponents of a plural, postextractivist economy stress the importance of recycling, and manufacturing that relies heavily on recycled materials.[116] Recycling is key to Fioramonti's two critical shifts for mineral mining: (1) from extraction to recycling; (2) from centralized approaches to distributed networks.[117] Moving from extraction to recycling, he explains, entails shifting away from the default understanding of mining as 'digging holes in the ground'[118] – which poses immense threats to the environment, is unsafe for workers and mining-affected communities and generates enormous amounts of longstanding waste. Mining should rather entail developing more sophisticated systems for retrieving and reusing the substantial amount of metals, minerals and rare earths already in circulation. The 'future of mining', he

---

109 Brand (n 18) 37.
110 Gudynas (n 84) 9.
111 Ibid 9.
112 Hargreaves (n 82) 154.
113 Ibid.
114 Fioramonti (n 48) 362.
115 Ibid 361.
116 Hargreaves (n 82) 154.
117 Fioramonti (n 48) 368.
118 Ibid.

maintains, 'is about sifting through the vast amount of metal and mineral scrap (especially e-waste). This can generate economic value while helping solve the environmental problem of waste management and creating safe jobs for people'.[119] Further, with an eye towards the 'circular economy', the mining industry has a critical role to play in influencing conventional approaches to design in downstream manufacturing, to ensure modular approaches that allow for easier separation of minerals and metals in products after disposal. Mining companies can work with manufacturers to ensure that products are easier to disassemble into reusable segments.[120]

Fioramonti's proposal is provocative. But a commodity-specific approach would once again be necessary. For example, while titanium metal might be infinitely recyclable, the pigments produced from ilmenite and rutile would not be recoverable. This highlights the need for degrowth/lifestyle change in addition to a switch to recycling. The equity of a recycling economy – in the light of a historic imperial and colonial transfer of minerals and metals from the global South to the global North – must also be constantly foregrounded. This raises questions around how a global 'reuse value' can be calculated and paid for metals and minerals that enables a portion of recycled value to be transferred to host regions. Blockchain technologies may well have an important role to play here.

Fioramonti's second shift (from centralized approaches to distributed networks) is based on a vision of nodal recyclers fed by a nationwide distribution of small mineral/scrap metal businesses. These businesses could include artisanal and smallscale miners who would sell minerals/metals gleaned directly from the soil, waste rock or tailings, and a host of waste collection businesses, who could 'mine' piles of waste, including e-waste.[121]

The future vision is thus of economies that are smaller, more diverse, more customized to local and regional needs, offering new opportunities.

3.2.4 Role of the State

The State does not disappear in postextractivist accounts. Indeed, in some instances the role of the State in mining production should expand, where is it critical to exploit a mineral resource from the perspective of wellbeing and the protection of ecosystems.[122] But States will need to become far more circumspect in how they promote the mining industries in their territories, and

---

[119] Ibid.
[120] Ibid 370.
[121] Ibid 376.
[122] Alcoreza (n 12) 154.

far more rigorous in how they support healthy social relations and ecosystems. This implies abandoning the double movement.

Brand highlights a distinction between the need for the State to transform itself, and the need for it to instigate policies that will stimulate thoroughgoing social change.[123] He also makes a further distinction between transition (led by public policies) and transformation (a more thoroughgoing change, instigated by the innovations of State and non-State actors).[124] This implies that the State has a role to play in a shift to postextractivism, even if its role is necessary but not sufficient.

States firstly have an important role to play in fundamentally altering their narratives of 'development', 'progress' and 'economic growth'. Even if the contradictions around neoextractivism and the Rights of Nature are rife in Bolivia and Ecuador, the constitutional and statutory frameworks these countries have enacted to respect the plural creation of value in society, and to protect ecosystems, stand out as beacons of hope. The State plays a critical role in naturalizing the 'generalised discourses' on social and economic life in the minds of the majority.[125] In addition to affirming development alternatives centred on wellbeing and ecosystem protection, this will entail refusing to engage in magical and misleading language around the potential of the extractive industries to alleviate poverty and inequality. Even the mining industry, as this book has pointed out, qualifies these claims.[126] At the same time, the State must acknowledge some of the harsh realities: that in addition to positive externalities, the mineral extractives industry fuels inequality, fosters corruption, sickens workers and communities, weakens the social fabric, consumes more resources than it generates, exports the value of natural capital and leads to longterm and even perpetuity problems of pollution and waste. As a result, this industry contributes to an economy that can only be characterized as underperforming and underdeveloped.[127]

Second, States should understand how their recognition and protection of a range of public and private property rights reinforces dominant social relations in a manner that perpetuates a global system of unsustainable mineral extraction. The three property rights of significance here are the 'public', centralized rights to minerals in themselves; the private rights to explore or exploit (heavily influenced by the security of mineral tenure discourse); and rights to land and water affected by the mining industry, inclusive of Indigenous Peoples' rights. There is work to be done, for example, in elaborating the

---

123 Brand (n 68) 105.
124 Ibid.
125 Ibid 108.
126 See Chapter 2, section 2.2.2.
127 Fioramonti (n 48) 362.

fiduciary duties of the State in its role as national landlord of mineral rights, and how these duties should be linked to public-facing systems of monitoring and accountability. States also need to grapple with and reconcile different systems of authority for allocating rights to mineral exploitation, land and water, which should include respecting indigenous and customary systems of land allocation. The State's all encompassing 'sovereignty' over natural resources should have an outward looking focus only (that is, protection from interference and domination by foreign powers), but inwardly there should be different jurisdictional layers, with enough space for authorities to protect community, cooperative or local economies.

There is scope, third, to rethink the relationship between States and mineral resource revenues. Despite States' well-founded concerns around tax avoidance, tax evasion and illicit financial flows in the mining industry, resource revenues inevitably tie the State to extractive projects. While tax revenues are based on levels of production or profit, the State is inevitably biased towards the mining industry's growth and expansion. Proposals relating to a green fiscal regime for mining already chart a promising alternative way forward.[128] Rather than taxing production output or throughput, States can tax atmospheric emissions, the loss of biodiversity, the generation of mining waste or the generation of mining wastewater. States should additionally investigate models for taxing distributed networks of artisanal and smallscale mining, and the collection and recycling of scrap metal.

Fourth, States can model full cost accounting and a more balanced approach to the creation of value in their economies by changing the design of their national accounts. Systems of Environmental Economic Accounting are already well developed,[129] and even the World Bank sustains a unit that attempts to measure wealth more accurately, through the measure of adjusted net savings.[130] Although the 'bean counting' of natural capital has drawn strong criticism from mining dissenters, Bond argues that it serves as an additional *economic* argument that reinforces existing intellectual arguments about the resource curse.[131] In an era of 'big data' and 'open data', however, the State can do much more to invest in information systems that capture the negative externalities of mining. If States can invest in geological systems, then they can also invest in inventories on the extent of land disturbed by mining, or on closing and abandoned mines.

---

128 See Chapter 5, section 2.3.2.
129 See Chapter 3, section 2.
130 Bond (n 60) 6.
131 Ibid 7.

If the State abandons the double movement, fifth, it must transform the institutional structures responsible for decisionmaking around mining exploration and exploitation. At present, the double movement is reflected in the general pattern of government agencies responsible for mining or investment promotion approving mining developments, and separate agencies responsible for the 'environment' granting environmental approvals. A far more integrated approach is required that can allow the State to consider the necessity of a mining development in the context of existing market conditions, the potential for value addition within the jurisdiction concerned, the short, medium and longterm costs to the State, the position of various other 'sovereignties' on the development concerned, and so forth. Instruments other than environmental impact assessment may need to be developed, such as an externally audited market impact statement, or a resource depletion statement. At an international level there is scope for States, mining producers and civil society organizations to collaborate on the governance of mineral value chains in a manner that enables the end use of different mineral commodities and the value addition by and allocation to different groups in society to become apparent. Institutional reform must also keep in mind that democratization lies at the core of a project of postextractivism – matters of development must be decided by ordinary citizens.[132] Conflicts must be addressed in transparent and democratic ways.[133]

4. CONCLUSION

How will the transition to a state of postextractivism proceed? Who and what are the drivers of change? Will the transition proceed chaotically or is it possible to effect orderly change?

The answers to these questions are not obvious. On the one hand, some maintain that only the State is capable of providing continuity to the changing relationships of forces.[134] On the other hand, others insist that 'it is only the unified struggles of workers, communities and women, acting on the basis of consensus that will be able to advance [the postextractivist] agenda'.[135] Transition discourses and postextractivist positions, however, tend to favour diversity and plurality over 'silver bullet' solutions, leading to the conclusion that the 'great transformation' we need to effect on a planetary scale leaves space for everyone to contribute.

---

[132] Hargreaves (n 82) 154.
[133] Brand (n 18) 37.
[134] Brand (n 68) 105.
[135] Hargreaves (n 82) 154.

It is possible that changes will come chaotically. In the past, mining, oil and gas ventures have been the first to benefit from neoliberal economic reforms in natural resource-rich jurisdictions, following conditions of actual war or acute economic distress. Advocates of postextractivism advocate for a more measured, orderly transition. Gudynas, for example, envisions a swift move from 'predatory extractivism' to 'sensible extractivism'. Predatory extractivism predominates in much of South America (and other developing countries): '[A]ctivities take place on a large scale or are intensive, their social and environmental impacts are substantial, and their costs are externalised'. Economic growth takes place within enclaves dependent on globalization, with scarce benefits for national economies or job creation. National societies are left to cope with the aftermath of negative externalities.[136] Sensible extractivism (which is not synonymous with the policy prescriptions of the sustainable mineral development consensus), would entail substantial compliance with the social and environmental laws of mineral-rich jurisdictions, the full internalization of social and environmental impacts, effective and rigorous controls, use of the best available technologies, proper measures for remediation and mine closure and effective mitigation and social compensation strategies.[137] Thereafter, a focus on 'indispensable extractivism' would need to occur, 'where the only enterprises left operating are those that are really necessary to meet national and regional needs', that is, to ensure quality of life, flanked on either side by broadscale societal consensus on the limits to poverty and opulence.[138]

The changes required will be profound, Gudynas warns. They will not be brought about overnight. They must be rooted in a deep and growing societal support base, not from messianic (or worse) authoritarian leadership. 'Because the transition requires democratic support', he concludes, 'the focus should be on broadening the consensus and presenting compelling arguments in favour of it'.[139]

In its essence, this book has aimed to contribute to this broadening societal consensus. Drawing on law, political economy, history and philosophy, it has traversed the different varieties of extractivism, past, contemporary and imagined. Taking the perspective of the State, it has elaborated on a particular mental model – the double movement – to explain the persistence of a system of globalized, unsustainable mineral extraction. In its conclusion, it holds out the hope of a third way – one not (neo)liberal, socialist or communist, but

---

136 Gudynas (n 95) 167.
137 Ibid 175.
138 Ibid.
139 Ibid 170.

rooted in a new and growing understanding of the pluriverse of cooperation in a world where we have never been more connected.

Index